Thoreau in
the Mountains

COMMENTARY BY

William Howarth

Farrar . Straus . Giroux

NEW YORK

Thoreau in the Mountains

WRITINGS BY

Henry David Thoreau

Introduction and commentary
copyright © 1982 by William Howarth
All rights reserved
First printing, 1982
Printed in the United States of America
Published simultaneously in Canada by
McGraw-Hill Ryerson Ltd., Toronto
Designed by Cynthia Krupat

Grateful acknowledgment is made to the Graphic Arts
Collection of the Princeton University Library for
assistance in obtaining the nineteenth-century American
woodcuts that illustrate *Thoreau in the Mountains;* and to
Princeton University Press for permission to reprint
portions of *The Writings of Henry D. Thoreau*

Library of Congress Cataloging in Publication Data
Thoreau, Henry David, 1817–1862.
Thoreau in the mountains.
Bibliography: p.   /   Includes index.
1. Appalachian Mountains—Collected works.
2. Mountains—New England—Collected works.
I. Howarth, William L.   II. Title.
PS3042.H6   1982   917.4′043   82–2356
AACR2

For Warren Elmer

———————

I doubt if in the landscape there can be

anything finer than a distant mountain-range.

They are a constant elevating influence.

THOREAU'S JOURNAL

MAY 17, 1858

Foreword

For the past few years I have spent my summers in the New England mountains, following the trails of Henry David Thoreau. Thoreau climbed several peaks in the northern Appalachians, long before backpackers arrived. He wrote accounts of all his trips, but published only a few; most went into his private Journal, a document unpublished in his lifetime—and largely unread today, because of its two-million-word length.

Thoreau's stories about mountain climbing, when extracted from the Journal and his other works, amount to less than two percent of his life's total wordage. I gathered these writings because they deserve to be better known; I hiked Thoreau's trails to see if the country still resembles what he saw.

The result is this volume, where Thoreau's text and my commentary provide a set of responses to the mountains. My aim was twofold: to act as a guide to his journeys (for readers who may want to follow him) and as an interpreter of his stories. He explored mountains, I am exploring him. The range of his interests is wide: I have touched upon his study of flowers, birds, and maps, and tried to clarify his forays in literature and philosophy.

I have adapted my texts from *Excursions* (Boston: Ticknor & Fields, 1863); *A Week on the Concord and Merrimack Rivers*, ed. C. Hovde (Princeton: Princeton University Press, 1980); *The Maine Woods*, ed. J. Moldenhauer (Princeton: Princeton University Press, 1972); and *The Journal of Henry David Thoreau*, 14 vols., eds. B. Torrey and F. H. Allen (Boston: Houghton Mifflin Co., 1906). Ellipses (...) indicate my abridgment of Thoreau's texts; the deletion of his drawings is noted throughout.

My footnotes are signed WH; all other notes are Thoreau's.

All illustrations are from the Sinclair Hamilton Collection of American Illustrated Books at Firestone Library, Princeton University. These woodcuts date from the early nineteenth century, and several were in books that Thoreau read. Readers interested in Thoreau's Journal drawings can refer to the 1906 text. The maps are by Tom Funk.

For help with this book I want to thank especially its editor and its designer, Pat Strachan and Cynthia Krupat; also Lydia Ostenson for valued early counsel. Eugene and Mary Walker read the manuscript and advised me on points about geology and alpine botany. Ruth and Don Brown loaned me their quiet, sunny place to write. Several persons at Firestone Library provided generous assistance: Larry Spellman of the Map Division; Dale Roylance and Nancy Finlay of the Graphic Arts Collection; Beth Witherell, Carolyn Kappes, Mark Patterson, and Kevin Van Anglen of the Thoreau Textual Center. John Williamson, Princeton '81, helped me gather texts and locate sources. My good companions on the trails were Mary and Eugene Walker, Lydia and Dana Ostenson, Jeff and Jenny and Bonnie Howarth. John McPhee gave me sound advice at the start and throughout. On every mountain Warren Elmer was my trusted guide; this book is dedicated to him and his favorite country.

W. H.

Princeton, New Jersey
May 1982

Contents

INTRODUCTION *3*

Massachusetts

WACHUSETT *23*
GREYLOCK *54*

Maine

KATAHDIN *85*
KINEO *162*

Vermont & New Hampshire

WANTASTIQUET *191*
FALL MOUNTAIN *200*
THE WHITE MOUNTAINS *205*
Washington *206*
Tuckerman Ravine *250*
Lafayette *266*
MONADNOCK *287*

Selected Bibliography *369*
Notes on Illustrations *377*
Index *381*

Thoreau in
the Mountains

Introduction

He lived on a flood plain, the low ground of Concord, Massachusetts, and from his earliest days Henry Thoreau heard stories about mountains. His mother spoke of Monadnock, near her girlhood home in New Hampshire. The Bible told him of Ararat, Sinai, Golgotha—sacred places where history made a turn. In school his classical texts described Olympus, Parnassus, Caucasus—the homes of gods that mortals feared to climb. Dante's image of Purgatory was a mountain; Petrarch climbed Ventoux and wrote about his journey of the spirit. At Harvard, Thoreau read Milton, Johnson, Gibbon; their mountains were places of chaos and barbarian hordes. But Rousseau, Goethe, and Wordsworth made him see the Alps as a vast, deep space, where ideas and emotions could be just as immense.

After receiving his college degree in 1837, Thoreau took work in Concord as a schoolteacher and tender of odd jobs. He started a Journal, wrote poems, took daily walks in the countryside. For climbing he had some modest hills, many with Indian names: Nawshawtuct, Annursnuck, Ponkawtasset. From their summits he could see the blue slopes of Wachusett and Monadnock out on the western horizon. In search of fresh myths, he read the Hindu scriptures and absorbed a vision of Himalaya, the highest mountains of all. He also read travel books; then he decided that Concord would be the center of his world.

Mountains on the horizon were his far boundaries, presiding over this river valley like a highland crown. At sunset he saw the earth become a succession of great stairs, falling from a high rim to the plain far below. Mountains enlarged the world of Concord, reminded him of distance and eternity. More than once, he imagined regions farther north, where the earth and heaven meet. That was Unappropriated Land, isolated and remote, a country so different that he would be changed by going there.

.   .   .

In 1839 Thoreau began to make his mountain trips, which continued at regular intervals until his death in 1862. He climbed Greylock in the Berkshires, Washington and Lafayette in the White Mountains of New Hampshire, Katahdin in northern Maine. Wachusett and Monadnock he visited several times, as well as many smaller rises throughout New England: Uncannunuc, Wantastiquet, Fall Mountain, Red Hill, Kineo. (He also hiked in the Catskills of New York, but only a partial account has survived.) Every height gave him a prospect, threw the terrain into relief and perspective. He went up the hill that gave Montreal its name, surveyed Cape Cod from a high dune called Ararat—and said the scenery was not exactly Biblical: "You would think you might be in Labrador, or some other place you have imagined."

The experience of climbing mountains tempered some of his imagination, for traveling there was hard work. For transport he relied on boats, coaches, his own legs; lodging came at farms or inns, where the fare was crude and scant. Often he packed his own food and shelter, carrying in a knapsack the rudiments of camping: food, tools, a blanket or sheet of canvas. Few college graduates traveled in this manner. In his day, "camps" were usually set up for musters or revivals, masses of people on transient business. Solitaries went to the woods for game or timber, not for rest and recreation.

To his friends Thoreau seemed an expert camper, but many of his feats now look amateurish. On Greylock he siphoned his water from a nearby puddle, then built a hovel from rocks and scrap lumber. His huts of spruce on Monadnock were more substantial; but a companion said one "would make a good sieve." Fires were a nagging problem: in these exposed, windy places, the dry undergrowth often caught up flying sparks. He caused one major fire in Concord, where the neighbors called him "woods-burner" for years. Sometimes his mountain fires were also too generous, but he was not alarmed—after all, the forest was in ample supply. He also took for granted that every stream ran pure and clear. When he poured a skillet of grease into Lake Moosehead, his Indian guide only observed: "That make hard paddlum thro'; hold 'em canoe. So say old times."

Thoreau was not a prodigal; mostly he camped in the Spartan style of his life at Walden Pond. Meals often consisted of tea, rice, and wild berries—some so tart it was a triumph to eat them. On longer journeys he took bread, meat, and coffee to satisfy his companions. One personal luxury was a moist, rich plum cake, taken in pinches for energy —an early version of trail "gorp." His garb was plain and patched, in keeping with the credo of *Walden:* "Beware of all enterprises that require new clothes." He wore thick coats and pants, in earthen colors; checked shirts and a slouch hat; wool socks and stout shoes. He kept the shoes greased with tallow and put wooden pegs in their soles— wood was cheaper and tougher, he claimed, than newfangled zinc.

Pitifully underequipped on some early trips, in later years Thoreau filled his pack with ample gear. He made partitions out of heavy paper, kept his reading and writing materials dry in "India-rubber" bags. Into the pack went needles, thread, and stamps; a spyglass and microscope; fishing tackle; cooking utensils made of iron or tin. An average load weighed about fifty pounds, not suspended on a frame (as with modern packs) but hanging from narrow, unpadded straps. With that load he climbed the steepest trails, setting a faster pace than most of his companions.

Thoreau planned his mountain trips carefully, but often the maps were misleading. In Maine he was confused by place names, Algonquian and English in variant spellings. No map existed for Monadnock; being a professional surveyor, he supplied his own with crude finesse—a pocket compass for his bearings, the toss of a stone to measure distance (one toss equaled six rods, more or less). This semblance of precision impressed others; Emerson called it "a natural skill for mensuration" and said Thoreau gave all his dimensions exactly. In fact, most of his linear figures are only rough estimates, and those for altitude are merely prayers.

Still, he was a good man with a chart and compass, and his natural obstinacy made him seek out new routes. His favorite mode of walking was "across-lots" on a compass line, ignoring roads and fences, deviating only to avoid houses or people. He thought this habit was evidence of his genius, a desire to see places from the side. In truth, he was shy and secretive, uneasy with the stares or questions of strangers.

He climbed mountains the same way, drawing a bead on some distant point, then plunging into the fog with reckless confidence. Although not averse to trails and bridle paths, often he followed a stream bed up to the mountaintop. Splashing over slick, mossy rock was hazardous, but the route was direct and private. This method worked poorly on Katahdin, where he should have climbed along a rockslide, and in Tuckerman Ravine the stream cut beneath a melting snowfield. Thoreau fell on the snow and ripped his nails; later he sprained an ankle. The wonder is that he was not hurt or lost more often.

For all his quirks as a mountain hiker, Thoreau knew that others would follow him—in Maine he advised: "I will give the names and distances, for the benefit of future tourists." He could see the growth of tourism in his own lifetime, as hotels, summit houses, and stagecoaches began to appear in mountain areas. He preferred the gypsy life, with its primitive style of traveling. His one trip with a horse and wagon was inconvenient; he complained: "I frequently envied the independence of the walker, who can spend the midday hours and take his lunch in the most agreeable spot on his route." Yet he said New Hampshire should develop facilities for wagon campers, in areas that functioned as public parks.

That attitude will surprise readers who think of Thoreau as an enemy of the state, the radical who refused to pay his taxes and defended crazy John Brown. Thoreau held the line on anti-slavery, but in wilderness matters he was pro-government. Often he called for the preservation of forest and mountain areas, free of private interests. Late in life he heard that two rivals were claiming the Mt. Washington summit: "Thank God, men cannot as yet fly, and lay waste to the sky as well as the earth. We are safe on that side for the present." Today that hope has long been dashed, but he would be glad to know that all his mountains lie within federal or state preserves. Many of his routes now follow the Appalachian Trail, a 2,000-mile footpath from Maine to Georgia.

·   ·   ·

Thoreau lived during the great era of mountain climbing in Europe, when the Alps swarmed every summer with athletic tourists. Most climbers were British, for the reign of Victoria inspired a rush of imperial adrenaline. Flush with the profits of industrial power, her sporting gentlemen raced to conquer these last monuments of primitive nature. Climbing asserted their cultural pride, conspicuously expended money and time. British climbers created "mountaineering," a competitive blend of adventure and science. They pushed exploration into little-known pockets of high terrain, and they greatly improved techniques for survival in cold, thin air.

Thoreau was aware of Alpinism. He read about the climbs of early Swiss naturalists like Gesner and de Saussure; he went vicariously along with English poets and journalists to the highest peaks. He knew John Ruskin's descriptions of Alpine scenery in *Modern Painters* (1849–56), especially his two famous chapters "The Mountain Gloom" and "The Mountain Glory." Ruskin was critical of climbing expeditions, for he wanted the mountains to remain a place of sanctuary and meditation. So did Thoreau, yet his own trips were both sporting and scientific.

Any comparison of Thoreau with the Alpinists is bound to make him suffer. The Appalachians are of modest size, and in New England few summits rise above 5,000 feet, a level Thoreau exceeded only on Mt. Washington. The Alps are twice as high, the Himalayans twice again. On the other hand, climbers rate a slope by its vertical relief—how sharply does it rise over surrounding terrain? The great mountains Thoreau climbed have bases of a thousand feet; they rise three to five times that height over short horizontal distances. On those peaks a hiker quickly turns to climber, using hands and feet to scramble up steep grades, where the coarse rock is abrasive.

Even so, the British would call Thoreau's trips hill-walking and bouldering, for he worked mostly on paths and soil slopes, with occasional passages up rock, but without ropes or other technical aids. A true mountaineer could make a list, long as his ice ax, of the thrills Thoreau missed: no winter trips, no mastery of foot- or handholds, no encounter with an exposed pitch or "route of character," where the sense of danger and altitude is paramount. Thoreau never saw an avalanche or a permanent snow line; his one traverse of a small snowfield ended in a fall. The only times he made a bivouac, camping without a tent, were below 3,000 feet—and even then he complained of the cold.

As long as the comparison deals with quantities alone, Thoreau will seem a poor second: he spent more time traveling to and from mountains than he did climbing them, and he never climbed as high or as often as other mountaineers. Herman Melville never harpooned a whale, either, nor did Stephen Crane fight in the Civil War. Physical feats are not required of writers; their achievements lie in the imagination and on paper. Thoreau's value as a climber is that of an artist, one who can re-create his journeys vividly. His mission was to interpret facts, translate them into language, and thereby heighten our feelings and ideas.

Judged on the scale of literary quality, he rises considerably in stature. As writers, most climbers succumb to cliché and inept phrasing: the mountains are too immense for their fumbling words. Edward Whymper, first to climb the Matterhorn, paled before his memory of Monte Rosa, "more brilliant than man knows how to depict." Thoreau was articulate, and he managed to travel far within a narrow circle. The mountains on his horizon answered the purpose of the Rockies or the Andes, because he made the most of self-imposed limits: "As I cannot go upon a Northwest Passage, then I will find a passage round the actual world where I am."

Having this set of values, he thought life could not be small or mean enough, if he were to know it well. At Walden he saw the universe in one house and a pond; mountains were grander, but still he studied them for small signs of large import. In this respect he echoed his mentors, from Kant to Emerson, who said that ideas and earthly forms are synonymous; that knowledge of this kinship is *transcendental,* surpassing the limits of our senses. *Transcend* (in its Latin root) means to climb over, to rise above the ordinary plane. When Thoreau described himself as "a mystic, a transcendentalist, and a natural philosopher to boot," he also defined the higher purpose behind his mountain stories.

As with those of many romantic artists, Thoreau's landscapes represent human consciousness, the outer world expressing his mind's unseen, inner realm. A journey for him was both actual and imaginative, and his challenge as a writer was to make those two ventures balance. In his early work he harped strongly on ideas; later he set down facts rather plainly—too fully, some readers may think.

For him, the change was necessary. His early models—Chaucer, Milton, Wordsworth—used the landscape to portray established ideas, but during the 1850s he was more drawn to books of factual reportage, chiefly travel and natural history. Facts became his means of finding new ideas, providing a ground of reality for higher implications. No fact could therefore be too homely, he wrote: "Familiar and surrounding objects are the best symbols of [a reporter's] life."

Thoreau's mountain stories clearly reflect this growth of mind and art. His early accounts of Wachusett and Greylock are transcendentalist "excursions," journeys that have an appropriate climax on the highest ground, most elevating to his thoughts. His greatest triumph in this vein is *A Week on the Concord and Merrimack Rivers* (1849), parts of which appear here in the sections on Massachusetts and New Hampshire. Written as a memorial for his deceased brother John, with whom he climbed Mt. Washington in 1839, *A Week* retraces their route, moving upstream to the mountains where rivers—and youthful friendships—are endlessly reborn. Reconciled to the flow of time and events, the brothers at last head downstream to Concord, where one day the survivor can write this invocation:

> *Where'er thou sail'st who sailed with me,*
> *Though now thou climbest loftier mounts,*
> *And fairer rivers dost ascend,*
> *Be thou my Muse, my Brother—.*

Although published earlier (1848), "Ktaadn" (Thoreau's spelling of Katahdin) begins to depart from this pattern in several significant ways: in the story Thoreau challenges his own preconceptions of mountain scenery. Significantly, his climax occurs upon descent, for he never actually reached the Katahdin summit. But one view of its desolate lower slopes was enough: "This was that Earth of which we have heard, made out of Chaos and Old Night. Here was no man's garden, but the unhandselled globe." Katahdin changed many of his ideas, especially of how to see and describe the wilderness.

His later narratives, written mostly as entries for the Journal, are not as artless as they seem: Thoreau wrote them in retrospect, often weeks after the event, adding ideas and facts gathered from later research. These journeys to Vermont, Maine, and New Hampshire are not pyramidal but circular, each one serving as a rounded statement of theme, variation, and reprise. His concluding inferences, drawn from the story just told, deliver the sort of "wholesale, hearty statements" he admired in works of natural history, where writers plainly stated their human concerns.

This bias is worth noting, for no matter how "scientific" Thoreau's later stories seem, their main purpose is humanistic: to celebrate experience, not merely to explain it as physical laws. Generally, Thoreau's prose retains the emotion that expresses human consciousness. His description of some shadows on Mt. Lafayette even lends a name to this style: "It several times disappeared and was then brought out again with wonderful brilliancy, as it were an invisible writing, or a fluid which required to be held to the sun to be brought out."

This later prose, which can seem either dense or transparent, shapes the Journal entry for October 29, 1857, in which Thoreau describes a recurrent dream. Dreams are a rare subject in his Journal; this account verifies his fusion of conscious and unconscious meaning.

There are some things of which I cannot at once tell whether I have dreamed them or they are real; as if they were just, perchance, establishing, or else losing, a real basis in my world. This is especially the case in the early morning hours, when there is a gradual transition from dreams to waking thoughts, from illusions to actualities, as from darkness, or perchance moon and star light, to sunlight. Dreams are real, as is the light of the stars and moon, and theirs is said to be a *dreamy* light. Such early morning thoughts as I speak of occupy a debatable ground between dreams and waking thoughts. They are a sort of permanent dream in my mind. At least, until we have for some time changed our position from prostrate to erect, and commenced or faced some of the duties of the day, we cannot tell what we have dreamed from what we have actually experienced.

This morning, for instance, for the twentieth time at least, I thought of that mountain in the easterly part of our town (where no high hill actually is) which once or twice I had ascended, and often allowed my thoughts alone to climb. I now contemplate it in my mind as a familiar thought which I have surely had for many years from time to time, but whether anything could have reminded me of it in the middle of yesterday, whether I ever before remembered it in broad daylight, I doubt. I can now eke out the vision I had of it this morning with my old and yesterday forgotten dreams.

My way up used to lie through a dark and unfrequented wood at its base,—I cannot now tell exactly, it was so long ago, under what circumstances I first ascended, only that I shuddered as I went along (I have an indistinct remembrance of having been out overnight alone),—and then I steadily ascended along a rocky ridge half clad with stinted trees, where wild beasts haunted, till I lost myself quite in the upper air and clouds, seeming to pass an imaginary line which separates a hill, mere earth heaped up, from a mountain, into a super-terranean grandeur and sublimity. What distinguishes that summit above the earthy line, is that it is unhandselled, awful, grand. It can never become familiar; you are lost the moment you set foot there. You know no path, but wander, thrilled, over the bare and pathless rock, as if it were solidified air and cloud. That rocky, misty summit, secreted in the clouds, was far more thrillingly awful and sublime than the crater of a volcano spouting fire.

This is a business we can partly understand. The perfect mountain height is already thoroughly purified. It is as if you trod with awe the face of a god turned up, unwittingly but helplessly, yielding to the laws of gravity. And are there not such mountains, east or west, from which you may look down on Concord in your thought, and on all the world? In dreams I am shown this height from time to time, and I seem to have asked my fellow once to climb there with me, and yet I am constrained to believe that I never actually ascended it. It chances, now I think of it,* that it rises in my mind where lies the Burying-Hill. You might go through its gate to enter that dark wood,† but that hill and its graves are so concealed and obliterated by the

---

*Now *first think of it*, at this stage of my description, which makes it the more singularly symbolical. The interlineations on the last page were made before this. ["Only that I shuddered . . . overnight alone" in the last paragraph.—WH]
†Perchance that was the grave.

awful mountain that I never thought of them as underlying it. Might not the graveyards of the just always be hills, ways by which we ascend and over look the plain?

But my old way down was different, and, indeed, this was another way up, though I never so ascended. I came out, as I descended, breathing the thicker air. I came out the belt of wood into a familiar pasture, and along down by a wall. Often, as I go along the low side of this pasture, I let my thoughts ascend toward the mount, gradually entering the stinted wood (Nature subdued) and the thinner air, and drape themselves with mists. There are ever two ways up: one is through the dark wood, the other through the sunny pasture. That is, I reach and discover the mountain only through the dark wood, but I see to my surprise, when I look off between the mists from its summit, how it is ever adjacent to my native fields, nay, imminent over them, and accessible through a sunny pasture. Why is it that in the lives of men we hear more of the dark wood than of the sunny pasture?

A hard-featured god reposing, whose breath hangs about his forehead.

Though the pleasure of ascending the mountain is largely mixed with awe, my thoughts are purified and sublimed by it, as if I had been translated.

To Thoreau, this mountain was both real and imaginary: it rose in the eastern part of Concord (where no mountains exist); his way up lay along a ridge of dwarfed trees, of the sort he had often seen above 3,500 feet. Finally (as on Katahdin), he became lost on the clouded upper heights, wandering through scenes of grand sublimity. Ruskin may have prompted this description (Thoreau referred to him the next day), but so did a long series of actual experiences.

Romance and reality fused in Thoreau's later mind, as his mountain stories make clear. On Monadnock the summit became a lodestone, drawing together all his knowledge of alpine life—plants, birds, rocks, clouds, views—to make a final, integrated statement. Some of his notes and cross-references suggest that he wanted to publish this material, a possibility cut short by his death in 1862. The Monadnock entries make a fitting coda, for they depict a world of Chaos passing toward

Cosmos, the order he sought in nature. On this mountain—from which Thoreau saw many of the peaks he had climbed—he found a rough, uneven surface that suggested many ideas within a small space: "We no longer thought and reasoned as in the plain." That theme has inspired many later writers—Nietzsche, Mann, Hemingway—who also saw mountains as a symbol of the human will.

.   .   .

Thoreau's interest in mountains was not purely literary. Their very shape, rising suddenly above the plains, stirred his curiosity: "What is it lifts them upward so? Why not rest level along the horizon?" Many early climbers were also men of thought, drawn to intellectual work in outdoor settings. These scholar-mountaineers, as Wilfrid Noyce calls them, shared a common need for challenge and isolation on the heights, but also for imparting their knowledge to the lower world.

During his last ten years, Thoreau attempted to learn the natural history of North America: Indians, European explorers, plant and animal relations, the development of land forms. He read hundreds of books and articles on these subjects, copied passages into the Journal and his notebooks. The work was preliminary, its ultimate purpose undefined. When he died, friends like Emerson lamented: "The scale on which his studies proceeded was so large as to require longevity, and we were the less prepared for his sudden disappearance." Speculation later arose about various "books" Thoreau might have written about Indians, the seasons, his favorite haunts in Concord. The purpose of *Thoreau in the Mountains* is not to launch yet another mythical book but to present what he wrote and knew about mountains. Even so, when his narratives are brought together, certain themes and subjects begin to stand out.

Thoreau's central preoccupation was clearly with plant life, but his own knowledge of botany was not systematic. He learned a bit just after college, then made a serious study of scientific nomenclature in the 1850s. He read Linnaeus with a literary bias, reacting at once to the abundance and precision of botanical language. Plant names were a kind of sensuous Latin poetry, pure liquid on the tongue: *Chelone glabra, Potentilla tridentata, Festuca ovina.* The Linnaean *Systema Naturae* (1758), a vast complex of phyla, orders, and species, impressed Thoreau with its coherence and rigor. Linnaeus could classify anything, even a miscellaneous *Botanophilist* from Concord.

In Concord, Thoreau managed to locate all of Linnaeus's twenty-five types of plant environments, from *Mare* to *Ruderata,* except for high meadows *(Alpes),* but several American authorities told him where to look nearby. The writings of William Oakes, Jacob Bigelow, and Edward Tuckerman all pointed to the White Mountains. Tuckerman, who taught botany at Amherst in the 1850s and published important studies of alpine lichens, did his principal fieldwork near Mt. Washington (hence the naming of Tuckerman Ravine), where he located many plants normally found only in the Arctic.

Inspired by this work, Thoreau made his journeys of 1858 and 1860 and verified the presence of six vegetative zones on mountain slopes. Von Humboldt saw as much in the Andes half a century earlier, but Thoreau was surveying a northern latitude, in far greater detail. Moreover, the sequence of plants (each higher level grew simpler and more primitive) suggested to him a model for the historical succession of species. That theme, worked out to a finer degree in his study of Concord's forests, coincided with the evolutionary theory unfolded by Darwin in 1859.

Linnaeus and Darwin were the bookends to Thoreau's career as a naturalist, and their influence led him to study the species of given areas—what ecologists now call "plant communities." On the mountain summits he found a regular alternation between wet and dry communities, the grassy bogs and "scars" of loose gravel, and this rhythm continued down the lower slopes: moist and shaded on the north, drier with more sun on the south. Many factors—light, wind, water, surface contour—influenced these patterns, which in turn affected the feeding or nesting habits of animals. The idea of an "ecosystem" was years away, but Thoreau was heading toward it.

His ultimate concern was not with individual species, the endless particulars that break down nature into Variety, but with integrating these elements into a holistic Unity—a concord, like his town's symbolic name. He was therefore drawn to studying and describing large natural processes, the events that link together many species into complex phenomena. Because he was an artist, not a scientist, he made bold, inclusive arguments. Undoubtedly, he also made mistakes, left wide gaps in the evidence and theories he was building. But his work on forest succession, the distribution of species, the transitional patterns of seasons, were all original contributions to ecological study—which in his day had not even reached infancy.

The mountains helped him advance this work, taught him to refine concepts and develop new ones. He found that a summit in New Hampshire resembled the coast of Labrador, because altitude and latitude were equivalents. Later alpine botanists have worked out this relationship more precisely; to Thoreau it was a proof of his strongest belief, that the mind can travel far within its single circle.

The slopes also gave him fresh evidence about birds, insects, and mammals, but he chose not to explore zoology closely. His descriptions of animals are mostly appreciative, limited to sympathetic thoughts about wildlife, the creatures who survive by their own laws and needs. The winter "yards" of moose and deer on Katahdin, the booming of nighthawks on Monadnock, all portray a vigorous form of life that he admires but does not examine thoroughly.

Even less rigorous was his knowledge of geology, the field of study that mountains inspired. Lyell's *Principles of Geology* (1830–33) was available when Thoreau studied at Harvard, but there his scientific training was minimal—physics, astronomy, entomology, a bit of mineralogy. He learned about graphite mining to help his father's pencil business, but mineral elements seemed a poor resource to him, as he wrote in 1844: "It is hard to know rocks. They are crude and inaccessible to our nature." Thoreau met Louis Agassiz in 1846, and in April 1854 he borrowed a copy of the Swiss scientist's three-volume work (called by Thoreau in a letter "Agassiz sur les Glaciers"). Yet either Thoreau forgot about glaciation or he regarded it as an unproven theory. He read a few geological reports and recognized fossil plants, but he wrote nothing about the main controversies of his day: whether geological events were uniform, catastrophic, contrary to Scripture, and so on.

Despite this background, he was an accurate observer of geological evidence. On every mountain, he could identify the principal types of rock, including varieties of granite, mica schist, and quartz at Monadnock. He also noted forms wrought by uplift and erosion: ridges, gullies, ravines, slides. Although silent about glaciers, he described (and sketched) virtually all the souvenirs of our last Ice Age: the cirque, or deep eroded hollow, of Tuckerman Ravine; the debris and ponds of moraines, dropped at the edges of glacial flow; the grooves and scratches left on mountaintops. On Katahdin and Monadnock he saw strange rounded outcrops, smooth on one side, rough and fleecy on the other. His homely analogy: "flocks and herds that pastured, chewing a rocky cud." Alpinists call them *roches moutonnées,* or fleecy-mutton rocks.

Thoreau's ignorance is understandable, because geology was so youthful in his day, and perhaps also because this science demands so much of an observer, who must leap from present evidence back into immense stretches of time. Rocks are complex, subject to varied interpretation, and knowledge of them has evolved rapidly since Thoreau's time. New theories seem to appear each decade; countertheories bubble to the surface like magma in a volcanic caldera. In the 1960s, a great revision of geological thought began which provided a new explanation for the origins of mountains.

This theory, known as plate tectonics, holds that mountains arise from the movement of vast, irregular plates in the earth's outer layer. On top of the plates are continents, and mountains ride atop them. When the plates collide along their edges, one edge gives way and slides under the other; if continents are riding above, the flatland buckles, rising into mountains. On the rise, mountains are falling as well, gradually eroding into plains and lowlands. Later, uplift may build new mountains, which in turn erode away. The process is slow, imperceptible, ceaseless. It has occurred countless times in the earth's total history. All the mountains Thoreau saw arose from recent versions of these great cycles.

The forces that built contemporary New England took more than 500 million years, or eleven percent of earthly time. Oceans were once there, then volcanoes (forming the Berkshires); after collisions of the North American and European plates, successive waves of mountain building occurred, a process of uplift, downwarp, and folding that produced the Appalachian chain (and White Mountains) 100 million years ago. Erosion followed, wearing down all but the chain and some isolated knobs of resistant rock, standing alone as monadnocks (Wachusett, Greylock, Monadnock, Katahdin). Two million years ago, glaciation ensued, building up ice sheets two miles thick. They flowed and receded in successive cycles, plucking and scraping the mountains bare, dropping till and outwash farther south. The ice began its most recent retreat 25,000 years ago and now abides in Greenland. Vegetation returned from the south; human beings appeared thereafter. Indians have lived in New England for ten thousand years, Europeans for five hundred.

The numbers are big and hard to grasp; geologists often suggest that novices imagine earth history in smaller units of time. For example, let one calendar year represent the entire four and a half billion years. If the earth began at midnight on January 1, then the Berkshires emerged late in the fall (November 28), the White Mountains just after winter solstice (December 23), and the glaciers departed two seconds before midnight on December 31. Human beings have lived in New England for one second. Henry Thoreau first saw mountains on his horizon just an instant ago.

Massachusetts

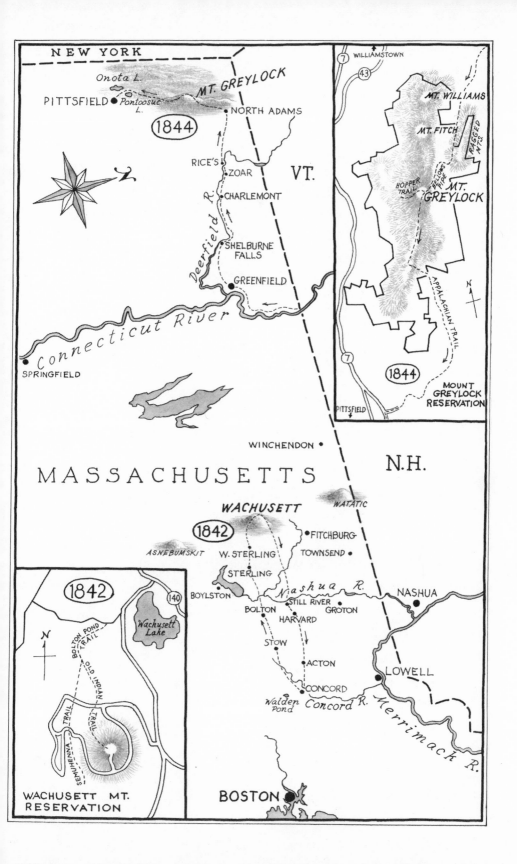

NEW YORK

Onota L.
PITTSFIELD ● ●Pontoosuc L.
MT. GREYLOCK
1844
● NORTH ADAMS

VT.

RICE'S
● ZOAR
Deerfield R.
● CHARLEMONT

● SHELBURNE FALLS
● GREENFIELD

Connecticut River

● SPRINGFIELD

7
WILLIAMSTOWN
43
MT. WILLIAMS
MT. FITCH
RAGGED MTS
BELLOWS PIPE
HOPPER TRAIL
MT. GREYLOCK
APPALACHIAN TRAIL
7
1844
PITTSFIELD
N
MOUNT GREYLOCK RESERVATION

WINCHENDON ●

MASSACHUSETTS

N.H.

WACHUSETT
WATATIC
1842
● FITCHBURG
ASNEBUMSKIT
W. STERLING
TOWNSEND ●
STERLING
Nashua R.
NASHUA ●
BOYLSTON ●
BOLTON ●
STILL RIVER ●
GROTON ●
HARVARD
STOW ●
ACTON ●
CONCORD ●
Walden Pond
Concord R.
Merrimack R.
LOWELL ●

1842
140
Wachusett Lake
BOLTON POND TRAIL
OLD INDIAN TRAIL
N
SEMUHENNA TRAIL
WACHUSETT MT. RESERVATION

BOSTON ●

Wachusett

---

*A mountain chain determines many things for the
statesman and philosopher. The improvements of
civilization rather creep along its sides than
cross its summit.*

From the top of Annursnuck Hill in Concord, Wachusett lies
nearly due west, twenty-six miles away. Wachusett is a lump of rock
that defied the glaciers. Its tough granite resisted millennia of scouring and weathering, while all around it the land surface eroded
away. A string of similar mountains runs from south to north across
central Massachusetts: Asnebumskit (1,395'), Wachusett (2,006'), and
Watatic (1,840'). Geologists call them *monadnocks,* after the Grand
Monadnock (3,165') that stands in New Hampshire, thirty miles
north. The monadnocks are upstarts in an otherwise compliant landscape: conspicuous and solitary, they surprise the traveler who meets
them unprepared.

In July of 1842, Thoreau felt he was ready to see Wachusett. On his
first mountain trip he had gone north, to New Hampshire, with his
brother John in 1839. Since boyhood, they had also looked west to
Wachusett, imagining a vast continent on the other side. Wachusett
lay on a path of discovery and exploration, the arc of progress that
marched from Greece to America. When John suddenly died in January of 1842, Henry's vision of progress nearly expired as well. Yet
slowly he recovered from grief, and after his twenty-fifth birthday on
July 12, he decided to step westward at last.

On July 19, 1842, Thoreau left Concord with Richard Fuller, a Harvard undergraduate and the brother of Margaret Fuller, Thoreau's
editor at *The Dial.* The hikers had knapsacks, some provisions, and a
tent. The tent was heavy, so they took turns carrying it. Starting before

dawn, they marched over twenty-five miles to a village (now West Sterling) on the Stillwater River. In the morning, they ascended Wachusett and camped there overnight, enjoying a fine sunrise view on July 21. Then they descended and walked to Harvard, where they spent the night. On July 22 they parted company, Fuller going home to Groton and Thoreau back to Concord.

Fuller wrote an account of this journey which survives in part, covering the trip as far as Stow. His style was florid and pompous, much given to citing the classics: his hikers went west into "the broad realm of Pan," away from the lands of Minerva (Cambridge) and Mammon (Boston). Fuller was not an ideal companion. He had no taste for puns or paradox, even less for the unorthodoxy of transcendentalism. His sister Margaret was less conventional, yet twice she had rejected Thoreau's submissions to *The Dial,* insisting (with cause) that a "mosaic" of his Journal passages was a poor contrivance.

In writing an essay about Wachusett, Thoreau decided to use the simpler pattern of a travel story. Within this frame, time and space became an orderly sequence, pulling his ideas into a logical chain. He had produced an "excursion," the story pattern that shapes most of his later works: a traveler leaves home, seeking the novelty of a new land. There he encounters something—a lake, a mountain, the ocean shore—that gives him a fresh view of nature and his place in its order. With this insight he returns home, ready to resume his ties with society.

This narrative form was hardly unique, as Thoreau's allusions indicate: he cited the epic voyages of Homer and Virgil, the moral journeys of Rasselas and Peter Bell. In the latter works, travel was a moral enterprise, an opportunity to test the mind and see God's power. To this tradition Thoreau added a historical dimension, the going west that is America's Manifest Destiny. His single excursion was therefore a national story: "In the spaces of thought are the reaches of land and water, where men go and come. The landscape lies far and fair within, and the deepest thinker is the farthest traveled."

One of Thoreau's friends in Concord was Nathaniel Hawthorne, a writer with more commercial instinct than those who published in *The Dial.* He probably encouraged Thoreau to take the following essay, "A Walk to Wachusett," to *The Boston Miscellany,* where it appeared in January 1843. Another version later appeared in a posthumous volume of travel and nature essays, *Excursions* (1863), edited by Thoreau's sister and friends.

A WALK

TO WACHUSETT

Concord, July 19, 1842.

The needles of the pine
All to the west incline.

Summer and winter our eyes had rested on the dim outline of the mountains in our horizon, to which distance and indistinctness lent a grandeur not their own, so that they served equally to interpret all the allusions of poets and travelers; whether with Homer, on a spring morning, we sat down on the many-peaked Olympus, or with Virgil and his compeers roamed the Etrurian and Thessalian hills, or with Humboldt measured the more modern Andes and Teneriffe. Thus we spoke our mind to them, standing on the Concord cliffs:—

> *With frontier strength ye stand your ground,*
> *With grand content ye circle round,*
> *Tumultuous silence for all sound,*
> *Ye distant nursery of rills,*
> *Monadnock, and the Peterboro' hills;*
> *Like some vast fleet,*
> *Sailing through rain and sleet,*
> *Through winter's cold and summer's heat;*
> *Still holding on, upon your high emprise,*
> *Until ye find a shore amid the skies;*
> *Not skulking close to land,*

With cargo contraband,
For they who sent a venture out by ye
Have set the sun to see
Their honesty.
Ships of the line, each one,
Ye to the westward run,
Always before the gale,
Under a press of sail,
With weight of metal all untold.
I seem to feel ye, in my firm seat here,
Immeasurable depth of hold,
And breadth of beam, and length of running gear.

Methinks ye take luxurious pleasure
In your novel western leisure;
So cool your brows, and freshly blue,
As Time had nought for ye to do;
For ye lie at your length,
An unappropriated strength,
Unhewn primeval timber,
For knees so stiff, for masts so limber;
The stock of which new earths are made
One day to be our western trade,
Fit for the stanchions of a world
Which through the seas of space is hurled.

While we enjoy a lingering ray,
Ye still o'ertop the western day,
Reposing yonder, on God's croft,
Like solid stacks of hay.
Edged with silver, and with gold,
The clouds hang o'er in damask fold,
And with such depth of amber light
The west is dight,
Where still a few rays slant,
That even heaven seems extravagant.
On the earth's edge mountains and trees

Stand as they were on air graven,
Or as the vessels in a haven
Await the morning breeze.
I fancy even
Through your defiles windeth the way to heaven;
And yonder still, in spite of history's page,
Linger the golden and the silver age;
Upon the laboring gale
The news of future centuries is brought,
And of new dynasties of thought,
From your remotest vale.

But special I remember thee,
Wachusett, who like me
Standest alone without society.
Thy far blue eye,
A remnant of the sky,
Seen through the clearing or the gorge
Or from the windows of the forge,
Doth leaven all it passes by.
Nothing is true,
But stands 'tween me and you,
Thou western pioneer,
Who know'st not shame nor fear
By venturous spirit driven,
Under the eaves of heaven.
And canst expand thee there,
And breathe enough of air?
Upholding heaven, holding down earth,
Thy pastime from thy birth,
Not steadied by the one, nor leaning on the other;
May I approve myself thy worthy brother!

At length, like Rasselas, and other inhabitants of happy valleys, we resolved to scale the blue wall which bounded the western horizon, though not without misgivings that thereafter no visible fairyland would exist for us. But we will not leap at once to our journey's end, though near, but imitate Homer, who conducts his reader over the plain, and along the resounding sea, though it be but to the tent of Achilles. In the spaces of thought are the reaches of land and water, where men go and come. The landscape lies far and fair within, and the deepest thinker is the farthest traveled.

> Thoreau sprinkled literary references throughout this essay, a hallmark of his early style. He began with allusions to Homer, Virgil, and Humboldt to suggest that mountains, whether in the Old or the New World, have long been associated with discovery. His poem, written in shaggy couplets, addressed both the future and the past: Wachusett was a "frontier" mountain but also a "worthy brother," like the recently deceased John Thoreau, Jr. The allusion to Samuel Johnson's *Rasselas* was equally sober: in leaving home and wandering the earth, Rasselas learned that all experiences and moods eventually fade away.
>
> *ROUTE FROM CONCORD: Lexington Road (MA 2A) to Main Street (MA 62) to Concord Turnpike (MA 2)* Thoreau's trip began in Concord at Emerson's house, on the corner of Lexington Road and the old Cambridge Turnpike. Across the street today is the Concord Antiquarian Society, a museum that displays the furniture from Thoreau's house at Walden Pond. (The Thoreau Lyceum, 158 Belknap Street, has a replica of the Walden house.) Thoreau lived at the Emersons' in 1841–43 and 1845–47. His second-floor room is now a storage closet. On Main Street are the Free Public Library (Thoreau books, manuscripts, and artifacts) and the house (No. 255, private) where Thoreau lived with his parents in 1850–62.

At a cool and early hour on a pleasant morning in July, my companion and I passed rapidly through Acton and Stow, stopping to rest and refresh us on the bank of a small stream, a tributary of the Assabet, in the latter town. As we traversed the cool woods of Acton, with stout staves in our hands, we were cheered by the song of the red-eye, the

*This summary always follows Thoreau's route of travel, using modern names and highway numbers. Any necessary deviations from his route are noted in the commentary.—WH

thrushes, the phœbe, and the cuckoo; and as we passed through the open country, we inhaled the fresh scent of every field, and all nature lay passive, to be viewed and traveled. Every rail, every farmhouse, seen dimly in the twilight, every tinkling sound told of peace and purity, and we moved happily along the dank roads, enjoying not such privacy as the day leaves when it withdraws, but such as it has not profaned. It was solitude with light; which is better than darkness. But anon, the sound of the mower's rifle was heard in the fields, and this, too, mingled with the lowing of kine.

Emerson's home, Concord, Mass.

This part of our route lay through the country of hops, which plant perhaps supplies the want of the vine in American scenery, and may remind the traveler of Italy and the South of France, whether he traverses the country when the hop-fields, as then, present solid and regular masses of verdure, hanging in graceful festoons from pole to pole, the cool coverts where lurk the gales which refresh the way-farer; or in September, when the women and children, and the neigh-bors from far and near, are gathered to pick the hops into long troughs; or later still, when the poles stand piled in vast pyramids in the yards, or lie in heaps by the roadside.

The culture of the hop, with the processes of picking, drying in the kiln, and packing for the market, as well as the uses to which it is applied, so analogous to the culture and uses of the grape, may afford a theme for future poets.

The mower in the adjacent meadow could not tell us the name of the brook on whose banks we had rested, or whether it had any, but his younger companion, perhaps his brother, knew that it was Great Brook. Though they stood very near together in the field, the things they knew were very far apart; nor did they suspect each other's reserved knowledge, till the stranger came by. In Bolton, while we rested on the rails of a cottage fence, the strains of music which issued from within, probably in compliment to us, sojourners, reminded us that thus far men were fed by the accustomed pleasures. So soon did we, wayfarers, begin to learn that man's life is rounded with the same few facts, the same simple relations everywhere, and it is vain to travel to find it new. The flowers grow more various ways than he. But coming soon to higher land, which afforded a prospect of the mountains, we thought we had not traveled in vain, if it were only to hear a truer and wilder pronunciation of their names from the lips of the inhabitants; not *Way*-tatic, *Way*-chusett, but *Wor*-tatic, *Wor*-chusett. It made us ashamed of our tame and civil pronunciation, and we looked upon them as born and bred farther west than we. Their tongues had a more generous accent than ours, as if breath was cheaper where they wagged. A countryman, who speaks but seldom, talks copiously, as it were, as his wife sets cream and cheese before you without stint. Before noon we had reached the highlands overlooking the valley of Lancaster (affording the first fair and open prospect into the west), and there, on the top of a hill, in the shade of some oaks, near to where a spring bubbled out from a leaden pipe, we rested during the heat of the day, reading Virgil and enjoying the scenery. It was such a place as one feels to be on the outside of the earth; for from it we could, in some measure, see the form and structure of the globe. There lay Wachusett, the object of our journey, lowering upon us with unchanged proportions, though with a less ethereal aspect than had greeted our morning gaze, while further north, in successive order, slumbered its sister mountains along the horizon.

We could get no further into the Æneid than

—atque altae moenia Romae,
—and the wall of high Rome,

before we were constrained to reflect by what myriad tests a work of genius has to be tried; that Virgil, away in Rome, two thousand years off, should have to unfold his meaning, the inspiration of Italian vales, to the pilgrim on New England hills. This life so raw and modern, that so civil and ancient; and yet we read Virgil mainly to be reminded of the identity of human nature in all ages, and, by the poet's own account, we are both the children of a late age, and live equally under the reign of Jupiter.

"He shook honey from the leaves, and removed fire,
And stayed the wine, everywhere flowing in rivers;
That experience, by meditating, might invent various arts
By degrees, and seek the blade of corn in furrows,
And strike out hidden fire from the veins of the flint."

The old world stands serenely behind the new, as one mountain yonder towers behind another, more dim and distant. Rome imposes her story still upon this late generation. The very children in the school we had that morning passed had gone through her wars, and recited her alarms, ere they had heard of the wars of neighboring Lancaster. The roving eye still rests inevitably on her hills, and she still holds up the skirts of the sky on that side, and makes the past remote.

The hour of departure on July 19 was early; Fuller said they were underway "about quarter to five." The small stream where they rested (see p. 30) is Great Brook, which crosses MA 117 just east of Meadow Road. Fuller said they cut the walking staves in a woods "between Concord and Stowe." Their hilltop view of Wachusett (see p. 30) was possibly from Wataquadock Hill (600'). The passages from Virgil allude to the building of Rome and Carthage, two cities with strikingly different fates.

ROUTE FROM CONCORD TURNPIKE: *MA 2 to Acton, MA 111 to Willow Street, West Acton Road to Stow, MA 117 to Bolton, MA 62 to Sterling*

The lay of the land hereabouts is well worthy the attention of the traveler. The hill on which we were resting made part of an extensive range, running from southwest to northeast, across the country, and separating the waters of the Nashua from those of the Concord, whose banks we had left in the morning, and by bearing in mind this fact, we could easily determine whither each brook was bound that crossed our path. Parallel to this, and fifteen miles further west, beyond the deep and broad valley in which lie Groton, Shirley, Lancaster, and Boylston, runs the Wachusett range, in the same general direction. The descent into the valley on the Nashua side is by far the most sudden; and a couple of miles brought us to the southern branch of the Nashua, a shallow but rapid stream, flowing between high and gravelly banks. But we soon learned that these were no *gelidae valles* into which we had descended, and, missing the coolness of the morning air, feared it had become the sun's turn to try his power upon us.

> *"The sultry sun had gained the middle sky,*
> *And not a tree, and not an herb was nigh,"*

and with melancholy pleasure we echoed the melodious plaint of our fellow-traveler, Hassan, in the desert,—

> *"Sad was the hour, and luckless was the day,*
> *When first from Schiraz' walls I bent my way."*

The air lay lifeless between the hills, as in a seething caldron, with no leaf stirring, and instead of the fresh odor of grass and clover, with which we had before been regaled, the dry scent of every herb seemed merely medicinal. Yielding, therefore, to the heat, we strolled into the woods, and along the course of a rivulet, on whose banks we loitered, observing at our leisure the products of these new fields. He who traverses the woodland paths, at this season, will have occasion to remember the small, drooping, bell-like flowers and slender red stem of the dogsbane, and the coarser stem and berry of the poke, which are both common in remoter and wilder scenes; and if "the sun casts such a reflecting heat from the sweet-fern" as makes him faint, when he is climbing the bare hills, as they complained who first penetrated into these parts, the cool fragrance of the swamp-pink restores him again, when traversing the valleys between.

As we went on our way late in the afternoon, we refreshed ourselves by bathing our feet in every rill that crossed the road, and anon, as we were able to walk in the shadows of the hills, recovered our morning elasticity. Passing through Sterling, we reached the banks of the Stillwater, in the western part of the town, at evening, where is a small village collected. We fancied that there was already a certain western look about this place, a smell of pines and roar of water, recently confined by dams, belying its name, which were exceedingly grateful. When the first inroad has been made, a few acres leveled, and a few houses erected, the forest looks wilder than ever. Left to herself, nature is always more or less civilized, and delights in a certain refinement; but where the axe has encroached upon the edge of the forest, the dead and unsightly limbs of the pine, which she had concealed with green banks of verdure, are exposed to sight. This village had, as yet, no post-office, nor any settled name. In the small villages which we entered, the villagers gazed after us, with a complacent, almost compassionate look, as if we were just making our *début* in the world at a late hour. "Nevertheless," did they seem to say, "come and study us, and learn men and manners." So is each one's world but a clearing in the forest, so much open and inclosed ground. The landlord had not yet returned from the field with his men, and the cows had yet to be milked. But we remembered the inscription on the wall of the Swedish inn, "You will find at Trolhate excellent bread, meat, and wine, provided you bring them with you," and were contented. But I must confess it did somewhat disturb our pleasure, in this withdrawn spot, to have our own village newspaper handed us by our host, as if the greatest charm the country offered to the traveler was the facility of communication with the town. Let it recline on its own everlasting hills, and not be looking out from their summits for some petty Boston or New York in the horizon.

Thoreau was determined to see this landscape as pasto- ral, a mid-ground between civilization and wilderness. He quoted alternately from two sources of pastoral poetry, ancient and modern: the *Georgics* of Virgil and the

ROUTE FROM STERLING: *MA 62 and MA 140 to West Sterling*

(see page 32) *Persian Eclogues* of William Collins. The "rivulet" is still unnamed; it crosses MA 62 just before the Conrail tracks.

(see page 33) But the "small village" is now West Sterling, on the banks of the Stillwater River. Thoreau and Fuller had hiked twenty-five miles in one day; they probably lodged here in a private home.

At intervals we heard the murmuring of water, and the slumberous breathing of crickets, throughout the night; and left the inn the next morning in the gray twilight, after it had been hallowed by the night air, and when only the innocent cows were stirring, with a kind of regret. It was only four miles to the base of the mountain, and the scenery was already more picturesque. Our road lay along the course of the Stillwater, which was brawling at the bottom of a deep ravine, filled with pines and rocks, tumbling fresh from the mountains, so

Wachusett

soon, alas! to commence its career of usefulness. At first, a cloud hung between us and the summit, but it was soon blown away. As we gathered the raspberries, which grew abundantly by the roadside, we fancied that that action was consistent with a lofty prudence; as if the traveler who ascends into a mountainous region should fortify himself by eating of such light ambrosial fruits as grow there, and drinking of the springs which gush out from the mountain-sides, as he gradually inhales the subtler and purer atmosphere of those elevated places, thus propitiating the mountain gods by a sacrifice of their own fruits. The gross products of the plains and valleys are for such as dwell therein; but it seemed to us that the juices of this berry had relation to the thin air of the mountain-tops.

In due time we began to ascend the mountain, passing, first, through a grand sugar maple wood, which bore the marks of the auger, then a denser forest, which gradually became dwarfed, till there were no trees whatever. We at length pitched our tent on the summit. It is but nineteen hundred feet above the village of Princeton, and three thousand above the level of the sea; but by this slight elevation it is infinitely removed from the plain, and when we reached it we felt a sense of remoteness, as if we had traveled into distant regions, to Arabia Petræa, or the farthest East. A robin upon a staff was the highest object in sight. Swallows were flying about us, and the chewink and cuckoo were heard near at hand. The summit consists of a few acres, destitute of trees, covered with bare rocks, interspersed with blueberry bushes, raspberries, gooseberries, strawberries, moss, and a fine, wiry grass. The common yellow lily and dwarf cornel grow abundantly in the crevices of the rocks. This clear space, which is gently rounded, is bounded a few feet lower by a thick shrubbery of oaks, with maples, aspens, beeches, cherries, and occasionally a mountain-ash intermingled, among which we found the bright blue berries of the Solomon's-seal, and the fruit of the pyrola. From the foundation of a wooden observatory, which was formerly erected on the highest point, forming a rude, hollow structure of stone, a dozen feet in diameter, and five or six in height, we could see Monadnock, in simple grandeur, in the northwest, rising nearly a thousand feet higher, still the "far blue mountain," though with an altered profile. The first day the weather was so hazy that it was in vain we endeavored to unravel the obscurity. It was like looking into the sky again, and the patches of forest here and there seemed to flit like clouds over a lower heaven. As to voyagers of an aerial Polynesia, the earth seemed like a larger island in the ether; on every side, even as low as we, the sky shutting down, like an unfathomable deep, around it, a blue Pacific island, where who knows what islanders inhabit? and as we sail near its shores we see the waving of trees and hear the lowing of kine.

We read Virgil and Wordsworth in our tent, with new pleasure there, while waiting for a clearer atmosphere, nor did the weather prevent our appreciating the simple truth and beauty of Peter Bell:

> *"And he had lain beside his asses,*
>   *On lofty Cheviot Hills:*

> *"And he had trudged through Yorkshire dales,*
>   *Among the rocks and winding* scars;
>   *Where deep and low the hamlets lie*
>   *Beneath their little patch of sky*
>   *And little lots of stars."*

Who knows but this hill may one day be a Helvellyn, or even a Parnassus, and the Muses haunt here, and other Homers frequent the neighboring plains?

> *Not unconcerned Wachusett rears his head*
>   *Above the field, so late from nature won,*
> *With patient brow reserved, as one who read*
>   *New annals in the history of man.*

The blueberries which the mountain afforded, added to the milk we had brought, made our frugal supper, while for entertainment the even-song of the wood thrush rang along the ridge. Our eyes rested on no painted ceiling nor carpeted hall, but on skies of Nature's painting, and hills and forests of her embroidery. Before sunset, we rambled along the ridge to the north, while a hawk soared still above us. It was a place where gods might wander, so solemn and solitary, and removed from all contagion with the plain. As the evening came on, the haze was condensed in vapor, and the landscape became more distinctly visible, and numerous sheets of water were brought to light.

> *"Et jam summa procul villarum culmina fumant,*
>   *Majoresque cadunt altis de montibus umbrae."*
> *And now the tops of the villas smoke afar off,*
>   *And the shadows fall longer from the high mountains.*

As we stood on the stone tower while the sun was setting, we saw the shades of night creep gradually over the valleys of the east; and the inhabitants went into their houses, and shut their doors, while the moon silently rose up, and took possession of that part. And then the same scene was repeated on the west side, as far as the Connecticut and the Green Mountains, and the sun's rays fell on us two alone, of all New England men.

It was the night but one before the full of the moon, so bright that we could see to read distinctly by moonlight, and in the evening strolled over the summit without danger. There was, by chance, a fire blazing on Monadnock that night, which lighted up the whole western horizon, and, by making us aware of a community of mountains, made our position seem less solitary. But at length the wind drove us to the shelter of our tent, and we closed its door for the night, and fell asleep.

Wachusett Reservation is a year-round state park, replete with Visitor Center (maps and displays) and auto road. Carriage roads first appeared here in the 1850s; today's paved surface is a two-mile, one-way loop. The road is free, easy to "climb," and just two hours' driving time from greater Boston. Hence, Wachusett is one of the busiest mountains in North America. A quarter of a million visitors ascend each year; ten thousand a day come during the fall foliage season. Not all of them leave behind "the gross products of plains and valleys." Near the lower gate a sign reads: NO SKATEBOARDING ON ROAD.

ROUTE FROM WEST STERLING: *MA 140 to Wachusett Mountain State Reservation, Bolton Pond Trail to Old Indian Trail, same to summit*

(see page 35)

Walking time via Thoreau's route, the Bolton Pond and Old Indian trails, is about forty-five minutes. Changes in mountain vegetation since his visit reflect the species succession that occurs on undisturbed land. The sugar maples he saw have given way to hemlocks, part of the climax forest. Fallen hemlock needles, rich in tannin, create an acidic "duff" or humus for evergreen shrubs like mountain laurel and rhododendron. This soil is thick and damp, but easily eroded by rain and hikers. Along the path, most tree roots are exposed, making dark

(see page 35)

gnarled shapes against the gray-green lichens on rock shelves and ledges.

The trail is steep and wet, but at intervals it crosses flat shoulders open to the sky. These "benches" are forested or farmed patches where trees were cleared early in the twentieth century. Recovery is slow at this elevation: the new growth is small and wind-stunted. At 1,200 feet, the trail enters a large artificial clearing, the West and Long John ski trails. Both trails form long slashes of meadow, attracting flowers and birds, but also human traffic. New trails and chair lifts are planned, enough to accommodate 1,900 skiers an hour.

The exact elevations of Wachusett (2,006′) and Princeton (1,175′) differ from Thoreau's figures. Wachusett is not above the normal tree line, yet its summit is bare. Three hundred years of erosion, partially induced by fires and storms, have removed the thin topsoil and exposed sandstone, shale, and gray-banded gneiss. On the same observatory foundation that Thoreau climbed, Harvard University built a weather station in the 1850s. A long succession of summit houses (offering meals and beds) ensued; last in this line was a refreshment stand,

(see page 35)

now boarded up. A fire tower and microwave antenna are the main structures today. Monadnock (3,165′) is twenty-eight miles northwest.

On the summit, Thoreau's literary pastoralism reached a climax, with citations of Virgil's *Georgics* and Wordsworth's *Peter Bell.* Peter was a lawless rover who repented and became "a good and honest man," a theme that echoes the hikers' conciliatory mood. The ridge they walked lies along the Sumehenna Trail, and *(see page 36)* the best view of hawks is in September–October, when observers have counted several thousand raptors, gliding south on the updrafts. Thoreau had a clear view at sunset, for the Connecticut River valley and the Green Mountains are seventy miles northwest. Fires were a common event on Monadnock after 1800, as he discov- *(see page 292)* ered on a later visit.

It was thrilling to hear the wind roar over the rocks, at intervals when we waked, for it had grown quite cold and windy. The night was, in its elements, simple even to majesty in that bleak place,—a bright moonlight and a piercing wind. It was at no time darker than twilight within the tent, and we could easily see the moon through its transparent roof as we lay; for there was the moon still above us, with Jupiter and Saturn on either hand, looking down on Wachusett, and it was a satisfaction to know that they were our fellow-travelers still, as high and out of our reach as our own destiny. Truly the stars were given for a consolation to man. We should not know but our life were fated to be always groveling, but it is permitted to behold them, and surely they are deserving of a fair destiny. We see laws which never fail, of whose failure we never conceived; and their lamps burn all the night, too, as well as all day,—so rich and lavish is that nature which can afford this superfluity of light.

The morning twilight began as soon as the moon had set, and we arose and kindled our fire, whose blaze might have been seen for thirty miles around. As the daylight increased, it was remarkable how rapidly the wind went down. There was no dew on the summit, but coldness supplied its place. When the dawn had reached its prime, we enjoyed the view of a distinct horizon line, and could fancy ourselves at sea, and the distant hills the waves in the horizon, as seen from the deck of a vessel. The cherry-birds flitted around us, the nuthatch and flicker were heard among the bushes, the titmouse perched within a few feet, and the song of the wood thrush again rang along the ridge. At length we saw the sun rise up out of the sea, and shine on Massachusetts; and from this moment the atmosphere grew more and more transparent till the time of our departure, and we began to realize the extent of the view, and how the earth, in some degree, answered to the heavens in the breadth, the white villages to the constellations in the sky. There was little of the sublimity and grandeur which belong to mountain scenery, but an immense landscape to ponder on a summer's day. We could see how ample and roomy is nature. As far as the eye could reach there was little life in the landscape; the few birds that flitted past did not crowd. The travelers on the remote highways, which intersect the country on every side, had no fellow-travelers for miles, before or behind. On every side, the eye ranged over successive circles of towns, rising one above another, like the terraces of a vineyard, till they were lost in the horizon. Wachusett is, in fact, the observatory of the State. There lay Massachusetts, spread out before us in its length and breadth, like a map. There was the level horizon which told of the sea on the east and south, the well-known hills of New Hampshire on the north, and the misty summits of the Hoosac and Green Mountains, first made visible to us the evening before, blue and unsubstantial, like some bank of clouds which the morning wind would dissipate, on the northwest and west. These last distant ranges, on which the eye rests unwearied, commence with an abrupt boulder in the north, beyond the Connecticut, and travel southward, with three or four peaks dimly seen. But Monadnock, rearing its masculine front in the northwest, is the grandest feature. As we beheld it, we knew that it was the height of land between the two rivers, on this side the valley of the Merrimack, on that of the Connecticut, fluctuating with their blue seas of air,—these rival vales, already teeming with Yankee men along their respective streams, born to what destiny who shall tell? Watatic and the neighboring hills, in this State and in New Hampshire, are a continuation of the same elevated range on which we were standing. But that New Hampshire bluff,—that promontory of a State,—lowering day and night on this our State of Massachusetts, will longest haunt our dreams.

We could at length realize the place mountains occupy on the land, and how they come into the general scheme of the universe. When first we climb their summits and observe their lesser irregularities, we do not give credit to the comprehensive intelligence which shaped them; but when afterward we behold their outlines in the horizon, we confess that the hand which moulded their opposite slopes, making one to balance the other, worked round a deep centre, and was privy to the plan of the universe. So is the least part of nature in its bearings referred to all space. These lesser mountain ranges, as well as the Alleghanies, run from northeast to southwest, and parallel with these mountain streams are the more fluent rivers, answering to the general direction of the coast, the bank of the great ocean stream itself. Even the clouds, with their thin bars, fall into the same direction by preference, and such even is the course of the prevailing winds, and the migration of men and birds. A mountain chain determines many things for the statesman and philosopher. The improvements of civilization rather creep along its sides than cross its summit. How often is it a barrier to prejudice and fanaticism! In passing over these heights of land, through their thin atmosphere, the follies of the plain are refined and purified; and as many species of plants do not scale their summits, so many species of folly, no doubt, do not cross the Alleghanies; it is only the hardy mountain-plant that creeps quite over the ridge, and descends into the valley beyond.

We get a dim notion of the flight of birds, especially of such as fly high in the air, by having ascended a mountain. We can now see what landmarks mountains are to their migrations; how the Catskills and Highlands have hardly sunk to them, when Wachusett and Monadnock open a passage to the northeast; how they are guided, too, in their course by the rivers and valleys; and who knows but by the stars, as well as the mountain ranges, and not by the petty landmarks which we use. The bird whose eye takes in the Green Mountains on the one side, and the ocean on the other, need not be at a loss to find its way.

Camping is no longer permitted on Wachusett, but the
auto road is open at sunrise and sunset, when low-angled

light provides the best views. Thoreau's cold, windy night in July was no exaggeration. Evening temperatures can drop to 50 degrees, and gusts of 20 m.p.h. will produce a wind-chill equivalent of 32 degrees.

(see page 40) The "immense landscape" Thoreau saw after sunrise was about forty-five miles in diameter. Maximum visibility attained has been 120 miles, but today's hazy, polluted air usually reduces the view to twenty or thirty miles. To the east is Boston, with its prominent Hancock tower; north and west are Monadnock and Hoosac, where Thoreau was to travel in 1844. He was mistaken to think of these mountains as parts of a common *(see page 40)* "range," but accurate in describing their similar configurations.

(see page 41) His ensuing passage on "the place mountains occupy" turned this dawn into a moment of lofty vision, connecting the land below with the destiny of its inhabitants. In describing how the mind travels from confusion to clarity, Thoreau was trying to emulate the "comprehensive intelligence" that shaped these mountains. For him, Wachusett reflected Nature's orderly design, its opposing slopes balanced and centered into a model of the universe. Wachusett also revealed to him the larger Appalachian structure, a northeast-to-southwest chain that directed the course of rivers, climate, animal and human migration. To Thoreau, the historical implications were clear: this natural barrier held back the early colonists; by passing over it, later settlers were charting the course of national destiny. East lay the past and its errors; west was the future, a hope for redemption.

If America's subsequent history has not confirmed this optimism, Wachusett still poses the alternatives Thoreau saw. East of the mountain are Fitchburg and Lowell, once thriving industrial centers but now fallen into decay. West and southwest are many acres of forest and wildlife sanctuary, a protected land where "progress" may never come.

At noon we descended the mountain, and, having returned to the abodes of men, turned our faces to the east again; measuring our progress, from time to time, by the more ethereal hues which the mountain assumed. Passing swiftly through Stillriver and Sterling, as with a downward impetus, we found ourselves almost at home again in the green meadows of Lancaster, so like our own Concord, for both are watered by two streams which unite near their centres, and have many other features in common. There is an unexpected refinement

Lancaster, Mass.

about this scenery; level prairies of great extent, interspersed with elms and hop-fields and groves of trees, give it almost a classic appearance. This, it will be remembered, was the scene of Mrs. Rowlandson's capture, and of other events in the Indian wars, but from this July afternoon, and under that mild exterior, those times seemed as remote as the irruption of the Goths. They were the dark age of New England. On beholding a picture of a New England village as it then appeared, with a fair open prospect, and a light on trees and river, as if it were broad noon, we find we had not thought the sun shone in those days, or that men lived in broad daylight then. We do not imagine the sun shining on hill and valley during Philip's war, nor on the war-path of Paugus, or Standish, or Church, or Lovewell, with serene summer weather, but a dim twilight or night did those events transpire in. They must have fought in the shade of their own dusky deeds.

At length, as we plodded along the dusty roads, our thoughts became as dusty as they; all thought indeed stopped, thinking broke down, or proceeded only passively in a sort of rhythmical cadence of the confused material of thought, and we found ourselves mechanically repeating some familiar measure which timed with our tread; some verse of the Robin Hood ballads, for instance, which one can recommend to travel by:—

> *"Sweavens are swift, sayd lyttle John,*
> *As the wind blows over the hill;*
> *For if it be never so loud this night,*
> *To-morrow it may be still."*

And so it went, up-hill and down, till a stone interrupted the line, when a new verse was chosen:—

> *"His shoote it was but loosely shott,*
> *Yet flewe not the arrowe in vaine,*
> *For it mett one of the sheriffe's men,*
> *And William a Trent was slaine."*

There is, however, this consolation to the most wayworn traveler, upon the dustiest road, that the path his feet describe is so perfectly symbolical of human life,—now climbing the hills, now descending into the vales. From the summits he beholds the heavens and the horizon, from the vales he looks up to the heights again. He is treading his old lessons still, and though he may be very weary and travelworn, it is yet sincere experience.

Leaving the Nashua, we changed our route a little, and arrived at Stillriver Village, in the western part of Harvard, just as the sun was setting. From this place, which lies to the northward, upon the western slope of the same range of hills on which we had spent the noon before, in the adjacent town, the prospect is beautiful, and the grandeur of the mountain outlines unsurpassed. There was such a repose and quiet here at this hour, as if the very hillsides were enjoying the scene; and as we passed slowly along, looking back over the country we had traversed, and listening to the evening song of the robin, we could not help contrasting the equanimity of Nature with the bustle and impatience of man. His words and actions presume always a crisis near at hand, but she is forever silent and unpretending.

And now that we have returned to the desultory life of the plain, let us endeavor to import a little of that mountain grandeur into it. We will remember within what walls we lie, and understand that this level life too has its summit, and why from the mountain-top the deepest valleys have a tinge of blue; that there is elevation in every hour, as no part of the earth is so low that the heavens may not be seen from, and we have only to stand on the summit of our hour to command an uninterrupted horizon.

We rested that night at Harvard, and the next morning, while one bent his steps to the nearer village of Groton, the other took his separate and solitary way to the peaceful meadows of Concord; but let him not forget to record the brave hospitality of a farmer and his wife, who generously entertained him at their board, though the poor wayfarer could only congratulate the one on the continuance of hay weather, and silently accept the kindness of the other. Refreshed by this instance of generosity, no less than by the substantial viands set before him, he pushed forward with new vigor, and reached the banks of the Concord before the sun had climbed many degrees into the heavens.

Homeward bound, Thoreau passed signs of harmony and reconciliation. The streams in Lancaster, the Nashua and North Nashua, matched those in Concord, the Assabet and Sudbury. Mary Rowlandson was held hostage by Indians from February to May 1676. She endured many privations and forced marches, but was finally ransomed (by John Hoar of Concord) at "Redemption Rock," now in Leominster State Forest. Her story is part of the region's bloody past, when Indians and colonists clashed in warfare. Yet Thoreau's allusions to Robin Hood, a figure of woodland justice, suggest that history still moves in compensatory rhythms.

Near Harvard, the finest "prospect" is from Prospect Hill Road, also the site of Fruitlands Museums, a

ROUTE FROM WACHUSETT: *MA 140 to Sterling, MA 62 to Still River, MA 110 to Harvard, MA 2 to Concord*

(see page 43)

(see page 44)

National Historic Landmark. In 1843 Bronson Alcott founded a utopian community here, but it failed after a few months. Today the Fruitlands site has several collections devoted to early America: paintings, Indian artifacts (and Thoreau's arrowheads), Shaker furnishings, the history of Transcendentalism. Ending their day's hike at Harvard, Thoreau and Fuller had walked thirty-one miles. They may have stayed at the Shaker community near Harvard, where guests were lodged free.

On the following day, Thoreau probably stopped for lunch in Acton, the midpoint of his fourteen-mile walk to Concord. Although the journey ended with him going his solitary way, echoing his early reference to Wa- *(see page 45)* chusett, the closing images were of hospitality. The traveler returned to his lowlands, even as the sun climbed toward the heights he had briefly shared.

Thoreau used a small portion of his essay on Wachusett in *A Week* (1849), there to reinforce the elegiac theme of grief transcended. (The references to Thoreau's companion, Richard Fuller, were so veiled that he could have been John Thoreau instead.)

Although Henry did not return to Wachusett for many years, he kept his eye on Concord's western horizon. Several Journal entries in the early 1850s described his view.

J O U R N A L

April 30 [*1852*]. 2 P.M.—Down the Boston road and across to Turn-pike, etc., etc. . . . When I look hence to the hills on the Boston road under which the inhabitants are beginning to plant in their gardens, the air is so fine and peculiar that I seem to see the hills and woods through a mirage. I am doubtful about their distance and exact form and elevation. The sound of a spade, too, sounds musical on the spring air. (To-night for the first time I sit without a fire.) One plower in a red flannel shirt, who looks picturesquely under the hill, suggests that our dress is not commonly of such colors as to adorn the landscape. (To-night and last night the spearer's light is seen on the meadows; he has been delayed by the height of the water.) I like very well to walk here on the low ground on the meadow; to see the churches and houses in the horizon against the sky and the now very blue Mt. Wachusett seeming to rise from amid them. When you get still further off on the lowest ground, you see distant barns and houses against the horizon, and the mountain appears to preside over this vale alone, which the adjacent hills on right and left fence in. . . .

May 18 [*1852*]. P.M.—To Cliffs. . . .

It is fine clear atmosphere, only the mountains blue. A slight seeth-ing but no haze. Shall we have much of *this* weather after this? There is scarcely a flock of cloud in the sky. The heaven is now broad and open to the earth in these longest days. The world can never be more beautiful than now, for, combined with the tender fresh green, you have this remarkable clearness of the air. I doubt if the landscape will be any greener.

The landscape is most beautiful looking towards the sun (in the orchard on Fair Haven) at four. First, there is this green slope on which I sit, looking down between the rows of apple trees just being clothed with tender green,—sometimes underneath them to the sparkling water, or over through them, or seeing them against the sky. Secondly, the outline of this bank or hill is drawn against the water far below; the river still high, a beautifully bright sheen on the water there, though it is elsewhere a dull slaty-blue color, a sober rippled surface. A fine sparkling shimmer in front, owing to the remarkable clearness of the atmosphere (clarified by the May storm?). Thirdly, on either side of the wood beyond the river are patches of bright, tender, yellowish, velvety green grass in meadows and on hillsides. It is like a short furred mantle now and bright as if it had the sun on it. Those great fields of green affect me as did those early green blades by the Corner Spring,—like a fire flaming up from the earth. The earth proves itself well alive even in the skin. No scurf on it, only a browner color on the barren tops of hills. Fourthly, the forest, the dark-green pines, wonderfully distinct, near and erect, with their distinct dark stems, spiring tops, regularly disposed branches, and silvery light on their needles. They seem to wear an aspect as much fresher and livelier as the other trees,—though their growth can hardly be perceptible yet,—as if they had been washed by the rains and the air. They are now being invested with the light, sunny, yellowish-green of the deciduous trees. This tender foliage, putting so much light and life into the landscape, is the remarkable feature at this date. The week when the deciduous trees are generally and conspicuously expanding their leaves. The various tints of gray oaks and yellowish-green birches and aspens and hickories, and the red or scarlet tops where maple keys are formed (the blossoms are now over),—these last the high color (rosaceous?) in the bouquet. And fifthly, I detect a great stretch of high-backed, mostly bare, grassy pasture country between this and the Nashua, spotted with pines and forests, which I had formerly taken for forest uninterrupted. And finally, sixthly, Wachusett rising in the background, slightly veiled in bluish mist,—toward which all these seem to slope gradually upward,—and those grassy hillsides in the foreground, seen but as patches of bare grassy ground on a spur of that distant mountain.˙. . .

Aug. 2, [*1852*]; . . .Wachusett from Fair Haven Hill looks like this: —[drawing]* the dotted line being the top of the surrounding forest.

*Thoreau's sketch deleted.—WH

Even on the low principle that misery loves company and is relieved by the consciousness that it is shared by many, and therefore is not so insignificant and trivial, after all, this blue mountain outline is valuable. In many moods it is cheering to look across hence to that blue rim of the earth, and be reminded of the invisible towns and communities, for the most part also unremembered, which lie in the further and deeper hollows between me and those hills. Towns of sturdy uplandish fame, where some of the morning and primal vigor still lingers, I trust. Ashburnham, Rindge, Jaffrey, etc.,—it is cheering to think that it is with such communities that we survive or perish. Yes, the mountains do thus impart, in the mere prospect of them, some of the New Hampshire vigor. The melancholy man who had come forth to commit suicide on this hill might be saved by being thus reminded how many brave and contented lives are lived between him and the horizon. Those hills extend our plot of earth; they make our native valley or indentation in the earth so much the larger. There is a whitish line along the base of Wachusett more particularly, as if the reflection of bare cliffs there in the sun. Undoubtedly it is the slight vaporous haze in the atmosphere seen edgewise just above the top of the forest, though it is a clear day. It, this line, makes the mountains loom, in fact, a faint whitish line separating the mountains from their bases and the rest of the globe.

[*May 10, 1853*]. . . . From the hill, I look westward over the landscape. The deciduous woods are in their hoary youth, every expanding bud swaddled with downy webs. From this more eastern hill, with the whole breadth of the river valley on the west, the mountains appear higher still, the width of the blue border is greater,—not mere peaks, or a short and shallow sierra, but a high blue table-land with broad foundations, a deep and solid base or tablet, in proportion to the peaks that rest on it. As you ascend, the near and low hills sink and flatten into the earth; no sky is seen behind them; the distant mountains rise. The truly great are distinguished. Vergers, crests of the waves of earth, which in the highest break at the summit into granitic rocks over which the air beats. A part of their hitherto concealed base is seen blue. You see, not the domes only, but the body, the façade, of these terrene temples. You see that the foundation answers to the superstructure. Moral structures. (The sweet-fern leaves among odors now.) The successive lines of haze which divide the western landscape, deeper and more misty over each intervening valley, are not yet very dense; yet there is a light atmospheric line along the base of the mountains for their whole length, formed by this denser and grosser atmosphere through which we look next the earth, which almost melts them into the atmosphere, like the contact of molten metal with that which is unfused; but their pure, sublimed tops and main body rise, palpable sky-land above it, like the waving signal of the departing who have already left these shores. It will be worth the while to observe carefully the direction and altitude of the mountains from the Cliffs. The value of the mountains in the horizon,—would not that be a good theme for a lecture? The text for a discourse on real values, and permanent; a sermon on the mount. They are stepping-stones to heaven,—as the rider has a horse-block at his gate,—by which to mount when we would commence our pilgrimage to heaven; by which we gradually take our departure from earth, from the time when our youthful eyes first rested on them,—from this bare actual earth, which has so little of the hue of heaven. They make it easier to die and easier to live. They let us off. . . .

Whether any picture by a human master hung on our western wall could supply their place. Whether to shovel them away and level them would really smooth the way to the true west. Whether the skies would not weep over their scars. They are valuable to mankind as is the iris of the eye to a man. They are the path of the translated. The undisputed territory between earth and heaven. In our travels rising higher and higher, we at length got to where the earth was blue. Suggesting that this earth, unless our conduct curse it, is as celestial as that sky. They are the pastures to which we drive our thoughts on these 20ths of May. (George Baker told me the other day that he had driven cows to Winchendon, forty miles, in one day.) Men often spend a great deal on a border to their papered walls, of the costliest figure and colors, ultramarine (or what other?). This color bears a price like precious stones. We may measure our wealth, then, by the number of square rods of superficial *blue* earth in our earth border. Such proportion as it bears to the area of the visible earth, in such proportion are we heavenly-minded. Yet I doubt if I can find a man in this country who would not think it better if they were converted into solid gold,

which could in no case be a blessing to all, but only a curse to a few,
—and so they would be stepping-stones to hell. . . .

Dec. 27 [*1853*]. The wind has now shaken the snow from the
trees, and it lies in irregular little heaps on the snow beneath, except
that there is a white ridge up and down their trunks on the northwest side, showing which side the storm came from, which, better
than the moss, would enable one to find his way in the night. I went
to hear the pond whoop, but did not hear much. I look far, but see
no rainbow flocks in the sky. It is a true winter sunset, almost cloudless, clear, cold indigo-y along the horizon. The evening (?) star is
seen shining brightly, before the twilight has begun. A rosy tint
suffuses the eastern horizon. The outline of the mountains is wonderfully distinct and hard, and they are a dark blue and very near.
Wachusett looks like a right whale over our bow, plowing the continent, with his flukes well down. He has a vicious look, as if he had
a harpoon in him. . . .

Some of these passages may have been intended for
Walden, but the book (published in August 1854) had few
references to mountains, and none directly to Wachusett.
Two months later, Thoreau suddenly went there on a
brief return trip, one quite different from his romantic
journey of 1842. The idealistic ardor of Transcendentalism was beginning to cool, as he turned to the task of
learning natural history. Margaret Fuller was dead,
Emerson's influence had waned. Now Thoreau had a
new circle of admiring friends, a private Journal for
hours of daily writing. Most of his income came from
surveying, an outdoor trade that was agreeably irregular.

This trip to Wachusett was a pleasure jaunt, timed to
coincide with the show of autumn leaves. Thoreau's
companions were an odd pair: Harrison Blake from
Worcester, a frequent correspondent on intellectual
themes; and an English aristocrat named Thomas Cholmondeley, an author and traveler then boarding with the
Thoreaus. The three men traveled in comfort, using the

train for all but six miles, then hiking up Wachusett via the new coach road. They did not camp on the mountain, but instead lodged overnight at a farm. After climbing to the summit twice in two days, they returned to Concord via a train from Westminster.

As was his custom, Thoreau made field notes on the journey and used them to write Journal entries at home. This time he had relatively little to say. Almost nothing reminded him of 1842, except for the sunrise view looking west. His concern for facts, his use of Latin names, the absence of allusions or figurative devices were all significant changes. Thoreau was becoming the factual reporter of his later years.

ROUTE FROM CONCORD: *MA 2 to Westminster, MA 140 to Wachusett Mountain State Reservation, Stage Coach and Harrington trails to summit*

—*Oct. 19* [*1854*]. 7.15 A.M.—To Westminster by cars; thence on foot to Wachusett Mountain, four miles to Foster's, and two miles thence to mountain-top by road.

The country above Littletown (plowed ground) more or less sugared with snow, the first I have seen. We find a little on the mountain-top. The prevailing tree on this mountain, top and all, is apparently the red oak, which toward and on the top is very low and spreading. Other trees and shrubs which I remember on the top are beech, *Populus tremuliformis,* mountain-ash (looking somewhat like sumach), witch-hazel, white and yellow birch, white pine, black spruce, etc., etc. Most of the deciduous woods *look as if* dead. On the sides, beside red oak, are rock maple, yellow birch, lever-wood, beech, chestnut, shagbark, hemlock, striped maple, witch-hazel, etc., etc.

With a glass you can see vessels in Boston Harbor from the summit, just north of the Waltham hills.

Two white asters, the common ones, not yet quite out of bloom,— *A. acuminatus* and perhaps *cordifolius* (hearted, with long sharp teeth). The *Geranium Robertianum* in bloom below the woods on the east side.

Oct. 20. Saw the sun rise from the mountain-top. This is the time to look westward. All the villages, steeples, and houses on that side were revealed; but on the east all the landscape was a misty and gilded obscurity. It was worth the while to see westward the countless hills and fields all apparently flat, now white with frost. A little white fog marked the site of many a lake and the course of the Nashua, and in the east horizon the great pond had its own fog mark in a long, low bank of cloud.

Soon after sunrise I saw the pyramidal shadow of the mountain reaching quite across the State, its apex resting on the Green or Hoosac Mountains, appearing as a deep-blue section of a cone there. It rapidly contracted, and its apex approached the mountain itself, and when about three miles distant the whole conical shadow was very distinct. The shadow of the mountain makes some minutes' difference in the time of sunrise to the inhabitants of Hubbardston, within a few miles west.

F. hyemalis, how long?

Saw some very tall and large dead chestnuts in the wood between Foster's and the mountain. Wachusett Pond appeared the best place from which to view the mountain (from a boat). Our host had picked thirty-four bushels of shagbarks last year. *For the most part* they do not rattle out yet, but it is time to gather them. On account of squirrels now is the time.

Greylock

As I had climbed above storm and cloud, so by
successive days' journeys I might reach the region of
eternal day beyond the tapering show of the earth. . . .

On Wachusett, Thoreau saw mountains to the north and west, but he did not climb them for another two years. During that interval, his fortunes sank to a nadir. In 1843 he tried living near New York and writing for popular magazines; after six months he quit, having sold only two pieces. He returned to Concord and mostly worked in his father's pencil shop throughout 1844. After *The Dial* shut down in April, he had virtually no market for his writings. Then came a public disgrace: on a day's outing near Fairhaven Bay he accidentally set fire to several hundred acres of forest land, the town's main source of fuel and lumber.

Late in July, he left Concord on an undefined mission, traveling alone. Carrying a small leather pouch, he took few supplies—just some books and a blanket. His exact route is unknown, but apparently he went first to Monadnock, a journey of two or more days, and slept one night on the summit (see p. 288). Over the next few days he headed toward the Connecticut River, probably going south to Greenfield, Mass., before turning west along the Deerfield River valley. At Shelburne Falls he examined potholes cut into the rock by the river current. He went far up the valley to its western terminus, where he stayed one night with a mountain farmer named Rice.

By now a week had elapsed, and Thoreau was travel-worn but still looking for adventure. After buying food in North Adams, he hiked up the north slope of "Saddleback," or Mt. Greylock. At one of the highest farms he paused to chat with a handsome young woman, clad in a dressing gown, who mistook him for a student from Williams College, "a pretty wild set of fellows." Thoreau considered staying at her house for an extra week. But he climbed on, at last leaving the trail and using his compass to reach the summit. He could have used a tent also; the night was so cold he had to pile loose "boards" over himself to keep off the wind. At dawn he saw a spectacular sunrise, the world below him completely shrouded in thick white clouds.

This moment seemed both to justify and to end his solitary quest. Thoreau descended the south slope of Greylock and hiked to Pittsfield, where by prior agreement he met Ellery Channing, a new acquaintance from Concord. Channing later recalled that Thoreau was unshaven, poorly dressed, and rather seedy from sleeping out. For another week they traveled together, down the Hudson River to the Catskill Mountains, before returning to Concord.

At home Thoreau found a letter from Isaac Hecker, a former boarder with the family, who proposed a hiking tour in Europe. Thoreau was tempted, but the recent journey had helped him turn a corner. He would stay in Concord and get back to his writing. "Better trivial days with faith," he wrote Hecker, "than the fairest ones lighted by sunshine alone." Early the next spring he built his one-room house on the shore of Walden Pond. There he lived for two years, writing early drafts of *A Week* and *Walden.* The first book contained his story of hiking to Greylock. He omitted Monadnock and barely mentioned the Catskills; only a partial Journal account of those days has survived (see p. 78).

In writing of the Greylock trip, Thoreau described how space and solitude on a mountain journey had restored his dignity and self-confidence. His exile became a lesson in civil manners, the graces that override good or bad fortune. Eventually *Walden* repeated this story, that exile can clear away the "quiet desperation" of a life spent at home. In *A Week* the Greylock story is a digression from Thoreau's journey along the Merrimack River, but Greylock anticipates his later climax atop Mt. Washington (see p. 219) and enlivens a sluggish stretch of early narrative. For his book, Thoreau split and rearranged the 1844 trip; the following version restores his original sequence of travel.

A WEEK ON THE

CONCORD AND

MERRIMACK RIVERS

Early one summer morning I had left the shores of the Connecticut, and for the livelong day travelled up the bank of a river, which came in from the west; now looking down on the stream, foaming and rippling through the forest a mile off, from the hills over which the road led, and now sitting on its rocky brink and dipping my feet in its rapids, or bathing adventurously in mid-channel. The hills grew more and more frequent, and gradually swelled into mountains as I advanced, hemming in the course of the river, so that at last I could not see where it came from, and was at liberty to imagine the most wonderful meanderings and descents. At noon I slept on the grass in the shade of a maple, where the river had found a broader channel than usual, and was spread out shallow, with frequent sand-bars exposed. In the names of the towns I recognized some which I had long ago read on teamsters' wagons, that had come from far up country, quiet, uplandish towns, of mountainous fame. I walked along musing, and enchanted by rows of sugar-maples, through the small and uninquisitive villages, and sometimes was pleased with the sight of a boat drawn up on a sand-bar, where there appeared no inhabitants to use it. It seemed, however, as essential to the river as a fish, and to lend a certain dignity to it. It was like the trout of mountain streams to the fishes of the sea, or like the young of the land crab born far in the interior, who have never yet heard the sound of the ocean's surf. The hills approached nearer and nearer to the stream, until at last they closed behind me, and I found myself just before night-fall, in a romantic and retired valley, about half a mile in length, and barely wide enough for the stream at its bottom. I thought that there could be no finer site for a cottage among mountains. You could any where run across the stream on the rocks, and its constant murmuring would quiet the passions of mankind forever. Suddenly the road, which seemed aiming for the mountain side, turned short to the left, and another valley opened, concealing the former, and of the same character with it. It was the most remarkable and pleasing scenery I had ever seen. I found here a few mild and hospitable inhabitants, who, as the day was not quite spent, and I was anxious to improve the light, directed me four or five miles further on my way to the dwelling of a man whose name was Rice, who occupied the last and highest of the valleys that lay in my path, and who, they said, was a rather rude and uncivil man. But, "What is a foreign country to those who have science? Who is a stranger to those who have the habit of speaking kindly?"

At length, as the sun was setting behind the mountains in a still

Deerfield and Connecticut Rivers

darker and more solitary vale, I reached the dwelling of this man. Except for the narrowness of the plain, and that the stones were solid granite, it was the counterpart of that retreat to which Belphœbe bore the wounded Timias;—

> *"in a pleasant glade,*
> *With mountains round about environed,*
> *And mighty woods, which did the valley shade,*
> *And like a stately theatre it made,*
> *Spreading itself into a spacious plain;*
> *And in the midst a little river played*
> *Amongst the pumy stones which seemed to plain,*
> *With gentle murmur that his course they did restrain."*

ROUTE FROM GREENFIELD, MASS.: *MA 2 (Mohawk Trail) to Charlemont, Zoar River Road*

Thoreau's trail followed the Deerfield River closely, along the present Conrail tracks. At Shelburne Falls he saw large potholes "worn quite through the rock, so that a portion of the river leaks through in anticipation of

that fall." (This phrase appears in a later passage of *A* *to Florida town line*
Week, describing Amoskeag Falls, N.H.) His spot for a
nap was probably near the Shelburne town line, where *(see page 57)*
the river forms a large oxbow turn, then flows by several
big islands. The small villages he passed were Shelburne
Falls and East Charlemont (then called Lower Village).
The two valleys were in Charlemont: between Mill Brook *(see page 57)*
and Rice's Brook, and (farther west) between Hawk's
Brook and the Deerfield River.

Rice's farm was just at the Florida town line, on the
south bank of the Deerfield River. Thoreau introduced
Rice with stately allusions to courtesy books: the ancient
Hindu code, *Heetopades of Veeshnoo-Sarma,* and Spenser's *The Faerie Queene.* Spenser's allegory plays heavily
on the conflict between appearance and reality. In this
passage (repeated on p. 63), Belphoebe heals the wounds
of Timias, but later she spurns his love.

I observed, as I drew near, that he was not so rude as I had anticipated, for he kept many cattle and dogs to watch them, and I saw
where he had made maple sugar on the sides of the mountains, and

Charlemont, Mass.

above all distinguished the voices of children mingling with the murmur of the torrent before the door. As I passed his stable I met one
whom I supposed to be a hired man, attending to his cattle, and
inquired if they entertained travellers at that house. "Sometimes we
do," he answered, gruffly, and immediately went to the farthest stall
from me, and I perceived that it was Rice himself whom I had addressed. But pardoning this incivility to the wildness of the scenery,
I bent my steps to the house. There was no sign-post before it, nor any
of the usual invitations to the traveller, though I saw by the road that
many went and came there, but the owner's name only was fastened
to the outside, a sort of implied and sullen invitation, as I thought. I
passed from room to room without meeting any one, till I came to
what seemed the guests' apartment, which was neat, and even had an
air of refinement about it, and I was glad to find a map against the
wall which would direct me on my journey on the morrow. At length
I heard a step in a distant apartment, which was the first I had
entered, and went to see if the landlord had come in; but it proved to
be only a child, one of those whose voices I had heard, probably his
son, and between him and me stood in the door-way a large watch-dog,
which growled at me, and looked as if he would presently spring, but
the boy did not speak to him; and when I asked for a glass of water,
he briefly said, "It runs in the corner." So I took a mug from the
counter and went out of doors, and searched round the corner of the
house, but could find neither well nor spring, nor any water but the
stream which ran all along the front. I came back, therefore, and
setting down the mug, asked the child if the stream was good to drink;
whereupon he seized the mug and going to the corner of the room,
where a cool spring which issued from the mountain behind trickled
through a pipe into the apartment, filled it, and drank, and gave it to
me empty again, and calling to the dog, rushed out of doors. Ere long
some of the hired men made their appearance, and drank at the
spring, and lazily washed themselves and combed their hair in silence,
and some sat down as if weary, and fell asleep in their seats. But all
the while I saw no women, though I sometimes heard a bustle in that
part of the house from which the spring came.

  At length Rice himself came in, for it was now dark, with an ox whip
in his hand, breathing hard, and he too soon settled down into his seat

not far from me, as if now that his day's work was done he had no
further to travel, but only to digest his supper at his leisure. When
I asked him if he could give me a bed, he said there was one ready,
in such a tone as implied that I ought to have known it, and the less
said about that the better. So far so good. And yet he continued to look
at me as if he would fain have me say something further like a
traveller. I remarked, that it was a wild and rugged country he inhabited, and worth coming many miles to see. "Not so very rough neither," said he, and appealed to his men to bear witness to the breadth
and smoothness of his fields, which consisted in all of one small interval, and to the size of his crops; "and if we have some hills," added
he, "there's no better pasturage any where." I then asked if this place
was the one I had heard of, calling it by a name I had seen on the map,
or if it was a certain other; and he answered, gruffly, that it was
neither the one nor the other; that he had settled it and cultivated it,
and made it what it was, and I could know nothing about it. Observing
some guns and other implements of hunting hanging on brackets
around the room, and his hounds now sleeping on the floor, I took
occasion to change the discourse, and inquired if there was much
game in that country, and he answered this question more graciously,
having some glimmering of my drift; but when I inquired if there

were any bears, he answered impatiently, that he was no more in danger of losing his sheep than his neighbors, he had tamed and civilized that region. After a pause, thinking of my journey on the morrow, and the few hours of daylight in that hollow and mountainous country, which would require me to be on my way betimes, I remarked, that the day must be shorter by an hour there than on the neighboring plains; at which he gruffly asked what I knew about it, and affirmed that he had as much daylight as his neighbors; he ventured to say, the days were longer there than where I lived, as I should find if I stayed; that in some way, I could not be expected to understand how, the sun came over the mountains half an hour earlier, and stayed half an hour later there than on the neighboring plains.—And more of like sort he said. He was, indeed, as rude as a fabled satyr. But I suffered him to pass for what he was, for why should I quarrel with nature? and was even pleased at the discovery of such a singular natural phenomenon. I dealt with him as if to me all manners were indifferent, and he had a sweet wild way with him. I would not question nature, and I would rather have him as he was, than as I would have him. For I had come up here not for sympathy, or kindness, or society, but for novelty and adventure, and to see what nature had produced here. I therefore did not repel his rudeness, but quite innocently welcomed it all, and knew how to appreciate it, as if I were reading in an old drama a part well sustained. He was indeed a coarse and sensual man, and, as I have said, uncivil, but he had his just quarrel with nature and mankind, I have no doubt, only he had no artificial covering to his ill humors. He was earthy enough, but yet there was good soil in him, and even a long-suffering Saxon probity at bottom. If you could represent the case to him, he would not let the race die out in him, like a red Indian.

At length I told him that he was a fortunate man, and I trusted that he was grateful for so much light, and rising, said I would take a lamp, and that I would pay him then for my lodging, for I expected to recommence my journey, even as early as the sun rose in his country; but he answered in haste, and this time civilly, that I should not fail to find some of his household stirring, however early, for they were no sluggards, and I could take my breakfast with them before I started if I chose; and as he lighted the lamp I detected a gleam of true hospitality and ancient civility, a beam of pure and even gentle humanity from his bleared and moist eyes. It was a look more intimate with me, and more explanatory, than any words of his could have been if he had tried to his dying day. It was more significant than any Rice of those parts could even comprehend, and long anticipated this man's culture,—a glance of his pure genius, which did not much enlighten him, but did impress and rule him for the moment, and faintly constrain his voice and manner. He cheerfully led the way to my apartment, stepping over the limbs of his men who were asleep on the floor in an intervening chamber, and showed me a clean and comfortable bed. For many pleasant hours, after the household was asleep, I sat at the open window, for it was a sultry night, and heard the little river

"*Amongst the pumy stones, which seemed to plain*
With gentle murmur that his course they did restrain."

But I arose as usual by starlight the next morning, before my host, or his men, or even his dogs, were awake; and having left a ninepence on the counter, was already half way over the mountain with the sun, before they had broken their fast.

Thoreau's encounter with Rice was an object lesson in the differences between town and country manners. This mountain farm was well kept and hospitable, after its own fashion. The momentary confusion over running water, the apparent absence of women, the faltering talk of fields and crops—all illustrate Thoreau's alien status here, in a place where he was not even certain of proper geographic names. (His confusion may have arisen because Rice's farm stood near three different town lines: Charlemont, Florida, and Savoy.)

Rice's gruff manner apparently stemmed from a desire to protect the farm's reputation: he was insisting that his land had no more bears, and no less sunlight, than elsewhere. If he was "a fabled satyr," the wild goat- *(see page 62)* man of Greek legend, Rice most resembled Silenus, the sly tutor of Dionysius, god of wine and fertility. (In an

early Journal version, Rice was first called "Satyrus.")
Eventually, Thoreau saw Rice as a natural element,
rough on the surface, good-natured within. He expressed
the coherence of a life spent close to nature; an ideal
Thoreau later pursued at Walden Pond.

For all his allegorical trappings, "Rice" was not a
fictional character: Captain Luke Rice helped to found
the town of Florida, Mass., in 1805. He served as the first
Moderator, then successively as Selectman, Treasurer,
and Town Clerk; later still, he was part owner of a hotel
near the Hoosac Tunnel. Many of his descendants still
live in the vicinity of Charlemont.

Before I had left the country of my host, while the first rays of the
sun slanted over the mountains, as I stopped by the way-side to gather
some raspberries, a very old man, not far from a hundred, came along
with a milking pail in his hand, and turning aside began to pluck the
berries near me;—

> —*"his reverend locks*
> *In comelye curles did wave;*
> *And on his aged temples grew*
> *The blossoms of the grave."*—

But when I inquired the way, he answered in a low, rough voice,
without looking up or seeming to regard my presence, which I im-
puted to his years; and presently, muttering to himself, he proceeded
to collect his cows in a neighboring pasture; and when he had again
returned near to the way-side, he suddenly stopped, while his cows
went on before, and, uncovering his head, prayed aloud in the cool
morning air, as if he had forgotten this exercise before, for his daily
bread, and also that He who letteth his rain fall on the just and on the
unjust, and without whom not a sparrow falleth to the ground, would
not neglect the stranger, (meaning me,) and with even more direct and
personal applications, though mainly according to the long established formula common to lowlanders and the inhabitants of mountains. When he had done praying, I made bold to ask him if he had any

cheese in his hut which he would sell me, but he answered without looking up, and in the same low and repulsive voice as before, that they did not make any, and went to milking. It is written, "The stranger who turneth away from a house with disappointed hopes, leaveth there his own offences, and departeth, taking with him all the good actions of the owner."

Introduced by an Elizabethan ballad, "The Beggar's Daughter of Bednall-Green," this elderly man was a direct contrast to Rice: pious in deed, craven at heart. His invocation of Scripture echoed a similar lament by King Lear, an old man who came to regret his lack of charity. That hope Thoreau confirmed by again quoting from the *Heetopades* and then departing.

ROUTE FROM FLORIDA: *River Road to Whitcomb Hill Road, Monroe Road to MA 2 and Whitcomb summit*

.   .   .

In an earlier section of *A Week,* Thoreau and his brother left their campsite near Nashville, N.H., before 3 A.M. and headed upstream, into a thick fog. As they waited for dawn, Thoreau described a similar morning in the Berkshires.

I had come over the hills on foot and alone in serene summer days, plucking the raspberries by the way-side, and occasionally buying a loaf of bread at a farmer's house, with a knapsack on my back, which held a few traveller's books and a change of clothing, and a staff in my hand. I had that morning looked down from the Hoosack Mountain, where the road crosses it, on the village of North Adams in the valley, three miles away under my feet, showing how uneven the earth may sometimes be, and making it seem an accident that it should ever be level and convenient for the feet of man. Putting a little rice and sugar and a tin cup into my knapsack at this village, I began in the afternoon to ascend the mountain, whose summit is three thousand six hundred feet above the level of the sea, and was seven or eight miles distant by the path. My route lay up a long and spacious valley called the Bellows, because the winds rush up or down it with violence in storms, sloping up to the very clouds between the principal

North Adams, Mass.

range and a lower mountain. There were a few farms scattered along
at different elevations, each commanding a fine prospect of the mountains to the north, and a stream ran down the middle of the valley, on
which near the head there was a mill. It seemed a road for the pilgrim
to enter upon who would climb to the gates of heaven. Now I crossed
a hay-field, and now over the brook on a slight bridge, still gradually
ascending all the while, with a sort of awe, and filled with indefinite
expectations as to what kind of inhabitants and what kind of nature
I should come to at last. It now seemed some advantage that the earth
was uneven, for one could not imagine a more noble position for a
farm house than this vale afforded, further from or nearer to its head,
from a glen-like seclusion overlooking the country at a great elevation
between these two mountain walls.

It reminded me of the homesteads of the Hugunots, on Staten
Island, off the coast of New Jersey. The hills in the interior of this
island, though comparatively low, are penetrated in various directions
by similar sloping valleys on a humble scale, gradually narrowing and
rising to the center, and at the head of these the Hugunots, who were
the first settlers, placed their houses, quite within the land, in rural
and sheltered places, in leafy recesses where the breeze played with
the poplar and the gum tree, from which, with equal security in calm
and storm, they looked out through a widening vista, over miles of

forest and stretching salt marsh, to the Hugunots' Tree, an old elm on the shore at whose root they had landed, and across the spacious outer bay of New York to Sandy Hook and the Highlands of Neversink, and thence over leagues of the Atlantic, perchance to some faint vessel in the horizon, almost a day's sail on her voyage to that Europe whence they had come. When walking in the interior there, in the midst of rural scenery, where there was as little to remind me of the ocean as amid the New Hampshire hills, I have suddenly, through a gap, a cleft or "clove road," as the Dutch settlers called it, caught sight of a ship under full sail, over a field of corn, twenty or thirty miles at sea. The effect was similar, since I had no means of measuring distances, to seeing a painted ship passed backwards and forwards through a magic lantern.

Greylock (Saddleback)

"Saddleback" and "Greylock" have been common names for the same peak since the nineteenth century. From the west, the mountain's profile resembles a giant saddle; "Greylock" probably refers to its snow-covered appearance in winter. Thoreau's foot trail began at the present junction of Pattison and West Mountain roads; the latter continues to the summit.

ROUTE FROM WHITCOMB SUMMIT: *MA 2 to North Adams, Notch Road to Pattison Road and West Mountain Road*

(see page 65)

Greylock is another monadnock, with several differences from Wachusett. Both mountains contain gneiss and granite of similar origin, but Greylock is much higher and more densely forested. Both mountains recovered from the glacial scalping, but Wachusett has

suffered constant erosion since 1700. The region around
Greylock was settled later, and farms had crept far up
the mountain slopes when Thoreau visited in 1844. After
the Civil War, this rural population declined and a heavy
forest cover returned. Today a hike up Greylock leads
through vigorous hardwood stands well over a century
old. Only at the summit does a clearing appear for structures and visitors, and even there the ground cover is a
thick, fertile sod.

Thoreau's trail was a long and gradual ascent of "Bellows Pipe," a broad ravine cut by Notch Brook between
Greylock and Ragged Mountain. For its first mile this
trail is smooth and wide enough for vehicles; then it
crosses a small brook and begins a more narrow ascent.
(see page 66) Thoreau saw farms and many open views here, but now
the ravine has a thick growth of mixed deciduous forest,
about fifty to eighty years old. The signs of abandoned
farms are clear: tumbled stone fences mark old boundaries, clumps of apple orchard languish in the shade of
taller trees. This north slope was not ideal for farming,
but its cool, wet grounds help the maple and beech to
build a high, dense canopy.

The trail crosses several brooks and enters Greylock
State Reservation. At 1,700 feet, the path becomes a rocky
gully, lined with alternate beds of stinging nettles and
jewelweed. The two plants look similar, but nettles give
a smart sting, while jewelweed soothes it away. Beds of
apparent "pine seedlings" are in fact scouring rush, a
relative of grass that favors wet, boggy ground. At each
brook, partial clearings and faint, grown-over paths appear; signs of previous cultivation. Now the only edible
plant is Indian cucumber, its plump root having the faint
taste of radish. Near 2,000 feet, the first true clearing
emerges, an open pasture of wild timothy and blackberries.

In July 1844 Thoreau could look down this valley and
(see page 66) recall a scene from Staten Island, where he had lived in

1843 while trying to sell his writings in New York. The
Huguenots were French Calvinists, many of whom came
to America after losing their political security. Their
comfortable homes on Staten Island were in sharp contrast to Thoreau's fortunes there.

But to return to the mountain. It seemed as if he must be the most
singular and heavenly-minded man whose dwelling stood highest up
the valley. The thunder had rumbled at my heels all the way, but the
shower passed off in another direction, though if it had not, I half
believed that I should get above it. I at length reached the last house
but one, where the path to the summit diverged to the right, while the
summit itself rose directly in front. But I determined to follow up the
valley to its head, and then find my own route up the steep, as the
shorter and more adventurous way. I had thoughts of returning to
this house, which was well kept and so nobly placed, the next day, and
perhaps remaining a week there, if I could have entertainment. Its
mistress was a frank and hospitable young woman, who stood before
me in a dishabille, busily and unconcernedly combing her long black
hair while she talked, giving her head the necessary toss with each
sweep of the comb, with lively, sparkling eyes, and full of interest in
that lower world from which I had come, talking all the while as
familiarly as if she had known me for years, and reminding me of a
cousin of mine. She had at first taken me for a student from Williamstown, for they went by in parties, she said, either riding or walking,
almost every pleasant day, and were a pretty wild set of fellows; but
they never went by the way I was going. As I passed the last house,
a man called out to know what I had to sell, for seeing my knapsack,
he thought that I might be a pedler, who was taking this unusual
route over the ridge of the valley into South Adams. He told me that
it was still four or five miles to the summit by the path which I had
left, though not more than two in a straight line from where I was,
but that nobody ever went this way; there was no path, and I should
find it as steep as the roof of a house. But I knew that I was more used
to woods and mountains than he, and went along through his cowyard, while he, looking at the sun, shouted after me that I should not
get to the top that night. I soon reached the head of the valley, but

as I could not see the summit from this point, I ascended a low mountain on the opposite side, and took its bearing with my compass. I at once entered the woods, and began to climb the steep side of the mountain in a diagonal direction, taking the bearing of a tree every dozen rods. The ascent was by no means difficult or unpleasant, and occupied much less time than it would have taken to follow the path. Even country people, I have observed, magnify the difficulty of travelling in the forest, especially among mountains. They seem to lack their usual common sense in this. I have climbed several higher mountains without guide or path, and have found, as might be expected, that it takes only more time and patience commonly than to travel the smoothest highway. It is very rare that you meet with obstacles in this world, which the humblest man has not faculties to surmount. It is true, we may come to a perpendicular precipice, but we need not jump off, nor run our heads against it. A man may jump down his own cellar stairs, or dash his brains out against his chimney, if he is mad. So far as my experience goes, travellers generally exaggerate the difficulties of the way. Like most evil, the difficulty is imaginary; for what's the hurry? If a person lost would conclude that after all he is not lost, he is not beside himself, but standing in his own old shoes on the very spot where he is, and that for the time being he will live there; but the places that have known him, *they* are lost,—how much anxiety and danger would vanish. I am not alone if I stand by myself. Who knows where in space this globe is rolling? Yet we will not give ourselves up for lost, let it go where it will.

(see page 69) The trail continues north, crossing a fourth brook. The "last house but one" possibly stood at this site, which is elevated and close to running water. But the exact site seems as ambiguous as the young woman Thoreau met. Was the Concord bachelor attracted to this "mistress"? On balance, his estimate seems fairly chaste: like farmer Rice, she had unpolished manners yet was frank and hospitable. If her attire, her loose hair, and her reference to the students were meant as provocations, then Thoreau missed the point: to him she seemed familiar and wholesome, like a cousin he knew. Today not a trace of

her home remains; only the forest, the wind, the sound of running water.

Nor is the path that Thoreau left any longer visible; *(see page 69)* possibly it crossed the north slope of Mt. Williams and went on to Greylock, three miles distant. The Bellows Pipe trail, from this point on marked with paint blazes, most nearly follows his route. At the head of the ravine is a T-junction, with the left spur going up Ragged Mountain (2,451'), where Thoreau took his compass bearing. *(see page 70)* The Bellows Pipe trail goes right, past a lean-to shelter for overnight campers. Following Thoreau's compass course through the heavy forest is risky; the dirt path is challenging enough, especially when wet. His emphasis on overcoming obstacles and fears may allude to the troubling events before his journey in 1844. Since *A Week* was published in 1849, he could include with those "several higher mountains" his experience on Katahdin in *(see page 70)* 1846.

I made my way steadily upward in a straight line through a dense undergrowth of mountain laurel, until the trees began to have a scraggy and infernal look, as if contending with frost goblins, and at length I reached the summit, just as the sun was setting. Several acres here had been cleared, and were covered with rocks and stumps, and there was a rude observatory in the middle which overlooked the woods. I had one fair view of the country before the sun went down, but I was too thirsty to waste any light in viewing the prospect, and set out at once to find water. First, going down a well-beaten path for half a mile through the low scrubby wood, till I came to where the water stood in the tracks of the horses which had carried travellers up, I lay down flat, and drank these dry one after another, a pure, cold, spring-like water, but yet I could not fill my dipper, though I contrived little syphons of grass stems and ingenious aqueducts on a small scale; it was too slow a process. Then remembering that I had passed a moist place near the top on my way up, I returned to find it again, and here with sharp stones and my hands, in the twilight, I made a well about two feet deep, which

was soon filled with pure cold water, and the birds too came and
drank at it. So I filled my dipper, and making my way back to the
observatory, collected some dry sticks and made a fire on some flat
stones, which had been placed on the floor for that purpose, and so
I soon cooked my supper of rice, having already whittled a wooden
spoon to eat it with.

I sat up during the evening, reading by the light of the fire the
scraps of newspapers in which some party had wrapped their lunch-
eon; the prices current in New York and Boston, the advertisements,
and the singular editorials which some had seen fit to publish, not
foreseeing under what critical circumstances they would be read. I
read these things at a vast advantage there, and it seemed to me that
the advertisements, or what is called the business part of a paper,
were greatly the best, the most useful, natural, and respectable. Almost all the opinions and sentiments expressed were so little considered, so shallow and flimsy, that I thought the very texture of the
paper must be weaker in that part and tear the more easily. The
advertisements and the prices current were more closely allied to
nature, and were respectable in some measure as tide and meteorolog-
ical tables are; but the reading matter, which I remembered was most
prized down below, unless it was some humble record of science, or
an extract from some old classic, struck me as strangely whimsical,
and crude, and one-idea'd, like a school-boy's theme, such as youths
write and afterward burn. The opinions were of that kind that are
doomed to wear a different aspect to-morrow, like last year's fashions;
as if mankind were very green indeed, and would be ashamed of
themselves in a few years, when they had outgrown this verdant
period. There was, moreover, a singular disposition to wit and humor,
but rarely the slightest real success; and the apparent success was a
terrible satire on the attempt; as if the Evil Genius of man laughed
the loudest at his best jokes. The advertisements, as I have said, such
as were serious, and not of the modern quack kind, suggested pleasing and poetic thoughts; for commerce is really as interesting as
nature. The very names of the commodities were poetic, and as suggestive as if they had been inserted in a pleasing poem,—Lumber,
Cotton, Sugar, Hides, Guano, and Logwood. Some sober, private, and
original thought would have been grateful to read there, and as much

in harmony with the circumstances as if it had been written on a mountain top; for it is of a fashion which never changes, and as respectable as hides and logwood, or any natural product. What an inestimable companion such a scrap of paper would have been, containing some fruit of a mature life. What a relic! What a recipe! It seemed a divine invention, by which not mere shining coin, but shining and current thoughts, could be brought up and left there.

As it was cold, I collected quite a pile of wood and lay down on a board against the side of the building, not having any blanket to cover me, with my head to the fire, that I might look after it, which is not the Indian rule. But as it grew colder towards midnight, I at length encased myself completely in boards, managing even to put a board on top of me, with a large stone on it, to keep it down, and so slept comfortably. I was reminded, it is true, of the Irish children, who inquired what their neighbors did who had no door to put over them in winter nights as they had; but I am convinced that there was nothing very strange in the inquiry. Those who have never tried it can have no idea how far a door, which keeps the single blanket down, may go toward making one comfortable. We are constituted a good deal like chickens, which taken from the hen, and put in a basket of cotton in the chimney corner, will often peep till they die nevertheless, but if you put in a book, or any thing heavy, which will press down the cotton, and feel like the hen, they go to sleep directly. My only companions were the mice, which came to pick up the crumbs that had been left in those scraps of paper; still, as every where, pensioners on man, and not unwisely improving this elevated tract for their habitation. They nibbled what was for them; I nibbled what was for me. Once or twice in the night, when I looked up, I saw a white cloud drifting through the windows, and filling the whole upper story.

This observatory was a building of considerable size, erected by the students of Williamstown College, whose buildings might be seen by daylight gleaming far down in the valley. It would be no small advantage if every college were thus located at the base of a mountain, as good at least as one well-endowed professorship. It were as well to be educated in the shadow of a mountain as in more classical shades. Some will remember, no doubt, not only that they went to the college, but that they went to the mountain. Every visit to its summit would, as it were, generalize the particular information gained below, and subject it to more catholic tests.

Williams College, Williamstown, Mass.

The present trail is more serpentine than Thoreau's course, rising through steep switchbacks at 2,700 feet. Here the trees are fewer and larger, for these dry slopes encourage species like yellow birch—some specimens have a six- to eight-foot girth. At 3,000 feet the Appalachian Trail enters, a wide course lined with raspberry bushes. Just below the summit area is a small pavilion with fireplaces, in a sad state of repair.

The summit itself is a busy place, with roads and parking lots, a modern guest lodge (meals and overnight bunks) and a hundred-foot observation tower which—though damp and poorly ventilated—affords a view in all *(see page 71)* directions. Thoreau's "well-beaten path" down to water probably followed the Overlook and Hopper trails, which head toward Williamstown. They pass by the Reservation campground, where space is available for tents and vehicles.

Thoreau's odd habits of drinking, cooking, and reading on this summit were equivalent, for he was stressing how solitude on the mountain condoned his eccentricity. He was always an ardent reader of the press, but his failure at Staten Island soured him on city editors. "My bait will not tempt the rats," he wrote his mother in 1843; "they are too well fed."

Williams College built several towers on Greylock for scientific observation. The structure Thoreau saw was *(see page 73)* erected in 1841; at first, it was a simple wooden rectangle with a hipped roof. By 1844, part of the central tower had been added; eventually, its two stories rose to sixty feet. The loose boards may have been part of this project; they were sawed at a mill below and hauled up the Hopper Trail. The building was a community enterprise: financed by local citizens, designed by two faculty members, and built with student labor.

Sleeping in a nest of boards *is* absurd, and Thoreau's account seems deliberately grotesque—as though he had built a makeshift coffin. Apparently, he made a rough lean-to; the boards pinned down his blanket, the stone was an anchor against cold night winds. The whole experience has a morbid air, even a hint of self-punishment. Later, at Walden Pond, Thoreau continued to experiment with poverty.

I was up early and perched upon the top of this tower to see the daybreak, for some time reading the names that had been engraved there before I could distinguish more distant objects. An "untameable fly" buzzed at my elbow with the same non-chalance as on a molasses hogshead at the end of Long-wharf. Even there I must attend to his stale humdrum. But now I come to the pith of this long digression.— As the light increased I discovered around me an ocean of mist, which by chance reached up exactly to the base of the tower, and shut out every vestige of the earth, while I was left floating on this fragment of the wreck of a world, on my carved plank in cloudland; a situation which required no aid from the imagination to render it impressive. As the light in the east steadily increased, it revealed to me more clearly the new world into which I had risen in the night, the new terra-firma perchance of my future life. There was not a crevice left through which the trivial places we name Massachusetts, or Vermont, or New York, could be seen, while I still inhaled the clear atmosphere of a July morning,—if it were July there. All around beneath me was spread for a hundred miles on every side, as far as the eye could reach, an undulating country of clouds, answering in the varied swell of its surface to the terrestrial world it veiled. It was such a country as we might see in dreams, with all the delights of paradise. There were immense snowy pastures, apparently smooth-shaven and firm, and shady vales between the vaporous mountains, and far in the horizon I could see where some luxurious misty timber jutted into the prairie, and trace the windings of a water course, some unimagined Amazon or Orinoko, by the misty trees on its brink. As there was wanting the symbol, so there was not the substance of impurity, no spot nor stain. It was a favor for which to be forever silent to be shown this vision. The earth beneath had become such a flitting thing of lights and shadows as the clouds had been before. It was not merely veiled to me, but it had passed away like the phantom of a shadow, σκιᾶς ὄναρ, and this new platform was gained. As I had climbed above storm and cloud, so by successive days' journeys I might reach the region of eternal day beyond the tapering shadow of the earth; aye,

> *"Heaven itself shall slide,*
> *And roll away, like melting stars that glide*
> *Along their oily threads."*

But when its own sun began to rise on this pure world, I found myself a dweller in the dazzling halls of Aurora, into which poets have had but a partial glance over the eastern hills,—drifting amid the saffron-colored clouds, and playing with the rosy fingers of the Dawn, in the very path of the Sun's chariot, and sprinkled with its dewy dust, enjoying the benignant smile, and near at hand the far-darting glances of the god. The inhabitants of earth behold commonly but the dark and shadowy under-side of heaven's pavement; it is only when seen at a favorable angle in the horizon, morning or evening, that some faint streaks of the rich lining of the clouds are revealed. But my muse would fail to convey an impression of the gorgeous tapestry by which I was surrounded, such as men see faintly reflected afar off in the chambers of the east. Here, as on earth, I saw the gracious god

> *"Flatter the mountain tops with sovereign eye,*
> *Gilding pale streams with heavenly alchemy."*

But never here did "Heaven's sun" stain himself. But alas, owing as I think to some unworthiness in myself, my private sun did stain himself, and

> *"Anon permit the basest clouds to ride*
> *With ugly wrack on his celestial face,"*—

for before the god had reached the zenith the heavenly pavement rose and embraced my wavering virtue, or rather I sank down again into that "forlorn world," from which the celestial Sun had hid his visage.

> *"How may a worm, that crawls along the dust,*
> *Clamber the azure mountains, thrown so high,*
> *And fetch from thence thy fair idea just,*
> *That in those sunny courts doth hidden lie,*
> *Cloth'd with such light, as blinds the angel's eye?*
> *How may weak mortal ever hope to file*
> *His unsmooth tongue, and his deprostrate style?*
> *O, raise thou from his corse thy now entombed exile!"*

In the preceding evening I had seen the summits of new and yet higher mountains, the Catskills, by which I might hope to climb to heaven again, and had set my compass for a fair lake in the south-west, which lay in my way, for which I now steered, descending the mountain by my own route, on the side opposite to that by which I had

ascended, and soon found myself in the region of cloud and drizzling
rain, and the inhabitants affirmed that it had been a cloudy and drizzling day wholly. . . .

ROUTE FROM · SUMMIT: *Rockwell Road to MA 7 and Pittsfield* (see page 76)

Before dawn, Thoreau climbed the tower's outside stair-
case and watched the sun rise over a broad "country of
clouds." His ensuing description was a Transcendentalist *aubade,* the serenade of morning found in traditional lyrics by the three poets cited—Pindar, Fletcher,
and Shakespeare. This visual climax to his story verified
its central theme, that greatness abides in "trivial
places" and people, that physical challenge rewards the
mind and spirit. Greylock allowed him to dwell amid the
paradise of "vaporous mountains," the clouds that most

(see page 76) men see only from far below.

(see page 77) When Thoreau descended later that morning, the
clouds opened to give him a bearing on "a fair lake,"
either Pontoosuc or Onota, twelve and sixteen miles
southwest. His route down the south side may have followed the present Appalachian Trail, which crosses several lesser peaks on the Saddleback ridge. Channing
awaited at Pittsfield; from there, the two men went down
the Hudson to hike in the Catskills.

For the Catskill part of his journey, only a partial account survives, which Thoreau wrote into his Journal a
year later, after settling at Walden Pond.

Walden Sat. July 5th—[18]45

Yesterday I came here to live. My house makes me think of some
mountain houses I have seen, which seemed to have a fresher auroral
atmosphere about them, as I fancy of the halls of Olympus. I lodged
at the house of a saw-miller last summer, on the Caatskills mountains,
high up as Pine orchard in the blue-berry & raspberry region, where
the quiet and cleanliness & cool coolness seemed to be all one, which
had this ambrosial character. He was the miller of the Kauterskill
Falls. They were a clean & wholesome family inside and out—like
their house. The latter was not plastered—only lathed and the inner

Catskill Mountains

doors were not hung. The house seemed high placed, airy, and per-
fumed, fit to entertain a travelling God. It was so high indeed that all
the music, the broken strains, the waifs & accompaniments of tunes,
that swept over the ridge of the Caatskills, passed through its aisles.
Could not man be man in such an abode? And would he ever find out
this grovelling life?

It was the very light & atmosphere in which the works of Grecian
art were composed, and in which they rest. They have appropriated
to themselves a loftier hall than mortals ever occupy, at least on a
level with the mountain brows of the world.

There was wanting a little of the glare of the lower vales and in its
place a pure twilight as became the precincts of heaven. Yet so equable and calm was the season there that you could not tell whether it
was morning or noon or evening. Always there was the sound of the
morning cricket.

(see page 78) Only one phrase from this entry reached *Walden,* there
to describe the "auroral atmosphere" of his house at
Walden Pond. Not much of the Catskill journey emerges
from this entry. Thoreau and Channing must have
disembarked at the village of Catskill, then hiked west
along the present course of NY 23A, Rip Van Winkle
Trail. At Kaaterskill Creek they probably left the road
and hiked upstream to the hamlet of Kaaterskill Falls.
The miller was Ira Scribner, and he was then enlarging
his house (hence the lack of doors or plaster) in order to
(see page 80) run an inn, later called "Glen Mary." The "ridge" was
Kaaterskill Clove (1,800′), which lies south of Kaaterskill
Falls. The rest of Thoreau's itinerary was later recorded
by Channing in his copy of *A Week:* walking south to
Massachusetts, through Mt. Washington and Chester,
then via railroad to a point south of Concord, from which
they walked home.

Maine

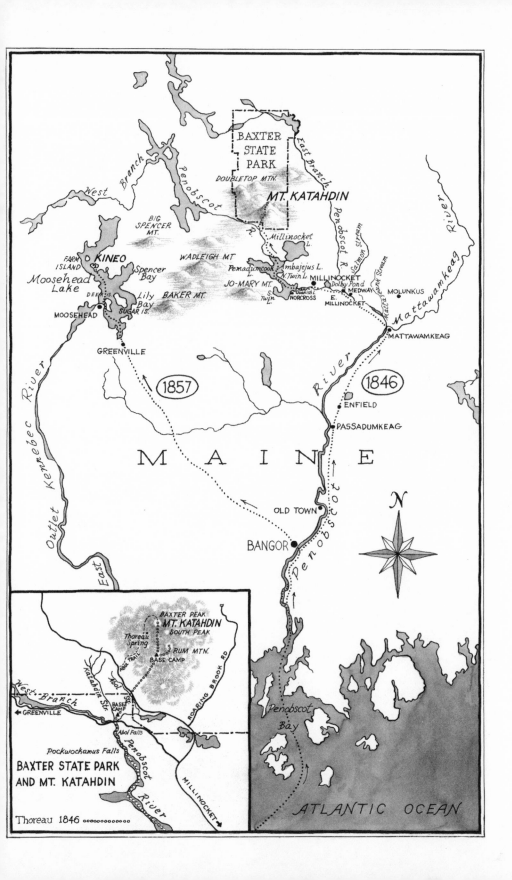

BAXTER
STATE
PARK

DOUBLETOP MTN.

MT. KATAHDIN

East Branch

BIG
SPENCER
MT.

West
Branch

Penobscot

Millinocket L.

FARM
ISLAND

KINEO

WADLEIGH MT

Pemadumcook L.

Ambajejus L.

N. Twin L.

MILLINOCKET

Penobscot R.

Salmon Stream

MOLUNKUS

Moosehead
Lake

Spencer
Bay

JO-MARY MT.

S.
Twin
L.

Quakish L.

NORCROSS

Dolby Pond

MEDWAY

Lily
Bay

BAKER MT.

DEER IS.

Mattawamkeag Stream

Mattawamkeag River

SUGAR IS.

E.
MILLINOCKET

MOOSEHEAD

GREENVILLE

MATTAWAMKEAG

1857

River

1846

Kennebec River

Outlet

ENFIELD

PASSADUMKEAG

M A I N E

Penobscot

N

OLD TOWN

BANGOR

East

Penobscot
Bay

BAXTER PEAK
MT. KATAHDIN
SOUTH PEAK

Thoreau
Spring

RUM MTN.

ABOL TRAIL

BASE CAMP

West Branch

Abol Str.

BASE
CAMP

ROARING BROOK RD

GREENVILLE

Katahdin Str.

Abol Falls

Penobscot

ATLANTIC OCEAN

Pockwockamus Falls

BAXTER STATE PARK
AND MT. KATAHDIN

MILLINOCKET

River

Thoreau 1846 ∘∘∘∘∘∘∘∘∘∘∘∘∘

Katahdin

It is even more grim and wild than you had anticipated,
a damp and intricate wilderness, in the spring
everywhere wet and miry.

Thoreau first went to Maine in May 1838, looking for a job as a schoolteacher. For several weeks he made the rounds of small towns in the Penobscot River valley, finding no work but gaining a vivid impression of this rough frontier world. At Oldtown, an Indian settlement north of Bangor, he talked with a tribal elder about fishing and hunting. When they spoke of travel, the old man pointed north: "Two or three mile up the river one beautiful country."

Thoreau went home to Concord and opened his own school, but over the next few years he did not forget Maine. By 1845 he was living at Walden Pond, which reminded him of "a tarn high upon the side of a mountain." His cousin in Bangor, George Thatcher, knew that country upriver well. There stood Katahdin, the highest mountain in Maine, so remote it had been climbed only by a few surveyors and scientists. In August 1845, Thoreau saw a story in the Boston *Daily Advertiser* of an ascent by two young Harvard men, Edward Everett Hale and William Francis Channing. One year later, Thoreau headed north on a similar expedition.

He was looking for literary material, something solid and dramatic that might sell to a magazine in New York. He was also leaving Concord, where a month earlier he had spent a night in jail as an antislavery gesture. Maine would be a respite from village life—and from the dog-day heat of late summer. He planned to go up the Penobscot River to North Twin Lake, where Thatcher wanted to see some property. Thoreau would then secure other companions (perhaps Indian guides) and continue upriver, carrying around a series of rapids and waterfalls. They would ascend Katahdin from its southern slope, a steep but direct route to the summit.

This trip took him into the wildest country he had yet seen, and while his anticipation was keen and romantic, the actual experience was not. The Indians were ignoble savages; one agreed to serve as guide but then was delayed by "a drunken frolic." Thoreau's journey upstream was difficult, especially the long portages of food and equipment. Maps of the area were inadequate: he carried two, yet he rarely knew his true location. Although previous parties had climbed via the great Abol slide, Thoreau chose a more difficult route; going along a stream to its head, then following a compass line. That method had worked on Greylock two years ago, but here the terrain was far more hazardous. His route gave him poor views, and heavy clouds allowed him only to reach a great plateau, 1,200 feet below the actual summit.

These experiences affected the following story, which Thoreau published in the *Union* magazine in 1848 and revised for *The Maine Woods* (1864). He seems to tell the story just as it happened, but in fact the events have merged with later ideas and research (most of his footnotes refer to sources he read after 1850). "Ktaadn" turns away from his early techniques: the style is spare and precise, devoted to physical details; description takes more space than thought; other characters become nearly as important as himself.

The famous climactic passage, an impassioned sermon on "Matter, vast, terrific," is an afterthought, inserted in the story at a strategic point. Many readers of this passage see it as Thoreau's first recognition of a brutal force in nature. Clearly, his idyllic dreams do give way to a tempered, observant realism. But nature itself is not brutal; only a human mind can assign it that value. From the days of his earliest visit, Maine was schooling him. He first saw it as one beautiful country, far from the restraints of town and law. On the mountain he found another form of order, one that profoundly changed his ideas and art.

THE

MAINE WOODS

On the 31st of August, 1846, I left Concord in Massachusetts for Bangor and the backwoods of Maine, by way of the railroad and steamboat, intending to accompany a relative of mine engaged in the lumber trade in Bangor, as far as a dam on the west branch of the Penobscot, in which property he was interested. From this place, which is about one hundred miles by the river above Bangor, thirty miles from the Houlton military road, and five miles beyond the last log hut, I proposed to make excursions to mount Ktaadn, the second highest mountain in New England, about thirty miles distant, and to some of the lakes of the Penobscot, either alone or with such company as I might pick up there. It is unusual to find a camp so far in the woods at that season, when lumbering operations have ceased, and I was glad to avail myself of the circumstance of a gang of men being employed there at that time in repairing the injuries caused by the great freshet in the spring. The mountain may be approached more easily and directly on horseback and on foot from the north-east side, by the Aroostook road, and the Wassataquoik river; but in that case you see much less of the wilderness, none of the glorious river and lake scenery, and have no experience of the batteau and the boatman's life. I was fortunate also in the season of the year, for in the summer myriads of black flies, mosquitoes, and midges, or, as the Indians call them, "no-see-ems," make travelling in the woods almost impossible; but now their reign was nearly over.

Ktaadn, whose name is an Indian word signifying highest land, was first ascended by white men in 1804. It was visited by Professor J. W. Bailey of West Point in 1836, by Dr. Charles T. Jackson, the State Geologist, in 1837, and by two young men from Boston in 1845. All these have given accounts of their expeditions. Since I was there, two or three other parties have made the excursion and told their stories. Besides these, very few, even among backwoodsmen and hunters, have ever climbed it, and it will be a long time before the tide of fashionable travel sets that way. The mountainous region of the State of Maine stretches from near the White Mountains, northeasterly one hundred and sixty miles, to the head of the Aroostook river, and is about sixty miles wide. The wild or unsettled portion is far more extensive. So that some hours only of travel in this direction will carry the curious to the verge of a primitive forest, more interesting, perhaps, on all accounts, than they would reach by going a thousand miles westward.

ROUTE FROM BOSTON: *I-95 to Bangor* Like other glaciated monadnocks, Katahdin is steepest on its south face, rising 4,000 feet in less than three miles. Thoreau climbed this face; most of the previous ascents, including Hale and Channing's in 1845, came from the east. Thoreau's spelling of "Ktaadn" followed that of Jackson's report (1837), and most translations agree that the word is a superlative, meaning greatest, largest, or preeminent mountain. Besides the three ascents Thoreau cited, surveying parties climbed Katahdin in 1819, 1820, and 1825.

The next forenoon, Tuesday, Sept. 1st, I started with my companion* in a buggy from Bangor for "up river," expecting to be overtaken the next day night, at Mattawamkeag Point, some sixty miles off, by two more Bangoreans, who had decided to join us in a trip to the mountain. We had each a knapsack or bag filled with such clothing and other articles as were indispensable, and my companion carried his gun.

Within a dozen miles of Bangor we passed through the villages of Stillwater and Oldtown, built at the falls of the Penobscot, which

*George Thatcher, Thoreau's cousin from Bangor, who was active in the lumber trade.—WH

furnish the principal power by which the Maine woods are converted into lumber. The mills are built directly over and across the river. Here is a close jam, a hard rub, at all seasons; and then the once green tree, long since white, I need not say as the driven snow, but as a driven log, becomes lumber merely. Here your inch, your two and your three inch stuff begin to be, and Mr. Sawyer marks off those spaces which decide the destiny of so many prostrate forests. Through this steel riddle, more or less coarse, is the arrowy Maine forest, from Ktaadn and Chesuncook, and the head waters of the St. John, relentlessly sifted, till it comes out boards, clapboards, laths, and shingles such as the wind can take, still perchance to be slit and slit again, till men get a size that will suit. Think how stood the white-pine tree on the shore of Chesuncook, its branches soughing with the four winds, and every individual needle trembling in the sunlight—think how it stands with it now—sold, perchance to the New England Friction Match Company! There were in 1837, as I read, two hundred and fifty saw mills on the Penobscot and its tributaries above Bangor, the greater part of them in this immediate neighborhood, and they sawed two hundred millions of feet of boards annually. To this is to be added, the lumber of the Kennebeck, Androscoggin, Saco, Passamaquoddy, and other streams. No wonder that we hear so often of vessels which are becalmed off our coast, being surrounded a week at a time by floating lumber from the Maine woods. The mission of men there seems to be, like so many busy demons, to drive the forest all out of the country, from every solitary beaver swamp, and mountain side, as soon as possible.

At Oldtown we walked into a batteau manufactory. The making of batteaux is quite a business here for the supply of the Penobscot river. We examined some on the stocks. They are light and shapely vessels, calculated for rapid and rocky streams, and to be carried over long portages on men's shoulders, from twenty to thirty feet long, and only four or four and a half wide, sharp at both ends like a canoe, though broadest forward on the bottom, and reaching seven or eight feet over the water, in order that they may slip over rocks as gently as possible. They are made very slight, only two boards to a side, commonly secured to a few light maple or other hard-wood knees, but inward are of the clearest and widest white-pine stuff, of which there

is a great waste on account of their form, for the bottom is left
perfectly flat, not only from side to side, but from end to end. Sometimes they become "hogging" even, after long use, and the boatmen
then turn them over and straighten them by a weight at each end.
They told us that one wore out in two years, or often in a single trip,
on the rocks, and sold for from fourteen to sixteen dollars. There was
something refreshing and wildly musical to my ears in the very name
of the white man's canoe, reminding me of Charlevoix and Canadian
Voyageurs. The batteau is a sort of mongrel between the canoe and
the boat, a fur-trader's boat.

The ferry here took us past the Indian island. As we left the shore,
I observed a short shabby washer-woman-looking Indian; they commonly have the woe-begone look of the girl that cried for spilt milk
—just from "up river,"—land on the Oldtown side near a grocery, and
drawing up his canoe, take out a bundle of skins in one hand, and an
empty keg or half-barrel in the other, and scramble up the bank with
them. This picture will do to put before the Indian's history, that is,
the history of his extinction. In 1837, there were three hundred and
sixty-two souls left of this tribe. The island seemed deserted to-day,
yet I observed some new houses among the weather-stained ones, as
if the tribe had still a design upon life; but generally they have a very
shabby, forlorn, and cheerless look, being all back side and woodshed,
not homesteads, even Indian homesteads, but instead of home or
abroad-steads, for their life is *domi aut militiæ*, at home or at war,
or now rather *venatus*, that is, a hunting, and most of the latter. The
church is the only trim-looking building, but that is not Abenaki, that
was Rome's doings. Good Canadian it may be, but it is poor Indian.
These were once a powerful tribe. Politics are all the rage with them
now. I even thought that a row of wigwams, with a dance of pow-
wows, and a prisoner tortured at the stake, would be more respectable
than this.

We landed in Milford, and rode along on the east side of the Penobscot, having a more or less constant view of the river, and the Indian
islands in it, for they retain all the islands as far up as Nickatow, at
the mouth of the East Branch. They are generally well-timbered, and
are said to be better soil than the neighboring shores. The river
seemed shallow and rocky, and interrupted by rapids, rippling and

gleaming in the sun. We paused a moment to see a fish-hawk dive for a fish down straight as an arrow, from a great height, but he missed his prey this time. It was the Houlton Road on which we were now travelling, over which some troops were marched once towards Mars' Hill, though not to Mars' *field*, as it proved. It is the main, almost the only, road in these parts, as straight and well made, and kept in as good repair, as almost any you will find anywhere. Everywhere we saw signs of the great freshet—this house standing awry, and that where it was not founded, but where it was found, at any rate, the next day; and that other with a water-logged look, as if it were still airing and drying its basement, and logs with everybody's marks upon them, and sometimes the marks of their having served as bridges, strewn along the road. We crossed the Sunkhaze, a summery Indian name, the Olemmon, Passadumkeag, and other streams, which make a greater show on the map than they now did on the road. At Passadumkeag, we found anything but what the name implies, earnest politicians, to wit—white ones, I mean—on the alert, to know how the election was likely to go; men who talked rapidly, with subdued voice, and a sort of factitious earnestness, you could not help believing, hardly waiting for an introduction, one on each side of your buggy, endeavoring to say much in little, for they see you hold the whip impatiently, but always saying little in much. Caucuses they have had, it seems, and caucuses they are to have again—victory and defeat: somebody may be elected, somebody may not. One man, a total stranger, who stood by our carriage, in the dusk, actually frightened the horse with his asseverations, growing more solemnly positive as there was less in him to be positive about. So Passadumkeag did not look on the map. At sundown, leaving the river-road awhile for shortness, we went by way of Enfield, where we stopped for the night. This, like most of the localities bearing names on this road, was a place to name, which, in the midst of the unnamed and unincorporated wilderness, was to make a distinction without a difference, it seemed to me. Here, however, I noticed quite an orchard of healthy and well-grown apple trees, in a bearing state, it being the oldest settler's house in this region, but all natural fruit, and comparatively worthless for want of a grafter. And so it is generally lower down the river. It would be a good speculation, as well as a favor conferred on the settlers, for a

Massachusetts boy to go down there with a trunk full of choice scions, and his grafting apparatus, in the spring.

ROUTE FROM
BANGOR: *US 2 to
Passadumkeag,
Enfield Road to
Enfield* Thoreau traveled with three lumbermen, yet he opened his story with a blast at their trade. As in *Walden,* his economics sarcastically inverted normal values: logging was ultimately trivial, he argued, for it reduced the forest to shingles and matches. This work was a travesty of the injunction in Genesis, to subdue and dominate the earth: that "mission" had turned men into "so many busy (see page 89) demons."

Batteaux and Indians exemplified the character of Maine: one were "sort of mongrel" boats; the others were tainted by contact with politics and religion. References to the Aroostook War of 1839–42 (Maine vs. New Brunswick) sustained this critique of property, and so did the absurd politicians, who were seeking the votes of travelers in a local election.

The next morning we drove along through a high and hilly country, in view of Cold-Stream Pond, a beautiful lake, four or five miles long, and came into the Houlton road again, here called the Military road, at Lincoln, forty-five miles from Bangor, where there is quite a village, for this country—the principal one above Oldtown. Learning that there were several wigwams here, on one of the Indian islands, we left our horse and wagon, and walked through the forest half a mile, to the river, to procure a guide to the mountain. It was not till after considerable search that we discovered their habitations—small huts, in a retired place, where the scenery was unusually soft and beautiful, and the shore skirted with pleasant meadows and graceful elms. We paddled ourselves across to the island-side in a canoe, which we found on the shore. Near where we landed, sat an Indian girl, ten or twelve years old, on a rock in the water, in the sun, washing, and humming or moaning a song meanwhile. It was an aboriginal strain. A salmon-spear, made wholly of wood, lay on the shore, such as they might have used before white men came. It had an elastic piece of wood fastened to one side of its point, which slipped over and closed upon the fish, somewhat like the contrivance for holding a bucket at the end of a well-pole. As we walked up to the nearest house, we were met by a sally of a dozen wolfish-looking dogs, which may have been lineal descendants from the ancient Indian dogs, which the first voyageurs describe as "their wolves." I suppose they were. The occupant soon appeared, with a long pole in his hand, with which he beat off the dogs, while he parleyed with us. A stalwart, but dull and greasy-looking fellow, who told us, in his sluggish way, in answer to our questions, as if it were the first serious business he had to do that day, that there *were* Indians going "up river,"—he and one other—to-day, before noon. And who was the other? Louis Neptune, who lives in the next house. Well, let us go over and see Louis together. The same doggish reception, and Louis Neptune makes his appearance—a small, wiry man, with puckered and wrinkled face, yet he seemed the chief man of the two; the same, as I remembered, who had accompanied Jackson to the mountain in '37. The same questions were put to Louis, and the same information obtained, while the other Indian stood by. It appeared, that they were going to start by noon, with two canoes, to go up to Chesuncook, to hunt moose—to be gone a month. "Well, Louis, suppose you get to the Point, [to the Five Islands, just below Mattawamkeag,] to camp, we walk on up the West Branch to-morrow—four of us—and wait for you at the dam, or this side. You overtake us to-morrow or next day, and take us into your canoes. We stop for you, you stop for us. We pay you for your trouble." "Ye!" replied Louis, "may be you carry some provision for all—some pork —some bread—and so pay." He said, "Me sure get some moose;" and when I asked, if he thought Pomola would let us go up, he answered that we must plant one bottle of rum on the top, he had planted good many; and when he looked again, the rum was all gone. He had been up two or three times: he had planted letter—English, German, French, &c. These men were slightly clad in shirt and pantaloons, like laborers with us in warm weather. They did not invite us into their houses, but met us outside. So we left the Indians, thinking ourselves lucky to have secured such guides and companions.

There were very few houses along the road, yet they did not altogether fail, as if the law by which men are dispersed over the globe were a very stringent one, and not to be resisted with impunity or for slight reasons. There were even the germs of one or two villages just beginning to expand. The beauty of the road itself was remarkable. The various evergreens, many of which are rare with us—delicate and beautiful specimens of the larch, arbor-vitæ, ball spruce, and fir-balsam, from a few inches to many feet in height, lined its sides, in some places like a long front yard, springing up from the smooth grassplots which uninterruptedly border it, and are made fertile by its wash; while it was but a step on either hand to the grim untrodden wilderness, whose tangled labyrinth of living, fallen, and decaying trees,—only the deer and moose, the bear and wolf, can easily penetrate. More perfect specimens than any front yard plot can show, grew there to grace the passage of the Houlton teams.

About noon we reached the Mattawamkeag, fifty-six miles from Bangor by the way we had come, and put up at a frequented house, still on the Houlton road, where the Houlton stage stops. Here was a substantial covered bridge over the Mattawamkeag, built, I think they said, some seventeen years before. We had dinner—where, by the way, and even at breakfast, as well as supper—at the public-houses on this road, the front rank is composed of various kinds of "sweet cakes," in a continuous line from one end of the table to the other. I think I may safely say that there was a row of ten or a dozen plates of this kind set before us two here. To account for which, they say, that when the lumberers come out of the woods, they have a craving for cakes and pies, and such sweet things, which there are almost unknown, and this is the *supply* to satisfy that *demand*—the supply is always equal to the demand,—and these hungry men think a good deal of getting their money's worth. No doubt, the balance of victuals is restored by the time they reach Bangor: Mattawamkeag takes off the raw edge. Well, over this front rank, I say, you coming from the "sweet cake" side, with a cheap philosophic indifference though it may be, have to assault what there is behind, which I do not by any means mean to insinuate is insufficient in quantity or quality to supply that other demand of men not from the woods, but from the towns, for venison and strong country fare. After dinner, we strolled down to the "Point," formed by the junction of the two rivers, which is said to be the scene of an ancient battle between the Eastern Indians and the Mohawks, and searched there carefully for relics, though the men at the bar-room had never heard of such things; but we found only some flakes of arrow-head stone, some points of arrow-heads, one small leaden-bullet, and some colored beads, the last to be referred, perhaps, to early fur-trader days. The Mattawamkeag, though wide, was a mere river's bed, full of rocks and shallows at this time, so that you could cross it almost dry-shod in boots; and I could hardly believe my companion, when he told me that he had been fifty or sixty miles up it in a batteau, through distant and still uncut forests. A batteau could hardly find a harbor now at its mouth. Deer, and caribou, or reindeer, are taken here in the winter, in sight of the house.

Before our companions arrived, we rode on up the Houlton road seven miles, to Molunkus, where the Aroostook road comes into it, and where there is a spacious public house in the woods, called the "Molunkus House," kept by one Libbey, which looked as if it had its hall for dancing and for military drills. There was no other evidence of man but this huge shingle palace in this part of the world; but sometimes even this is filled with travellers. I looked off the piazza round the corner of the house up the Aroostook road, on which there was no clearing in sight. There was a man just adventuring upon it this evening, in a rude, original, what you may call Aroostook, wagon —a mere seat, with a wagon swung under it, a few bags on it, and a dog asleep to watch them. He offered to carry a message for us to anybody in that country, cheerfully. I suspect, that if you should go to the end of the world, you would find somebody there going further, as if just starting for home at sundown, and having a last word before he drove off. Here, too, *was* a small trader, whom I did not see at first, who kept a store—but no great store, certainly—in a small box over the way, behind the Molunkus sign-post. It looked like the balance-box of a patent hay-scales. As for his house, we could only conjecture where that was; he may have been a boarder in the Molunkus House. I saw him standing in his shop-door—his shop was so small, that, if a traveller should make demonstrations of entering in, *he* would have to go out by the back way, and confer with his customer through a window, about his goods in the cellar, or, more probably, bespoken, and yet on the way. I should have gone in, for I felt a real impulse to trade, if I had not stopped to consider what would become of him.

The day before, we had walked into a shop, over against an inn where we stopped, the puny beginning of trade, which would grow at last into a firm copartnership, in the future town or city—indeed, it was already "Somebody & Co.," I forget who. The woman came forward from the penetralia of the attached house, for "Somebody & Co." was in the burning, and she sold us percussion-caps, canalés and smooth; and knew their prices and qualities, and which the hunters preferred. Here was a little of everything in a small compass to satisfy the wants and the ambition of the woods, a stock selected with what pains and care, and brought home in the wagon box, or a corner of the Houlton team; but there seemed to me, as usual, a preponderance of children's toys, dogs to bark, and cats to mew, and trumpets to blow, where natives there hardly are yet. As if a child, born into the Maine woods, among the pine cones and cedar berries, could not do without such a sugar-man, or skipping-jack, as the young Rothschild has.

I think that there was not more than one house on the road to Molunkus, or for seven miles. At that place we got over the fence into a new field, planted with potatoes, where the logs were still burning between the hills; and, pulling up the vines, found good-sized potatoes, nearly ripe, growing like weeds, and turnips mixed with them. The mode of clearing and planting, is, to fell the trees, and burn once what will burn, then cut them up into suitable lengths, roll into heaps, and burn again; then, with a hoe, plant potatoes where you can come at the ground between the stumps and charred logs, for a first crop, the ashes sufficing for manure, and no hoeing being necessary the first year. In the fall, cut, roll, and burn again, and so on, till the land is cleared; and soon it is ready for grain, and to be laid down. Let those talk of poverty and hard times who will, in the towns and cities; cannot the emigrant, who can pay his fare to New-York or Boston, pay five dollars more to get here,—I paid three, all told, for my passage from Boston to Bangor, 250 miles,—and be as rich as he pleases, where land virtually costs nothing, and houses only the labor of building, and he may begin life as Adam did? If he will still remember the distinction of poor and rich, let him bespeak him a narrower house forthwith.

When we returned to the Mattawamkeag, the Houlton stage had already put up there; and a Province man was betraying his greenness to the Yankees by his questions.—Why Province money won't pass here at par, when States' money is good at Frederickton—though this, perhaps, was sensible enough. From what I saw then, it appeared that the Province man was now the only real Jonathan, or raw country bumpkin, left so far behind by his enterprising neighbors, that he didn't know enough to put a question to them. No people can long continue provincial in character, who have the propensity for politics and whittling, and rapid travelling, which the Yankees have, and who are leaving the mother country behind in the variety of their notions and inventions. The possession and exercise of practical talent merely, are a sure and rapid means of intellectual culture and independence.

The last edition of Greenleaf's Map of Maine hung on the wall here, and, as we had no pocket map, we resolved to trace a map of the lake country: so dipping a wad of tow into the lamp, we oiled a sheet of paper on the oiled table-cloth, and, in good faith, traced what we afterwards ascertained to be a labyrinth of errors, carefully following the outlines of the imaginary lakes which that map contains. The Map of the Public Lands of Maine and Massachusetts is the only one I have seen that at all deserves the name. It was while we were engaged in this operation that our companions arrived. They had seen the Indians' fire on the Five Islands, and so we concluded that all was right.

Louis Neptune affected the trip, largely through his absence. He apparently knew Katahdin from the Jackson survey and did not fear "Pomola" (English for "Bumole," the mountain's evil spirit), but the allusion to rum anticipates his later appearance in the story, barely detoxified.

ROUTE FROM ENFIELD: *ME 155 to Lincoln, US 2 to Mattawamkeag and Molunkus*

(see page 93)

Thoreau prepared to meet the "grim, untrodden wilderness" with an air of enthusiasm. This road is less impressive today, but among the trees and trailer homes are still the covered bridge at Mattawamkeag, the "Point" or long gravel bar between the West Branch and Mattawamkeag River, where Indian hunting parties once camped. The source of this river is Mattawamkeag Lake, fifty miles northeast.

At Molunkus, Thoreau recalled the shop he saw in Enfield on Tuesday night; his hope that commerce will not follow him into the wilderness proves unfounded, just as naïve as the "Province man" from New Brunswick, who thought his money could pass in Maine. Similar difficulties plagued Thoreau when he tried to copy "Greenleaf's Map" (3rd ed., 1844), then later found it to be full of errors.

Early the next morning we had mounted our packs, and prepared for a tramp up the West Branch, my companion having turned his horse out to pasture for a week or ten days, thinking that a bite of fresh grass, and a taste of running water, would do him as much good as backwoods fare, and new country influences his master. Leaping over a fence, we began to follow an obscure trail up the northern bank of the Penobscot. There was now no road further, the river being the only highway, and but half a dozen log huts confined to its banks, to be met with for thirty miles; on either hand, and beyond, was a wholly uninhabited wilderness, stretching to Canada. Neither horse, nor cow, nor vehicle of any kind, had ever passed over this ground. The cattle, and the few bulky articles which the loggers use, being got up in the winter on the ice, and down again before it breaks up. The evergreen woods had a decidedly sweet and bracing fragrance; the air was a sort of diet-drink, and we walked on buoyantly in Indian file, stretching our legs. Occasionally there was a small opening on the bank, made for the purpose of log-rolling, where we got a sight of the river—always a rocky and rippling stream. The roar of the rapids, the note of a whistler-duck on the river, of the jay and chicadee around us, and of the pigeon-woodpecker in the openings, were the sounds that we heard. This was what you might call a bran new country; the only roads were of Nature's making, and the few houses were camps. Here, then, one could no longer accuse institutions and society, but must front the true source of evil.

    There are three classes of inhabitants, who either frequent or inhabit the country which we had now entered; first, the loggers, who, for a part of the year, the winter and spring, are far the most numerous, but in the summer, except a few explorers for timber, completely desert it; second, the few settlers I have named, the only permanent inhabitants, who live on the verge of it, and help raise supplies for the former; third, the hunters, mostly Indians, who range over it in their season.

At the end of three miles we came to the Mattaseunk stream and mill, where there was even a rude wooden railroad running down to the Penobscot, the last railroad we were to see. We crossed one tract, on the bank of the river, of more than a hundred acres of heavy timber, which had just been felled and burnt over, and was still smoking. Our trail lay through the midst of it, and was well nigh blotted out. The trees lay at full length, four or five feet deep, and crossing each other in all directions, all black as charcoal, but perfectly sound within, still good for fuel or for timber; soon they would be cut into lengths and burnt again. Here were thousands of cords, enough to keep the poor of Boston and New-York amply warm for a winter, which only cumbered the ground, and were in the settler's way. And the whole of that solid and interminable forest is doomed to be gradually devoured thus by fire, like shavings, and no man be warmed by it. At Crocker's log hut, at the mouth of Salmon River, seven miles from the Point, one of the party commenced distributing a store of small cent picture-books among the children, to teach them to read; and also newspapers, more or less recent, among the parents, than which nothing can be more acceptable to a backwoods people. It was really an important item in our outfit, and, at times, the only currency that would circulate. I walked through Salmon River with my shoes on, it being low water, but not without wetting my feet. A few miles further we came to "Marm Howard's," at the end of an extensive clearing, where there were two or three log huts in sight at once, one on the opposite side of the river, and a few graves, even surrounded by a wooden paling, where already the rude forefathers of *a* hamlet lie; and a thousand years hence, perchance, some poet will write his "Elegy in a Country Churchyard." The "Village Hampdens," the "mute, inglorious Miltons," and Cromwells, "guiltless of" their "country's blood," were yet unborn.

> *"Perchance in this <u>wild</u> spot <u>there will be</u> laid*
> *Some heart once pregnant with celestial fire;*
> *Hands that the rod of empire might have swayed,*
> *Or waked to ecstasy the living lyre."*

The next house was Fisk's, ten miles from the Point, at the mouth
of the East Branch, opposite to the island Nickatow, or the Forks, the
last of the Indian islands. I am particular to give the names of the
settlers and the distances, since every log hut in these woods is a
public house, and such information is of no little consequence to those
who may have occasion to travel this way. Our course here crossed
the Penobscot, and followed the southern bank. One of the party, who
entered the house in search of some one to set us over, reported a very
neat dwelling, with plenty of books, and a new wife, just imported
from Boston, wholly new to the woods. We found the East Branch a
large and rapid stream at its mouth, and much deeper than it appeared. Having with some difficulty discovered the trail again, we
kept up the south side of the West Branch, or main river, passing by
some rapids called Rock-Ebeeme, the roar of which we heard through
the woods, and, shortly after, in the thickest of the wood, some empty
loggers' camps, still new, which were occupied the previous winter.
Though we saw a few more afterwards, I will make one account serve
for all. These were such houses as the lumberers of Maine spend the
winter in, in the wilderness. There were the camps and the hovel for
the cattle, hardly distinguishable, except that the latter had no chimney. These camps were about twenty feet long by fifteen wide, built
of logs—hemlock, cedar, spruce, or yellow birch—one kind alone, or
all together, with the bark on; two or three large ones first, one

directly above another, and notched together at the ends, to the height of three or four feet, then of smaller logs resting upon transverse ones at the ends, each of the last successively shorter than the other, to form the roof. The chimney was an oblong square hole in the middle, three or four feet in diameter, with a fence of logs as high as the ridge. The interstices were filled with moss, and the roof was shingled with long and handsome splints of cedar, or spruce, or pine, rifted with a sledge and cleaver. The fire-place, the most important place of all, was in shape and size like the chimney, and directly under it, defined by a log fence or fender on the ground, and a heap of ashes a foot or two deep within, with solid benches of split logs running round it. Here the fire usually melts the snow, and dries the rain before it can descend to quench it. The faded beds of arbor-vitæ leaves extended under the eaves on either hand. There was the place for the water-pail, pork-barrel, and wash-basin, and generally a dingy pack of cards left on a log. Usually a good deal of whittling was expended on the latch, which was made of wood, in the form of an iron one. These houses are made comfortable by the huge fires that can be afforded night and day. Usually the scenery about them is drear and savage enough; and the logger's camp is as completely in the woods as a fungus at the foot of a pine in a swamp; no outlook but to the sky overhead; no more clearing than is made by cutting down the trees of which it is built, and those which are necessary for fuel. If only it be well sheltered and convenient to his work, and near a spring, he wastes no thought on the prospect. They are very proper forest houses, the stems of the trees collected together and piled up around a man to keep out wind and rain: made of living green logs, hanging with moss and lichen, and with the curls and fringes of the yellow-birch bark, and dripping with resin, fresh and moist, and redolent of swampy odors, with that sort of vigor and perennialness even about them that toad-stools suggest.* The logger's fare consists of tea,

---

*Springer, in his "Forest Life" (1851), says that they first remove the leaves and turf from the spot where they intend to build a camp, for fear of fire; also, that "the spruce-tree is generally selected for camp-building, it being light, straight, and quite free from sap"; that "the roof is finally covered with the boughs of the fir, spruce, and hemlock, so that when the snow falls upon the whole, the warmth of the camp is preserved in the coldest weather"; and that they make the log seat before the fire, called the "Deacon's Seat," of a spruce or fir split in halves, with three or four stout limbs left on one side for legs, which are not likely to get loose.

molasses, flour, pork,—sometimes beef,—and beans. A great proportion of the beans raised in Massachusetts find their market here. On
expeditions it is only hard bread and pork, often raw, slice upon slice,
with tea or water, as the case may be.

The primitive wood is always and everywhere damp and mossy, so
that I travelled constantly with the impression that I was in a swamp;
and only when it was remarked that this or that tract, judging from
the quality of the timber on it, would make a profitable clearing, was
I reminded, that if the sun were let in it would make a dry field, like
the few I had seen, at once. The best shod for the most part travel with
wet feet. If the ground was so wet and spongy at this, the driest part
of a dry season, what must it be in the spring? The woods hereabouts
abounded in beech and yellow-birch, of which last there were some
very large specimens; also spruce, cedar, fir, and hemlock; but we saw
only the stumps of the white pine here, some of them of great size,
these having been already culled out, being the only tree much sought
after, even as low down as this. Only a little spruce and hemlock
beside had been logged here. The eastern wood, which is sold for fuel
in Massachusetts, all comes from below Bangor. It was the pine alone,
chiefly the white pine, that had tempted any but the hunter to precede
us on this route.

Waite's farm, thirteen miles from the Point, is an extensive and
elevated clearing, from which we got a fine view of the river, rippling
and gleaming far beneath us. My companions had formerly had a
good view of Ktaadn and the other mountains here, but to-day it was
so smoky that we could see nothing of them. We could overlook an
immense country of uninterrupted forest, stretching away up the
East Branch toward Canada, on the north and northwest, and toward
the Aroostook valley on the northeast: and imagine what wild life was
stirring in its midst. Here was quite a field of corn for this region,
whose peculiar dry scent we perceived a third of a mile off before we
saw it.

Eighteen miles from the Point brought us in sight of McCauslin's,
or "Uncle George's," as he was familiarly called by my companions,
to whom he was well known, where we intended to break our long
fast. His house was in the midst of an extensive clearing of intervale,
at the mouth of the Little Schoodic River, on the opposite or north

bank of the Penobscot. So we collected on a point of the shore, that we might be seen, and fired our gun as a signal, which brought out his dogs forthwith, and thereafter their master, who in due time took us across in his batteau. This clearing was bounded abruptly on all sides but the river, by the naked stems of the forest, as if you were to cut only a few feet square in the midst of a thousand acres of mowing, and set down a thimble therein. He had a whole heaven and horizon to himself, and the sun seemed to be journeying over his clearing only, the live-long day. Here we concluded to spend the night, and wait for the Indians, as there was no stopping place so convenient above. He had seen no Indians pass, and this did not often happen without his knowledge. He thought that his dogs sometimes gave notice of the approach of Indians, half an hour before they arrived.

McCauslin was a Kennebec man, of Scotch descent, who had been a waterman twenty-two years, and had driven on the lakes and head waters of the Penobscot five or six springs in succession, but was now settled here to raise supplies for the lumberers and for himself. He entertained us a day or two with true Scotch hospitality, and would accept no recompense for it. A man of a dry wit and shrewdness, and a general intelligence which I had not looked for in the backwoods. In fact, the deeper you penetrate into the woods, the more intelligent, and, in one sense, less countrified do you find the inhabitants; for always the pioneer has been a traveller, and, to some extent, a man of the world; and, as the distances with which he is familiar are greater, so is his information more general and far reaching than the villager's. If I were to look for a narrow, uninformed, and countrified mind, as opposed to the intelligence and refinement which are thought to emanate from cities, it would be among the rusty inhabitants of an old-settled country, on farms all run out and gone to seed with life-ever-lasting, in the towns about Boston, even on the high road in Concord, and not in the backwoods of Maine.

Supper was got before our eyes, in the ample kitchen, by a fire which would have roasted an ox; many whole logs, four feet long, were consumed to boil our tea-kettle—birch, or beech, or maple, the same summer and winter; and the dishes were soon smoking on the table, late the arm-chair, against the wall, from which one of the party was expelled. The arms of the chair formed the frame on which the table rested; and, when the round top was turned up against the wall, it formed the back of the chair, and was no more in the way than the wall itself. This, we noticed, was the prevailing fashion in these log houses, in order to economize in room. There were piping hot wheaten-cakes, the flour having been brought up the river in batteaux,—no Indian bread, for the upper part of Maine, it will be remembered, is a wheat country,—and ham, eggs, and potatoes, and milk and cheese, the produce of the farm; and, also, shad and salmon, tea sweetened with molasses, and sweet cakes in contradistinction to the hot cakes not sweetened, the one white, the other yellow, to wind up with. Such, we found, was the prevailing fare, ordinary and extraordinary, along this river. Mountain cranberries *(Vaccinium Vitis-Idæa)*, stewed and sweetened, were the common dessert. Everything here was in profusion, and the best of its kind. Butter was in such plenty, that it was commonly used, before it was salted, to grease boots with.

ROUTE FROM MATTAWAMKEAG: *ME 157 to Millinocket Lake* The journey to Katahdin took Thoreau into totally unin-habited country, where the "true source of evil" was not nature or society, but man alone. During his trip he faced the problem of knowing humanity *independent* of all external supports, a test that reflected on his experiment with solitude at Walden.

Most of his landmarks are still clear: Mattaseunk Stream crosses ME 157 at Jordan Mills, three miles north. *(see page 99)* "Crocker's" was two miles south of Medway, where Salmon Stream crosses ME 157. "Marm Howard's" was *(see page 100)* near the present Lynch Cemetery, and "Fisk's" was prob-ably near Fiske Cemetery in Medway, where the East and West branches of the Penobscot meet. A dam now lies beyond Nicatou Island, and Rockabema Stream en-ters just above the island.

No loggers' camps are at Medway any longer, but the Lumberman's Museum in Patten, thirty-five miles north on ME 11, has exact replicas. This description, probably *(see page 101)* of a camp Thoreau saw later, is sharp and physical, simi-lar to his account of house building in *Walden.* Like that shelter, these camps are an appropriate use of natural resources. Yet the loggers are also destructive: white pine, once perhaps the most abundant species of tree in aboriginal America, no longer survives in virgin stands. The now-dominant balsam fir makes poor firewood, and it had little commercial use until the pulp industry developed. "Waite's farm" stood near East Millinocket, *(see page 102)* now the site of a pulp and paper mill run by Great Northern, the principal employer and landowner in Maine.

Logging has also drastically changed the watershed in Maine: George McCauslin lived on the West Branch, at Schoodic Stream; that whole area was later "flowed out" as dams and logging pens backed up water to create the vast Dolby Pond. McCauslin, who came from Kennebec River country in southern Maine, was an expert handler of batteaux and about the best guide available. His woods lore contrasted strongly with the "narrow, uninformed, countrified mind" Thoreau brought from Con- *(see page 103)* cord. Yet McCauslin's house was more civil than anticipated: good furniture and lavish meals were part of its solid, abundant life.

In the night we were entertained by the sound of rain-drops on the cedar splints which covered the roof, and awaked the next morning with a drop or two in our eyes. It had set in for a storm, and we made up our minds not to forsake such comfortable quarters with this prospect, but wait for Indians and fair weather. It rained and drizzled, and gleamed by turns, the live-long day. What we did there, how we killed the time, would, perhaps, be idler to tell; how many times we buttered our boots, and how often a drowsy one was seen to sidle off to the bedroom. When it held up, I strolled up and down the bank and gathered the harebell and cedar berries, which grew there; or else we tried by turns the long-handled axe on the logs before the door. The axe-helves here were made to chop standing on the log—a primitive log of course—and were, therefore, nearly a foot longer than with us. One while we walked over the farm, and visited his well-filled barns with McCauslin. There were one other man and two women only here. He kept horses, cows, oxen, and sheep. I think he said that he was the first to bring a plough and a cow so far; and, he might have added, the last, with only two exceptions. The potato rot had found him out here, too, the previous year, and got half or two-thirds of his crop, though the seed was of his own raising. Oats, grass, and potatoes, were his staples; but he raised, also, a few carrots and turnips, and "a little corn for the hens," for this was all that he dared risk, for fear that it would not ripen. Melons, squashes, sweet-corn, beans, tomatoes, and many other vegetables, could not be ripened there.

The very few settlers along this stream were obviously tempted by the cheapness of the land mainly. When I asked McCauslin why more settlers did not come in, he answered, that one reason was, they could not buy the land, it belonged to individuals or companies who were afraid that their wild lands would be settled, and so incorporated into towns, and they be taxed for them; but to settling on the States' land there was no such hinderance. For his own part, he wanted no neighbors—he didn't wish to see any road by his house. Neighbors, even the best, were a trouble and expense, especially on the score of cattle and fences. They might live across the river, perhaps, but not on the same side.

The chickens here were protected by the dogs. As McCauslin said, "The old one took it up first, and she taught the pup, and now they had got it into their heads that it wouldn't do to have anything of the bird kind on the premises." A hawk hovering over was not allowed to alight, but barked off by the dogs circling underneath; and a pigeon, or a "yellow hammer," as they called the pigeon-woodpecker, on a dead limb or stump, was instantly expelled. It was the main business of their day, and kept them constantly coming and going. One would rush out of the house on the least alarm given by the other.

When it rained hardest, we returned to the house, and took down a tract from the shelf. There was the Wandering Jew, cheap edition, and fine print, the Criminal Calendar, and Parish's Geography, and flash novels two or three. Under the pressure of circumstances, we read a little in these. With such aid, the press is not so feeble an engine after all. This house, which was a fair specimen of those on this river, was built of huge logs, which peeped out everywhere, and were chinked with clay and moss. It contained four or five rooms. There were no sawed boards, or shingles, or clapboards, about it; and scarcely any tool but the axe had been used in its construction. The partitions were made of long clapboard-like splints, of spruce or cedar, turned to a delicate salmon color by the smoke. The roof and sides were covered with the same, instead of shingles and clapboards, and some of a much thicker and larger size were used for the floor. These were all so straight and smooth, that they answered the purpose admirably; and a careless observer would not have suspected that they were not sawed and planed. The chimney and hearth were of vast size, and made of stone. The broom was a few twigs of arborvitæ tied to a stick; and a pole was suspended over the hearth, close to the ceiling, to dry stockings and clothes on. I noticed that the floor was full of small, dingy holes, as if made with a gimlet, but which were, in fact, made by the spikes, nearly an inch long, which the lumberers wear in their boots to prevent their slipping on wet logs. Just above McCauslin's, there is a rocky rapid, where logs jam in the spring; and many "drivers" are there collected, who frequent his house for supplies: these were their tracks which I saw.

At sundown, McCauslin pointed away over the forest, across the river, to signs of fair weather amid the clouds—some evening redness there. For even there the points of compass held; and there was a quarter of the heavens appropriated to sunrise and another to sunset.

Stuck with a day of cool, rainy weather, Thoreau re-
sorted to minor subjects, all for the benefit of his distant
readers: methods of farming, neighbors, available books,
house shingles. The nearby rapid was either Pond Falls *(see above)*
or Grand Falls, both near Shad Pond.

The next morning, the weather proving fair enough for our purpose, we prepared to start; and, the Indians having failed us, persuaded McCauslin, who was not unwilling to re-visit the scenes of his driving, to accompany us in their stead, intending to engage one other boatman on the way. A strip of cotton-cloth for a tent, a couple of blankets, which would suffice for the whole party, fifteen pounds of hard bread, ten pounds of "clear" pork, and a little tea, made up "Uncle George's" pack. The last three articles were calculated to be provision enough for six men for a week, with what we might pick up. A tea-kettle, a frying-pan and an axe, to be obtained at the last house, would complete our outfit.

We were soon out of McCauslin's clearing, and in the ever-green woods again. The obscure trail made by the two settlers above, which even the woodman is sometimes puzzled to discern, ere long crossed a narrow open strip in the woods overrun with weeds, called the Burnt Land, where a fire had raged formerly, stretching northward nine or ten miles, to Millinocket Lake. At the end of three miles we reached Shad Pond, or Noliseemack, an expansion of the river. Hodge, the Assistant State Geologist, who passed through this on the twenty-fifth of June, 1837, says, "We pushed our boat through an acre or more of buck-beans, which had taken root at the bottom, and bloomed above the surface in the greatest profusion and beauty." Thomas Fowler's house is four miles from McCauslin's, on the shore of the Pond, at the mouth of the Millinocket River, and eight miles from the lake of the same name, on the latter stream. This lake affords a more direct course to Ktaadn, but we preferred to follow the Penobscot and the Pamadumcook Lakes. Fowler was just completing a new log hut, and was sawing out a window through the logs nearly two feet thick when we arrived. He had begun to paper his house with spruce bark, turned inside out, which had a good effect, and was in keeping with the circumstances. Instead of water we got here a draught of beer, which, it was allowed, would be better; clear and thin, but strong and stringent as the cedar sap. It was as if we sucked at the very teats of Nature's pine-clad bosom in these parts—the sap of all Millinocket botany commingled—the topmost most fantastic and spiciest sprays of the primitive wood, and whatever invigorating and stringent gum or essence it afforded, steeped and dissolved in it—a lumberer's drink, which would acclimate and naturalize a man at once—which would make him see green, and, if he slept, dream that he heard the wind sough among the pines. Here was a fife, praying to be played on, through which we breathed a few tuneful strains,—brought hither to tame wild beasts. As we stood upon the pile of chips by the door, fish-hawks were sailing over head; and here, over Shad Pond, might daily be witnessed, the tyranny of the bald-eagle over that bird. Tom pointed away over the Lake to a bald-eagle's nest, which was plainly visible more than a mile off, on a pine, high above the surrounding forest, and was frequented from year to year by the same pair, and held sacred by him. There were these two houses only there, his low hut, and the eagles' airy cart-load of fagots. Thomas Fowler, too, was persuaded to join us, for two men were necessary to manage the batteau, which was soon to be our carriage, and these men needed to be cool and skilful for the navigation of the Penobscot. Tom's pack was soon made, for he had not far to look for his waterman's boots, and a red flannel shirt. This is the favorite color with lumbermen; and red flannel is reputed to possess some mysterious virtues, to be most healthful and convenient in respect to perspiration. In every gang there will be a large proportion of red birds. We took here a poor and leaky batteau, and began to pole up the Millinocket two miles, to the elder Fowler's, in order to avoid the Grand Falls of the Penobscot, intending to exchange our batteau there for a better. The Millinocket is a small, shallow and sandy stream, full of what I took to be lamprey-eels' or suckers' nests, and lined with musquash cabins,* but free from rapids, according to Fowler, excepting at its outlet from the Lake. He was at this time engaged in cutting the native grass—rush grass and meadow-clover, as he called it—on the meadows and small, low islands, of this stream. We noticed flattened places in the grass on either side, where, he said, a moose had lain down the night before, adding, that there were thousands in these meadows.

Old Fowler's, on the Millinocket, six miles from McCauslin's, and twenty-four from the Point, is the last house. Gibson's, on the Sowad-nehunk, is the only clearing above, but that had proved a failure, and was long since deserted. Fowler is the oldest inhabitant of these woods. He formerly lived a few miles from here, on the south side of the West Branch, where he built his house sixteen years ago, the first house built above the Five Islands. Here our new batteau was to be carried over the first portage of two miles, round the Grand Falls of the Penobscot, on a horse-sled made of saplings, to jump the numerous rocks in the way, but we had to wait a couple of hours for them to catch the horses, which were pastured at a distance, amid the stumps, and had wandered still further off. The last of the salmon for this season had just been caught, and were still fresh in pickle, from

*Muskrat nests, or lodges.—WH

which enough was extracted to fill our empty kettle, and so graduate
our introduction to simpler forest fare. The week before, they had lost
nine sheep here out of their first flock, by the wolves. The surviving
sheep came round the house, and seemed frightened, which induced
them to go and look for the rest, when they found seven dead and
lacerated, and two still alive. These last they carried to the house, and,
as Mrs. Fowler said, they were merely scratched in the throat, and had
no more visible wound than would be produced by the prick of a pin.
She sheared off the wool from their throats, and washed them and put
on some salve, and turned them out, but in a few moments they were
missing, and had not been found since. In fact, they were all poisoned,
and those that were found swelled up at once, so that they saved
neither skin nor wool. This realized the old fables of the wolves and
the sheep, and convinced me that that ancient hostility still existed.
Verily, the shepherd boy did not need to sound a false alarm this time.
There were steel traps by the door of various sizes, for wolves, otter,
and bears, with large claws instead of teeth, to catch in their sinews.
Wolves are frequently killed with poisoned bait.

At length, after we had dined here on the usual backwoods fare, the
horses arrived, and we hauled our batteau out of the water, and
lashed it to its wicker carriage, and, throwing in our packs, walked on
before, leaving the boatmen and driver, who was Tom's brother, to
manage the concern. The route, which led through the wild pasture
where the sheep were killed, was in some places the roughest ever
travelled by horses, over rocky hills, where the sled bounced and slid
along, like a vessel pitching in a storm; and one man was as necessary
to stand at the stern, to prevent the boat from being wrecked, as a
helmsman in the roughest sea. The philosophy of our progress was
something like this: when the runners struck a rock three or four feet
high, the sled bounced back and upwards at the same time; but, as the
horses never ceased pulling, it came down on the top of the rock, and
so we got over. This portage probably followed the trail of an ancient
Indian carry round these falls. By 2 o'clock we, who had walked on
before, reached the river above the falls, not far from the outlet of
Quakish Lake, and waited for the batteau to come up. We had been
here but a short time, when a thunder-shower was seen coming up
from the west, over the still invisible lakes, and that pleasant wilder-

Indian carry

ness which we were so eager to become acquainted with; and soon the heavy drops began to patter on the leaves around us. I had just selected the prostrate trunk of a huge pine, five or six feet in diameter, and was crawling under it, when, luckily, the boat arrived. It would have amused a sheltered man to witness the manner in which it was unlashed, and whirled over, while the first waterspout burst upon us. It was no sooner in the hands of the eager company than it was abandoned to the first revolutionary impulse, and to gravity, to adjust it; and they might have been seen all stooping to its shelter, and wriggling under like so many eels, before it was fairly deposited on the ground. When all were under, we propped up the lee side, and busied ourselves there, whittling thole pins for rowing, when we should reach the lakes; and made the woods ring, between the claps of thunder, with such boat-songs as we could remember. The horses stood sleek and shining with the rain, all drooping and crestfallen, while deluge after deluge washed over us; but the bottom of a boat may be relied on for a tight roof. At length, after two hours' delay at this place, a streak of fair weather appeared in the northwest, whither our course now lay, promising a serene evening for our voyage; and the driver returned with his horses, while we made haste to launch our boat, and commence our voyage in good earnest.

There were six of us, including the two boatmen. With our packs heaped up near the bows, and ourselves disposed as baggage to trim the boat, with instructions not to move in case we should strike a rock, more than so many barrels of pork, we pushed out into the first rapid, a slight specimen of the stream we had to navigate. With Uncle George in the stern, and Tom in the bows, each using a spruce pole about twelve feet long, pointed with iron,* and poling on the same side, we shot up the rapids like a salmon, the water rushing and roaring around, so that only a practised eye could distinguish a safe course, or tell what was deep water and what rocks, frequently grazing the latter on one or both sides, with a hundred as narrow escapes as ever the Argo had in passing through the Symplegades. I, who had had some experience in boating, had never experienced any half so exhilarating before. We were lucky to have exchanged our Indians, whom we did not know, for these men, who, together with Tom's brother, were reputed the best boatmen on the river, and were at once indispensable pilots and pleasant companions. The canoe is smaller, more easily upset, and sooner worn out; and the Indian is said not to be so skilful in the management of the batteau. He is, for the most part, less to be relied on, and more disposed to sulks and whims. The utmost familiarity with dead streams, or with the ocean, would not prepare a man for this peculiar navigation; and the most skilful boatman anywhere else would here be obliged to take out his boat and carry round a hundred times, still with great risk, as well as delay, where the practised batteau man poles up with comparative ease and safety. The hardy "voyageur" pushes with incredible perseverance and success quite up to the foot of the falls, and then only carries round some perpendicular ledge, and launches again in "the torrent's smoothness, ere it dash below," to struggle with the boiling rapids above. The Indians say, that the river once ran both ways, one half up and the other down, but, that since the white man came, it all runs down, and now they must laboriously pole their canoes against the stream, and carry them over numerous portages. In the summer, all stores, the grindstone and the plough of the pioneer, flour, pork, and utensils for the ex-

---

*The Canadians call it *picquer de fond*.

plorer, must be conveyed up the river in batteaux; and many a cargo and many a boatman is lost in these waters. In the winter, however, which is very equable and long, the ice is the great highway, and the loggers' team penetrates to Chesuncook Lake, and still higher up, even two hundred miles above Bangor. Imagine the solitary sled-track running far up into the snowy and evergreen wilderness, hemmed in closely for a hundred miles by the forest, and again stretching straight across the broad surfaces of concealed lakes!

Thoreau's route can be followed from Millinocket Road to Shad Pond, where travelers enter Baxter State Park. Before leaving Millinocket, stop at the Park headquarters for information. A limited number of reservations are available for overnight camping; fees are charged for camping and for driving on the park roads. ROUTE FROM MILLINOCKET LAKE: *ME 11 to Millinocket, Millinocket Road to Roaring Brook Road, to Togue Pond Gate*

Thomas Fowler, Jr. (1822–1902), was the son of Thomas Fowler and Betsy Martin, who settled here in 1828. At twenty-four, young Fowler was a skilled carpenter and brewer. The drink he offered Thoreau was black spruce-beer, made from the tree's young twigs; its resinous flavor suggested the "essence" or spirit of primitive wilderness. *(see page 108)*

Thomas Fowler, Sr. (1792–1874), first built at Grand Falls, where ledges and a twenty-foot drop prevented navigation into the upper lakes. Fowler later moved to Millinocket Stream, a tributary of the West Branch, and (following an old Indian carry) cut a road west to Rines Pitch, at the foot of Quakish Lake. A private road still follows this route to Quakish Dam. *(see page 109)*

"Tom's brother" was George W. Fowler (1824–90). Thoreau's account of "the philosophy of our progress" across the carry was a whimsical forecast of the difficulties that lay ahead, in a region where "progress" was more desire than reality. Changes occurred rapidly in the wilderness; a sudden rainstorm instantly converted the batteau into a shelter. This "first revolutionary impulse" character- *(see page 110)* *(see page 111)*

ized the entire journey, on which Thoreau learned to
accept the dominant course of events.

With Thatcher apparently changing his plans and
going on to Katahdin, the party had six men and several
hundred pounds of gear, yet one batteau could hold them
all. Like salmon or the Argonauts, the boatmen's passage
(see page 112) upstream was a heroic enterprise, dangerous and de-
fiant, enacting a proud impulse to ascend to higher
ground. This rhythm now began to accelerate Thoreau's
story.

We were soon in the smooth water of the Quakish Lake, and took our
turns at rowing and paddling across it. It is a small, irregular, but
handsome lake, shut in on all sides by the forest, and showing no
traces of man but some low boom in a distant cove, reserved for
spring use. The spruce and cedar on its shores, hung with gray lichens, looked at a distance like the ghosts of trees. Ducks were sailing
here and there on its surface, and a solitary loon, like a more living
wave—a vital spot on the lake's surface—laughed and frolicked, and
showed its straight leg, for our amusement. Joe Merry Mountain
appeared in the northwest, as if it were looking down on this lake
especially; and we had our first, but a partial view of Ktaadn, its
summit veiled in clouds, like a dark isthmus in that quarter, connecting the heavens with the earth. After two miles of smooth rowing
across this lake, we found ourselves in the river again, which was a
continuous rapid for one mile, to the dam, requiring all the strength
and skill of our boatmen to pole up it.

This dam is a quite important and expensive work for this country,
whither cattle and horses cannot penetrate in the summer, raising the
whole river ten feet, and flooding, as they said, some sixty square
miles by means of the innumerable lakes with which the river connects. It is a lofty and solid structure, with sloping piers some distance
above, made of frames of logs filled with stones, to break the ice.*
Here every log pays toll as it passes through the sluices.

*Even the Jesuit missionaries, accustomed to the St. Lawrence and other rivers of Canada, in their first
expeditions to the Abnaquiois, speak of rivers *ferrées de rochers*, shod with rocks. . . .

We filed into the rude loggers' camp at this place, such as I have described, without ceremony, and the cook, at that moment the sole occupant, at once set about preparing tea for his visitors. His fire-place, which the rain had converted into a mud-puddle, was soon blazing again, and we sat down on the log benches around it to dry us. On the well-flattened, and somewhat faded beds of arbor-vitæ leaves, which stretched on either hand under the eaves behind us, lay an odd leaf of the Bible, some genealogical chapter out of the Old Testament; and, half buried by the leaves, we found Emerson's Address on West India Emancipation, which had been left here formerly by one of our company; and *had made two converts to the Liberty party here*, as I was told; also, an odd number of the Westminster Review, for 1834, and a pamphlet entitled History of the Erection of the Monument on the Grave of Myron Holley. This was the readable, or reading matter, in a lumberer's camp in the Maine woods, thirty miles from a road, which would be given up to the bears in a fortnight. These things were well thumbed and soiled. This gang was headed by one John Morrison, a good specimen of a Yankee; and was necessarily composed of men not bred to the business of dam-building, but who were Jacks-at-all-trades, handy with the axe, and other simple implements, and well skilled in wood and water craft. We had hot cakes for our supper even here, white as snow-balls, but without butter, and the never-failing sweet cakes, with which we filled our pockets, foreseeing that we should not soon meet with the like again. Such delicate puffballs seemed a singular diet for backwoodsmen. There was also tea without milk, sweetened with molasses. And so, exchanging a word with John Morrison and his gang when we had returned to the shore, and also exchanging our batteau for a better still, we made haste to improve the little daylight that remained. This camp, exactly twenty-nine miles from Mattawamkeag Point, by the way we had come, and about one hundred from Bangor by the river, was the last human habitation of any kind in this direction. Beyond, there was no trail; and the river and lakes, by batteaux and canoes, was considered the only practicable route. We were about thirty miles by the river from the summit of Ktaadn, which was in sight, though not more than twenty, perhaps, in a straight line.

It being about the full of the moon, and a warm and pleasant

evening, we decided to row five miles by moonlight to the head of the
North Twin Lake, lest the wind should rise on the morrow. After one
mile of river, or what the boatmen call "thoroughfare,"—for the river
becomes at length only the connecting link between the lakes,—and
some slight rapids which had been mostly made smooth water by the
dam, we entered the North Twin Lake just after sundown, and steered
across for the river "thoroughfare," four miles distant. This is a noble
sheet of water, where one may get the impression which a new country and a "lake of the woods" are fitted to create. There was the
smoke of no log-hut nor camp of any kind to greet us, still less was
any lover of nature or musing traveller watching our batteau from
the distant hills; not even the Indian hunter was there, for he rarely
climbs them, but hugs the river like ourselves. No face welcomed us
but the fine fantastic sprays of free and happy evergreen trees, waving one above another in their ancient home. At first the red clouds
hung over the western shore as gorgeously as if over a city, and the
lake lay open to the light with even a civilized aspect, as if expecting
trade and commerce, and towns and villas. We could distinguish the
inlet to the South Twin, which is said to be the larger, where the shore
was misty and blue, and it was worth the while to look thus through
a narrow opening across the entire expanse of a concealed lake to its
own yet more dim and distant shore. The shores rose gently to ranges
of low hills covered with forests; and though in fact the most valuable
white pine timber, even about this lake, had been culled out, this
would never have been suspected by the voyager. The impression,
which indeed corresponded with the fact, was as if we were upon a
high table land between the States and Canada, the northern side of
which is drained by the St. John and Chaudiere, the southern by the
Penobscot and Kennebec. There was no bold mountainous shore, as
we might have expected, but only isolated hills and mountains rising
here and there from the plateau. The country is an archipelago of
lakes,—the lake-country of New England. Their levels vary but a few
feet, and the boatmen, by short portages, or by none at all, pass easily
from one to another. They say that at very high water the Penobscot
and the Kennebec flow into each other, or at any rate, that you may
lie with your face in the one and your toes in the other. Even the
Penobscot and St. John have been connected by a canal, so that the

lumber of the Allagash, instead of going down the St. John, comes down the Penobscot; and the Indian's tradition that the Penobscot once ran both ways for his convenience, is, in one sense, partially realized to-day.

None of our party but McCauslin had been above this lake, so we trusted to him to pilot us, and we could not but confess the importance of a pilot on these waters. While it is river, you will not easily forget which way is up stream; but when you enter a lake, the river is completely lost, and you scan the distant shores in vain to find where it comes in. A stranger is, for the time at least, lost, and must set about a voyage of discovery first of all to find the river. To follow the windings of the shore when the lake is ten miles or even more in length, and of an irregularity which will not soon be mapped, is a wearisome voyage, and will spend his time and his provisions. They tell a story of a gang of experienced woodmen sent to a location on this stream, who were thus lost in the wilderness of lakes. They cut their way through thickets, and carried their baggage and their boats over from lake to lake, sometimes several miles. They carried into Millinocket lake, which is on another stream, and is ten miles square, and contains a hundred islands. They explored its shores thoroughly, and then carried into another and another, and it was a week of toil and anxiety before they found the Penobscot river again, and then their provisions were exhausted, and they were obliged to return.

While Uncle George steered for a small island near the head of the lake, now just visible like a speck on the water, we rowed by turns swiftly over its surface, singing such boat-songs as we could remember. The shores seemed at an indefinite distance in the moonlight. Occasionally we paused in our singing and rested on our oars, while we listened to hear if the wolves howled, for this is a common serenade, and my companions affirmed that it was the most dismal and unearthly of sounds; but we heard none this time.—If we did not *hear*, however, we did *listen*, not without a reasonable expectation; that at least I have to tell,—only some utterly uncivilized, big-throated owl hooted loud and dismally in the drear and boughy wilderness, plainly not nervous about his solitary life, nor afraid to hear the echoes of his voice there. We remembered also that possibly moose were silently watching us from the distant coves, or some surly bear, or timid caribou had been startled by our singing. It was with new emphasis that we sang there the Canadian boat-song—

> *"Row, brothers, row, the stream runs fast,*
> *The Rapids are near and the daylight's past!"*—

which described precisely our own adventure, and was inspired by the experience of a similar kind of life,—for the rapids were ever near, and the daylight long past; the woods on shore looked dim, and many an Utawas' tide here emptied into the lake.

> *"Why should we yet our sail unfurl?*
> *There is not a breath the blue wave to curl!*
> *But, when the wind blows off the shore,*
> *O sweetly we'll rest our weary oar."*

> *"Utawas' tide! this trembling moon,*
> *Shall see us float o'er thy surges soon."*

At last we glided past the "green isle" which had been our landmark, all joining in the chorus; as if by the watery links of rivers and of lakes we were about to float over unmeasured zones of earth, bound on unimaginable adventures.

> *"Saint of this green isle! hear our prayers,*
> *O grant us cool heavens and favoring airs!"*

About nine o'clock we reached the river, and ran our boat into a natural haven between some rocks, and drew her out on the sand. This camping ground McCauslin had been familiar with in his lumbering days, and he now struck it unerringly in the moonlight, and we heard the sound of the rill which would supply us with cool water emptying into the lake. The first business was to make a fire, an operation which was a little delayed by the wetness of the fuel and the ground, owing to the heavy showers of the afternoon. The fire is the main comfort of a camp, whether in summer or winter, and is about as ample at one season as at another. It is as well for cheerfulness, as for warmth and

dryness. It forms one side of the camp; one bright side at any rate. Some were dispersed to fetch in dead trees and boughs, while Uncle George felled the birches and beeches which stood convenient, and soon we had a fire some ten feet long by three or four high, which rapidly dried the sand before it. This was calculated to burn all night. We next proceeded to pitch our tent; which operation was performed by sticking our two spike poles into the ground in a slanting direction, about ten feet apart, for rafters, and then drawing our cotton cloth over them, and tying it down at the ends, leaving it open in front, shed-fashion. But this evening the wind carried the sparks on to the tent and burned it. So we hastily drew up the batteau just within the edge of the woods before the fire, and propping up one side three or four feet high, spread the tent on the ground to lie on; and with the corner of a blanket, or what more or less we could get to put over us, lay down with our heads and bodies under the boat, and our feet and legs on the sand toward the fire. At first we lay awake, talking of our course, and finding ourselves in so convenient a posture for studying the heavens, with the moon and stars shining in our faces, our conversation naturally turned upon astronomy, and we recounted by turns the most interesting discoveries in that science. But at length we composed ourselves seriously to sleep. It was interesting, when awakened at midnight, to watch the grotesque and fiendlike forms and motions of some one of the party, who, not being able to sleep, had got up silently to arouse the fire, and add fresh fuel, for a change; now stealthily lugging a dead tree from out the dark, and heaving it on, now stirring up the embers with his fork, or tiptoeing about to observe the stars, watched, perchance, by half the prostrate party in breathless silence; so much the more intense because they were awake, while each supposed his neighbor sound asleep. Thus aroused, I too brought fresh fuel to the fire, and then rambled along the sandy shore in the moonlight, hoping to meet a moose come down to drink, or else a wolf. The little rill tinkled the louder, and peopled all the wilderness for me; and the glassy smoothness of the sleeping lake, laving the shores of a new world, with the dark, fantastic rocks rising here and there from its surface, made a scene not easily described. It has left such an impression of stern yet gentle wildness on my memory as will not soon be effaced. Not far from midnight, we were one after another awakened by rain falling on our extremities; and as each was made aware of the fact by cold or wet, he drew a long sigh and then drew up his legs, until gradually we had all sidled round from lying at right angles with the boat, till our bodies formed an acute angle with it, and were wholly protected. When next we awoke, the moon and stars were shining again, and there were signs of dawn in the east. I have been thus particular in order to convey some idea of a night in the woods.

> In Quakish Lake (still relatively unsettled), the diving loon and Jo-Mary Mountain (2,904', twelve miles west) were early signs of wild country. The first sight of Katahdin, fifteen miles northwest, was of a summit veiled in clouds—and thus imagined as Olympus, an "isthmus

... connecting the heavens with the earth." Beyond the *(see page 114)*
dam at the south end of Twin Lakes (now the village of
Norcross) lay unbroken wilderness, a country with no
outposts or trails.

Because winds are generally light after dusk, rowing
by bright moonlight was a prudent course. This sequence made a seemingly peaceful interlude in the story,
yet it carried a faint air of unease as familiar country
slipped away. The scene in Twin Lakes is more settled
today; it has become a mile-wide stretch of water, on
which canoeists can easily find outlets to the other lakes.
Thoreau's account of the night sounds and sights, especially when his friends became "fiendlike forms" in the
firelight, prepared him for the coming ascent. Realities *(see page 120)*
were beginning to displace his romantic hunger for "unimaginable" adventures.

The connection between Twin and Pemadumcook
lakes is no longer a river, but a broad neck, half a mile
wide. The camp spot was probably near Wadleigh Brook,
on a point just off Little Porus Island.

We had soon launched and loaded our boat, and, leaving our fire
blazing, were off again before breakfast. The lumberers rarely trouble themselves to put out their fires, such is the dampness of the
primitive forest; and this is one cause, no doubt, of the frequent fires
in Maine, of which we hear so much on smoky days in Massachusetts.
The forests are held cheap after the white pine has been culled out;
and the explorers and hunters pray for rain only to clear the atmosphere of smoke. The woods were so wet today, however, that there
was no danger of our fire spreading. After poling up half a mile of
river, or thoroughfare, we rowed a mile across the foot of Pamadumcook Lake, which is the name given on the map to this whole chain
of lakes, as if there was but one, though they are, in each instance,
distinctly separated by a reach of the river, with its narrow and rocky
channel and its rapids. This lake, which is one of the largest, stretched
north-west ten miles, to hills and mountains in the distance. McCauslin pointed to some distant and, as yet, inaccessible forests of white

pine, on the sides of a mountain in that direction. The Joe Merry Lakes, which lay between us and Moosehead, on the west, were recently, if they are not still, "surrounded by some of the best timbered land in the state." By another thoroughfare we passed into Deep Cove, a part of the same lake, which makes up two miles, toward the north-east, and rowing two miles across this, by another short thoroughfare, entered Ambejijis Lake.

At the entrance to a lake we sometimes observed what is technically called "fencing stuff," or the unhewn timbers of which booms are formed, either secured together in the water, or laid up on the rocks and lashed to trees, for spring use. But it was always startling to discover so plain a trail of civilized man there. I remember that I was strangely affected when we were returning, by the sight of a ring-bolt well drilled into a rock, and fastened with lead, at the head of this solitary Ambejijis Lake.

It was easy to see, that driving logs must be an exciting as well as arduous and dangerous business. All winter long the logger goes on piling up the trees which he has trimmed and hauled in some dry ravine at the head of a stream, and then in the spring he stands on the bank, and whistles for Rain and Thaw, ready to wring the perspiration out of his shirt to swell the tide, till suddenly, with a whoop and halloo from him, shutting his eyes, as if to bid farewell to the existing state of things, a fair proportion of his winter's work goes scrambling down the country, followed by his faithful dogs, Thaw, and Rain, and Freshet, and Wind, the whole pack in full cry, toward the Orono Mills. Every log is marked with the owner's name, cut in the sapwood with an axe, or bored with an auger, so deep as not to be worn off in the driving, and yet not so as to injure the timber; and it requires considerable ingenuity to invent new and simple marks where there are so many owners. They have quite an alphabet of their own, which only the practised can read. One of my companions read off from his memorandum book some marks of his own logs, among which there were crosses, belts, crow's feet, girdles, &c., as Y—girdle—crow-foot, and various other devices. When the logs have run the gauntlet of innumerable rapids and falls, each on its own account, with more or less jamming and bruising, those bearing various owners' marks being mixed up together, since all must take advantage of the same freshet, they are collected together at the heads of the lakes, and surrounded by a boom fence of floating logs, to prevent their being dispersed by the wind, and are thus towed all together, like a flock of sheep, across the lake, where there is no current, by a windlass, or boom-head, such as we sometimes saw standing on an island or head-land, and, if circumstances permit, with the aid of sails and oars. Sometimes, not-withstanding, the logs are dispersed over many miles of lake surface in a few hours by winds and freshets, and thrown up on distant shores, where the driver can pick up only one or two at a time, and return with them to the thoroughfare; and, before he gets his flock well through Ambejijis or Pamadumcook, he makes many a wet and

uncomfortable camp on the shore. He must be able to navigate a log as if it were a canoe, and be as indifferent to cold and wet as a muskrat. He uses a few efficient tools,—a lever commonly of rock-maple, six or seven feet long, with a stout spike in it, strongly ferruled on, and a long spike-pole, with a screw at the end of the spike to make it hold. The boys along shore learn to walk on floating logs as city boys on sidewalks. Sometimes the logs are thrown up on rocks in such positions as to be irrecoverable but by another freshet as high, or they jam together at rapids and falls, and accumulate in vast piles, which the driver must start at the risk of his life. Such is the lumber busi-ness, which depends on many accidents, as the early freezing of the rivers, that the teams may get up in season, a sufficient freshet in the

spring, to fetch the logs down, and many others.* I quote Michaux on
Lumbering on the Kennebec, then the source of the best white-pine
lumber carried to England. "The persons engaged in this branch of
industry are generally emigrants from New Hampshire. . . . In the
summer they unite in small companies, and traverse these vast soli-
tudes in every direction, to ascertain the places in which the pines
abound. After cutting the grass and converting it into hay for the
nourishment of the cattle to be employed in their labor, they return
home. In the beginning of the winter they enter the forests again,
establish themselves in huts covered with the bark of the canoe-birch,
or the arborvitæ; and, though the cold is so intense that the mercury
sometimes remains for several weeks from 40° to 50° [Fahr.] below the
point of congelation, they persevere, with unabated courage, in their
work." According to Springer, the company consists of choppers,
swampers,—who make roads,—barker and loader, teamster, and
cook. "When the trees are felled, they cut them into logs from fourteen to eighteen feet long, and, by means of their cattle, which they
employ with great dexterity, drag them to the river, and after stamp-
ing on them a mark of property, roll them on its frozen bosom. At the
breaking of the ice, in the spring, they float down with the current.
. . . The logs that are not sawn the first year," adds Michaux, "are
attacked by large worms, which form holes about two lines in diameter, in every direction; but, if stripped of their bark, they will remain
uninjured for thirty years."

Ambejijis, this quiet Sunday morning, struck me as the most beautiful lake we had seen. It is said to be one of the deepest. We had the
fairest view of Joe Merry, Double Top, and Ktaadn, from its surface.
The summit of the latter had a singularly flat tableland appearance,
like a short highway, where a demi-god might be let down to take a
turn or two in an afternoon, to settle his dinner. We rowed a mile and
a half to near the head of the lake, and, pushing through a field of lily
pads, landed, to cook our breakfast by the side of a large rock, known
to McCauslin. Our breakfast consisted of tea, with hard bread and

---

*"A steady current or pitch of water is preferable to one either rising or diminishing; as, when rising
rapidly, the water at the middle of the river is considerably higher than at the shores,—so much so as
to be distinctly perceived by the eye of a spectator on the banks, presenting an appearance like a turnpike
road. The lumber, therefore, is always sure to incline from the centre of the channel toward either shore."
—Springer

pork, and fried salmon, which we ate with forks neatly whittled from alder-twigs, which grew there, off strips of birch-bark for plates. The tea was black tea, without milk to color or sugar to sweeten it, and two tin dippers were our tea cups. This beverage is as indispensable to the loggers as to any gossiping old women in the land, and they, no doubt, derive great comfort from it. Here was the site of an old loggers' camp, remembered by McCauslin, now overgrown with weeds and bushes. In the midst of a dense underwood, we noticed a whole brick, on a rock, in a small run, clean, and red, and square, as in a brick-yard, which had been brought thus far formerly for tamping. Some of us afterward regretted that we had not carried this on with us to the top of the mountain, to be left there for our mark. It would certainly have been a simple evidence of civilized man. McCauslin said, that large wooden crosses made of oak, still sound, were sometimes found standing in this wilderness, which were set up by the first Catholic missionaries who came through to the Kennebec.

In the next nine miles, which were the extent of our voyage, and which it took us the rest of the day to get over, we rowed across several small lakes, poled up numerous rapids and thoroughfares, and carried over four portages. I will give the names and distances, for the benefit of future tourists. First, after leaving Ambejijis Lake, we had a quarter of a mile of rapids to the portage, or carry of ninety rods around Ambejijis Falls; then a mile and a half through Passamagamet Lake, which is narrow and river-like, to the falls of the same name— Ambejijis stream coming in on the right; then two miles through Katepskonegan Lake to the portage of ninety rods around Katepskonegan Falls, which name signifies "carrying place"—Passamagamet stream coming in on the left; then three miles through Pockwockomus Lake, a slight expansion of the river, to the portage of forty rods around the falls of the same name—Katepskonegan stream coming in on the left; then three quarters of a mile through Aboljacarmegus Lake, similar to the last, to the portage of forty rods around the falls of the same name; then half a mile of rapid water to the Sowadnehunk dead-water, and the Aboljacknagesic stream.

This is generally the order of names as you ascend the river:—First, the lake, or, if there is no expansion, the dead-water; then the falls; then the stream emptying into the lake or river above, all of the same name. First we came to Passamagamet Lake, then to Passamagamet Falls, then to Passamagamet stream, emptying in. This order and identity of names, it will be perceived, is quite philosophical, since the dead-water or lake is always at least partially produced by the stream emptying in above; and the first fall below, which is the inlet of that lake, and where that tributary water makes its first plunge, also naturally bears the same name.

At the portage around Ambejijis Falls, I observed a pork-barrel on the shore, with a hole eight or nine inches square cut in one side, which was set against an upright rock; but the bears, without turning or upsetting the barrel, had gnawed a hole in the opposite side, which looked exactly like an enormous rat hole, big enough to put their heads in; and at the bottom of the barrel were still left a few mangled and slabbered slices of pork. It is usual for the lumberers to leave such supplies as they cannot conveniently carry along with them at carries or camps, to which the next comers do not scruple to help themselves, they being the property commonly not of an individual, but a company, who can afford to deal liberally.

I will describe particularly how we got over some of these portages and rapids, in order that the reader may get an idea of the boatman's life. At Ambejijis Falls, for instance, there was the roughest path imaginable cut through the woods; at first up hill at an angle of nearly forty-five degrees, over rocks and logs without end. This was the manner of the portage:—We first carried over our baggage, and deposited it on the shore at the other end; then returning to the batteau, we dragged it up the hill by the painter, and onward, with frequent pauses, over half the portage. But this was a bungling way, and would soon have worn out the boat. Commonly, three men walk over with a batteau weighing from three to five or six hundred pounds on their heads and shoulders, the tallest standing under the middle of the boat, which is turned over, and one at each end, or else there are two at the bows. More cannot well take hold at once. But this requires some practice, as well as strength, and is in any case extremely laborious, and wearing to the constitution, to follow. We were, on the whole, rather an invalid party, and could render our boatmen but little assistance. Our two men at length took the batteau upon their shoulders, and, while two of us steadied it, to prevent it from rocking and wearing into their shoulders, on which they placed their hats folded, walked bravely over the remaining distance, with two or three pauses. In the same manner they accomplished the other portages. With this crushing weight they must climb and stumble along over fallen trees and slippery rocks of all sizes, where those who walked by the sides were continually brushed off, such was the narrowness of the path. But we were fortunate not to have to cut our path in the first place. Before we launched our boat, we scraped the bottom smooth again with our knives, where it had rubbed on the rocks, to save friction.

Any visitors who now want to build open fires in Maine *(see page 121)* must have written permits from the state Forest Service; and of course all fires must be thoroughly extinguished before leaving camp! The virgin forest of Thoreau's day was constantly damp, but today the second and third growth has a dry, combustible understory. The lakes he

crossed are also different: Pemadumcook is no longer a
chain, but a single broad arm of water, twelve miles long
and two wide.

(see page 122)   Thoreau's view of the loggers was ambivalent. They
cut down the wild forest, marked it as property, drove it
along the lakes; yet strong winds and fatal logjams constantly threatened their lives. Hence he tended to admire
their skill and bravery, in contrast to the investors from
Bangor, whose risks were merely financial.

Beyond Ambajejus Lake, the landscape became his in-
structor, as the West Branch alternated between long,
still pools and narrow rapids. The rapids are formed by
clusters of granite boulders, which back up the "dead-
water" of pools. At each fall a ridge or ledge of granite
cuts across the stream, forcing it to rise and drop over the
lower shelf. The symmetry of this natural chain impressed Thoreau as "philosophical," like the sequence of
(see page 126) storm and clearing he saw on Saturday. In describing
(see page 127) "particularly" how the party traveled up these rapids, he
was adapting the same principle to his story's progress.

To avoid the difficulties of the portage, our men determined to "warp
up" the Passamagamet Falls; so while the rest walked over the portage with the baggage, I remained in the batteau, to assist in warping
up. We were soon in the midst of the rapids, which were more swift
and tumultuous than any we had poled up, and had turned to the side
of the stream for the purpose of warping, when the boatmen, who felt
some pride in their skill, and were ambitious to do something more
than usual, for my benefit, as I surmised, took one more view of the
rapids, or rather the falls; and in answer to one's question, whether
we couldn't get up there, the other answered that he guessed he'd try
it: so we pushed again into the midst of the stream, and began to
struggle with the current. I sat in the middle of the boat, to trim it,
moving slightly to the right or left as it grazed a rock. With an
uncertain and wavering motion we wound and bolted our way up,
until the bow was actually raised two feet above the stern at the
steepest pitch; and then, when everything depended upon his exer-

tions, the bowman's pole snapped in two; but before he had time to take the spare one, which I reached him, he had saved himself with the fragment upon a rock; and so we got up by a hair's breadth; and Uncle George exclaimed, that that was never done before; and he had not tried it, if he had not known whom he had got in the bow—nor he in the bow, if he had not known him in the stern. At this place there was a regular portage cut through the woods; and our boatmen had never known a batteau to ascend the falls. As near as I can remember, there was a perpendicular fall here, at the worst place, of the whole Penobscot River, two or three feet at least. I could not sufficiently admire the skill and coolness with which they performed this feat, never speaking to each other. The bowman, not looking behind, but knowing exactly what the other is about, works as if he worked alone; now sounding in vain for a bottom in fifteen feet of water, while the boat falls back several rods, held straight only with the greatest skill and exertion; or, while the sternman obstinately holds his ground, like a turtle, the bowman springs from side to side with wonderful suppleness and dexterity, scanning the rapids and the rocks with a thousand eyes; and now, having got a bite at last, with a lusty shove which makes his pole bend and quiver, and the whole boat tremble, he gains a few feet upon the river. To add to the danger, the poles are liable at any time to be caught between the rocks, and wrenched out of their hands, leaving them at the mercy of the rapids—the rocks, as it were, lying in wait, like so many alligators, to catch them in their teeth, and jerk them from your hands, before you have stolen an effectual shove against their palates. The pole is set close to the boat, and the prow is made to overshoot, and just turn the corners of the rocks, in the very teeth of the rapids. Nothing but the length and lightness, and the slight draught of the batteau, enables them to make any headway. The bowman must quickly choose his course; there is no time to deliberate. Frequently the boat is shoved between rocks where both sides touch, and the waters on either hand are a perfect maelstrom.

Half a mile above this, two of us tried our hands at poling up a slight rapid; and we were just surmounting the last difficulty, when an unlucky rock confounded our calculations; and while the batteau was sweeping round irrecoverably amid the whirlpool, we were obliged to resign the poles to more skilful hands.

Katepskonegan is one of the shallowest and weediest of the lakes, and looked as if it might abound in pickerel. The falls of the same name, where we stopped to dine, are considerable and quite picturesque. Here Uncle George had seen trout caught by the barrel-full; but they would not rise to our bait at this hour. Half way over this carry, thus far in the Maine wilderness on its way to the Provinces, we noticed a large flaming Oak Hall hand-bill, about two feet long, wrapped round the trunk of a pine, from which the bark had been stript, and to which it was fast glued by the pitch. This should be recorded among the advantages of this mode of advertising, that so, possibly, even the bears and wolves, moose, deer, otter, and beaver, not to mention the Indian, may learn where they can fit themselves according to the latest fashion, or, at least, recover some of their own lost garments. We christened this the Oak Hall carry.

The forenoon was as serene and placid on this wild stream in the woods as we are wont to imagine that Sunday in summer usually is in Massachusetts. We were occasionally startled by the scream of a bald-eagle, sailing over the stream in front of our batteau; or of the fish-hawks, on whom he levies his contributions. There were, at intervals, small meadows of a few acres on the sides of the stream, waving with uncut grass, which attracted the attention of our boatmen, who regretted that they were not nearer to their clearings, and calculated how many stacks they might cut. Two or three men sometimes spend the summer by themselves, cutting the grass in these meadows, to sell to the loggers in the winter, since it will fetch a higher price on the spot than in any market in the state. On a small isle, covered with this kind of rush, or cut grass, on which we landed, to consult about our further course, we noticed the recent track of a moose, a large, roundish hole, in the soft wet ground, evincing the great size and weight of the animal that made it. They are fond of the water, and visit all these island-meadows, swimming as easily from island to island as they make their way through the thickets on land. Now and then we passed what McCauslin called a pokelogan, an Indian term for what the drivers might have reason to call a poke-logs-in, an inlet that leads nowhere: if you get in you have got to get out again the same way. These, and the frequent "run-rounds," which come into the

river again, would embarrass an inexperienced voyager not a little.

The carry around Pockwockomus Falls was exceedingly rough and rocky, the batteau having to be lifted directly from the water up four or five feet on to a rock, and launched again down a similar bank. The rocks on this portage were covered with the dents made by the spikes in the lumberers' boots while staggering over under the weight of their batteaux; and you could see where the surface of some large rocks on which they had rested their batteaux was worn quite smooth

with use. As it was, we had carried over but half the usual portage
at this place for this stage of the water, and launched our boat in the
smooth wave just curving to the fall, prepared to struggle with the
most violent rapid we had to encounter. The rest of the party walked
over the remainder of the portage, while I remained with the boatmen
to assist in warping up. One had to hold the boat while the others got
in to prevent it from going over the falls. When we had pushed up the
rapids as far as possible, keeping close to the shore, Tom seized the
painter and leaped out upon a rock just visible in the water, but he lost
his footing notwithstanding his spiked boots, and was instantly amid
the rapids; but recovering himself by good luck, and reaching another
rock, he passed the painter to me, who had followed him, and took his
place again in the bows. Leaping from rock to rock in the shoal water
close to the shore, and now and then getting a bite with the rope round
an upright one, I held the boat while one reset his pole, and then all
three forced it upward against any rapid. This was "warping up."
When a part of us walked round at such a place, we generally took
the precaution to take out the most valuable part of the baggage, for
fear of being swamped.

As we poled up a swift rapid for half a mile above Aboljacarmegus
Falls, some of the party read their own marks on the huge logs which
lay piled up high and dry on the rocks on either hand, the relics
probably of a jam which had taken place here in the Great Freshet in
the spring. Many of these would have to wait for another great
freshet, perchance, if they lasted so long, before they could be got off.
It was singular enough to meet with property of theirs which they had
never seen, and where they had never been before, thus detained by
freshets and rocks when on its way to them. Methinks that must be
where all my property lies, cast up on the rocks on some distant and
unexplored stream, and waiting for an unheard-of freshet to fetch it
down. O make haste, ye gods, with your winds and rains, and start
the jam before it rots!

The last half mile carried us to the Sowadnehunk dead-water, so
called from the stream of the same name, signifying "running between mountains," an important tributary which comes in a mile
above. Here we decided to camp, about twenty miles from the Dam,
at the mouth of Murch Brook and the Aboljacknagesic, mountain

streams, broad off from Ktaadn, and about a dozen miles from its summit; having made fifteen miles this day.

We had been told by McCauslin that we should here find trout enough: so while some prepared the camp, the rest fell to fishing. Seizing the birch poles which some party of Indians or white hunters had left on the shore, and baiting our hooks with pork, and with trout, as soon as they were caught, we cast our lines into the mouth of the Aboljacknagesic, a clear, swift, shallow stream, which came in from Ktaadn. Instantly a shoal of white chivin, (leucisci pulchelli,) silvery roaches, cousin-trout, or what not, large and small, prowling there-abouts, fell upon our bait, and one after another were landed amidst the bushes. Anon their cousins, the true trout, took their turn, and alternately the speckled trout, and the silvery roaches, swallowed the bait as fast as we could throw in; and the finest specimens of both that I have ever seen, the largest one weighing three pounds, were heaved upon the shore, though at first in vain, to wriggle down into the water again, for we stood in the boat; but soon we learned to remedy this evil: for one, who had lost his hook, stood on shore to catch them as they fell in a perfect shower around him—sometimes, wet and slip-pery, full in his face and bosom, as his arms were outstretched to receive them. While yet alive, before their tints had faded, they glis-tened like the fairest flowers, the product of primitive rivers; and he could hardly trust his senses, as he stood over them, that these jewels should have swum away in that Aboljacknagesic water for so long, so many dark ages;—these bright fluviatile flowers, seen of Indians only, made beautiful, the Lord only knows why, to swim there! I could understand better, for this, the truth of mythology, the fables of Proteus, and all those beautiful sea-monsters,—how all history, in-deed, put to a terrestrial use, is mere history; but put to a celestial, is mythology always.

But there is the rough voice of Uncle George, who commands at the frying-pan, to send over what you've got, and then you may stay till morning. The pork sizzles, and cries for fish. Luckily for the foolish race, and this particularly foolish generation of trout, the night shut down at last, not a little deepened by the dark side of Ktaadn, which, like a permanent shadow, reared itself from the eastern bank. Lescar-bot, writing in 1609, tells us that the Sieur Champdoré, who, with one of the people of the Sieur de Monts, ascended some fifty leagues up the St. John in 1608, found the fish so plenty, "qu'en mettant la chaudière sur le feu ils en avoient pris suffisamment pour eux dîsner avant que l'eau fust chaude." Their descendants here are no less numerous. So we accompanied Tom into the woods, to cut cedar-twigs for our bed. While he went ahead with the axe, and lopped off the smallest twigs of the flat-leaved cedar, the arbor-vitæ of the gardens, we gathered them up, and returned with them to the boat, until it was loaded. Our bed was made with as much care and skill as a roof is shingled; beginning at the foot, and laying the twig end of the cedar upward, we advanced to the head, a course at a time, thus successively covering the stub-ends, and producing a soft and level bed. For us six it was about ten feet long by six in breadth. This time we lay under our tent, having pitched it more prudently with reference to the wind and the flame, and the usual huge fire blazed in front. Supper was eaten off a large log, which some freshet had thrown up. This night we had a dish of arbor-vitæ, or cedar tea, which the lumberer sometimes uses when other herbs fail,—

> "*A quart of* arbor-*vitæ,*
> *To make him strong and mighty,*"—

but I had no wish to repeat the experiment. It had too medicinal a taste for my palate. There was the skeleton of a moose here, whose bones some Indian hunters had picked on this very spot.

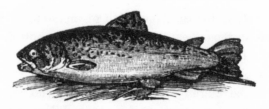

In the night I dreamed of trout-fishing; and, when at length I awoke, it seemed a fable, that this painted fish swam there so near my couch, and rose to our hooks the last evening—and I doubted if I had not dreamed it all. So I arose before dawn to test its truth, while my companions were still sleeping. There stood Ktaadn with distinct and cloudless outline in the moonlight; and the rippling of the rapids was the only sound to break the stillness. Standing on the shore, I once more cast my line into the stream, and found the dream to be real, and the fable true. The speckled trout and silvery roach, like flying fish, sped swiftly through the moonlight air, describing bright arcs on the dark side of Ktaadn, until moonlight, now fading into daylight, brought satiety to my mind, and the minds of my companions, who had joined me.

The boatmen had difficult work, carrying heavy loads over the rough ground of carries, then poling up the falls with great skill. This arduous ascent, which rose a hundred feet along the course of five falls, anticipated the mountain climb that would follow. Their achievement is still impressive, for today's canoeing maps rate this sequence of falls as Class IV, Very Difficult, "dangerous even for experts." The batteau was well suited for poling upstream because it had a shallow draft. ROUTE FROM TOGUE POND ROAD: *Millinocket Road to Abol Stream road (private)*

At Pockwockamus Falls, where the elevation was fifty feet, poling was impossible; but still the batteau was light enough to "warp" or drag with a rope. At the end of this exhausting trek, the party took out where two streams (now called Abol and Katahdin) enter, and the land is bare. The elevation there is 580 feet, and the place today is known as Abol.

Thoreau made some disparaging remarks here about investors and their notions of property, offering for contrast his still untested vision of Katahdin, the place of high romance. The authorities who manage Baxter State Park today find that some visitors have little sense of property; they deface rocks, trees, and signs at will, and thus require strong regulations—which are intended to protect the park's free, wild state. *(see page 132)*

Because of his poor maps, Thoreau was confused about distances in this area. Neosowadnehunk dead water is four miles west, not one; Katahdin is five miles northeast, not a dozen. Place names were not yet a settled *(see page 132)* matter in this raw country; "Murch Brook" (probably suggested by his companions) has the distinction of being unique—no one has used it since. By "Murch" he probably meant the upper (and then unnamed) stream, now called Katahdin.

The season for trout is now over by September, when fish generally move to colder streams. Thoreau's catch would seem fantastic today, for the fish are no longer as big or abundant. Indeed, his description of them as jew-
(see page 133) els, flowers, and Protean creatures seems a deliberate exaggeration, the sort of mythologizing that will cease after his mountain climb. Although a supper of broiled trout and cedar tea (rich in vitamin C) should have subdued his fanciful tendencies, that night he still envisioned the fish as "bright arcs on the dark side of
(see page 135) Ktaadn."

By six o'clock, having mounted our packs and a good blanket full of trout, ready dressed, and swung up such baggage and provision as we wished to leave behind upon the tops of saplings, to be out of the reach of bears, we started for the summit of the mountain, distant, as Uncle George said the boatmen called it, about four miles, but as I judged, and as it proved, nearer fourteen. He had never been any nearer the mountain than this, and there was not the slightest trace of man to guide us further in this direction. At first, pushing a few rods up the Aboljacknagesic, or "open-land stream," we fastened our batteau to a tree, and travelled up the north side, through burnt lands, now partially overgrown with young aspens, and other shrubbery; but soon, recrossing this stream, where it was about fifty or sixty feet wide, upon a jam of logs and rocks, and you could cross it by this means almost anywhere, we struck at once for the highest peak, over a mile or more of comparatively open land still, very gradually ascending the while. Here it fell to my lot, as the oldest mountain-climber, to take the lead: so scanning the woody side of the mountain, which lay still at an indefinite distance, stretched out some seven or eight miles in length before us, we determined to steer directly for the base of the highest peak, leaving a large slide, by which, as I have since learned, some of our predecessors ascended, on our left. This course would lead us parallel to a dark seam in the forest, which marked the bed of a torrent, and over a slight spur, which extended southward from the main mountain, from whose bare summit we could get an outlook over the country, and climb directly up the peak, which would then be close at hand. Seen from this point, a bare ridge at the extremity of the open land, Ktaadn presented a different aspect from any mountain I have seen, there being a greater proportion of naked rock, rising abruptly from the forest; and we looked up at this blue barrier as if it were some fragment of a wall which anciently bounded the earth in that direction. Setting the compass for a north-east course, which was the bearing of the southern base of the highest peak, we were soon buried in the woods.

We soon began to meet with traces of bears and moose, and those of rabbits were everywhere visible. The tracks of moose, more or less recent, to speak literally covered every square rod on the sides of the mountain; and these animals are probably more numerous there now than ever before, being driven into this wilderness from all sides by the settlements. The track of a full-grown moose is like that of a cow, or larger, and of the young, like that of a calf. Sometimes we found ourselves travelling in faint paths, which they had made, like cow-paths in the woods, only far more indistinct, being rather openings, affording imperfect vistas through the dense underwood, than trodden paths; and everywhere the twigs had been browsed by them, clipt as smoothly as if by a knife. The bark of trees was stript up by them to the height of eight or nine feet, in long narrow strips, an inch wide, still showing the distinct marks of their teeth. We expected nothing less than to meet a herd of them every moment, and our Nimrod held his shooting-iron in readiness; but we did not go out of our way to look for them, and, though numerous, they are so wary, that the unskilful hunter might range the forest a long time before he could get sight of one. They are sometimes dangerous to encounter, and will not turn out for the hunter, but furiously rush upon him, and trample him to death, unless he is lucky enough to avoid them by dodging round a tree. The largest are nearly as large as a horse, and weigh sometimes one thousand pounds; and it is said that they can step over a five-foot gate in their ordinary walk. They are described as exceedingly awk-

ward-looking animals, with their long legs and short bodies, making
a ludicrous figure when in full run, but making great headway nevertheless. It seemed a mystery to us how they could thread these woods,
which it required all our suppleness to accomplish, climbing, stooping,
and winding, alternately. They are said to drop their long and branch-
ing horns, which usually spread five or six feet, on their backs, and
make their way easily by the weight of their bodies. Our boatmen
said, but I know not with how much truth, that their horns are apt to
be gnawed away by vermin while they sleep. Their flesh, which is
more like beef than venison, is common in Bangor market.

We had proceeded on thus seven or eight miles, till about noon, with
frequent pauses to refresh the weary ones, crossing a considerable
mountain stream, which we conjectured to be Murch Brook, at whose
mouth we had camped, all the time in woods, without having once seen
the summit, and rising very gradually, when the boatmen, beginning
to despair a little, and fearing that we were leaving the mountain on
one side of us, for they had not entire faith in the compass, McCauslin
climbed a tree, from the top of which he could see the peak, when it
appeared that we had not swerved from a right line, the compass
down below still ranging with his arm, which pointed to the summit.
By the side of a cool mountain rill, amid the woods, where the water
began to partake of the purity and transparency of the air, we stopped
to cook some of our fishes, which we had brought thus far in order
to save our hard bread and pork, in the use of which we had put
ourselves on short allowance. We soon had a fire blazing, and stood
around it, under the damp and sombre forest of firs and birches, each
with a sharpened stick, three or four feet in length, upon which he had
spitted his trout, or roach, previously well gashed and salted, our
sticks radiating like the spokes of a wheel from one centre, and each
crowding his particular fish into the most desirable exposure, not with
the truest regard always to his neighbor's rights. Thus we regaled
ourselves, drinking meanwhile at the spring, till one man's pack, at
least, was considerably lightened, when we again took up our line of
march.

At length we reached an elevation sufficiently bare to afford a view
of the summit, still distant and blue, almost as if retreating from us.
A torrent, which proved to be the same we had crossed, was seen

tumbling down in front, literally from out of the clouds. But this glimpse at our whereabouts was soon lost, and we were buried in the woods again. The wood was chiefly yellow birch, spruce, fir, mountain-ash, or round-wood, as the Maine people call it, and moose-wood. It was the worst kind of travelling; sometimes like the densest scrub-oak patches with us. The cornel, or bunch-berries, were very abundant, as well as Solomon's seal and moose-berries. Blue-berries were dis-tributed along our whole route; and in one place the bushes were drooping with the weight of the fruit still as fresh as ever. It was the seventh of September. Such patches afforded a grateful repast, and served to bait the tired party forward. When any lagged behind, the cry of "blue-berries" was most effectual to bring them up. Even at this elevation we passed through a moose-yard, formed by a large flat rock, four or five rods square, where they tread down the snow in winter. At length, fearing that if we held the direct course to the summit, we should not find any water near our camping-ground, we gradually swerved to the west, till, at four o'clock, we struck again the torrent which I have mentioned, and here, in view of the summit, the weary party decided to camp that night.

While my companions were seeking a suitable spot for this purpose, I improved the little daylight that was left in climbing the mountain alone. We were in a deep and narrow ravine, sloping up to the clouds, at an angle of nearly forty-five degrees, and hemmed in by walls of rock, which were at first covered with low trees, then with impenetra-ble thickets of scraggy birches and spruce-trees, and with moss, but at last bare of all vegetation but lichens, and almost continually draped in clouds. Following up the course of the torrent which occu-pied this—and I mean to lay some emphasis on this word *up*—pulling myself up by the side of perpendicular falls of twenty or thirty feet, by the roots of firs and birches, and then, perhaps, walking a level rod or two in the thin stream, for it took up the whole road, ascending by huge steps, as it were, a giant's stairway, down which a river flowed, I had soon cleared the trees, and paused on the successive shelves, to look back over the country. The torrent was from fifteen to thirty feet wide, without a tributary, and seemingly not diminishing in breadth as I advanced; but still it came rushing and roaring down, with a copious tide, over and amidst masses of bare rock, from the very

clouds, as though a water-spout had just burst over the mountain.
Leaving this at last, I began to work my way, scarcely less arduous
than Satan's anciently through Chaos, up the nearest, though not the
highest peak. At first scrambling on all fours over the tops of ancient
black spruce-trees, *(Abies nigra,)* old as the flood, from two to ten or
twelve feet in height, their tops flat and spreading, and their foliage
blue and nipt with cold, as if for centuries they had ceased growing
upward against the bleak sky, the solid cold. I walked some good rods
erect upon the tops of these trees, which were overgrown with moss
and mountain-cranberries. It seemed that in the course of time they
had filled up the intervals between the huge rocks, and the cold wind
had uniformly levelled all over. Here the principle of vegetation was
hard put to it. There was apparently a belt of this kind running quite
round the mountain, though, perhaps, nowhere so remarkable as
here. Once, slumping through, I looked down ten feet, into a dark and
cavernous region, and saw the stem of a spruce, on whose top I stood,
as on a mass of coarse basket-work, fully nine inches in diameter at
the ground. These holes were bears' dens, and the bears were even
then at home. This was the sort of garden I made my way *over*, for
an eighth of a mile, at the risk, it is true, of treading on some of the
plants, not seeing any path *through* it—certainly the most treacherous and porous country I ever travelled.

> "—nigh founder'd, on he fares,
> Treading the crude consistence, half on foot,
> Half flying."

But nothing could exceed the toughness of the twigs,—not one
snapped under my weight, for they had slowly grown. Having
slumped, scrambled, rolled, bounced, and walked, by turns, over this
scraggy country, I arrived upon a side-hill, or rather side-mountain,
where rocks, gray, silent rocks, were the flocks and herds that pastured, chewing a rocky cud at sunset. They looked at me with hard
gray eyes, without a bleat or a low. This brought me to the skirt of
a cloud, and bounded my walk that night. But I had already seen that
Maine country when I turned about, waving, flowing, rippling, down
below.

When I returned to my companions, they had selected a camping-ground on the torrent's edge, and were resting on the ground; one was on the sick list, rolled in a blanket, on a damp shelf of rock. It was a savage and dreary scenery enough; so wildly rough, that they looked long to find a level and open space for the tent. We could not well camp higher, for want of fuel; and the trees here seemed so evergreen and sappy, that we almost doubted if they would acknowledge the influence of fire; but fire prevailed at last, and blazed here, too, like a good citizen of the world. Even at this height we met with frequent traces of moose, as well as of bears. As here was no cedar, we made our bed of coarser feathered spruce; but at any rate the feathers were plucked from the live tree. It was, perhaps, even a more grand and desolate place for a night's lodging than the summit would have been, being in the neighborhood of those wild trees, and of the torrent. Some more aerial and finer-spirited winds rushed and roared through the ravine all night, from time to time arousing our fire, and dispersing the embers about. It was as if we lay in the very nest of a young whirlwind. At midnight, one of my bedfellows, being startled in his dreams by the sudden blazing up to its top of a fir-tree, whose green boughs were dried by the heat, sprang up, with a cry, from his bed, thinking the world on fire, and drew the whole camp after him.

Thoreau's hike cannot be followed exactly today, but park trails provide a close approximation. His route lay mostly along Abol Stream, which is hard walking over jagged rubble, especially at low water. On land, Thoreau was expected to guide the party, but he did not do so well. The "highest peak" he selected was really South Peak, a lower but more obvious prominence from this angle. (Baxter Peak is twenty-seven feet higher and one third of a mile farther north.) By keeping Abol Stream on his left, he avoided Abol Slide, used by all previous climbers on the south slope. Today the Abol Trail follows this slide, which fell in 1816, a spectacular (but largely unwitnessed) moment of downwasting.

ROUTE FROM ABOL: *Trail to Abol Falls and Pond, Park road to Abol campground, Abol Slide Trail to summit*

(see page 136)

Animal traces are still plentiful on the trail; moose go up to 4,000 feet and "yard" there in winter. They should

(see page 137)

be avoided in the September rutting season, when bulls can be aggressive.

(see page 138) By noon, the party had hiked only five miles (not seven or eight), and the stream they crossed was not "Murch" but Abol; Katahdin Stream lies seven miles west. The boatmen (having watched him pole a batteau) were wise to check Thoreau's compass readings. The torrent they saw was Abol Stream, which cuts down through a narrow ravine. By swerving west, Thoreau returned to Abol Stream, at 3,200 feet, just parallel to the base of Abol Slide, farther west. The Abol Trail begins to rise quite steeply here; hikers can look off to the right and imagine having to struggle over that rugged country on a misty, overcast day. This open trail is hard enough walking, full of loose cobblestones and moderate granite boulders. Thoreau did not exaggerate the hazards of walking Abol (see page 139) Stream; for a small taste of that adventure, try the Little Abol Falls trail at the Abol campground.

The experience of climbing this "giant's stairway" rapidly altered Thoreau's tone and imagery. He became Milton's Satan, struggling up out of Chaos, a vengeful (see page 140) figure driven by his pride. The mood turned melodramatic, exaggerated. Possibly the dwarf spruce *were* thick enough to support him, but looking down into bears' dens seems farfetched. Walking off the trail should be avoided today, for the trees and plants damage easily and take years to recover.

(see page 140) The "side hill" Thoreau climbed was possibly Rum Mountain (3,361'), which lies due south of South Peak. His description of rocks as sheep, "chewing a rocky cud," revises the pastoralism of his hikes on Wachusett and Greylock. On this solo climb Thoreau probably did not go beyond the headwall of the ravine, or 3,000 feet. The (see page 141) party's camp was near the tree line, at the edge of Abol Stream. At night Thoreau's rising trepidation was apparent, as the wind and rain conspired to bring on fearsome dreams.

In the morning, after whetting our appetite on some raw pork, a wafer of hard bread, and a dipper of condensed cloud or water-spout, we all together began to make our way up the falls, which I have described; this time choosing the right hand, or highest peak, which was not the one I had approached before. But soon my companions were lost to my sight behind the mountain ridge in my rear, which still seemed ever retreating before me, and I climbed alone over huge rocks, loosely poised, a mile or more, still edging toward the clouds —for though the day was clear elsewhere, the summit was concealed by mist. The mountain seemed a vast aggregation of loose rocks, as if sometime it had rained rocks, and they lay as they fell on the mountain sides, nowhere fairly at rest, but leaning on each other, all rocking-stones, with cavities between, but scarcely any soil or smoother shelf. They were the raw materials of a planet dropped from an unseen quarry, which the vast chemistry of nature would anon work up, or work down, into the smiling and verdant plains and valleys of earth. This was an undone extremity of the globe; as in lignite we see coal in the process of formation.

At length I entered within the skirts of the cloud which seemed forever drifting over the summit, and yet would never be gone, but was generated out of that pure air as fast as it flowed away; and when, a quarter of a mile further, I reached the summit of the ridge, which those who have seen in clearer weather say is about five miles long, and contains a thousand acres of table-land, I was deep within the hostile ranks of clouds, and all objects were obscured by them. Now the wind would blow me out a yard of clear sunlight, wherein I stood; then a gray, dawning light was all it could accomplish, the cloud-line ever rising and falling with the wind's intensity. Sometimes it seemed as if the summit would be cleared in a few moments and smile in sunshine: but what was gained on one side was lost on another. It was like sitting in a chimney and waiting for the smoke to blow away. It was, in fact, a cloud-factory,—these were the cloud-works, and the wind turned them off done from the cool, bare rocks. Occasionally, when the windy columns broke in to me, I caught sight of a dark, damp crag to the right or left; the mist driving ceaselessly between it and me. It reminded me of the creations of the old epic and dramatic poets, of Atlas, Vulcan, the Cyclops, and Prometheus. Such was Caucasus and the rock where Prometheus was bound. Æschylus had no doubt visited such scenery as this. It was vast, Titanic, and such as man never inhabits. Some part of the beholder, even some vital part, seems to escape through the loose grating of his ribs as he ascends. He is more lone than you can imagine. There is less of substantial thought and fair understanding in him, than in the plains where men inhabit. His reason is dispersed and shadowy, more thin and subtile like the air. Vast, Titanic, inhuman Nature has got him at disadvantage, caught him alone, and pilfers him of some of his divine faculty. She does not smile on him as in the plains. She seems to say sternly, why came ye here before your time? This ground is not prepared for you. Is it not enough that I smile in the valleys? I have never made this soil for thy feet, this air for thy breathing, these rocks for thy neighbors. I cannot pity nor fondle thee here, but forever relentlessly drive thee hence to where I *am* kind. Why seek me where I have not called thee, and then complain because you find me but a stepmother? Shouldst thou freeze or starve, or shudder thy life away, here is no shrine, nor altar, nor any access to my ear.

> *"Chaos and ancient Night, I come no spy*
> *With purpose to explore or to disturb*
> *The secrets of your realm, but · · ·*
> *· · · as my way*
> *Lies through your spacious empire up to light."*

The tops of mountains are among the unfinished parts of the globe, whither it is a slight insult to the gods to climb and pry into their secrets, and try their effect on our humanity. Only daring and insolent men, perchance, go there. Simple races, as savages, do not climb mountains—their tops are sacred and mysterious tracts never visited by them. Pomola is always angry with those who climb to the summit of Ktaadn.

According to Jackson, who in his capacity of geological surveyor of the state, has accurately measured it—the altitude of Ktaadn is 5,300 feet, or a little more than one mile above the level of the sea—and he adds: "It is then evidently the highest point in the State of Maine, and is the most abrupt granite mountain in New England." The peculiarities of that spacious table-land on which I was standing, as well as the remarkable semicircular precipice or basin on the eastern side, were all concealed by the mist. I had brought my whole pack to the top, not knowing but I should have to make my descent to the river, and possibly to the settled portion of the state alone and by some other route, and wishing to have a complete outfit with me. But at length, fearing that my companions would be anxious to reach the river before night, and knowing that the clouds might rest on the mountain for days, I was compelled to descend. Occasionally, as I came down, the wind would blow me a vista open through which I could see the country eastward, boundless forests, and lakes, and streams, gleaming in the sun, some of them emptying into the East Branch. There were also new mountains in sight in that direction. Now and then some small bird of the sparrow family would flit away before me, unable to command its course, like a fragment of the gray rock blown off by the wind.

I found my companions where I had left them, on the side of the peak, gathering the mountain cranberries, which filled every crevice between the rocks, together with blue berries, which had a spicier flavor the higher up they grew, but were not the less agreeable to our palates. When the country is settled and roads are made, these cranberries will perhaps become an article of commerce. From this elevation, just on the skirts of the clouds, we could overlook the country west and south for a hundred miles. There it was, the State of Maine, which we had seen on the map, but not much like that. Immeasurable forest for the sun to shine on, that eastern *stuff* we hear of in Massachusetts. No clearing, no house. It did not look as if a solitary traveller had cut so much as a walking-stick there. Countless lakes,—Moosehead in the southwest, forty miles long by ten wide, like a gleaming silver platter at the end of the table; Chesuncook, eighteen long by three wide, without an island; Millinocket, on the south, with its hundred islands; and a hundred others without a name; and mountains also, whose names, for the most part, are known only to the Indians. The forest looked like a firm grass sward, and the effect of these lakes in its midst has been well compared by one who has since visited this same spot, to that of a "mirror broken into a thousand fragments, and wildly scattered over the grass, reflecting the full blaze of the sun."

It was a large farm for somebody, when cleared. According to the Gazetteer, which was printed before the boundary question was settled, this single Penobscot county in which we were, was larger than the whole State of Vermont, with its fourteen counties; and this was only a part of the wild lands of Maine. We are concerned now, however, about natural, not political limits. We were about eighty miles as the bird flies from Bangor, or one hundred and fifteen as we had ridden, and walked, and paddled. We had to console ourselves with the reflection that this view was probably as good as that from the peak, as far as it went, and what were a mountain without its attendant clouds and mists? Like ourselves, neither Bailey nor Jackson had obtained a clear view from the summit.

Ahead of his companions, Thoreau crossed the tree line and reached huge rocks, parallel with the upper part of Abol Slide, 4,000 feet. Climbers need to concentrate here, keeping the trail blazes in sight and working some stretches of boulders on hands and knees. Thoreau's description *(see page 143)* tion of this erosional matter was accurate, but he did not understand the processes involved. The geologist Charles Hamlin gives a succinct explanation: "Ktaadn has thus been buried under its own ruins."

At the top of a last ridge (near 4,600 feet), Thoreau was confused about his exact location: he had to be either on the tableland or near the base of South peak. This misty, shrouded realm awoke for him references to Prometheus, Satan, Pomola; figures of demonic power who hold *(see page 144)* the secrets of gods. Since he failed to reach the summit, one secret that eluded Thoreau was the exact height of Katahdin (now determined to be one mile, 5,280 feet).

From the tableland, hikers to the summit will pass Thoreau Spring (which he never saw) and take the last steps of the Appalachian Trail up a moderate ridge to Baxter Peak. On clear days, the views up here are powerful. Charles Hamlin, in an otherwise dry report, describes the scene as "a savage and chaotic desolation . . . without a parallel in North America." Thoreau had

to rely on a written source, and thus he reported some
errors: the view west and south is closer to sixty or sev- *(see page 145)*
enty miles (rather than the one hundred he gives); and
by 1846 this region was no longer one county but four.

Setting out on our return to the river, still at an early hour in the day,
we decided to follow the course of the torrent, which we supposed to
be Murch Brook, as long as it would not lead us too far out of our way.
We thus travelled about four miles in the very torrent itself, continually crossing and recrossing it, leaping from rock to rock, and jumping
with the stream down falls of seven or eight feet, or sometimes sliding
down on our backs in a thin sheet of water. This ravine had been the
scene of an extraordinary freshet in the spring, apparently accompanied by a slide from the mountain. It must have been filled with a
stream of stones and water, at least twenty feet above the present
level of the torrent. For a rod or two on either side of its channel, the
trees were barked and splintered up to their tops, the birches bent
over, twisted, and sometimes finely split like a stable-broom; some a
foot in diameter snapped off, and whole clumps of trees bent over with
the weight of rocks piled on them. In one place we noticed a rock two
or three feet in diameter, lodged nearly twenty feet high in the crotch
of a tree. For the whole four miles, we saw but one rill emptying in,
and the volume of water did not seem to be increased from the first.
We travelled thus very rapidly with a downward impetus, and grew
remarkably expert at leaping from rock to rock, for leap we must, and
leap we did, whether there was any rock at the right distance or not.
It was a pleasant picture when the foremost turned about and looked
up the winding ravine, walled in with rocks and the green forest, to
see at intervals of a rod or two, a red-shirted or green-jacketed mountaineer against the white torrent, leaping down the channel with his
pack on his back, or pausing upon a convenient rock in the midst of
the torrent to mend a rent in his clothes, or unstrap the dipper at his
belt to take a draught of the water. At one place we were startled by
seeing, on a little sandy shelf by the side of the stream, the fresh print
of a man's foot, and for a moment realized how Robinson Crusoe felt
in a similar case; but at last we remembered that we had struck this
stream on our way up, though we could not have told where, and one

had descended into the ravine for a drink. The cool air above, and the continual bathing of our bodies in mountain water, alternate foot, sitz, douche, and plunge baths, made this walk exceedingly refreshing, and we had travelled only a mile or two after leaving the torrent, before every thread of our clothes was as dry as usual, owing perhaps to a peculiar quality in the atmosphere.

After leaving the torrent, being in doubt about our course, Tom threw down his pack at the foot of the loftiest spruce tree at hand, and shinned up the bare trunk some twenty feet, and then climbed through the green tower, lost to our sight, until he held the topmost spray in his hand.* McCauslin, in his younger days, had marched through the wilderness with a body of troops, under General Somebody, and with one other man did all the scouting and spying service. The General's word was: "Throw down the top of that tree," and there was no tree in the Maine woods so high that it did not lose its top in such a case. I have heard a story of two men being lost once in these woods, nearer to the settlements than this, who climbed the loftiest pine they could find, some six feet in diameter at the ground, from whose top they discovered a solitary clearing and its smoke. When at this height, some two hundred feet from the ground, one of them became dizzy, and fainted in his companion's arms, and the latter had to accomplish the descent with him, alternately fainting and reviving, as best he could. To Tom we cried, where away does the summit bear? where the burnt lands? The last he could only conjecture; he descried, however, a little meadow and pond, lying probably in our course, which we concluded to steer for. On reaching this secluded meadow, we found fresh tracks of moose on the shore of the pond, and the water was still unsettled as if they had fled before us. A little further, in a dense thicket, we seemed to be still on their trail. It was a small meadow, of a few acres, on the mountain side, concealed by the forest,

* "The spruce-tree," says Springer in '51, "is generally selected, principally for the superior facilities which its numerous limbs afford the climber. To gain the first limbs of this tree, which are from twenty to forty feet from the ground, a smaller tree is undercut and lodged against it, clambering up which the top of the spruce is reached. In some cases, when a very elevated position is desired, the spruce-tree is lodged against the trunk of some lofty pine, up which we ascend to a height twice that of the surrounding forest."

To indicate the direction of pines, he throws down a branch, and a man at the ground takes the bearing.

and perhaps never seen by a white man before, where one would think that the moose might browse and bathe, and rest in peace. Pursuing this course, we soon reached the open land, which went sloping down some miles toward the Penobscot.

Perhaps I most fully realized that this was primeval, untamed, and forever untameable *Nature*, or whatever else men call it, while coming down this part of the mountain. We were passing over "Burnt Lands," burnt by lightning, perchance, though they showed no recent marks of fire, hardly so much as a charred stump, but looked rather like a natural pasture for the moose and deer, exceedingly wild and desolate, with occasional strips of timber crossing them, and low poplars springing up, and patches of blueberries here and there. I found myself traversing them familiarly, like some pasture run to waste, or partially reclaimed by man; but when I reflected what man, what brother or sister or kinsman of our race made it and claimed it, I expected the proprietor to rise up and dispute my passage. It is difficult to conceive of a region uninhabited by man. We habitually presume his presence and influence everywhere. And yet we have not seen pure Nature, unless we have seen her thus vast, and drear, and inhuman, though in the midst of cities. Nature was here something savage and awful, though beautiful. I looked with awe at the ground I trod on, to see what the Powers had made there, the form and fashion and material of their work. This was that Earth of which we have heard, made out of Chaos and Old Night. Here was no man's garden, but the unhandselled globe. It was not lawn, nor pasture, nor mead, nor woodland, nor lea, nor arable, nor waste-land. It was the fresh and natural surface of the planet Earth, as it was made forever and ever,—to be the dwelling of man, we say,—so Nature made it, and many may use it if he can. Man was not to be associated with it. It was Matter, vast, terrific,—not his Mother Earth that we have heard of, not for him to tread on, or be buried in,—no, it were being too familiar even to let his bones lie there—the home this of Necessity and Fate. There was there felt the presence of a force not bound to be kind to man. It was a place for heathenism and superstitious rites,—to be inhabited by men nearer of kin to the rocks and to wild animals than we. We walked over it with a certain awe, stopping from time to time to pick the blueberries which grew there, and had a smart and spicy taste. Perchance where *our* wild pines stand, and leaves lie on their forest floor in Concord, there were once reapers, and husbandmen planted grain; but here not even the surface had been scarred by man, but it was a specimen of what God saw fit to make this world. What is it to be admitted to a museum, to see a myriad of particular things, compared with being shown some star's surface, some hard matter in its home! I stand in awe of my body, this matter to which I am bound has become so strange to me. I fear not spirits, ghosts, of which I am one,—*that* my body might,—but I fear bodies, I tremble to meet them. What is this Titan that has possession of me? Talk of mysteries! —Think of our life in nature,—daily to be shown matter, to come in contact with it,—rocks, trees, wind on our cheeks! the *solid* earth! the *actual* world! the *common sense! Contact! Contact! Who* are we? *where* are we?

Ere long we recognized some rocks and other features in the land-scape which we had purposely impressed on our memories, and quick-ening our pace, by two o'clock we reached the batteau.* Here we had expected to dine on trout, but in this glaring sunlight they were slow to take the bait, so we were compelled to make the most of the crumbs of our hard bread and our pork, which were both nearly exhausted. Meanwhile we deliberated whether we should go up the river a mile farther to Gibson's clearing on the Sowadnehunk, where there was a deserted log hut, in order to get a half-inch auger, to mend one of our spike-poles with. There were young spruce trees enough around us, and we had a spare spike, but nothing to make a hole with. But as it was uncertain whether we should find any tools left there, we patched up the broken pole as well as we could for the downward voyage, in which there would be but little use for it. Moreover, we were unwilling to lose any time in this expedition, lest the wind should rise before we reached the larger lakes, and detain us, for a moderate wind produces quite a sea on these waters, in which a batteau will not live for a moment; and on one occasion McCauslin had been delayed a week at the head of the North Twin, which is only four miles across. We were nearly out of provisions, and ill prepared in this respect for what

_____

*The bears had not touched things on our possessions. They sometimes tear a batteau to pieces for the sake of the tar with which it is besmeared.

might possibly prove a week's journey round by the shore, fording innumerable streams, and threading a trackless forest, should any accident happen to our boat.

It was with regret that we turned our backs on Chesuncook, which McCauslin had formerly logged on, and the Allagash lakes. There were still longer rapids and portages above; among the last the Rippogenus Portage, which he described as the most difficult on the river, and three miles long. The whole length of the Penobscot is two hundred and seventy-five miles, and we are still nearly one hundred miles from its source. Hodge, the assistant State Geologist, passed up this river in 1837, and by a portage of only one mile and three-quarters, crossed over into the Allagash, and so went down that into the St. John, and up the Madawaska to the Grand Portage across to the St. Lawrence. His is the only account that I know, of an expedition through to Canada in this direction. He thus describes his first sight of the latter river, which, to compare small things with great, is like Balboa's first sight of the Pacific from the mountains of the Isthmus of Darien. "When we first came in sight of the St. Lawrence," he says, "from the top of a high hill, the view was most striking, and much more interesting to me from having been shut up in the woods for the two previous months. Directly before us lay the broad river, extending across nine or ten miles, its surface broken by a few islands and reefs; and two ships riding at anchor near the shore. Beyond, extended ranges of uncultivated hills, parallel with the river. The sun was just going down behind them, and gilding the whole scene with its parting rays."

Having missed the summit, Thoreau reserved his climax for the descent, a sharp difference from the Wachusett or Greylock stories. He headed down Abol Stream (still calling it "Murch") and quickly found that descent is the harder part of climbing: it comes when energy is low, and the pull of gravity punishes knees and thighs. Hikers can now return on Abol or try the Hunt Trail, which descends along Katahdin Stream. Leaping down the rocks, turning and often looking back up, moved Thoreau into a contemplative state, evaluating events *post*

ROUTE FROM SUMMIT: *Appalachian Trail to Abol Trail, to Abol* campground

(see page 147)

facto—the rhythm of his later mountain trips. His route finally left the stream bed, reached twenty-foot spruce trees (at 2,000 feet), then came to small ponds (Meadow and Lost Pond), formed at the terminal moraine.

His trail (more direct than present footpaths) led across "Burnt Land," where the country was also passing from crisis back to a normal state. This appropriate set- *(see page 149)* ting inspired Thoreau's climactic meditation. Katahdin gave him a new vision of kinship and property; a sense of man's need to exist *in* nature, not above it. The mountain reminded him of his material existence, which at the same time was so mysterious. By asking *who* and *where* am I, he made a turn in his own thought and art, and sharing this moment with readers was a sign of his *(see page 151)* new direction. Hence, at the journey's end, he was looking forward to future trips in Maine, up Chesuncook and into the Allagash lakes.

About four o'clock the same afternoon, we commenced our return voyage, which would require but little if any poling. In shooting rapids, the boatmen use large and broad paddles, instead of poles, to guide the boat with. Though we glided so swiftly and often smoothly down, where it had cost us no slight effort to get up, our present voyage was attended with far more danger: for if we once fairly struck one of the thousand rocks by which we were surrounded, the boat would be swamped in an instant. When a boat is swamped under these circumstances, the boatmen commonly find no difficulty in keeping afloat at first, for the current keeps both them and their cargo up for a long way down the stream; and if they can swim, they have only to work their way gradually to the shore. The greatest danger is of being caught in an eddy behind some larger rock, where the water rushes up stream faster than elsewhere it does down, and being carried round and round under the surface till they are drowned. McCauslin pointed out some rocks which had been the scene of a fatal accident of this kind. Sometimes the body is not thrown out for several hours. He himself had performed such a circuit once, only his legs being visible to his companions; but he was fortunately thrown out in season to recover his breath.* In shooting the rapids, the boatman has this problem to solve: to choose a circuitous and safe course amid a thousand sunken rocks, scattered over a quarter or half a mile, at the same time that he is moving steadily on at the rate of fifteen miles an hour. Stop he cannot; the only question is, where will he go? The bow-man chooses the course with all his eyes about him, striking broad off with his paddle, and drawing the boat by main force into her course. The stern-man faithfully follows the bow.

We were soon at the Aboljacarmegus Falls. Anxious to avoid the delay as well as the labor of the portage here, our boatmen went forward first to reconnoitre, and concluded to let the batteau down the falls, carrying the baggage only over the portage. Jumping from rock to rock until nearly in the middle of the stream, we were ready to receive the boat and let her down over the first fall, some six or seven feet perpendicular. The boatmen stand upon the edge of a shelf of rock where the fall is perhaps nine or ten feet perpendicular, in from one to two feet of rapid water, one on each side of the boat, and let

*I cut this from a newspaper. "On the 11th (instant?) [May, '49], on Rappogenes Falls, Mr. John Delantee, of Orono, Me., was drowned while running logs. He was a citizen of Orono, and was twenty-six years of age. His companions found his body, enclosed it in bark, and buried it in the solemn woods."

it slide gently over, till the bow is run out ten or twelve feet in the air;
then letting it drop squarely, while one holds the painter, the other
leaps in, and his companion following, they are whirled down the
rapids to a new fall, or to smooth water. In a very few minutes they
had accomplished a passage in safety, which would be as fool-hardy
for the unskilful to attempt as the descent of Niagara itself. It seemed
as if it needed only a little familiarity, and a little more skill, to
navigate down such falls as Niagara itself with safety. At any rate,
I should not despair of such men in the rapids above Table-Rock, until
I saw them actually go over the falls, so cool, so collected, so fertile
in resources are they. One might have thought that these were falls,
and that falls were not to be waded through with impunity like a
mud-puddle. There was really danger of their losing their sublimity
in losing their power to harm us. Familiarity breeds contempt. The
boatman pauses, perchance, on some shelf beneath a table-rock under
the fall, standing in some cove of back-water two feet deep, and you
hear his rough voice come up through the spray, coolly giving directions how to launch the boat this time.

Having carried round Pockwockomus Falls, our oars soon brought
us to the Katepskonegan, or Oak Hall carry, where we decided to
camp half way over, leaving our batteau to be carried over in the
morning on fresh shoulders. One shoulder of each of the boatmen
showed a red spot as large as one's hand, worn by the batteau on this
expedition; and this shoulder, as it did all the work, was perceptibly
lower than its fellow, from long service. Such toil soon wears out the
strongest constitution. The drivers are accustomed to work in the cold
water in the spring, rarely ever dry; and if one falls in all over, he
rarely changes his clothes till night, if then, even. One who takes this
precaution is called by a particular nickname, or is turned off. None
can lead this life who are not almost amphibious. McCauslin said
soberly, what is at any rate a good story to tell, that he had seen where
six men were wholly under water at once, at a jam, with their shoulders to handspikes. If the log did not start, then they had to put out
their heads to breathe. The driver works as long as he can see, from
dark to dark, and at night has not time to eat his supper and dry his
clothes fairly, before he is asleep on his cedar bed. We lay that night
on the very bed made by such a party, stretching our tent over the

poles which were still standing, but reshingling the damp and faded bed with fresh leaves.

The return trip ran quickly downstream, and so took little time in the telling. As on the mountain, danger was constant: the batteau could strike rocks, founder and sink; the men could drown in eddies. But the boatmen had expert strokes; their progress was still "philosophical" as they returned to the lower world. In the boat, Thoreau no longer climbed high and alone, but rode and pulled with others. After much cool, resourceful action, all dangers subsided, and finally the travelers made their *(see page 154)* last camp.

In the morning, we carried our boat over and launched it, making haste lest the wind should rise. The boatmen ran down Passamagamet, and, soon after, Ambejijis Falls, while we walked round with the baggage. We made a hasty breakfast at the head of Ambejijis lake, on the remainder of our pork, and were soon rowing across its smooth surface again, under a pleasant sky, the mountain being now clear of clouds in the northeast. Taking turns at the oars, we shot rapidly across Deep Cove, the Foot of Pamadumcook, and the North Twin, at the rate of six miles an hour, the wind not being high enough to disturb us, and reached the Dam at noon. The boatmen went through one of the log sluices in the batteau, where the fall was ten feet at the bottom, and took us in below. Here was the longest rapid in our voyage, and perhaps the running this was as dangerous and arduous a task as any. Shooting down sometimes at the rate, as we judged, of fifteen miles an hour, if we struck a rock, we were split from end to end in an instant. Now like a bait bobbing for some river monster amid the eddies, now darting to this side of the stream, now to that, gliding swift and smooth near to our destruction, or striking broad off with the paddle and drawing the boat to right or left with all our might, in order to avoid a rock. I suppose that it was like running the rapids of the Sault de Ste. Marie, at the outlet of Lake Superior, and our boatmen probably displayed no less dexterity than the Indians there do. We soon ran through this mile, and floated in Quakish lake.

After such a voyage, the troubled and angry waters, which once had seemed terrible and not to be trifled with, appeared tamed and subdued; they had been bearded and worried in their channels, pricked and whipped into submission with the spike-pole and paddle, gone through and through with impunity, and all their spirit and their danger taken out of them, and the most swollen and impetuous rivers seemed but playthings henceforth. I began, at length, to understand the boatman's familiarity with and contempt for the rapids. "Those Fowler boys," said Mrs. McCauslin, "are perfect ducks for the water." They had run down to Lincoln, according to her, thirty or forty miles, in a batteau, in the night, for a doctor, when it was so dark that they could not see a rod before them, and the river was swollen so as to be almost a continuous rapid, so that the doctor *cried*, when they brought him up by daylight, "Why, Tom, how did you see to steer?" "We didn't steer much,—only kept her straight." And yet they met with no accident. It is true, the more difficult rapids are higher up than this.

When we reached the Millinocket opposite to Tom's house, and were waiting for his folks to set us over, for we had left our batteau above the Grand Falls, we discovered two canoes with two men in each, turning up this stream from Shad Pond, one keeping the opposite side of a small island before us, while the other approached the side where we were standing, examining the banks carefully for muskrats as they came along. The last proved to be Louis Neptune and his companion, now at last on their way up to Chesuncook after moose; but they were so disguised that we hardly knew them. At a little distance, they might have been taken for Quakers, with their broad-brimmed hats, and overcoats with broad capes, the spoils of Bangor, seeking a settlement in this Sylvania,—or, nearer at hand, for fashionable gentlemen, the morning after a spree. Met face to face, these Indians in their native woods looked like the sinister and slouching fellows whom you meet picking up strings and paper in the streets of a city. There is, in fact, a remarkable and unexpected resemblance between the degraded savage and the lowest classes in a great city. The one is no more a child of nature than the other. In the progress of degradation, the distinction of races is soon lost. Neptune at first was only anxious to know what we "kill," seeing some partridges in the hands of one of the party, but we had assumed too much anger to permit of a reply. We thought Indians had some honor before. But—"Me been sick. O, me unwell now. You make bargain, then me go." They had in fact been delayed so long by a drunken frolic at the Five Islands, and they had not yet recovered from its effects. They had some young musquash in their canoes, which they dug out of the banks with a hoe for food, not for their skins, for musquash are their principal food on these expeditions. So they went on up the Millinocket, and we kept down the bank of the Penobscot, after recruiting ourselves with a draught of Tom's beer, leaving Tom at his home.

Thus a man shall lead his life away here on the edge of the wilderness, on Indian Millinocket stream, in a new world, far in the dark of a continent, and have a flute to play at evening here, while his strains echo to the stars, amid the howling of wolves; shall live, as it were, in the primitive age of the world, a primitive man. Yet he shall spend a sunny day, and in this century be my contemporary; perchance shall read some scattered leaves of literature, and sometimes talk with me. Why read history then if the ages and the generations are now? He lives three thousand years deep into time, an age not yet described by poets. Can you well go further back in history than this? Ay! ay!—for there turns up but now into the mouth of Millinocket stream a still more ancient and primitive man, whose history is not brought down even to the former. In a bark vessel sewn with the roots of the spruce, with horn-beam paddles he dips his way along. He is but dim and misty to me, obscured by the æons that lie between the bark canoe and the batteau. He builds no house of logs, but a wigwam of skins. He eats no hot-bread and sweet-cake, but musquash and moose-meat and the fat of bears. He glides up the Millinocket and is lost to my sight, as a more distant and misty cloud is seen flitting by behind a nearer, and is lost in space. So he goes about his destiny, the red face of man.

After having passed the night and buttered our boots for the last time at Uncle George's, whose dogs almost devoured him for joy at his return, we kept on down the river the next day about eight miles on foot, and then took a batteau with a man to pole it to Mattawam-keag, ten more. At the middle of that very night, to make a swift conclusion to a long story, we dropped our buggy over the half-finished bridge at Oldtown, where we heard the confused din and clink of a hundred saws which never rest, and at six o'clock the next morning one of the party was steaming his way to Massachusetts.

At the end, Thoreau brought other characters to the fore: they told stories, shot rapids; and their valor contrasted sharply with the two Indians. Those fallen men, emblems of a faded past, were now meekly heading upstream. Since Thoreau had been there and seen the beginnings of time, he was now less optimistic about the future. A new realism dominated his view, more sober and calculating even in his praise of Maine and the *(see page 160)* "shores of America."

Heading home to Walden, he thought of the Maine *(see page 159)* lakes, "lying up so high and exposed to the light," always superior to their transient human observers. Up that river he had seen one beautiful country, where nature dwelled in all her aspects—grim, tender, and perpetual.

What is most striking in the Maine wilderness is, the continuousness of the forest, with fewer open intervals or glades than you had imagined. Except the few burnt lands, the narrow intervals on the rivers, the bare tops of the high mountains, and the lakes and streams, the forest is uninterrupted. It is even more grim and wild than you had anticipated, a damp and intricate wilderness, in the spring everywhere wet and miry. The aspect of the country indeed is universally stern and savage, excepting the distant views of the forest from hills, and the lake prospects, which are mild and civilizing in a degree. The lakes are something which you are unprepared for: they lie up so high exposed to the light, and the forest is diminished to a fine fringe on their edges, with here and there a blue mountain, like amethyst jewels set around some jewel of the first water,—so anterior, so superior to all the changes that are to take place on their shores, even now civil and refined, and fair, as they can ever be. These are not the artificial forests of an English king—a royal preserve merely. Here prevail no forest laws, but those of nature. The aborigines have never been dispossessed, nor nature disforested.

It is a country full of evergreen trees, of mossy silver birches and watery maples, the ground dotted with insipid, small red berries, and strewn with damp and moss-grown rocks—a country diversified with

Common loon

innumerable lakes and rapid streams, peopled with trout and various species of *leucisci,* with salmon, shad and pickerel, and other fishes; the forest resounding at rare intervals with the note of the chicadee, the blue-jay, and the woodpecker, the scream of the fish-hawk and the eagle, the laugh of the loon, and the whistle of ducks along the solitary streams; and at night, with the hooting of owls and howling of wolves; in summer, swarming with myriads of black flies and mosquitoes, more formidable than wolves to the white man. Such is the home of the moose, the bear, the caribou, the wolf, the beaver, and the Indian. Who shall describe the inexpressible tenderness and immortal life of the grim forest, where Nature, though it be mid-winter, is ever in her spring, where the moss-grown and decaying trees are not old, but seem to enjoy a perpetual youth; and blissful, innocent Nature, like a serene infant, is too happy to make a noise, except by a few tinkling, lisping birds and trickling rills?

What a place to live, what a place to die and be buried in! There certainly men would live forever, and laugh at death and the grave. There they could have no such thoughts as are associated with the village graveyard,—that make a grave out of one of those moist evergreen hummocks!

> *Die and be buried who will,*
> *I mean to live here still;*
> *My nature grows ever more young*
> *The primitive pines among.*

I am reminded by my journey how exceedingly new this country still is. You have only to travel for a few days into the interior and back parts even of many of the old states, to come to that very America which the Northmen, and Cabot, and Gosnold, and Smith and Raleigh visited. If Columbus was the first to discover the islands, Americus Vespucius, and Cabot, and the Puritans, and we their descendants, have discovered only the shores of America. While the republic has already acquired a history worldwide, America is still unsettled and unexplored. Like the English in New Holland, we live only on the shores of a continent even yet, and hardly know where the rivers come from which float our navy. The very timber and boards, and shingles, of which our houses are made, grew but yesterday in a wilderness where the Indian still hunts and the moose runs wild. New-York has her wilderness within her own borders; and though the sailors of Europe are familiar with the soundings of her Hudson, and Fulton long since invented the steamboat on its waters, an Indian is still necessary to guide her scientific men to its head-waters in the Adirondac country.

Have we even so much as discovered and settled the shores? Let a man travel on foot along the coast, from the Passamaquoddy to the Sabine, or to the Rio Bravo, or to wherever the end is now, if he is swift enough to overtake it, faithfully following the windings of every inlet and of every cape, and stepping to the music of the surf—with a desolate fishing-town once a week, and a city's port once a month to cheer him, and putting up at the light-houses, when there are any, and tell me if it looks like a discovered and settled country, and not rather, for the most part, like a desolate island, and No-man's Land.

We have advanced by leaps to the Pacific, and left many a lesser Oregon and California unexplored behind us. Though the railroad and the telegraph have been established on the shores of Maine, the Indian still looks out from her interior mountains over all these to the sea. There stands the city of Bangor, fifty miles up the Penobscot, at the head of navigation for vessels of the largest class, the principal lumber depot on this continent, with a population of twelve thousand, like a star on the edge of night, still hewing at the forests of which it is built, already overflowing with the luxuries and refinement of Europe, and sending its vessels to Spain, to England, and to the West Indies for its groceries,—and yet only a few axe-men have gone "up river" into the howling wilderness which feeds it. The bear and deer are still found within its limits; and the moose, as he swims the Penobscot, is entangled amid its shipping and taken by foreign sailors in its harbor. Twelve miles in the rear, twelve miles of railroad, are Orono and the Indian Island, the home of the Penobscot tribe, and then commence the batteau and the canoe, and the military road; and, sixty miles above, the country is virtually unmapped and unexplored, and there still waves the virgin forest of the New World.

Kineo

Standing on a mountain in the midst of a lake,
where would you look for the first sign of
approaching fair weather? Not into the heavens,
it seems, but into the lake.

True to his promise in "Ktaadn," Thoreau made return trips to the Penobscot River, seeing its West Branch in 1853, then its East Branch in 1857. On both journeys he hoped to climb Katahdin, but circumstances forced changes in his plans. At the beginning of his 1857 trip, he did climb the lesser peak of Mt. Kineo (1,789'), which stands on a peninsula in Moosehead Lake. This episode appears early in "The Allegash and the East Branch," written in 1858 for delivery as a lecture. He made further revisions in 1861–62 during his last illness, and the text was published as the final chapter of *The Maine Woods* (1864).

Thoreau planned the Allegash trip to complement his two previous ventures, when he traveled only one branch or the other of the Penobscot. Now he followed its entire circuit, passing from West to East Branch, always moving downstream with the current. His story reinforces this circular motif through images and events that simulate the round of travel, "a succession of curves from point to point." The opening pages launch the first of those curves, across the broad waters of Moosehead Lake to Mt. Kineo.

On Monday, July 20, 1857, Thoreau left Boston on a steamer, taking the outside passage to Bangor. His companion was Edward Hoar, a fellow Concordian and amateur botanist. They stayed at George Thatcher's that night, and on July 21 Thoreau went by wagon to Oldtown, where he engaged Joseph Polis as a guide. At forty-eight, Polis was a wealthy Penobscot Indian, "one of the aristocracy," but he charged modest fees: $1.50 a day for himself, $0.50 a week for his canoe.

The canoe (newly built by Polis) was birchbark, about eighteen feet long and weighing eighty pounds. Thoreau feared it might prove too small for three men and their baggage, a total of nearly 600 pounds; but the boat traveled well on both lakes and streams.

The three men left Bangor on July 23 by stagecoach, bound for Greenville, at the southern end of Moosehead Lake. They lashed the canoe and their gear atop the coach; because of steady rains and other delays, the eighty-five mile journey took all day. At Greenville they intended to paddle a mile or two up the lake and camp on one of its islands, but rain kept them overnight in a tavern. That was their last contact with civilization for the next twelve days.

T H E

M A I N E   W O O D S

About four o'clock the next morning, (July 24th,) though it was quite cloudy, accompanied by the landlord to the water's edge, in the twilight, we launched our canoe from a rock on the Moosehead Lake. When I was there four years before we had a rather small canoe for three persons, and I had thought that this time I would get a larger one, but the present one was even smaller than that. It was 18¼ feet long by 2 feet 6½ inches wide in the middle, and one foot deep within, as I found by measurement, and I judged that it would weigh not far from eighty pounds. The Indian had recently made it himself, and its smallness was partly compensated for by its newness, as well as stanchness and solidity, it being made of very thick bark and ribs. Our baggage weighed about 166 pounds, so that the canoe carried about 600 pounds in all, or the weight of four men. The principal part of the baggage was, as usual, placed in the middle of the broadest part, while we stowed ourselves in the chinks and crannies that were left before and behind it, where there was no room to extend our legs, the loose articles being tucked into the ends. The canoe was thus as closely packed as a market-basket, and might possibly have been upset without spilling any of its contents. The Indian sat on a cross-bar in the stern, but we flat on the bottom, with a splint or chip behind our backs, to protect them from the cross-bar, and one of us commonly paddled with the Indian. He foresaw that we should not want a pole till we reached the Umbazookskus River, it being either dead water or down stream so far, and he was prepared to make a sail of his blanket in the bows, if the wind should be fair; but we never used it.

It had rained more or less the four previous days, so that we thought we might count on some fair weather. The wind was at first southwesterly.

Lily Bay, Moosehead Lake

Paddling along the eastern side of the lake in the still of the morn-ing, we soon saw a few sheldrakes, which the Indian called *Shecor-ways*, and some peetweets *Naramekechus*, on the rocky shore; we also saw and heard loons, *medawisla*, which he said was a sign of wind. It was inspiriting to hear the regular dip of the paddles, as if they were our fins or flippers, and to realize that we were at length fairly embarked. We who had felt strangely as stage-passengers and tavern-lodgers were suddenly naturalized there and presented with the freedom of the lakes and the woods. Having passed the small rocky isles within two or three miles of the foot of the lake, we had a short consultation respecting our course, and inclined to the western shore for the sake of its lee; for otherwise, if the wind should rise, it would be impossible for us to reach Mount Kineo, which is about midway up the lake on the east side, but at its narrowest part, where probably we could recross if we took the western side. The wind is the chief obstacle to crossing the lakes, especially in so small a canoe. The Indian remarked several times that he did not like to cross the lakes "in littlum canoe," but nevertheless, "just as we say, it made no odds to him." He sometimes took a straight course up the middle of the lake between Sugar and Deer Islands, when there was no wind.

Measured on the map, Moosehead Lake is twelve miles wide at the widest place, and thirty miles long in a direct line, but longer as it lies. The captain of the steamer called it thirty-eight miles as he steered. We should probably go about forty. The Indian said that it was called *"Mspame,* because large water." Squaw Mountain rose darkly on our left, near the outlet of the Kennebec, and what the Indian called Spencer Bay Mountain, on the east, and already we saw Mount Kineo before us in the north.

Paddling near the shore, we frequently heard the *pe-pe* of the olive-sided fly-catcher, also the wood-pewee, and the kingfisher, thus early in the morning. The Indian reminding us that he could not work without eating, we stopped to breakfast on the main shore, southwest of Deer Island, at a spot where the *Mimulus ringens* grew abundantly. We took out our bags, and the Indian made a fire under a very large bleached log, using white-pine bark from a stump, though he said that hemlock was better, and kindling with canoe-birch bark. Our table was a large piece of freshly peeled birch-bark, laid wrong-side-up, and our breakfast consisted of hard bread, fried pork, and strong coffee, well sweetened, in which we did not miss the milk.

While we were getting breakfast a brood of twelve black dippers, half grown, came paddling by within three or four rods, not at all alarmed; and they loitered about as long as we stayed, now huddled close together, within a circle of eighteen inches in diameter, now moving off in a long line, very cunningly. The Indian thought that the mother had perhaps been killed. Yet they bore a certain proportion to the great Moosehead Lake on whose bosom they floated, and I felt as if they were under its protection.

Looking northward from this place it appeared as if we were entering a large bay, and we did not know whether we should be obliged to diverge from our course and keep outside a point which we saw, or should find a passage between this and the mainland. I consulted my map and used my glass, and the Indian did the same, but we could not find our place exactly on the map, nor could we detect any break in the shore. When I asked the Indian the way, he answered "I don't know," which I thought remarkable, since he had said that he was familiar with the lake; but it appeared that he had never been up this side. It was misty dog-day weather, and we had already penetrated a smaller bay of the same kind, and knocked the bottom out of it, though we had been obliged to pass over a small bar, between an island and the shore, where there was but just breadth and depth enough to float the canoe, and the Indian had observed, "Very easy makum bridge here," but now it seemed that, if we held on, we should be fairly embayed. Presently, however, though we had not stirred, the mist lifted somewhat, and revealed a break in the shore northward, showing that the point was a portion of Deer Island, and that our course lay westward of it. Where it had seemed a continuous shore even through a glass, one portion was now seen by the naked eye to be much more distant than the other which overlapped it, merely by the greater thickness of the mist which still rested on it, while the nearer or island portion was comparatively bare and green. The line of separation was very distinct, and the Indian immediately remarked, "I guess you and I go there,—I guess there's room for my canoe there." This was his common expression instead of saying we. He never addressed us by our names, though curious to know how they were spelled and what they meant, while we called him Polis. He had already guessed very accurately at our ages, and said that he was forty-eight.

Moosehead is the largest lake lying entirely within New England; its 350 miles of shoreline have been a sporting region since 1836, when Greenville was founded. Travelers today can launch canoes at Greenville—or take ME 15 north for eighteen miles to Rockwood, and there hire a canoe to cross the narrow, one-mile channel to Kineo Cove. During his passage across the lake, Thoreau referred frequently to his crossing of 1853, which he also described in "Chesuncook," the second part of *The Maine Woods.* ROUTE FROM BANGOR: *ME 15 to Greenville*

The size and location of this lake made it seem an open arena to Thoreau, where he felt "naturalized." The "rocky isles" they passed are west of Harford Point, two miles north of Greenville. The canoe had a favorable southeasterly wind and, accordingly, hugged the western shore. Polis was not familiar with this side; the usual route for canoes was on the east. The distant mountains were Big Squaw (six miles northwest), Big Spencer (seven miles northeast), and Kineo (sixteen miles northwest). Their breakfast spot was probably between Harford Point and Moose Island, on the west shore. *(see page 165)*

The "black dippers" Thoreau saw were either immature coots or grebes. In his Journal for 1857–58, he made several attempts to identify these birds; his "Appendix" to *The Maine Woods* lists *"Fuligula albeola* (spirit duck or dipper)." The young birds, floating in a circle, intro- *(see page 165) (see page 167)* duce the image of harmony and congruity that recurs throughout his story. Thoreau's relations with Joe Polis also develop: at first the white man was exact, the Indian casual, but gradually they adjusted to each other, not as "we" but as "you and I."

After breakfast I emptied the melted pork that was left into the lake, making what sailors call a "slick," and watching to see how much it spread over and smoothed the agitated surface. The Indian looked at it a moment and said, "That make hard paddlum thro'; hold 'em canoe. So say old times."

We hastily reloaded, putting the dishes loose in the bows, that they might be at hand when wanted, and set out again. The western shore, near which we paddled along, rose gently to a considerable height, and was everywhere densely covered with the forest, in which was a large proportion of hard wood to enliven and relieve the fir and spruce.

The Indian said that the usnea lichen which we saw hanging from the trees was called *chorchorque.* We asked him the names of several small birds which we heard this morning. The wood-thrush, which was quite common, and whose note he imitated, he said was called *Adelungquamooktum;* but sometimes he could not tell the name of some small bird which I heard and knew, but he said, "I tell all the birds about here,—this country; can't tell littlum noise, but I see 'em, then I can tell."

I observed that I should like to go to school to him to learn his language, living on the Indian island the while; could not that be done? "O, yer," he replied, "good many do so." I asked how long he thought it would take. He said one week. I told him that in this voyage I would tell him all I knew, and he should tell me all he knew, to which he readily agreed.

The birds sang quite as in our woods,—the red-eye, red-start, veery, wood-pewee, etc., but we saw no bluebirds in all our journey, and several told me in Bangor that they had not the bluebird there. Mt. Kineo, which was generally visible, though occasionally concealed by islands or the mainland in front, had a level bar of cloud concealing its summit, and all the mountain-tops about the lake were cut off at the same height. Ducks of various kinds—sheldrake, summer ducks, etc.—were quite common, and ran over the water before us as fast as a horse trots. Thus they were soon out of sight.

The Indian asked the meaning of *reality*, as near as I could make out the word, which he said one of us had used; also of *"interrent,"* that is, intelligent. I observed that he could rarely sound the letter r, but used l, as also r for l sometimes; as *load* for road, *pickelel* for pickerel, *Soogle* Island for Sugar Island, *lock* for rock, etc. Yet he trilled the r pretty well after me.

He generally added the syllable *um* to his words when he could,— as padl*um*, etc. I have once heard a Chippewa lecture, who made his audience laugh unintentionally by putting *m* after the word *too*, which word he brought in continually and unnecessarily, accenting and prolonging this sound into *m-ar* sonorously as if it were necessary to bring in so much of his vernacular as a relief to his organs, a compensation for twisting his jaws about, and putting his tongue into every corner of his mouth, as he complained that he was obliged to do when he spoke English. There was so much of the Indian accent resounding through his English, so much of the "bow-arrow tang" as my neighbor calls it, and I have no doubt that word seemed to him the best pronounced. It was a wild and refreshing sound, like that of the wind among the pines, or the booming of the surf on the shore.

I asked him the meaning of the word *Musketicook*, the Indian name of Concord River. He pronounced it *Muskéeticook*, emphasizing the second syllable with a peculiar guttural sound, and said that it meant "Dead-water," which it is, and in this definition he agreed exactly with the St. Francis Indian with whom I talked in 1853.

On a point on the mainland some miles southwest of Sand-bar Island, where we landed to stretch our legs and look at the vegetation, going inland a few steps, I discovered a fire still glowing beneath its ashes, where somebody had breakfasted, and a bed of twigs prepared for the following night. So I knew not only that they had just left, but that they designed to return, and by the breadth of the bed that there was more than one in the party. You might have gone within six feet of these signs without seeing them. There grew the beaked hazel, the only hazel which I saw on this journey, the *Diervilla*, rue seven feet high, which was very abundant on all the lake and river shores, and *Cornus stolonifera*, or red osier, whose bark, the Indian said, was good to smoke, and was called *maquoxigill,* "tobacco before white people came to this country, Indian tobacco."

The Indian was always very careful in approaching the shore, lest he should injure his canoe on the rocks, letting it swing round slowly sidewise, and was still more particular that we should not step into it on shore, nor till it floated free, and then should step gently lest we should open its seams, or make a hole in the bottom. He said that he would tell us when to jump.

> Thoreau's eye was constantly on the shoreline, his ear on the Penobscot language. After years of studying Indian books, he found Polis to be an excellent source of evidence about aboriginal life. Yet he was careful not to stereotype Polis, for the Indian's bilingualism and literacy made him atypical. The party landed for a stretch either at Deep Cove or Squaw Point, both four to six miles southwest of Sandbar Island.

(see page 169)

Soon after leaving this point we passed the mouth of the Kennebec, and heard and saw the falls at the dam there, for even Moosehead Lake is dammed. After passing Deer Island, we saw the little steamer from Greenville, far east in the middle of the lake, and she appeared nearly stationary. Sometimes we could hardly tell her from an island which had a few trees on it. Here we were exposed to the wind from over the whole breadth of the lake, and ran a little risk of being swamped. While I had my eye fixed on the spot where a large fish had leaped, we took in a gallon or two of water, which filled my lap; but we soon reached the shore and took the canoe over the bar, at Sandbar Island, a few feet wide only, and so saved a considerable distance. One landed first at a more sheltered place, and walking round caught the canoe by the prow, to prevent it being injured against the shore.

Again we crossed a broad bay opposite the mouth of Moose River, before reaching the narrow strait at Mount Kineo, made what the voyageurs call a *traverse,* and found the water quite rough. A very little wind on these broad lakes raises a sea which will swamp a canoe. Looking off from a lee shore, the surface may appear to be very little agitated, almost smooth, a mile distant, or if you see a few white crests they appear nearly level with the rest of the lake; but when you get out so far, you may find quite a sea running, and erelong, before you think of it, a wave will gently creep up the side of the canoe and fill your lap, like a monster deliberately covering you with its slime before it swallows you, or it will strike the canoe violently and break into it. The same thing may happen when the wind rises suddenly, though it were perfectly calm and smooth there a few minutes before; so that nothing can save you, unless you can swim ashore, for it is impossible to get into a canoe again when it is upset. Since you sit flat on the bottom, though the danger should not be imminent, a little water is a great inconvenience, not to mention the wetting of your provisions. We rarely crossed even a bay directly, from point to point, when there was wind, but made a slight curve corresponding somewhat to the shore, that we might the sooner reach it if the wind increased.

When the wind is aft, and not too strong, the Indian makes a spritsail of his blanket. He thus easily skims over the whole length of this lake in a day.

The Indian paddled on one side, and one of us on the other, to keep the canoe steady, and when he wanted to change hands he would say "t'other side." He asserted, in answer to our questions, that he had never upset a canoe himself, though he may have been upset by others.

Think of our little egg-shell of a canoe tossing across that great lake, a mere black speck to the eagle soaring above it!

My companion trailed for trout as we paddled along, but the Indian warning him that a big fish might upset us, for there are some very large ones there, he agreed to pass the line quickly to him in the stern if he had a bite. Beside trout, I heard of cusk, white-fish, &c., as found in this lake.

While we were crossing this bay, where Mount Kineo rose dark before us, within two or three miles, the Indian repeated the tradition respecting this mountain's having anciently been a cow moose,—how a mighty Indian hunter, whose name I forget, succeeded in killing this queen of the moose tribe with great difficulty, while her calf was killed somewhere among the islands in Penobscot Bay, and, to his eyes, this mountain had still the form of the moose in a reclining posture, its precipitous side presenting the outline of her head. He told this at some length, though it did not amount to much, and with apparent good faith, and asked us how we supposed the hunter could have killed such a mighty moose as that,—how we could do it. Whereupon a man-of-war to fire broadsides into her was suggested, etc. An Indian tells such a story as if he thought it deserved to have a good deal said about it, only he has not got it to say, and so he makes up for the deficiency by a drawling tone, long-windedness, and a dumb wonder which he hopes will be contagious.

We approached the land again through pretty rough water, and then steered directly across the lake, at its narrowest part, to the eastern side, and were soon partly under the lee of the mountain, about a mile north of the Kineo House, having paddled about twenty miles. It was now about noon.

We designed to stop there that afternoon and night, and spent half an hour looking along the shore northward for a suitable place to camp. We took out all our baggage at one place in vain, it being too rocky and uneven, and while engaged in this search we made our first acquaintance with the moose-fly. At length, half a mile further north, by going half a dozen rods into the dense spruce and fir wood on the side of the mountain, almost as dark as a cellar, we found a place sufficiently clear and level to lie down on, after cutting away a few bushes. We required a space only seven feet by six for our bed, the fire being four or five feet in front, though it made no odds how rough the hearth was; but it was not always easy to find this in those woods. The Indian first cleared a path to it from the shore with his axe, and we then carried up all our baggage, pitched our tent, and made our bed, in order to be ready for foul weather, which then threatened us, and for the night. He gathered a large armful of fir twigs, breaking them off, which he said were the best for our bed, partly, I thought, because they were the largest and could be most rapidly collected. It had been raining more or less for four or five days, and the wood was even damper than usual, but he got dry bark for the fire from the under-side of a dead leaning hemlock, which, he said, he could always do.

This noon his mind was occupied with a law question, and I referred him to my companion, who was a lawyer. It appeared that he had been buying land lately, (I think it was a hundred acres,) but there was probably an incumbrance to it, somebody else claiming to have bought some grass on it for this year. He wished to know to whom the grass belonged, and was told that if the other man could prove that he bought the grass before he, Polis, bought the land, the former could take it, whether the latter knew it or not. To which he only answered, "Strange!" He went over this several times, fairly sat down to it, with his back to a tree, as if he meant to confine us to this topic henceforth; but as he made no headway, only reached the jumping-off place of his wonder at white men's institutions after each explanation, we let the subject die.

He said that he had fifty acres of grass, potatoes, &c., somewhere above Oldtown, beside some about his house; that he hired a good deal of his work, hoeing, &c., and preferred white men to Indians, because "they keep steady, and know how."

What Thoreau called "the mouth of the Kennebec" is the *(see page 170)* East Outlet of the Kennebec River, at the village of Moosehead. Sandbar Island is three miles northeast; Spencer Bay lies opposite the mouth of the Moose River. His "traverse" began two or three miles below present- *(see page 170)* day Rockwood. A modern aluminum canoe, longer and heavier, should track better than birchbarks in the lake winds, which arise most afternoons. As Thoreau noted, the proper heading is cross-quarters to the wind, curving to correspond with the shore.

Mt. Kineo rises 769 feet above the lake's normal pool

(see page 171) elevation of 1,029 feet. Polis's tale resembles many old legends about Kineo, which was famous to Indians because its flintstone was a source for arrowpoints and tools. On his 1853 trip Thoreau described the mountain as a rounded peninsula, attached to the eastern shore by a slender causeway. The north end is wooded, the south end rocky; the western precipice overlooks North Bay, *(see page 172)* where the water is 540 feet deep. Kineo House is still on the lakeshore, beneath the mountain's southern base. The canoe party did not stay here, but made camp half a mile down shore, north of Kineo Cove.

After dinner we returned southward along the shore, in the canoe, on account of the difficulty of climbing over the rocks and fallen trees, and began to ascend the mountain along the edge of the precipice. But a smart shower coming up just then, the Indian crept under his canoe, while we, being protected by our rubber coats, proceeded to botanize. So we sent him back to the camp for shelter, agreeing that he should come there for us with his canoe toward night. It had rained a little in the forenoon, and we trusted that this would be the clearing-up shower, which it proved; but our feet and legs were thoroughly wet by the bushes. The clouds breaking away a little, we had a glorious wild view, as we ascended, of the broad lake with its fluctuating surface and numerous forest-clad islands, extending beyond our sight both north and south, and the boundless forest undulating away from its shores on every side, as densely packed as a rye-field, and enveloping nameless mountains in succession; but above all, looking westward over a large island was visible a very distant part of the lake, though we did not then suspect it to be Moosehead,—at first a mere broken white line seen through the tops of the island trees, like haycaps, but spreading to a lake when we got higher. Beyond this we saw what appears to be called Bald Mountain on the map, some twenty-five miles distant, near the sources of the Penobscot. It was a perfect lake of the woods. But this was only a transient gleam, for the rain was not quite over.

Looking southward, the heavens were completely overcast, the mountains capped with clouds, and the lake generally wore a dark and stormy appearance, but from its surface just north of Sugar Island, six or eight miles distant, there was reflected upward to us through the misty air a bright blue tinge from the distant unseen sky of another latitude beyond. They probably had a clear sky then at Greenville, the south end of the lake. Standing on a mountain in the midst of a lake, where would you look for the first sign of approaching fair weather? Not into the heavens, it seems, but into the lake.

Again we mistook a little rocky islet seen through the "drisk," with some taller bare trunks or stumps on it, for the steamer with its smoke-pipes, but as it had not changed its position after half an hour, we were undeceived. So much do the works of man resemble the works of nature. A moose might mistake a steamer for a floating isle, and not be scared till he heard its puffing or its whistle.

If I wished to see a mountain or other scenery under the most favorable auspices, I would go to it in foul weather, so as to be there when it cleared up; we are then in the most suitable mood, and nature is most fresh and inspiring. There is no serenity so fair as that which is just established in a tearful eye.

Jackson, in his Report on the Geology of Maine, in 1838, says of this mountain: "Hornstone, which will answer for flints, occurs in various parts of the State, where trap-rocks have acted upon silicious slate. The largest mass of this stone known in the world is Mount Kineo, upon Moosehead Lake, which appears to be entirely composed of it, and rises seven hundred feet above the lake level. This variety of hornstone I have seen in every part of New England in the form of Indian arrow-heads, hatchets, chisels, etc., which were probably obtained from this mountain by the aboriginal inhabitants of the country." I have myself found hundreds of arrow-heads made of the same material. It is generally slate-colored, with white specks, becoming a uniform white where exposed to the light and air, and it breaks with a conchoidal fracture, producing a ragged cutting edge. I noticed some conchoidal hollows more than a foot in diameter. I picked up a small thin piece which had so sharp an edge that I used it as a dull knife, and to see what I could do, fairly cut off an aspen one inch thick with it, by bending it and making many cuts; though I cut my fingers badly with the back of it in the meanwhile.

From the summit of the precipice which forms the southern and

eastern sides of this mountain peninsula, and is its most remarkable
feature, being described as five or six hundred feet high, we looked,
and probably might have jumped down to the water, or to the seemingly dwarfish trees on the narrow neck of land which connects it with
the main. It is a dangerous place to try the steadiness of your nerves.
Hodge says that these cliffs descend "perpendicularly ninety feet"
below the surface of the water.

The plants which chiefly attracted our attention on this mountain
were the mountain cinquefoil *(Potentilla tridentata)*, abundant and
in bloom still at the very base, by the water-side, though it is usually
confined to the summits of mountains in our latitude; very beautiful
harebells overhanging the precipice; bear-berry; the Canada blueberry *(Vaccinium Canadense)*, similar to the *V. Pennsylvanicum*,
our earliest one, but entire leaved and with a downy stem and leaf;
I have not seen it in Massachusetts; *Diervilla trifida; Microstylis
ophioglossoides*, an orchidaceous plant new to us; wild holly *(Nemopanthes Canadensis)*; the great round-leaved orchis *(Platanthera
orbiculata)*, not long in bloom; *Spiranthes cernua*, at the top; bunchberry, reddening as we ascended, green at the base of the mountain,
red at the top; and the small fern, *Woodsia ilvensis*, growing in tufts,
now in fruit. I have also received *Liparis liliifolia*, or twayblade,
from this spot. Having explored the wonders of the mountain, and the
weather being now entirely cleared up, we commenced the descent.
We met the Indian, puffing and panting, about one third of the way
up, but thinking that he must be near the top, and saying that it took
his breath away. I thought that superstition had something to do with
his fatigue. Perhaps he believed that he was climbing over the back
of a tremendous moose. He said that he had never ascended Kineo.
On reaching the canoe we found that he had caught a lake trout
weighing about three pounds, at the depth of twenty-five or thirty
feet, while we were on the mountain.

> The Mt. Kineo summit trail begins on the northwest
> shore, ascends northeast to 1,500 feet, makes a southerly
> switchback, then heads northeast again to a lookout
> tower. The total distance is one third of a mile, about
> forty-five minutes' walking time over a marked path.

Polis chose to stay put while Thoreau and Hoar climbed and botanized. During the ascent they followed the present trail, looking north and south at the lake and its surrounding forest. Their view northwest was over *(see page 174)* Farm Island; Boundary Bald Mountain is twenty-four miles northwest—eight miles from Canada, near the South Branch of the Penobscot River. Sugar Island is seven miles southeast, and the "rocky islet" is either Moody or Farm Island. Thoreau took the view here as a small but welcome reward; it demonstrated how the cycles of weather and mood could frame his life.

The mountain's hard, fine-grained flint also interested *(see page 175)* him; many visitors have found ancient artifacts at the southeast base, close by the precipice. His scrambling about the summit contrasted sharply with Polis's holding back. Polis was no mountain climber and so remained close to Indian tradition, in that respect.

When we got to the camp, the canoe was taken out and turned over, and a log laid across it to prevent its being blown away. The Indian cut some large logs of damp and rotten hard wood to smoulder and keep fire through the night. The trout was fried for supper. Our tent was of thin cotton cloth and quite small, forming with the ground a triangular prism closed at the rear end, six feet long, seven wide, and four high, so that we could barely sit up in the middle. It required two forked stakes, a smooth ridgepole, and a dozen or more pins to pitch it. It kept off dew and wind, and an ordinary rain, and answered our purpose well enough. We reclined within it till bedtime, each with his baggage at his head, or else sat about the fire, having hung our wet clothes on a pole before the fire for the night.

As we sat there, just before night, looking out through the dusky wood, the Indian heard a noise which he said was made by a snake. He imitated it at my request, making a low whistling note,—*pheet— pheet,*—two or three times repeated, somewhat like the peep of the hylodes, but not so loud. In answer to my inquiries, he said that he had never seen them while making it, but going to the spot he finds the snake. This, he said on another occasion, was a sign of rain.

When I had selected this place for our camp, he had remarked that there were snakes there,—he saw them. But they won't do any hurt, I said. "O no," he answered, "just as you say, it makes no difference to me."

He lay on the right side of the tent, because, as he said, he was partly deaf in one ear, and he wanted to lie with his good ear up. As we lay there, he inquired if I ever heard "Indian sing." I replied that I had not often, and asked him if he would not favor us with a song. He readily assented, and lying on his back, with his blanket wrapped around him, he commenced a slow, somewhat nasal, yet musical chant, in his own language, which probably was taught his tribe long ago by the Catholic missionaries. He translated it to us, sentence by sentence, afterward, wishing to see if we could remember it. It proved to be a very simple religious exercise or hymn, the burden of which was, that there was only one God who ruled all the world. This was hammered (or sung) out very thin, so that some stanzas wellnigh meant nothing at all, merely keeping up the idea. He then said that he would sing us a Latin song; but we did not detect any Latin, only one or two Greek words in it,—the rest may have been Latin with the Indian pronunciation.

His singing carried me back to the period of the discovery of America, to San Salvador and the Incas, when Europeans first encountered the simple faith of the Indian. There was, indeed, a beautiful simplicity about it; nothing of the dark and savage, only the mild and infantile. The sentiments of humility and reverence chiefly were expressed.

> The contrarities in Polis's character continued to emerge during their first evening in camp: his calls and songs were evocative, carrying Thoreau back in memory to the age of exploration. During the night, when he found a perfect ring of fox fire, he learned that discovery is always possible. This mystery would prevail over all the learning of science; it became a final message to him of
> *(see page 179)* nature's purpose, "the light that dwells in rotten wood."

It was a dense and damp spruce and fir wood in which we lay, and, except for our fire, perfectly dark; and when I awoke in the night, I either heard an owl from deeper in the forest behind us, or a loon from a distance over the lake. Getting up some time after midnight to collect the scattered brands together, while my companions were sound asleep, I observed, partly in the fire, which had ceased to blaze, a perfectly regular elliptical ring of light, about five inches in its shortest diameter, six or seven in its longer, and from one eighth to one quarter of an inch wide. It was fully as bright as the fire, but not reddish or scarlet like a coal, but a white and slumbering light, like the glowworm's. I could tell it from the fire only by its whiteness. I saw at once that it must be phosphorescent wood, which I had so often heard of, but never chanced to see. Putting my finger on it, with a little hesitation, I found that it was a piece of dead moose-wood *(Acer striatum)* which the Indian had cut off in a slanting direction the evening before. Using my knife, I discovered that the light proceeded from that portion of the sap-wood immediately under the bark, and thus presented a regular ring at the end, which, indeed, appeared raised above the level of the wood, and when I pared off the bark and cut into the sap, it was all aglow along the log. I was surprised to find the wood quite hard and apparently sound, though probably decay had commenced in the sap, and I cut out some little triangular chips, and placing them in the hollow of my hand, carried them into the camp, waked my companion, and showed them to him. They lit up the inside of my hand, revealing the lines and wrinkles, and appearing exactly like coals of fire raised to a white heat, and I saw at once how, probably, the Indian jugglers had imposed on their people and on travellers, pretending to hold coals of fire in their mouths.

I also noticed that part of a decayed stump within four or five feet of the fire, an inch wide and six inches long, soft and shaking wood, shone with equal brightness.

I neglected to ascertain whether our fire had anything to do with this, but the previous day's rain and long-continued wet weather undoubtedly had.

I was exceedingly interested by this phenomenon, and already felt paid for my journey. It could hardly have thrilled me more if it had taken the form of letters, or of the human face. If I had met with this ring of light while groping in this forest alone, away from any fire, I should have been still more surprised. I little thought that

there was such a light shining in the darkness of the wilderness for
me.

The next day the Indian told me their name for this light,—*Artoosoqu'*,—and on my inquiring concerning the will-o'-the-wisp, and
the like phenomena, he said that his "folks" sometimes saw fires
passing along at various heights, even as high as the trees, and making a noise. I was prepared after this to hear of the most startling and
unimagined phenomena witnessed by "his folks," they are abroad at
all hours and seasons in scenes so unfrequented by white men. Nature
must have made a thousand revelations to them which are still secrets
to us.

I did not regret my not having seen this before, since I now saw it
under circumstances so favorable. I was in just the frame of mind to
see something wonderful, and this was a phenomenon adequate to my
circumstances and expectation, and it put me on the alert to see more
like it. I exulted like "a pagan suckled in a creed" that had never been
worn at all, but was bran new, and adequate to the occasion. I let
science slide, and rejoiced in that light as if it had been a fellow-
creature. I saw that it was excellent, and was very glad to know that
it was so cheap. A scientific *explanation,* as it is called, would have
been altogether out of place there. That is for pale daylight. Science
with its *retorts* would have put me to sleep; it was the opportunity
to be ignorant that I improved. It suggested to me that there was
something to be seen if one had eyes. It made a believer of me more
than before. I believed that the woods were not tenantless, but choke-
full of honest spirits as good as myself any day,—not an empty chamber, in which chemistry was left to work alone, but an inhabited house,
—and for a few moments I enjoyed fellowship with them. Your so-
called wise man goes trying to persuade himself that there is no entity
there but himself and his traps, but it is a great deal easier to believe
the truth. It suggested, too, that the same experience always gives
birth to the same sort of belief or religion. One revelation has been
made to the Indian, another to the white man. I have much to learn
of the Indian, nothing of the missionary. I am not sure but all that
would tempt me to teach the Indian my religion would be his promise
to teach me *his.* Long enough I had heard of irrelevant things; now
at length I was glad to make acquaintance with the light that dwells

in rotten wood. Where is all your knowledge gone to? It evaporates completely, for it has no depth.

I kept those little chips and wet them again the next night, but they emitted no light.

. . .

Thoreau published an "Appendix" to *The Maine Woods* that lists his findings as a naturalist. Here are two segments of special interest.

VI. OUTFIT FOR AN EXCURSION

The following will be a good outfit for one who wishes to make an excursion of *twelve* days into the Maine woods in July, with a companion, and one Indian for the same purposes that I did.

Wear,—a check shirt, stout old shoes, thick socks, a neck ribbon, thick waistcoat, thick pants, old Kossuth hat, a linen sack.

Carry,—in an India-rubber knapsack, with a large flap, two shirts (check), one pair thick socks, one pair drawers, one flannel shirt, two pocket-handkerchiefs, a light India-rubber coat or a thick woollen one, two bosoms and collars to go and come with, one napkin, pins, needles, thread, one blanket, best gray, seven feet long.

Tent, six by seven feet, and four feet high in middle, will do; veil and gloves and insect-wash, or, better, mosquito-bars to cover all at night; best pocket-map, and perhaps description of the route; compass; plant-book and red blotting-paper; paper and stamps, botany, small pocket spy-glass for birds, pocket microscope, tape-measure, insect-boxes.

Axe, full size if possible, jackknife, fish-lines, two only apiece, with a few hooks and corks ready, and with pork for bait in a packet, rigged; matches (some also in a small vial in the waistcoat pocket); soap, two pieces; large knife and iron spoon (for all); three or four old newspapers, much twine, and several rags for dishcloths; twenty feet of strong cord, four-quart tin pail for kettle, two tin dippers, three tin plates, a fry-pan.

Provisions.—Soft hardbread, twenty-eight pounds; pork, sixteen pounds; sugar, twelve pounds; one pound black tea or three pounds coffee, one box or a pint of salt, one quart Indian meal, to fry fish in;

six lemons, good to correct the pork and warm water; perhaps two or three pounds of rice, for variety. You will probably get some berries, fish, &c., beside.

A gun is not worth the carriage, unless you go as hunters. The pork should be in an open keg, sawed to fit; the sugar, tea or coffee, meal, salt, &c., should be put in separate water-tight India-rubber bags, tied with a leather string; and all the provisions, and part of the rest of the baggage, put into two large India-rubber bags, which have been proved to be water-tight and durable. Expense of preceding outfit is twenty-four dollars.

An Indian may be hired for about one dollar and fifty cents per day, and perhaps fifty cents a week for his canoe (this depends on the demand). The canoe should be a strong and tight one. This expense will be nineteen dollars.

Such an excursion need not cost more than twenty-five dollars apiece, starting at the foot of Moosehead, if you already possess or can borrow a reasonable part of the outfit. If you take an Indian and canoe at Oldtown, it will cost seven or eight dollars more to transport them to the lake.

VII. A LIST OF INDIAN WORDS

I. *Katadn*, said to mean *Highest Land*. Rasles puts for mountain *Pemadené;* for *Grai, pierre à aiguiser, Kidadañgan.* (v. Potter.)

Mattawamkeag, place where two rivers meet. (Indian of carry.) (v. Williamson's History of Maine, and Willis.)

Molunkus.

Ebeeme, rock.

Noliseemack; other name, Shad Pond.

Kecunnilessu, chicadee.

Nipsquecohossus, woodcock.

Skuscumonsuk, kingfisher. Has it not the pl. termination *uk* here, or *suk?*

Wassus, bear. *Aouessous.* Rasles.

Lunxus, Indian-devil.

Upahsis, mountain-ash.

Moose, (is it called, or does it mean, wood-eater?) *Mous*, Rasles.

Joe.

Katahdinauguoh, said to mean mountains about Ktaadn.

Ebemena, tree-cranberry. *Ibimin, nar,* red, bad fruit. Rasles. ⎱ Joe.

Wighiggin, a bill or writing. *Aouixigan, "Livre, lettre, peinture, écriture."* Rasles. ⎱ Indian of carry.

Sebamook, Large-bay Lake. *Pegouasebem;* add *ar* for plural, *lac* or *étang.* Rasles. *Ouañrinañgamek, anse dans un lac.* Rasles. *Mspame,* large water. Polis. ⎱ Nicholai.

Sebago and *Sebec,* large open water.

Chesuncook, place where many streams empty in. (v. Willis and Potter.)

Caucomgomoc, Gull Lake. (*Caucomgomoc,* the lake; *Caucomgomoc-took,* the river, Polis.) ⎱ Tahmunt, &c.

Pammadumcook.

Kenduskieg, Little Eel River. (v. Willis.) ⎱ Nicholai.

Penobscot, Rocky River. *Pouapeskou,* stone. Rasles. (v. Springer.) ⎱ Indian of carry.

Umbazookskus, meadow stream. (Much-meadow river, Polis.)

Millinocket, place of Islands. ⎱ Nicholai.

Souneunk, that runs between Mountains.

Aboljacarmegus, Smooth-ledge Falls and Dead-water.

Aboljacarmeguscook, the river there.

Musketicook, Dead Stream. (Indian of carry.) *Meskikou,* or *Meskikouikou,* a place where there is grass. (Rasles.) *Muskéeticook,* Dead water. (Polis.)

Mattahumkeag, Sand-creek Pond.

Piscataquis, branch of a river. ⎱ Nicholai.

Shecorways, sheldrakes.

Naramekechus, peetweet. ⎱ Polis.

Medawisla, loon.

Orignal, Moosehead Lake. (Montresor.)

Chor-chor-que, usnea.

Adelungquamooktum, wood-thrush.

Bematinichtik, high land generally. (Mountain, *Pemadené,* Rasles.) ⎱ Polis.

Maquoxigil, bark of red osier, Indian tobacco.

Kineo, flint (Williamson); old Indian hunter (Hodge.)

Artoosoqu', phosphorescence.

Subekoondark, white spruce.

Skusk, black spruce.

Beskabekuk, the "Lobster Lake" of maps.

Beskabekukskishtook, the dead water below the island.

Paytaytequick, Burnt-Ground Stream, what Joe called *Ragmuff*.

Nonglangyis, the name of a dead-water between the last and Pine Stream.

Karsaootuk, Black River (or Pine Stream). *Mkazéouighen*, black. Rasles.

Michigan, fimus. Polis applied it to a sucker, or a poor, good-for-nothing fish. *Fiante (?), mitsegan*, Rasles. (Pickering puts the ? after the first word.)

Cowosnebagosar, Chiogenes hispidula; means, grows where trees have rotted.

Pockadunkquaywayle, echo. *Pagadañkouéouérre*. Rasles.

Bososquasis, moose-fly.

Nerlumskeechticook (or *quoik?*), (or *skeetcook*), Dead water, and applied to the mountains near.

Apmoojenegamook, lake that is crossed.

Allegash, hemlock-bark. (v. Willis.)

Paytaywecongomec, Burnt-Ground Lake, *Telos*.

Madunkehunk, Height-of-land Stream (Webster Stream).

Madunkehunk-gamooc, Height-of-land Lake.

Matungamooc, Grand Lake.

Uncardnerheese, Trout Stream.

Wassataquoik (or *-cook*), Salmon River, East Branch. (v. Willis.)

Pemoymenuk, Amelanchier berries. "*Pemouaïmin, nak*, a black fruit." Rasles. Has it not here the plural ending?

Polis.

Polis.

Sheepnoc, Lilium Canadense bulbs. *"Sipen, nak,* white, larger than *penak."* Rasles.

Paytgumkiss, Petticoat (where a small river comes into the Penobscot below Nickatow).

Burntibus, a lake-like reach in the Penobscot.

} Polis.

Passadumkeag, "where the water falls into the Penobscot above the falls." (Williamson.) *Pañsidañkioui* is, *au dessus de la montagne.* Rasles.

Olarmon, or *larmon,* (Polis) red paint. "Vermilion, paint, *Ourámañ."* Rasles.

Sunkhaze, "See canoe come out; no see 'em stream." (Polis.) The mouth of a river, according to Rasles, is *Sañghedétegoué.* The place where one stream empties into another, thus ∮, is *sañktaïoui.* (v. Willis.)

Tomhegan Brook (at Moosehead). "Hatchet, *temahígan."* Rasles.

Nickatow, "Niketaoutegoué, or *Niketoutegoué, rivière qui fourche."* Rasles.

Vermont &
New Hampshire

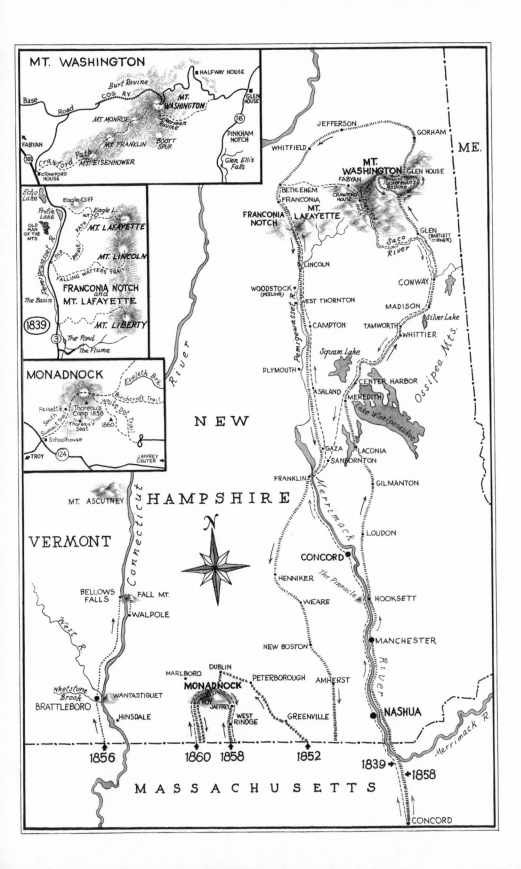

MT. WASHINGTON

HALFWAY HOUSE
Burt Ravine
COG. RY.
Base
Road
MT. WASHINGTON
GLEN HOUSE
MT. MONROE
Tuckerman Ravine
FABYAN
MT. FRANKLIN
BOOTT SPUR
16
PINKHAM NOTCH
302
Crawford Path
MT. EISENHOWER
CRAWFORD HOUSE
Glen Elli's Falls

Echo Lake
Eagle Cliff
Eagle L.
Profile Lake
HUT
OLD MAN OF THE MTS.
OLD BRIDLE PATH
MT. LAFAYETTE
Pemigewasset R.
MT. LINCOLN
FALLING WATERS TRAIL
FRANCONIA NOTCH *and* **MT. LAFAYETTE**
The Basin
1839
3
The Pond
MT. LIBERTY
The Flume

MONADNOCK

Eveleth Brk.
Birchcroft Trail
White Dot Trail
Fassetts
Thoreau's Camp 1858
Smith
Summit Trail
1860
Thoreau's Seat
Schoolhouse
TROY
124
JAFFREY CENTER

JEFFERSON
GORHAM
ME.
WHITFIELD
MT. WASHINGTON
GLEN HOUSE
FABYAN
Tuckerman's Ravine
BETHLEHEM
FRANCONIA
CRAWFORD HOUSE
FRANCONIA NOTCH
MT. LAFAYETTE
GLEN (BARTLETT CORNER)
Saco River
LINCOLN
CONWAY
WOODSTOCK (PEELING)
MADISON
WEST THORNTON
Pemigewasset R.
TAMWORTH
Silver Lake
CAMPTON
WHITTIER
PLYMOUTH
Squam Lake
Ossipee Mts.
ASHLAND
CENTER HARBOR
MEREDITH
Lake Winnipesaukee

N E W

GAZA
LACONIA
SANBORNTON
FRANKLIN
GILMANTON
Merrimack
MT. ASCUTNEY
H A M P S H I R E
LOUDON
CONCORD
N
VERMONT
HENNIKER
The Pinnacle
BELLOWS FALLS
FALL MT.
WEARE
HOOKSETT
WALPOLE
West R.
MANCHESTER
NEW BOSTON
Whetstone Brook
WANTASTIGUET
MARLBORO
DUBLIN
PETERBOROUGH
AMHERST
River
BRATTLEBORO
MONADNOCK
TROY
JAFFREY
GREENVILLE
NASHUA
HINSDALE
WEST RINDGE
Merrimack R.
1856
1860 1858
1852
1839
1858

M A S S A C H U S E T T S

CONCORD

Wantastiquet

*This town will be convicted of folly if they ever permit
this mountain to be laid bare.*

Up on Wantastiquet, the air is clear this afternoon. A light
breeze carries sounds from Brattleboro: dogs bark, traffic grinds
against a fire horn. Far west of town are the Green Mountains, blue in
a gathering haze. Sundown is coming on, the end of a warm day in
June. Yet the mountain rustles with a constant patter, a sound like
early drops of rain. The gypsy-moth larvae are feeding.

Millions of them are eating and casting, stripping the trees and
showering the ground with black-pepper crumbs of scat. Boot soles
make a soft, dry crunch. Gypsies, en masse: under the leaves, backlit
by sun, they form black lines and curls; from bare limbs they hang in
long festoons, making a slow descent to the earth. There they crawl
about blindly, searching for new trunks to climb.

With their yellow heads and blue-russet bodies, the larvae seem
enticing enough for predators—but few appetites can tolerate their
tannic acid. The gypsies are free to flourish. They dine on young
leaves, preferably oaks, but also birch or maple. On Wantastiquet this
June, the shrub oaks are bare, and bigger trees are going rapidly. Trees
can survive a broken foliage cycle for one or two years. But if the
gypsies return again and again, these trees may be doomed.

This infestation is a modern dilemma, caused by the accidental
release of moths in 1866. When Henry Thoreau came to Vermont in
1856, he could still hold to his benign view of nature. Yet his ideas were
changing, for he had become a self-taught naturalist. He spent many
hours collecting plants and animals, then writing accounts in his

Journal. On field trips he carried the tools of a scientist: tape measure, pocket microscope, spyglass for observing birds, and boxes to hold insects. He stored plants in the lining of his straw hat; at home he pressed them between sheets of blotting paper and the leaves of an old music book. (Hence his frequent aside in the Journal, "*Vide* [see] press.") He corresponded with noted scientists of the day, read the authorities in botany and zoology.

Thoreau's aims were not scientific, but neither did these studies clearly advance his literary career. By the fall of 1856 it had been two years since he had published *Walden,* and this quiet spell continued until 1858, when an essay on Maine appeared in the *Atlantic Monthly.* He kept busy writing, mostly in the Journal, but he managed to publish only small portions of that voluminous text before he died in 1862.

Bronson Alcott, who resided at Walpole, N.H., in 1856, had often invited Thoreau to visit; when he finally accepted, his motives were not wholly social. The Connecticut River valley, which lies on the Vermont–New Hampshire border, offered an opportunity to study plants in a high northern location, he wrote, "to get some hints from September on the Connecticut to help me understand that season on the Concord." He was beginning to move from the early stages of his work, identifying species and habitats, to examining the larger patterns of plant dispersal. His trip lasted one week, during which he explored both sides of the river, from Brattleboro north to Bellows Falls, then south to Walpole. Along the way, he climbed two rather low summits, Wantastiquet and Fall Mountain.

J O U R N A L

ROUTE FROM
CONCORD: *MA 2 to*
I-91, to
Brattleboro

Thoreau left Concord on Friday, September 5, 1856, taking the railway cars from his local depot to Fitchburg. There he discovered that the next train to Vermont would not arrive for several hours. Rather than wait, he shouldered his valise and walked along the tracks for six

miles, to Westminster. Along the way he botanized, noting the conditions of flowers and berries, finding a variety of willow that was rare in Concord. For the entire
course of his northern trip, he improvised in this fashion, making plans and then adjusting them to suit new
situations. In the decade since Katahdin, he had learned
to subdue his prejudices, discarding old ideas for the
sake of new evidence. His trip became a register of these
mental habits, the patience and tolerance that natural
history had taught him.

Brattleboro, Vt.

In Brattleboro, Thoreau stayed four days at the home
of Addison Brown, a former Unitarian minister then active in education and the local Lyceum. Thoreau spent
many hours consulting with Charles Frost, a shoemaker
who had become a prominent botanist. Frost had mas-
tered several languages and sciences; he was an en-
couraging example to a fellow amateur. From him, Thoreau obtained many plants and learned references; also

the surprising news that the famous polar explorer, Dr. Elisha Kane, had recently stayed in town. Kane had worked on the proof sheets of his book, *Arctic Explorations* (1856), which listed many alpine plants. Frost had a souvenir set of the proofs, which Thoreau borrowed and read. After publication, he used the book to study arctic-alpine species in the White Mountains.

(see page 243)

He made some quiet explorations of his own in Brattleboro, walking the Connecticut and West River banks, searching brooks and hillsides for evidence of new plants. Unimpressed by the Connecticut, he wrote: "The Concord is worth a hundred of it for my purposes." Yet on the Coldwater Path, a steep hillside trail along Whetstone Brook (now in West Brattleboro, north of VT 9), he found something that Concord lacked.

There for the first time I see growing indigenously the *Dirca palustris*, leather-wood, the largest on the low interval by the brook. I notice a bush there seven feet high. In its form it is somewhat like a quince bush, though less spreading, its leaves broad, like entire sassafras leaves; now beginning to turn yellow. It has a remarkably strong thick bark and soft white wood which bends like lead (Gray says it is brittle!), the different layers separating at the end. I cut a good-sized switch, which was singularly tough and flexible, just like a cowhide, and would answer the purpose of one admirably. The color of the bark is a very pale brown. I was much interested in this shrub, since it was the Indian's rope. Frost said that the farmers of Vermont used it to tie up their fences with. Certainly there can be no wood equal to it as a withe. He says it is still strong when dry. I should think it would be worth the while for the farmers to cultivate for this purpose. How often in the woods and fields we want a string or rope and cannot find one. This is the plant which Nature has made for this purpose. The Browns gave me some of the flowers, which appear very early in spring. Gray says that in northern New England it is called *wicopy*. Potter, in History of Manchester, says Indians sewed canoes with it. Beck says, "The bark has a sweetish taste, and when chewed excites a burning sensation in the fauces," and, according to Emerson, the bark of this family, "taken into the stomach causes heat and vomiting, or purging." According to the latter, cordage has been made from the bark of this family, also paper. Emerson says of this plant in particular, "The fresh bark produces a sensation of heat in the stomach, and at last brings on vomiting. . . . It has such strength that a man cannot pull apart so much as covers a branch of half or a third of an inch in diameter. It is used by millers and others for thongs." Indian cordage. I feel as if I had discovered a more indigenous plant than usual, it was so peculiarly useful to the aborigines.

On that wooded hillside, I find small-flowered asters, *A. miser*-like, hairy, but very long linear leaves; possibly the var. *hirsuta* of *A. miser* (Oakes gives of *A. miser*, only the var. *hirsuticaulis* to Vermont) or else a neighboring species, for they seem distinct. (*Vide* press.)* There is the hobble-bush with its berries and large roundish leaves, now beginning to turn a deep dull crimson red. Also mountain maples, with sharp-lobed leaves and downy beneath, the young plants numerous. The *Ribes cynosbati*, or prickly gooseberry, with its bur-like fruit, dry and still hanging here and there. Also the ground-hemlock, with its beautiful fruit, like a red waxen cup with a purple (?) fruit in it. By the edge of a ditch, where it had been overwhelmed and buried with mud by the later freshet, the *Solidago Muhlenbergii* in its prime. (*Vide* press.) Near by, on the bank of the ditch, leaves of coltsfoot. I had cut across the interval, but, taking to the Cold-water Path again near its southeast end, I found, at an angle in it near the canal, beech-drops under a beech, not yet out, and the *Equisetum scirpoides*, also radical leaves, very broad, perhaps of a sedge, some much longer. (*Vide* press.)

Gathered flowering raspberries in all my walks and found them a pleasant berry, large, but never abundant. In a wet place on the interval the *Veronica Americana*, according to Frost (*beccabunga* of some), not in bloom. Along this path observed the *Nabalus altissimus*, flowers in a long panicle of axillary and terminal branches, small-flowered, now in prime. Leaves apparently of *Oxalis Acetosella*. Large roundish radical leaves on the moist wooded hillside, which the Browns thought of the round-leaved violet. Low, flat-

---

**Thoreau's dried plant collection.—*WH

topped, very rough hairy, apparently *Aster acuminatus*. *Erigeron annuus*, broad, thin, toothed leaves. Also another, perhaps hirsute *A. miser*, with toothed leaves.

I hear that two thousand dollars' worth of huckleberries have been sold by the town of Ashby this season.

Also gathered on this walk the *Polypodium Dryopteris* and *Polystichum acrostichoides* and a short heavy-odored (like stramonium) plant with aspect of lilac, not in bloom. (*Vide* press.)

(see page 194) Leatherwood is distinctive in appearance, but not rare; it favors woods that have a damp, rich humus. The bark is rough and pliant, cannot be torn by hand, and thus was used by Indians for making lines and baskets. Gray, *(see page 195)* Emerson, and Oakes were botanical authorities. In his unscientific fashion, Thoreau saw this plant as an object nature made for a purpose, not one that man adapted to his needs.

The Connecticut River looked narrow, he decided, because it was "dwarfed by the mountain rising directly from it." On September 9, he climbed Wantastiquet (then called "Chesterfield Mountain") and later wrote the following account in the Journal.

Sept. 9. Tuesday. 8 A.M.—Ascend the Chesterfield Mountain with Miss Frances and Miss Mary Brown.

The Connecticut is about twenty rods wide between Brattleboro and Hinsdale. This mountain, according to Frost, 1064 feet high. It is the most remarkable feature here. The village of Brattleboro is peculiar for the nearness of the primitive wood and the mountain. Within three rods of Brown's house was excellent botanical ground on the side of a primitive wooded hillside, and still better along the Coldwater Path. But, above all, this everlasting mountain is forever lowering over the village, shortening the day and wearing a misty cap each morning. You look up to its top at a steep angle from the village streets. A great part belongs to the Insane Asylum. This town will be convicted of folly if they ever permit this mountain to be laid bare. Francis [*sic*] B. says its Indian name is Wantastiquet, from the name of West River above. Very abundant about B. the *Gerardia tenui-folia*, in prime, which I at first mistook for the *purpurea*. The latter I did not see. High up the mountain the *Aster macrophyllus* as well as *corymbosus*. The (apparently) *Platanthera orbiculata* (?) leaves, round and flat on ground (*vide* press); another by it with larger and more oblong leaves. Pine-sap. A tuft of five-divided leaves, fifteen or eighteen inches high, slightly fern-like (*vide* press). *Galium circazans* var. *lanceolatum*. Top of the mountain covered with wood. Saw Ascutney, between forty and fifty miles up the river, but not Monadnock on account of woods.

Wantastiquet (Mt. Chesterfield)

P.M.—To and up a brook north of Brown's house.

A large alternate cornel, four or five inches in diameter, a dark-gray stem. The kidney-shaped leaves of the *Asarum Canadense* common there. *Panax quinquefolium*, with peculiar flat scarlet fruit in a little umbel. *Clinopodium vulgare*, or basil, apparently flatted down by a freshet, rather past prime; and spearmint in brook just above. Close behind Brown's, *Liparis liliifolia*, or tway-blade, leaves and bulb.

A very interesting sight from the top of the mountain was that of the cars so nearly under you, apparently creeping along, you could see so much of their course.

The epigæa was very abundant on the hill behind Brown's and elsewhere in B. The *Populus monilifera* grows on West River, but I did not see it. The *Erigeron Philadelphicus* I saw pressed, with innumerable fine rays. Scouring-rush was common along the Coldwater Path and elsewhere. . . .

ROUTE FROM I-91:
VT 9 (Molly
Stark Trail) to
VT 119
Wantastiquet lies on the New Hampshire side of the river; visitors must cross the Hinsdale bridge and take the first left turn to a parking lot for Wantastiquet State Forest. An alternate route approaches from the north, via Mountain Road and a fire trail; but Thoreau's ascent was probably from the south end.

The Browns had five daughters: Frances was twenty-two and the eldest; Mary, the youngest at fourteen, was greatly interested in plants and had corresponded with Thoreau. In 1858 he thanked her for a gift of mayflowers, then sent his regards to the mountain, "if you communicate with it; I suppose it has not budged an inch."

Wantastiquet has a large variety of plant life, for southern Vermont is the northern limit of species like dogwood and sassafras. The walking trail begins as a wide jeep track, lined with banks of fern; the roadbed itself is at first cobblestone, then gravel. This forest is partly fire-scarred, but many mature red pines survive. In late June, the blooming mountain laurel spreads its white, star-blown clusters along the path. At these lower levels, sedimentary rock is exposed, especially a dark gray-blue slate, flecked with glints of black and silver. Higher up are shelves and boulders of granite, with large veins of pale white quartz and some red-orange stains of oxidized iron. The wildlife now consists mostly of chipmunks and toads.

(see page 196)
The presence of a large insane asylum in Brattleboro perhaps suggested Thoreau's jest about the "folly" of laying the mountain bare. Today's gypsy moths would have

astonished him, for the only insects he saw were ants who built large colony hills (he recalled them in a later *(see page 234)* entry). His view took in Ascutney (fifty-one miles north) and Monadnock (thirty miles east). The present view of Brattleboro is less impressive; many offices and factory buildings now crowd the riverside.

The mountaintop is more open than Thoreau found, but the best view is still west. At the summit is a stone pillar, with memorial inscription, and every Christmas the local Scouts put a great star up here. Wantastiquet is part of Brattleboro tradition, but hardly a tourist attraction. No one else is on the trail today—only the gypsy moths, laying it bare.

The other sight in Brattleboro that interested Thoreau was the skin and skull of a panther, killed in the Adirondack Mountains by a Vermont hunter. Impressed by the animal's size and apparent strength, Thoreau wrote: "It gave one a new idea of our American forests and the vigor of nature here." He interviewed the hunter, took measurements, wrote a precise description. This skin was the best evidence he ever saw of the Adirondacks, a mountain region he did not live to visit.

Fall Mountain

JOURNAL

ROUTE FROM
BRATTLEBORO: *VT
5 to Bellows
Falls, NH 12 to
Fall Mountain* On September 10, Thoreau took the railroad twenty-seven miles north to Bellows Falls, Vermont, where he examined the falls, rocks, and potholes, a feature that always attracted his interest. Dam construction has now lowered water levels, revealing a set of Indian rock carvings that would have fascinated Thoreau. In reading a history of this area, he encountered a literary style that suited him well.

Sept. 10. 10.30 A.M.—Took the cars to Bellows Falls, through Dummerston, Putney, and Westminster.

Looked at the falls and rocks. River higher than usual at this season, yet could cross all but about twenty feet on the rocks. Some pot-holes of this form: [drawing] real pot-holes, but commonly several curves commingled, thus: [drawing] or the whole more rounded. Found, spreading prostrate on the rocks amid the pot-holes, apparently a small willow,* with shining dark-red stems and smooth, spatu-

---

Prunus depressa.

late, rather obtuse serrate leaves. (*Vide* press.) I read that salmon passed these falls but not shad. When the water is lowest, it is contracted to sixteen feet here, and Peters's, an old history of Connecticut, says it was so condensed that you could not thrust a crowbar into it. It did me good to read his wholesale hearty statements,—strong,

Bellows Falls and Fall Mountain

living, human speech, so much better than the emasculated modern histories, like Bancroft's and the rest, cursed with a style. I would rather read such histories, though every sentence were a falsehood, than our dull emasculated reports which bear the name of histories. The former, having a human breath and interest behind them, are nearer to nature and to truth, after all. The historian is required to feel a human interest in his subject and to so express it. President Dwight, speaking of the origin of those pot-holes, says, "The river now is often fuller than it probably ever was before the country above was cleared of its forests: the snows in open ground melting much more suddenly, and forming much greater freshets, than in forested ground."

> After crossing the river into New Hampshire, Thoreau turned south and soon left the road for some climbing.

Ascended the Fall Mountain with a heavy valise on my back, against the advice of the toll-man. But when I got up so soon and easily I was amused to remember his anxiety. It is seven hundred and fifty feet high, according to Gazetteer. Saw great red oaks on this hill, particularly tall, straight, and bare of limbs, for a great distance, amid the woods. Here, as at Brattleboro, a fine view of the country immediately beneath you; but these views lack breadth, a distant horizon. There is a complete view of the falls from this height.

Saw a pair of middle-sized black hawks hovering about this cliff, with some white spots, with peculiar shrill snapping notes like a gull, a new kind to me.

Descending the steep south end of this hill, I saw an apparent *Corydalis glauca*, mostly withered, three feet or more, and more than usually broad and stout in proportion. (*Vide* press.) My shoes were very smooth, and I got many falls descending, battering my valise. By the railroad below, the *Solanum nigrum*, with white flowers but yet green fruit.

Just after crossing Cold River, bathed in the Connecticut, evidently not far from site of the old Kilbourn fort. Clay-muddy shore. Near the site of the old Bellows Fort, saw completely purple *Polygala verticillata* abundant in road. . . .

Bellows Falls bridge and Fall Mountain

The trail entrance to Fall Mountain is on NH 12, north of the Bellows Falls bridge. In three-quarters of a mile the path makes four sharp turns, reaching an elevation of 1,080 feet. Northern red oaks are still abundant, but other species have crowded in as well—hence, the views are largely obscured. Fall Mountain (also known as Mt. Kilbourne) was an incidental climb for Thoreau: though he safely ascended despite warnings, on the descent he "got many falls" after all.

(see page 202)

ROUTE FROM FALL MOUNTAIN: *NH 123 to North Road, to Main Street, Walpole*

In Walpole, Thoreau stayed with Alcott in his home (now the town library) on Main Street. During his visit, Thoreau climbed what Alcott called "Farm Hill" (Wentworth Road). From there he viewed the entire Connecticut Valley and Ascutney (thirty-two miles north), but again not Monadnock. He also visited the village graveyard (one mile north on VT 12) and saw a "recent monument" erected to Benjamin Bellows—its date is 1854. That evening he read an old pamphlet history of the Bellows family, enjoying its fabulous accounts of foxes, wolves, and panthers in this area. He counted up sixty-two species of plants collected on the trip, a goodly haul, and made his way home to Concord on September 12. There he reviewed his days spent in the hills and river valley, then turned with fresh gratitude to the pleasures of home.

Sept. 13. Saturday. At Concord.—After all, I am struck by the greater luxuriance of the same species of plants here than up-country, though our soil is considered leaner. Also I think that no view I have had of the Connecticut Valley, at Brattleboro or Walpole, is equal to that of the Concord from Nawshawtuct. Here is a more interesting horizon, more variety and richness. Our river is much the most fertile in every sense. Up there it is nothing but river-valley and hills. Here there is so much more that we have forgotten that we live in a valley.

The
White Mountains

*The scenery in Conway and onward to North Conway
is surprisingly grand. You are steadily advancing
into an amphitheatre of mountains.*

In the high country of northeast New Hampshire, more than thirty peaks rise above 4,000 feet. To the Indians who hunted in these mountain valleys, the "white rocks" were sacred heights, home of the Great Spirit and not to be scaled by mortals. The first recorded climb was made in 1642 by Darby Field, a colonist who hoped to find precious minerals in the "Crystal Hills." Settlement came slowly to the White Mountains, but in the early 1800s roads were finally cut through and travelers began to come north from Boston. Artists and writers awoke to the rugged scenery; stagecoaches and inns sprang up; and thus America's first touring region emerged.

Thoreau made two trips to the White Mountains—before and after they became a popular vacation area. The first journey was in August 1839 with his brother John; the second in July 1858, in the company of three friends and a local packer. The glaciers that rounded these mountains and widened their valley floors left three notches: Franconia Notch on the west, Pinkham Notch on the east, and Crawford Notch snaking between them. In 1839 Thoreau hiked up Franconia and down Crawford, going west to east; in 1858 he reversed directions, up Pinkham and down Franconia, east to west. He thus saw the entire area, climbed its mountains and ravines, and examined the major rock formations.

Yet the trips were different in character, because he changed over the decades, both as a traveler and writer. His 1839 excursion appears in *A Week* (1849), where it provides a brief, understated climax to the narrative.* He never published the 1858 account, which forms a long sequence in his Journal. That story is precise and detailed, an extended tribute to the wonders of mountain scenery.

Washington

J ohn and Henry Thoreau probably began to plan their trip to the White Mountains early in 1839. The two young schoolmasters had made brief day trips near home, but the White Mountains gave them a *Wanderjahr* on a small scale, nearly two full weeks of camping and travel. They planned to explore two river systems, going down the Concord and up the Merrimack to its highest source. For their journey, Henry built a boat that resembled a dory, flat-bottomed and narrow, with high sides and a sharp prow. He painted it green below, blue above, and called it *Musketaquid,* the old Indian name for Concord River. The brothers had oars for rowing and poles for the shallows, a mast and boom for sailing, wheels for rolling along the portage trails. Their camping gear included a large cotton cloth (for tent or sail), two buffalo skins (sleeping bags), a lantern, extra blanket, and kettle. The food was minimal: potatoes and melons from their garden; some rice, bread, sugar, and cocoa. En route they bought additional items at towns or farms.

Thoreau's story in A Week *is sketchy and generalized. I have added letters and Journal passages to create a more detailed account, along with commentary about specifics. The important early research of Christopher McKee was most helpful.*—WH

A WEEK ON
THE CONCORD AND
MERRIMACK RIVERS

After passing down the Concord River to Lowell, the ROUTE FROM CONCORD: *MA 62 to MA 3A and MA 3, to NH 3A* Thoreaus went up the Merrimack River to Hooksett, N.H. Boaters retracing this trip today will encounter many obstacles to navigation in the industrial sections of Lowell, Nashua, and Manchester. In *A Week,* Thoreau described the Merrimack and its northern watershed more happily.

We were thus entering the State of New Hampshire on the bosom of the flood formed by the tribute of its innumerable valleys. The river was the only key which could unlock its maze, presenting its hills and valleys, its lakes and streams, in their natural order and position. The MERRIMACK, or Sturgeon River, is formed by the confluence of the Pemigewasset, which rises near the Notch of the White Mountains, and the Winnepisiogee, which drains the lake of the same name, signifying "The Smile of the Great Spirit." From their junction it runs south seventy-eight miles to Massachusetts, and thence east thirty-five miles to the sea. I have traced its stream from where it bubbles out of the rocks of the White Mountains above the clouds, to where it is lost amid the salt billows of the ocean on Plum Island beach. At first it comes on murmuring to itself by the base of stately and retired mountains, through moist primitive woods whose juices it receives, where the bear still drinks it, and the cabins of settlers are far between, and there are few to cross its stream; enjoying in solitude its cascades still unknown to fame; by long ranges of mountains of Sandwich and of Squam, slumbering like tumuli of Titans, with the peaks of Moosehillock, the Haystack, and Kearsarge reflected in its waters; where the maple and the raspberry, those lovers of the hills, flourish amid temperate dews;—flowing long and full of meaning, but untranslatable as its name Pemigewasset, by many a pastured Pelion and Ossa, where unnamed muses haunt, tended by Oreads, Dryads, Naiads, and receiving the tribute of many an untasted Hippocrene. There are earth, air, fire, and water,—very well, this is water, and down it comes.

> *Such water do the gods distil,*
> *And pour down every hill*
> *For their New England men;*
> *A draught of this wild nectar bring,*
> *And I'll not taste the spring*
> *Of Helicon again.*

Falling all the way, and yet not discouraged by the lowest fall. By the law of its birth never to become stagnant, for it has come out of the clouds, and down the sides of precipices worn in the flood, through beaver dams broke loose, not splitting but splicing and mending itself,

until it found a breathing place in this low land. There is no danger
now that the sun will steal it back to heaven again before it reach the
sea, for it has a warrant even to recover its own dews into its bosom
again with interest at every eve.

It was already the water of Squam and Newfound Lake and
Winnepisiogee, and White Mountain snow dissolved, on which we
were floating, and Smith's and Baker's and Mad Rivers, and Nashua and Souhegan and Piscataquoag, and Suncook and Soucook
and Contoocook, mingled in incalculable proportions, still fluid,
yellowish, restless all, with an ancient, ineradicable inclination to the
sea.

The river journey took five days, from Saturday, August
31, to Wednesday, September 4. That night they camped
in "Hooksett, east bank, two or three miles below the
village, opposite Mr. Mitchel's." They intended to row
farther north, but rain the next day forced a change of
plans: "Sept. 5. Walked to Concord [N.H.], 10 miles." In *A
Week,* Thoreau explained why.

When we awoke this morning, we heard the faint deliberate and
ominous sound of rain drops on our cotton roof. The rain had pattered
all night, and now the whole country wept, the drops falling in the
river, and on the alders, and in the pastures, and instead of any bow
in the heavens, there was the trill of the chip-sparrow all the morning.
The cheery faith of this little bird atoned for the silence of the whole
woodland quire beside. When we first stepped abroad, a flock of sheep,
led by their rams, came rushing down a ravine in our rear, with
heedless haste and unreserved frisking, as if unobserved by man,
from some higher pasture where they had spent the night, to taste the
herbage by the river-side; but when their leaders caught sight of our
white tent through the mist, struck with sudden astonishment, with
their fore feet braced, they sustained the rushing torrent in their rear,
and the whole flock stood stock-still, endeavoring to solve the mystery
in their sheepish brains. At length, concluding that it boded no mis-
chief to them, they spread themselves out quietly over the field. We
learned afterward that we had pitched our tent on the very spot which

a few summers before had been occupied by a party of Penobscots. We could see rising before us through the mist a dark conical eminence called Hooksett Pinnacle, a landmark to boatmen, and also Uncannunuc Mountain, broad off on the west side of the river.

ROUTE FROM The brothers stored their boat with Mr. Mitchel. They
HOOKSETT: *NH 3A*
to Concord, N.H. also left the tent and buffalo robes, intending to lodge at roadside inns.

On foot, however, we continued up along the bank, feeling our way with a stick through the showery and foggy day, and climbing over the slippery logs in our path with as much pleasure and buoyancy as in brightest sunshine; scenting the fragrance of the pines and the wet clay under our feet, and cheered by the tones of invisible waterfalls; with visions of toadstools, and wandering frogs, and festoons of moss hanging from the spruce trees, and thrushes flitting silent under the leaves; our road still holding together through that wettest of weather, like faith, while we confidently followed its lead. We managed to keep our thoughts dry, however, and only our clothes were wet. It was altogether a cloudy and drizzling day, with occasional brightenings in the mist, when the trill of the tree-sparrow seemed to be ushering in sunny hours. . . .

Soon they passed the Pinnacle, which Thoreau later climbed during a trip in 1848.

The Pinnacle is a small wooded hill which rises very abruptly to the height of about two hundred feet, near the shore at Hooksett Falls. As Uncannunuc Mountain is perhaps the best point from which to view the valley of the Merrimack, so this hill affords the best view of the river itself. I have sat upon its summit, a precipitous rock only a few rods long, in fairer weather, when the sun was setting and filling the river valley with a flood of light. You can see up and down the Merrimack several miles each way. The broad and straight river, full of light and life, with its sparkling and foaming falls, the islet which divides the stream, the village of Hooksett on the shore almost directly under your feet, so near that you can converse with its inhabitants or throw a stone into its yards, the woodland lake at its western base, and the mountains in the north and north-east, make a scene of rare beauty and completeness, which the traveller should take pains to behold. . . .

That night they stayed in Concord, perhaps with family friends.

We were hospitably entertained in Concord in New Hampshire, which we persisted in calling *New* Concord, as we had been wont, to distinguish it from our native town, from which we had been told that it was named and in part originally settled. This would have been the proper place to conclude our voyage, uniting Concord with Concord by these meandering rivers, but our boat was moored some miles below its port.

On Friday, September 6, the pilgrims boarded a Concord stagecoach (the wagon that won the West) and traveled north to Sanbornton. "The scenery commences on Sanbornton Square, whence the White Mountains are first visible," Thoreau noted. At this elevation (520 feet) he

ROUTE FROM CONCORD, N.H.: *NH 3B to US 3, to West Thornton*

could see the Squam and Ossipee ranges, twenty-seven to thirty miles north. The coach continued north to Plymouth, partly along the Pemigewasset River, an upper tributary of the Merrimack. From Plymouth, reached in the late afternoon, the brothers hiked along the river through Campton ("decidedly mountainous," Thoreau wrote) to West Thornton, where they stayed at James Tilton's inn. Thoreau generalized about its primitive comforts.

Sometimes we lodged at an inn in the woods, where trout-fishers from distant cities had arrived before us, and where, to our astonishment, the settlers dropped in at night-fall to have a chat and hear the news, though there was but one road, and no other house was visible,—as if they had come out of the earth. There we sometimes read old newspapers, who never before read new ones, and in the rustle of their leaves heard the dashing of the surf along the Atlantic shore, instead of the sough of the wind among the pines. But then walking had given us an appetite even for the least palatable and nutritious food.

ROUTE FROM WEST THORNTON: *US 3 to NH 18, to Franconia* — On Saturday, September 7, the Thoreaus continued north through Franconia Notch: "Walked from Thornton through Peeling [Woodstock, N.H.] and Lincoln to Franconia." This route now follows the west bank of the Pemigewasset River into Franconia Notch State Reservation.

Suns rose and set and found us still on the dank forest path which meanders up the Pemigewasset, now more like an otter's or a marten's trail, or where a beaver had dragged his trap, than where the wheels of travel raise a dust; where towns begin to serve as gores, only to hold the earth together. The wild pigeon sat secure above our heads, high on the dead limbs of naval pines, reduced to a robin's size. The very yards of our hostelries inclined upon the skirts of mountains, and, as we passed, we looked up at a steep angle at the stems of maples waving in the clouds.

Pemigewasset River

Far up in the country,—for we would be faithful to our experience,—in Thornton, perhaps, we met a soldier lad in the woods, going to muster in full regimentals, and holding the middle of the road; deep in the forest with shouldered musket and military step, and thoughts of war and glory all to himself. It was a sore trial to the youth, tougher than many a battle, to get by us creditably and with soldierlike bearing. Poor man! He actually shivered like a reed in his thin military pants, and by the time we had got up with him, all the sternness that becomes the soldier had forsaken his face, and he skulked past as if he were driving his father's sheep under a sword-proof helmet. It was too much for him to carry any extra armor then, who could not easily dispose of his natural arms. And for his legs, they were like heavy artillery in boggy places; better to cut the traces and forsake them. His greaves chafed and wrestled one with another for want of other foes. But he did get by and get off with all his munitions, and lived to fight another day; and I do not

record this as casting any suspicion on his honor and real bravery in
the field.

Besides this forlorn young soldier, the brothers saw
many natural features in Franconia Notch: "In Lincoln
visited Stone Flume and Basin, and in Franconia the
Notch, and saw the Old Man of the Mountain." The
Flume, a deep stream-cut gorge, was first discovered in
1808 by "Aunt Jesse" Guernsey, who (at the age of ninety-
three) was looking for a place to fish. In 1839 a small
roadside inn, "Knight's Tavern," stood about a thousand
feet south of the present Flume entrance.

An admission fee to the Flume entitles visitors to a
half-mile bus ride up the slope and through a covered
bridge. From there a footpath skirts Table Rock, a large
granite outcrop, and passes (via a boardwalk) directly
into the gorge. Flume Brook tumbles below, sending up
billows of cool mist. Rising overhead are red granite
walls, sixty to seventy feet high, decked with heavy

clumps of ferns and mosses. The narrow gorge, barely twenty-five feet wide, echoes with roaring water; glints of rainbow shine when the sun is overhead.

Thoreau had no boardwalk to follow, so he must have walked along the gorge rim, sometimes crossing via fallen trees—and a large boulder—that formed natural bridges. The trees are gone now, and a flash flood removed the boulder in 1882. Walkways and stairs were not put in until the 1850s. (When his younger sister Sophia visited here in 1870, she walked on "a platform" through the gorge.) Above the gorge lies Avalanche Falls; from there, several footpaths lead to a smaller gorge, some cascades, a large kettle Pool, and the isolated boulders called "erratics." During the 1850s, when Flume House was erected, one John Merrill, called "the Philosopher of the Pool," gave boat rides there and preached that the world is flat. (Sophia saw Merrill in 1870 and concluded that he "had gone crazy upon cosmogony.")

Walking one and a half miles north, the Thoreau brothers passed Mt. Liberty (4,460') on the east; here the Appalachian Trail now crosses the highway. Viewed from this angle, Mt. Liberty supposedly resembles a face in repose; hence the traditional name of "Washington Lying in State." At the Basin, Thoreau stopped to examine the largest river pothole he had ever seen. In a passage drafted for *A Week* (but later cut) he wrote:

But the most remarkable instance of this kind is the well known Basin on the head waters of this stream—by the roadside in the town of Lincoln—where a mere brook, which may be passed at a stride, falling upon a rock has worn a basin from 30 to 40 feet in diameter—and proportionally deep—and passes out, probably after one revolution, or more when it is swollen—by a deep channel, scarcely more than a foot in width cut directly opposite to its entrance. It has a rounded brim of glassy water smoothness and is filled with cold transparent greenish water.

These holes may be observed at the flume, also at the head waters of this stream—at Bellows Falls—and more or less generally, I presume, about all falls.

> The Basin was formed by melting glacier ice; stones and sand carried downstream have cut the rock like a routing wheel. A fine suspension of rock dust, or "flour," tints the water dark green. Marked trails here lead to the waterfalls on Cascade Brook.
>
> Three miles north, the Thoreaus passed (without comment) Shelter Rock, scene of a famous White Mountains legend. Early in the 1800s, a Mr. Boise was trapped here when his horse suddenly died. As a winter storm came on, he skinned the horse, crawled into its hide, and took shelter under a rock ledge for the night. When found the next day, he had to be carried to a house, still rolled in the frozen hide, for thawing out.
>
> At Profile Lake (known as Ferrin's Pond in 1839), the Thoreaus stood at the source of the Pemigewasset River, and above them was the famous Old Man of the Mountains. Discovered in 1805 by two surveyors, this "profile" consists of three separate ledges, forty by one hundred feet, standing 1,200 feet above the lake. The surveyors saw a resemblance to Thomas Jefferson, then President. In his story "The Great Stone Face" (1851), Hawthorne mocked the vanity of such ideas; but Daniel Webster took a more popular view: ". . . up in the mountains of New Hampshire, God Almighty has hung out a sign to show that there He makes men." Fears later arose that God had not made this sign sufficiently permanent. The granite here lies in domed layers that exfoliate, rapidly peeling away in thin layers. Frost wedging accelerates this erosion, forcing slippage of the Old Man's dentures. In the early 1900s, he was anchored with blocks and turnbuckles, then waterproofed. These controls seem permanent, except to a geologist: in a few thousand years, the Profile will inevitably fall.

Old Man of the Mountains

One mile farther north, the Thoreaus turned toward Franconia village and passed Echo Lake. Surrounded by the slopes of Cannon Mountain, Echo Lake gives up a clear, layered resonance—seven distinct echoes, according to some ears. By 1853 a boating concession was in place here, taking visitors out on the lake to hear echoes from trumpets, shotguns, and a small cannon. Thoreau had his favorite echo spots in Concord; he said nothing about this place. (Sophia stopped here in 1870 to give off a few halloos; she also saw a bald eagle in flight, probably from Eagle Cliff across the road.) The brothers walked on to Franconia village, where they stayed the night.

ROUTE FROM FRANCONIA: *NH 142 to US 302, to Crawford House*   The Journal for Sunday, September 8, says: "Walked from Franconia to Thomas J. Crawford's." The following account in *A Week* is equally vague.

Wandering on through notches which the streams had made, by the side and over the brows of hoar hills and mountains, across the stumpy, rocky, forested and bepastured country, we at length crossed on prostrate trees over the Amonoosuck, and breathed the free air of Unappropriated Land. Thus, in fair days as well as foul, we had traced up the river to which our native stream is a tributary, until from Merrimack it became the Pemigewasset that leaped by our side, and when we had passed its fountain-head, the Wild Amonoosuck, whose puny channel was crossed at a stride, guiding us toward its distant source among the mountains, and at length, without its guidance, we were enabled to reach the summit of AGIOCOCHOOK.

The Thoreaus probably hiked north from Franconia village to Bethlehem and then east to the Ammonoosuc River, crossing at Pierce Bridge and going along the river to Washington House, an inn run by Horace Fabyan.

At this point, they had to make a choice. Two trails to the summit of Mt. Washington were available in 1839: one began here, passing west along the Ammonoosuc to a steep ridge, then ascending Burt Ravine directly to the peak. This trail, cut by Thomas Crawford in 1821, lay along the present Base Road and cog-railway track. The second trail, created by Crawford in 1819, began at his Notch House eleven miles farther south. Known today as Crawford Path, this trail climbs a low ridge and passes along the southern Presidential range to Mt. Washington.

Two trails: one steep but short, the other long and gradual; the Thoreaus were at the base of one, eleven miles from the other. They had hiked sixteen miles that day, and the time was probably noon or later. That would be too late to start climbing, for they could barely reach the summit before sunset. No shelter was available up there, and they had left their camping gear in Hooksett. For these reasons, they had to continue south to Notch House, where they arrived in the late afternoon.

Today's traveler might consider the first route, either taking the cog railway (as Sophia did in 1870) or climbing the Ammonoosuc Ravine trail. This path follows the Ammonoosuc River to its source at Lakes of the Clouds, site of the largest AMC hut in the White Mountains. From there, Mt. Washington is an easy ascent along the Crawford and Davis paths, both part of Thoreau's route. The ravine is a narrow, twisting gorge, cut by the river into thin cascades and deep, clear pools. Climbers pass through a twenty- to thirty-degree temperature change, and the vegetation alters from broadleaf forest to dwarf conifers, then to beds of damp, shaggy moss. Located on a warm western slope, the ravine protects many rare wild flowers, including the bright yellow Avens and white Bluet; both are alpine species found only here or in Nova Scotia and Newfoundland.

ROUTE FROM
CRAWFORD HOUSE:
*Crawford Path to
summit and
return*

(see page 219)

Thoreau's entry for Monday, September 9, is: "At Crawford's"—probably meaning he and John waited for clear weather (the summit is clouded sixty percent of the time). Tuesday was favorable: "Ascended the mountain and rode to Conway." Thoreau does not identify his route in *A Week,* and his description could apply to either of the two paths: at Fabyan, hikers could cross the Ammonoosuc River over "prostrate trees"; on the Crawford Path, that same river would seem a "puny channel." The Crawford Path seems their most likely choice, since it began at Notch House, rose gradually along a bridle path, and provided good views of surrounding terrain.

Crawford Path follows Gibbs Brook and a northeast ridge for almost three miles, joining the Appalachian Trail near the summit of Mt. Clinton (also called Mt. Pierce), then takes a steady course above the tree line, over the great swelling rises of the southern Presidentials. Cutoffs (bypasses) exist at Mt. Eisenhower (4,761') and Mt. Monroe (5,385'); the trail then proceeds to the AMC hut at Lakes of the Clouds. The hut offers hearty meals, cooked and served by cheerful collegians;

The Crawford Notch House

bunks accommodate ninety overnight guests. That's more society than some may prefer, especially on days of solid rain or fog, but the hut does provide an opportunity to explore, without backpack, the land above the tree line.

On the flats below Mt. Monroe lies the world of alpine flora, a ground-hugging cover of cushion plants that cling to life, slowly adding inches to their circumference. The low afternoon sun turns this assembly of grays into gold; light gleams on the dark bog pools and their borders of sedge, a thick grass with the incongruous look of clipped lawn. The gardeners here are altitude and the north winds, assigned on permanent duty.

Thoreau may have paused for a brief rest and a drink of cold Lakes water, but in 1839 he did not yet have the mind and eye of an alpine naturalist. Soon he would have taken the Crawford Path across Bigelow Lawn, a tableland covered with lichenous boulders. The trail here is fully exposed to winds that sweep across the col, or open ridge, between Ammonoosuc and Tuckerman ravines. Ahead lies some of the world's most dangerous weather. Fog—even hail or snow, in summer months— can close in swiftly and unpredictably. Hikers must exercise extreme caution; above the tree line, they can follow the rock cairns—sentinel markers visible even in heavy fog. For its last mile, the Crawford Path becomes steep and boulder-strewn; cairns and painted blazes lead up the northwest side to the summit.

The Thoreaus had a clear day here, with nothing to *(see page 219)* obstruct their view of "Unappropriated Land." Today's *(see page 249)* visitor will find a quite different situation. Two years later, Thoreau briefly described the view in a letter:

I see the stanzas rise around me, verse upon verse, far and near, like the mountains from Agiocochook, not all having a terrestrial existence as yet, even as some of them may be clouds; but I fancy I see the gleam of some Sebago Lake and Silver Cascade, at whose well I may drink one day.

Under the best possible conditions, landmarks nearly eighty miles distant have been identified. Agiocochook is an old Indian name for Mt. Washington; it means, approximately, "home of the Great Spirit." Thoreau's use of the name in *A Week* provides a climax to the memorial of his brother John. Having reached the summit together after their long journey, they will remain united in spirit forever.

ROUTE FROM SUMMIT: *Crawford Path to US 302, NH 16 to Conway*

If the Thoreaus hiked at a moderate pace, they probably reached the summit in five to six hours, rested an hour or so, descended to Crawford House in four hours, and continued south along the Saco River about three hours to Conway.

ROUTE FROM CONWAY: *NH 16 to NH 113, NH 25 to NH 109, to Concord, N.H.*

After an undoubtedly sound sleep, they rose before dawn on Wednesday, boarded a stage, and "Rode to Concord," passing directly along their earlier route (Meredith, Laconia, and Sanbornton) and arriving at Concord, N.H., that evening.

Mt. Washington

On Thursday, September 12, they "Rode to Hooksett," retrieved their boat, and set sail for Concord at noon. A good wind and the downstream current made brief work of their return voyage. They camped that night at Merrimack, and by the evening of Friday, September 13, they were rowing the last few miles home by starlight. They had been out exactly two weeks, taking what proved to be their first—and last—long journey together.

ROUTE FROM CONCORD, N.H.: *US 3 to Hooksett; NH 3A to MA 3 and 3A, to MA 62 and Concord, Mass.*

.   .   .

Thoreau's decision to return to the White Mountains nineteen years later was not sentimental. After 1855, he made a regular habit of summer excursions, leaving Concord during the hot, humid months and going either to the shore or to the mountains. These trips extended his daily journeys in Concord and also slightly improved his health. In his forties, he was still vigorous, but no longer endowed with endless stamina.

Edward Hoar, Thoreau's companion on the trip to Maine in 1857, was sensitive to these changes. When he and Thoreau first discussed a White Mountains venture, Hoar offered to hire a horse and covered wagon—at his own expense. A private wagon would offer more freedom of movement than stagecoaches, and it would spare them for the trip's main purpose, which Thoreau described when inviting Harrison Blake: "to explore the mountain-tops botanically, and camp on them at least several times."

From his reading of Edward Tuckerman's studies, Thoreau had learned that the White Mountains have many rare plants, most of them flowering in early July. (The mountains lie in a severe weather belt, but their low altitude sustains a full atmosphere, the carbon diox-

ide and water vapor so vital to plant growth.) He also
knew that many hazards could beset travelers in the
White Mountains. In February 1857 he commented in the
Journal on "Dr. Ball," who nearly died of exposure during a mountain storm. In the same entry, Thoreau pon-
tificated on the importance of carrying good supplies and
maps: "Do not take a dozen steps without which you
could not with tolerable accuracy protract on a chart. I
never do otherwise." (He and Hoar were lost twice in the
Maine woods in September 1857, and once again on Mt.
Lafayette in July 1858.)

Harrison Blake was a more experienced companion,
for he had hiked with Thoreau on Wachusett in 1854
and Monadnock in June 1858, and he made a solo trip *(see page 298)*
to the White Mountains in 1857. Thoreau urged Blake
to bring a map, a blanket and warm clothing for the
summit, and ample provisions, "for we intend to live
like gypsies," cooking meals and sleeping out. The
wagon was loaded with corned beef, sugar, tea, hard
and homemade bread, and "a moist, sweet plum cake
very good and lasting." They carried iron and tin
cooking implements, an ax, and a large canvas sheet
for a tent. Their botanical supplies included maps,
handbooks, magnifying glasses, and blotting paper for
specimens.

The trip lasted three weeks, one of them spent going
north along the Merrimack River, then through the New
Hampshire lakes region and into Pinkham Notch. The
ascent of Mt. Washington went smoothly, but in Tuckerman Ravine several mishaps occurred: Thoreau took
two bad falls and sustained injuries, his packer (a local
man) set a campfire that got out of control and burned
several acres of forest. (This point deserves emphasis,
for some locals here still blame Thoreau for that fire.)
Joined by Blake and Theo Brown, another friend from
Worcester, Thoreau stayed five days in Tuckerman Ravine. His forty-first birthday was July 12, a day spent

descending the trail to Pinkham Notch, carrying a full pack. The party then journeyed by wagon to Franconia Notch for two days on Mt. Lafayette before returning to Concord.

Thoreau kept the usual set of field notes; at home he immediately began to write Journal entries describing the trip in detail. The completed account was about 18,000 words, his longest piece of writing devoted entirely to mountains. (The following version is slightly abridged and divided into three sections.) One reader has said these entries contain "not one line of philosophical speculation or poetry," but the metaphors here lie in Thoreau's respectful handling of facts. He saw the trip in retrospect, added ideas and other data, gave his story a clear structure—beginning, middle, and end. To him, mountains were no longer just a poet's symbol, the great pyramid of inspiration, but a vast realm of knowledge, the environment where myriad creatures dwell. Thoreau hoped this country would always be Unappropriated Land, "if only to suggest that the earth has higher uses than we put her to."

JOURNAL

July 2. A.M.—Start for White Mountains in a private carriage with Edward Hoar.

Notice in a shallow pool on a rock on a hilltop, in road in North Chelmsford, a rather peculiar-looking *Alisma Plantago*, with long reddish petioles, just budded.

Spent the noon close by the old Dunstable graveyard, by a small stream north of it. Red lilies were abundantly in bloom in the burying-ground and by the river. Mr. Weld's monument is a large, thick, naturally flat rock, lying flat over the grave. Noticed the monument of Josiah Willard, Esq., "Captain of Fort Dummer." Died 1750, aged 58.

Walked to and along the river and bathed in it. There were hare-bells, well out, and much *Apocynum cannabinum*, well out, apparently like ours, prevailing along the steep sandy and stony shore. A marked peculiarity in this species is that the upper branches rise above the flowers. Also get the *A. androsæmifolium*, quite downy beneath. The *Smilacina stellata* going to seed, quite common in the copse on top of the bank.

What a relief and expansion of my thoughts when I come out from that inland position by the graveyard to this broad river's shore! This vista was incredible there. Suddenly I see a broad reach of blue beneath, with its curves and headlands, liberating me from the more terrene earth. What a difference it makes whether I spend my four hours' nooning between the hills by yonder roadside, or on the brink of this fair river, within a quarter of a mile of that! Here the earth is fluid to my thought, the sky is reflected from beneath, and around yonder cape is the highway to other continents. This current allies me to all the world. Be careful to sit in an elevating and inspiring place. There my thoughts were confined and trivial, and I hid myself from the gaze of travellers. Here they are expanded and elevated, and I am charmed by the beautiful river-reach. It is equal to a different season and country and creates a different mood. As you travel northward from Concord, probably the reaches of the Merrimack River, looking up or down them from the bank, will be the first inspiring sight. There is something in the scenery of a broad river equivalent to culture and civilization. Its channel conducts our thoughts as well as bodies to classic and famous ports, and allies us to all that is fair and great. I like to remember that at the end of half a day's walk I can stand on the bank of the Merrimack. It is just wide enough to interrupt the land and lead my eye and thoughts down its channel to the sea. A river is superior to a lake in its liberating influence. It has motion and indefinite length. A river touching the back of a town is like a wing, it may be unused as yet, but ready to waft it over the world. With its rapid current it is a slightly fluttering wing. River towns are winged towns.

I returned through the grass up the winding channel of our little brook to the camp again. Along the brook, in the rank grass and weeds, grew abundantly a slender umbelliferous plant mostly just out of bloom, one and a half to four feet high. Either *Thaspium aureum* or *Cryptotœnia Canadensis* (Sison). Saw also the scouring-rush, apparently just beginning to bloom!

In the southern part of Merrimack, passed a singular "Horseshoe Pond" between the road and the river on the interval. Belknap says in his History, speaking of the changes in river-courses, "In some places these ancient channels are converted into ponds, which, from their curved form, are called horseshoe ponds."

Put up at tavern in Merrimack, some miles after passing over a pretty high, flat-topped hill in road, whence we saw the mountains (with a steep descent to the interval on right).

7 P.M.—I walked by a path through the wood northeast to the Merrimack, crossing two branches of Babboosuck Brook, on which were handsome rocky falls in the woods.

The wood thrush sings almost wherever I go, eternally reconsecrating the world, morning and evening, for us. And again it seems habitable and more than habitable to us.

July 3. Continued along in a slight rain through Bedford, crossing to Manchester, and driving by a brook in Hookset just above Pinnacle. Then through Allenstown and Pembroke, with its long street, to Loudon, leaving Concord on the left. Along the sandy roadside in a pitch pine wood in Loudon, much apparent *Calystegia spithamœa* in bloom, but I think with reddish flowers. Probably same with my New Bedford plant.

After some initial particulars, the opening entry celebrated the "relief and expansion" of thoughts that travel can bring. The earth and his mind became allies, linked in a search for "all that is fair and great." The meditation recalls Thoreau's Concord-and-Merrimack trip of 1839, and it anticipates major discoveries that lie ahead. Horseshoe ponds are common near meandering rivers. Once a long, looping bend of current, the river eventually cuts straight across its neck and leaves a pond; the pond will in turn become marsh, then dry land. In July 1859, Thoreau began to study these and other limnological features on the rivers in Concord.

ROUTE FROM CONCORD: *MA 62 to US 3 and 3A, NH 106 to Loudon*

(see page 228)

July 4. Sunday. A.M.—Clears up after a rainy night. Get our breakfast apparently in the northern part of Loudon, where we find, in a beech and maple wood, *Panax quinquefolium,* apparently not quite out, *Osmorrhiza brevistylis* (or hairy uraspermum), gone to seed, which Bigelow refers to woods on Concord Turnpike, *i.e.,* hairy sweet cicely. Also ternate polypody (?). Saw a chestnut tree in Loudon.

Leaving Loudon Ridge on the right we continued on by the Hollow Road—a long way through the forest without houses—through a part of Canterbury into Gilmanton Factory village. I see the *Ribes prostratum,* or fetid currant, by roadside, already red, as also the red elder-berries, ripe or red.* Strawberries were abundant by the roadside and in the grass on hillsides everywhere, with the seeds conspicuous, sunk in pits on the surface. (*Vide* a leaf of same kind pressed.)

The Merrimack at Merrimack, where I walked,—half a mile or more below my last camp on it in '39,—had gone down two or three feet within a few days, and the muddy and slimy shore was covered with the tracks of many small animals, apparently three-toed sandpipers,

---

*This only in the northern part of New Hampshire.

minks, turtles, squirrels, perhaps mice, and some much larger quadrupeds. The *Solidago lanceolata*, not out, was common along the shore. Wool-grass without black sheaths, and a very slender variety with it; also *Carex crinita*.

We continue along through Gilmanton to Meredith Bridge, passing the Suncook Mountain on our right, a long, barren rocky range overlooking Lake Winnepiseogee. Turn down a lane five or six miles beyond the bridge and spend the midday near a bay of the lake. *Polygonum cilinode*, apparently not long. I hear song sparrows there among the rocks, with a totally new strain, ending *whit whit, whit whit, whit whit whit*. They had also the common strain. We had begun to see from Gilmanton, from high hills in the road, the sharp rocky peak of Chocorua in the north, to the right of the lower Red Hill. It was of a pale-buff color, with apparently the Sandwich Mountains west of it and Ossipee Mountain on the right. The goldfinch was more common than at home, and the fragrant fern was perceived oftener. The evergreen-forest note frequently heard.

It is far more independent to travel on foot. You have to sacrifice so much to the horse. You cannot choose the most agreeable places in which to spend the noon, commanding the finest views, because commonly there is no water there, or you cannot get there with your horse. New Hampshire being a more hilly and newer State than Massachusetts, it is very difficult to find a suitable place to camp near the road, affording water, a good prospect, and retirement. We several times rode on as much as ten miles with a tired horse, looking in vain for such a spot, and then almost invariably camped in some low, unpleasant spot. There are very few, scarcely any, lanes, or even paths and bars along the road. Having got beyond the range of the chestnut, the few bars that might be taken down are long and heavy planks or slabs, intended to confine sheep, and there is no passable road behind. And beside, when you have chosen a place one must stay behind to watch your effects, while the other looks about. I frequently envied the independence of the walker, who can spend the midday hours and take his lunch in the most agreeable spot on his route. The only alternative is to spend your noon at some trivial inn, pestered by flies and tavern loungers.

Camped within a mile south of Senter Harbor, in a birch wood on the right near the lake. Heard in the night a loon, screech owl, and cuckoo, and our horse, tied to a slender birch close by, restlessly pawing the ground all night and whinnering to us whenever we showed ourselves, asking for something more than meat to fill his belly with.

Center Harbor, N.H.

Nearing the lake country of New Hampshire, Thoreau watched the species change—trees, berries, sparrows—as he moved onto higher northern ground, a thousand feet, as compared to the 141 feet of Concord. The landmarks near Laconia were Suncook (now Belknap) Mountain (2,384'), Chocorua (3,475', twenty-five miles northeast), Red Hill (2,029', seven miles northeast), and Ossipee (now Mt. Shaw, 2,975'). Thoreau's spelling of "Winnipesaukee" is not incorrect; one authority reports 132 variant spellings of this Indian name.

ROUTE FROM LOUDON: *NH 129 to Lower Gilmanton, NH 107 to Meredith, NH 25 to Center Harbor*

(see page 230)

His complaints about horse and wagon were only temporary; today the roadside has no lack of accommodations, from modest clapboard houses to resorts proclaiming The Great Escape. The lake district also offers

miniature golf courses, water slides, and amusement
parks with names like Story Land and Fun Spot. Thoreau
had better fortune than he realized, only occasionally
passing some "trivial inn." After crossing the bridge at
Laconia, he camped that evening on Meredith Bay, in
the vicinity of Weirs Beach.

July 5. Monday. Continue on through Senter Harbor and ascend Red
Hill in Moultonboro. On this ascent I notice the *Erigeron annuus,*
which we have not, methinks, *i.e. purple* fleabane (for it is commonly
purplish), hairy with thin leaves and broader than the *strigosus.* Notice the *Comandra umbellata,* with leaves in three very regular
spiral lines. Dr. Jackson says that Red Hill is so called from the
uva-ursi on it turning red in the fall. On the top we boil a dipper of
tea for our dinner and spend some hours, having carried up water the
last half-mile.

Enjoyed the famous view of Winnepiseogee and its islands southeasterly and Squam Lake on the west, but I was as much attracted
at this hour by the wild mountain view on the northward. Chocorua
and the Sandwich Mountains a dozen miles off seemed the boundary
of cultivation on that side, as indeed they are. They are, as it were,
the impassable southern barrier of the mountain region, themselves
lofty and bare, and filling the whole northerly horizon, with the broad
vale or valley of Sandwich between you and them; and over their
ridges, in one or two places, you detected a narrow, blue edging or a
peak of the loftier White Mountains proper (or so called). Ossipee
Mountain is on the east, near by; Chocorua (which the inhabitants
pronounce She-corway or Corway), in some respects the wildest and
most imposing of all the White Mountain peaks, north of northeast,
bare rocks, slightly flesh-colored; some large mountains, perhaps the
Franconia, far northwesterly; Ragged (??) Mountain, south of west;
Kearsarge, southwest; Monadnock (?), dim and distant blue, and some
other mountains as distant, more easterly; Suncook Mountain, south-
southeast, and, beyond the lake, south of southeast, Copple-Crown
Mountain (?). When I looked at the near Ossipee Mountain (and some
others), I saw first smooth pastures around the base or extending part
way up, then the light green of deciduous trees (probably oak, birch,

Lake Winnipesaukee

maple, etc.), looking dense and shrubby, and above all the rest, looking like permanent shadows, dark saddles of spruce or fir or both on
the summits. Jackson says larch, spruce, and birch reach to the summit of Ossipee Mountain. The landscape is spotted, like a leopard-skin,
with large squarish patches of light-green and darker forests and blue
lakes, etc., etc.

On the top I found *Potentilla tridentata*, out a good while, choke-berry, red lily, dwarfish red oaks, *Carex Novæ-Angliæ* (?), and a carex *scoparia*-like. Apparently the common *Vaccinium Pennsylvanicum,* and just below, in the shrubbery, the *Vaccinium Canadense* was the prevailing one. Just below top, a clematis, and, as you descended, the red oak, growing larger, canoe birch, some small white birch, red maple, rock maple, *Populus tremuliformis,** diervilla (very common), etc., etc.†

Heard the chewink on the summit, and saw an ant-hill there, within six rods of apex, about seven by six feet in diameter and sixteen inches high, with grass growing on all sides of it. This reminded me of the great ant-hills I saw on Chesterfield Mountain, opposite Brattleboro.

Descended, and rode along the west and northwest side of Ossipee Mountain. Sandwich, in a large level space surrounded by mountains, lay on our left. Here first, in Moultonboro, I heard the *tea-lee* of the white-throated sparrow. We were all the afternoon riding along under Ossipee Mountain, which would not be left behind, unexpectedly large still, louring over your path. Crossed Bearcamp River, a shallow but unexpectedly sluggish stream, which empties into Ossipee Lake. Have new and memorable views of Chocorua, as we get round it eastward. Stop at Tamworth village for the night.

We are now near the edge of a wild and unsettlable mountain region, lying northwest, apparently including parts of Albany and Waterville. The landlord said that bears were plenty in it; that there was a little interval on Swift River that might be occupied, and that was all. Norcross gets his lumber in that region, on Mad and Swift Rivers, as I understood; and on Swift River, as near as I could learn, was the only road leading into it.

ROUTE FROM CENTER HARBOR: *NH 25 to Red Hill, trail to summit, NH 25 to Whittier, NH 113 to Tamworth*   Red Hill (2,029′) lies two miles northeast of Center Harbor: from NH 25 go left on Red Hill Road one and a half miles to a dirt road, then right to a parking area at 1,100 feet. Thoreau's ascent probably followed the present trail, laid out in the 1850s as a road and bridle path to the

---

*The common species afterward on sides and about the mountains.
†Diervilla and checkerberry common after on mountainsides.

summit. The mountains he saw from there were Win- *(see page 232)*
nipesaukee (five miles southwest), Squam (three miles
west), Chocorua (seventeen, not twelve, miles west). On
Ossipee/Shaw he could already see plant zones, later
described on Mt. Washington. *(see page 283)*

Squam Lake

On Red Hill today, the summit view is obscured by tall
trees. Thoreau could see far, but he got several locations
wrong: he saw not the Presidentials but Moat, Bear, Hancock, and Carrigan mountains; not Franconia but Moosilauke, Blue Ridge, and Mt. Kinsman. He also erred about
the direction of Copple-Crown; it lies north of southeast.
All the plants he noted are still visible, yet Dr. Jackson's
theory about the naming of Red Hill is suspect: the *uva-* *(see page 232)*
ursi (bearberry) has red fruits; its leaves are evergreen.

July 6. Tuesday. 5.35 A.M.—Keep on through North Tamworth, and
breakfast by shore of one of the Ossipee Lakes. Chocorua north-
northwest. Hear and see loons and see a peetweet's egg washed up.
A shallow-shored pond, too shallow for fishing, with a few breams
seen near shore; some pontederia and target-weed in it.

Travelling thus toward the White Mountains, the mountains fairly begin with Red Hill and Ossipee Mountain, but the White Mountain scenery proper on the high hillside road in Madison before entering Conway, where you see Chocorua on the left, Mote Mountain ahead, Doublehead, and some of the White Mountains proper beyond, *i.e.*, a sharp peak.

We fished in vain in a small clear pond by the roadside in Madison.

Chocorua is as interesting a peak as any to remember. You may be jogging along steadily for a day before you get round it and leave it behind, first seeing it on the north, then northwest, then west, and at last southwesterly, ever stern, rugged and inaccessible, and omnipresent. It was seen from Gilmanton to Conway, and from Moultonboro was the ruling feature.

The scenery in Conway and onward to North Conway is surprisingly grand. You are steadily advancing into an amphitheatre of mountains. I do not know exactly how long we had seen one of the highest peaks before us in the extreme northwest, with snow on its side just below the summit, but a little beyond Conway a boy called it Mt. Washington. I think it was visible just before entering Conway village. If Mt. Washington, the snow must have been in Tuckerman's Ravine, which, methinks, is rather too low. Perhaps it was that we afterward saw on Mt. Adams. There was the regular dark pyramid of Kearsarge at first in front, then, as you proceed to North Conway, on our right, with its deserted hotel on the summit, and Mote Mountain accompanies you on the left, and high, bare rocky precipices at last on the same side. The road, which is for the most part level, winds along the Saco through groves of maples, etc., on the level intervals, with so little of rugged New Hampshire under your feet, often soft and sandy road. The scenery is remarkable for this contrast of level interval with soft and shady groves, with mountain grandeur and ruggedness. Often from the midst of level maple groves, which remind you only of classic lowlands, you look out through a vista to the most rugged scenery of New England. It is quite unlike New Hampshire generally, quite unexpected by me, and suggests a superior culture. We at length crossed the Saco from the left to the right side of the valley, going over or through three channels. After leaving North Conway, the higher White Mountains were less seen, if at all. They had not appeared in pinnacles, as sometimes described, but

Conway Meadows

broad and massive. Only one of the higher peaks or summits (called by the boy Mt. Washington) was conspicuous. The snow near the top was conspicuous here thirty miles off. The summit appeared dark, the rocks just beneath pale-brown (forenoon) (not flesh-colored like Chocorua), and below, green, wooded.

The road to-day from Tamworth almost to the base of Mt. Washington was better on the whole, less hilly, than through Gilmanton to Tamworth; *i.e.*, the hills were not so long and tedious.

At Bartlett Corner we turned up the Ellis River and took our nooning on the bank of the river, by the bridge just this side of Jackson Centre, in a rock maple grove. Saw snow on Mt. Carter (?) from this road. There are but few *narrow* intervals on this road,—two or three only after passing Jackson,—and each is improved by a settler. We see the handsome *Malva sylvestris*, an introduced flower, by road-side, apparently in prime, and also in Conway, and hear the night-warbler all along thus far.

Saw the bones of a bear at Wentworth's house, and camped, rather late, on right-hand side of road just beyond, or a little more than four miles from Jackson. The wood was canoe birch and some yellow (see little of the small white birch as far as to the neighborhood of the mountains), rock maple, spruce, fir, *Populus tremuliformis*, and one *grandidentata*, etc. In this deep vale between the mountains, the sun set very early to us, but we saw it on the mountains long after. Heard at evening the wood thrush, veery, white-throated sparrow, etc., and I found a fresh nest in a fir, made of hemlock twigs, etc., when I was getting twigs, for a bed. The mosquitoes troubled us in the evening and just before dawn, but not seriously in the middle of the night. This, I find, is the way with them generally.

Wentworth said he was much troubled by the bears. They killed his sheep and calves and destroyed his corn when in the milk, close by his house. He has trapped and killed many of them and brought home and reared the young. When we looked up in the night we saw that the stars were bright as in winter, owing to the clear cold air.

ROUTE FROM TAMWORTH: *NH 113 to NH 16, to Glen*

(see page 235)

The region beyond Red Hill is no longer "wild and un-settable," yet Thoreau's route follows several quiet back roads which avoid the traffic that clogs up NH 16. His breakfast spot must have been on Silver Lake, and three-quarters of a mile west the road passes over Deer Hill (1,050′), where he first saw exposed mountain rock ahead. North of Madison, just off NH 113, is a feature he missed: Madison Boulder, one of the world's largest gla-cial erratics. This great hunk of rock, the size of a rail-road car, stands in splendid isolation, indifferent to the visitors who have scarred it with hammers and paint.

(see page 236)

The scenery Thoreau so admired beyond Conway and North Conway is still grand; but the towns are now clut-tered with signs (6,000 Salad Bowls!) and the motley hue of commerce. At this point he could see several northern peaks: Washington (6,288', twenty-three miles), Adams (5,798', twenty-seven miles), Kearsarge (3,268', seven miles), and North Moat (3,201'). Near the present village of Intervale, he was struck by the contrast between this mile-wide valley, soft and cultivated, and the rugged heights above. Today the "classic lowlands" are less suggestive of "superior culture." *(see page 236)*

Near Glen (then Bartlett Corner), Thoreau took his nooning, probably close to the trail entrance for Iron Mountain. Joining the men from Concord was William H. H. Wentworth (1818–?), whom Thoreau hired as a packer. The packer's job was to carry gear and help set up camp. Wentworth proved to be less than expert, but he offered Thoreau many observations about mountain life. Beyond Glen, the road now enters White Mountains National Forest, where commerce ends and the only signs are directional. These were the "Ungranted Lands" on Thoreau's maps, and today they still remain wild.

Glen Ellis Falls

July 7. Wednesday. Having engaged the services of Wentworth to carry up some of our baggage and to keep our camp, we rode onward to the Glen House, eight miles further, sending back our horse and wagon to his house. This road passes through what is called the Pinkham Notch, in Pinkham's Grant, the land, a large tract, having been given away to Pinkham for making the road a good while since. Wentworth has lived here thirty years and is a native. Have occasional views of Mt. Washington or a spur of it, etc. Get by roadside, in bloom some time, *Geum macrophyllum;* also, in a damp place, *Platanthera dilatata,* a narrow white spike. Turned off a little to the right to see Glen Ellis Falls.

Began the ascent by the mountain road at 11.30 A.M.

For about the first three quarters of a mile of steady (winding) ascent the wood was spruce, yellow birch (some, generally the largest, with a very rough, coarse, scaly bark, but other trees equally large had a beautifully smooth bark, and Wentworth called these "silver birch"; it appeared not to depend on age merely), hemlock, beech, canoe birch (according to Willey, "most abundant in the districts formerly burnt"), rock maple, fir, mountain maple (called by Wentworth bastard maple), northern wild cherry, striped maple, etc. At about a mile and three quarters spruce prevails, and rock maple, beech, and hemlock, etc., disappear. At three miles, or near the limit of trees, fir (increasing) and spruce chiefly prevail. And near by was the foot of the ledge and limit of trees, only their dead trunks standing, probably fir and spruce, about the shanty where we spent the night with the colliers.

I went on nearly a mile and a half further, and found many new alpine plants and returned to this shanty. A merry collier and his assistant, who had been making coal for the summit and were preparing to leave the next morning, made us welcome to this shanty and entertained us with their talk. We here boiled some of our beef-tongues, a very strong wind pouring in gusts down the funnel and scattering the fire about through the cracked stove. This man, named Page, had imported goats on to the mountain, and milked them to supply us with milk for our coffee. The road here ran north and south to get round the ledge. The wind, blowing down the funnel, set fire to a pile of dirty bed-quilts when I was out, and came near burning up the building. There were many barrels of spoiled beef in the cellar, and he said that a person coming down the mountain some time ago looked into the cellar and saw five wildcats *(loups-cerviers)* there. Page had heard two fighting like cats near by a few nights before. The wind blowed very strong and in gusts this night, but he said it was nothing to what it was sometimes, when the building rocked four inches.

Darby Field came through Pinkham Notch en route to Mt. Washington in 1642, when he also saw Glen Ellis Falls for the first time. The long, single cascade is a popular stop for visitors; as is Pinkham Notch AMC Camp, which provides supplies, meals, and rooms for hikers who are beginning or ending their journeys. The ambi-

ROUTE FROM GLEN: *NH 16 to Glen House, Mt. Washington Carriage Road to Half-way House*

ence here is super-ecologic: even the water cooler bears
a lab report, declaring the contents to be soft, bacteria-
free, and "excellant" [sic]. Hikers can obtain reports on
weather, trail conditions, and the latest fatalities. Over
the years, bad mountain weather has collected its dues.
Only three deaths were reported before 1858; since then,
almost ninety—half were persons under the age of
twenty-five. These numbers mostly reflect an increase in
traffic; hikers today are far better informed and
equipped than Thoreau was.

Glen House

His walking route began at the site of Glen House and
went up the present carriage/auto road. The walking is
easy (17,000 steps to the top!), with numbered mileage
posts and turnouts for good views. The main disadvantage on this route is heavy auto traffic; most hikers prefer
to ascend via the trails on Boott Spur, Tuckerman Ravine, or Huntington Ravine. Glen House today is home
for the Mt. Washington Summit Road Company, which
operates "stages" (auto vans) that make the ascent in

twenty minutes—fast enough to pop ears and induce altitude sickness. In 1858 this road was complete only four
miles to the shanty where Thoreau stayed overnight. A *(see page 241)*
second carriage road (on the west side) had just opened
that summer, and Sylvester Marsh was proposing to in-
stall a cog railway there. Thoreau was enjoying one of
the last summers on Mt. Washington before mechanical
transport reached the summit.

He moved easily with a backpack, apparently carrying a heavy load (at the summit his party tried to hire
an additional packer). But his mind was mostly on
plant life, as he watched the forest change from hard-
wood and conifers to spruce and fir. The shanty where
he stopped was at the tree line (3,840′); colliers were
posted there to make charcoal for the Summit House.
This area is now the site of Halfway House, the earliest
version of which was a cookhouse for road crews, probably in the 1860s. In 1858 the road ended here; Thoreau
hiked up Glen Bridle Path to a point near the present *(see page 241)*
five-mile post, where the road makes a steep switch-
back (4,500′).

July 8. Though a fair day, the sun did not rise clear. I started before
my companions, wishing to secure a clear view from the summit,
while they accompanied the collier and his assistant, who were con-
ducting up to the summit for the first time his goats. He led the old
one, and the rest followed.

I noticed these plants this morning and the night before at and
above the limit of trees: *Oxalis Acetosella,* abundant and in bloom
near the shanty and further down the mountain, all over the woods;
Cornus Canadensis, also abundantly in bloom about the shanty and
far above and below it. At shanty, or limit of trees, began to find
Alsine Grœnlandica abundant and in prime, the first mountain
flower.* Noticed one returning, in carriage-road more than half-way
down the mountain. It extended to within a mile of summit along

*Durand in Kane puts it at 73° + in Greenland.

path,* and grew about our camp at Hermit Lake. The second mountain plant I noticed was the ledum,† growing in dense continuous patches or fields, filling broad spaces between the rocks, but dwarfish compared with ours in Concord. It was still in bloom. It *prevailed* about two miles below the summit. At the same elevation I noticed the *Vaccinium uliginosum,* a prevailing plant from the ledge to perhaps one mile or more below summit, almost entirely out of bloom, a procumbent bilberry, growing well, not dwarfish, with peculiar glaucous roundish-obovate leaves.‡ About the same time and locality, *Salix Uva-ursi,* the prevailing willow of the alpine region, completely out of bloom and going or gone to seed, a flat, trailing, glossy-leaved willow with the habit of the bearberry, spreading in a close mat over the rocks or rocky surface. I saw one spreading flat for three or four feet over a rock in the ravine (as low as I saw it).§ *Diapensia Lapponica (Menziesia cœrulea),** beginning about same time, or just over the ledge, reached yet higher, or to within last mile. Quite out of bloom; only one flower seen. It grows in close, *firm,* and dense rounded tufts, just like a moss but harder, between the rocks, the flowers considerably elevated above its surface. *Empetrum nigrum,* growing somewhat like *Corema,* with berries green and some turning black.†† Mountain cranberry was abundant and in bloom, a very pretty flower, with, say, the *Vaccinium uliginosum* and to within last mile. Gold-thread in bloom, was abundant to within last mile. As high as the above, on this side or that extended dwarf shrubby canoe birches and almost impassable thickets of dwarf fir and spruce. The latter when dead exhibited the appearance of deer's horns, their hard, gnarled, slow-grown branches being twisted in every direction. Their roots were singularly knotted and swollen from time to time, from the size of the finger into oval masses like a ship's block, or a rabbit made of a handkerchief. Epigæa.‡‡ At this height, too, was a *Lycopodium*

---

*Aye, to summit.

†Loudon makes three (!) species, and says bees are very fond of the flower.

‡According to Durand at 78° N. in Smith's Sound.

§Durand in Kane places this at 65° N. in Greenland, but Kane (vol. i, p. 462) says that Morton and Hans saw it along the shore of Kennedy Channel, the furthest coast reached, and that with the southern Esquimaux it is reputed to cure scurvy.

**According to Durand, at 73° in Greenland.

††According to Durand, as far as Disco Island, 70° N.; "the ordinary food of deer and rabbits."

‡‡And after pretty high on Lafayette.

annotinum, a variety; and, probably, there, too, *L. Selago*, as at edge of ravine;* sedges, sorrel, moss, and lichens. Was surprised not to notice the *Potentilla tridentata* in bloom till quite high, though common on low mountains southward.† Here it was above the trailing spruce, answering to top of Monadnock, and with it came more sedge, *i.e.* a more grassy surface without many larger plants. (George Bradford says he has found this potentilla on Cape Ann, at Eastern Point, east side Gloucester Harbor.‡) About a mile below top, *Geum radiatum* var. *Peckii* in prime, and a little *Silene acaulis* (moss campion), still in bloom, a pretty little purplish flower growing like a moss in dense, hard tufts.§

The rocks of the alpine portion are of about uniform size, not large nor precipitous. Generally there is nothing to prevent ascending in any direction, and there is no climbing necessary on the summit. For the last mile the rocks are generally smaller and more bare and the ascent easier, and there are some rather large level grassy spaces. The rocks are not large and flat enough to hold water, as on Monadnock. I saw but little water on this summit, though in many places, commonly in small holes on the grassy flats, and I think the rocky portion under your feet is less interesting than at Monadnock. I sweated in a thick coat as I ascended. About half a mile below top I noticed dew on the mossy, tufted surface, with mountain cranberry in the sedge.

On the very summit I noticed moss, sedge (the kind I have tied together),** forming what is now to be called the Great Pasture there, they say; a little alsine and diapensia; a bright-green crustaceous lichen;†† and that small dark-brown umbilicaria-like one (of Monadnock), of which I have a specimen. The rocks, being small and not precipitous, have no such lichen-clad angles as at Monadnock, yet the general aspect of the rocks about you is dark-brown. All over the summit there is a great deal of that sedge grass, especially southeast

---

*Both, according to Durand, at 64° N. in Greenland.
†According to Durand at 79° N.
‡And Russell says in the college yard at Amherst.
§Durand says at 73° + in Greenland.
**Carex rigida*, with a black spike.
††Is this *Lecida geographica?* Oakes (in "Scenery," etc.) speaks of the geographic lichen as found on the summit; *viz.* "the yellow of the beautiful geographic lichen."

and east amid the smallish rocks. There was a solidago (or aster) quite near summit (not out), perhaps *S. Virgaurea.*

The only bird I had seen on the way up, above the limit of trees, was the *Fringilla hyemalis.* Willey says the swallow flies over the summit and that a bear has been seen there.

Mt. Washington, from Pinkham Notch

I got up about half an hour before my party and enjoyed a good view, though it was hazy, but by the time the rest arrived a cloud invested us all, a cool driving mist, which wet you considerably, as you squatted behind a rock. As I looked downward over the rock surface, I saw tinges of blue sky and a light as of breaking away close to the rocky edge of the mountain far below me instead of above, showing that there was the edge of the cloud. It was surprising to look down thus under the cloud at an angle of thirty or forty degrees for the only evidences of a clear sky and breaking away. There was a ring of light encircling the summit, thus close to the rocks under the thick cloud, and the evidences of a blue sky in that direction were just as strong as ordinarily when you look upward.

On our way up we had seen all the time, before us on the right, a large patch of snow on the southeast side of Mt. Adams, the first large summit north of Washington. I observed that the enduring snow-drifts were such as had lodged under the southeast cliffs, having been blown over the summit by the northwest wind. They lie up under such cliffs and at the head of the ravines on the southeast slopes.

A Mr. White, an artist taking views from the summit, had just returned from the Gulf of Mexico with the pretty purple-flowered *Phyllodoce taxifolia* and *Cassiope hypnoides*.

The landlords of the Tiptop and Summit Houses, Spaulding and Hall, assured me that my (Willey's) map was wrong, both in the names and height of Adams and Jefferson,—that the order should be reversed, Adams being the sharp peak, the second large one north of Washington,—but Boardman's map also calls this Jefferson.

Thoreau's morning climb followed the bridle path, which surveyors for the new road had staked all the way to the summit. Above the tree line, he had moved into the zone of sedge and cinquefoil, the alpine version of grass and roses. The ascent paused as he worked to get his botany straight, trying to draw a relationship between altitude and latitude. Every four hundred feet up is the equivalent of going seventy miles north; hence the plants here are those of Greenland or Labrador. Diapensia are the most prevalent "cushion plants," which adapt to their harsh environment with matted roots and tightly overlapped leaves. The flowers appear in early June, then use the remaining summer heat to ripen their seeds. Thoreau's "deer's horns" are dwarf

ROUTE FROM HALFWAY HOUSE: *Mt. Washington Carriage Road to summit* (see page 243) (see page 244) (see page 244)

The Mt. Washington Road

trees, or *krummholz* (German for "crooked wood"), that form the ultimate forest, their height no greater than winter snow.

The rocks above the tree line Thoreau could not inter- *(see page 245)* pret: once this folded mica schist was sedimentary (laid down on a seabed), then metamorphosed by heat and pressure, then lifted and folded up. A good example of folding appears halfway between mileposts 5 and 6. The "Great Pasture," used by horses and cows, was a sign of *(see page 245)* commerce lying ahead. Atop this peak, the highest in New England (6,288′), were two buildings: Summit House (rooms) and Tip-Top House (meals), both erected in 1852–53.

The scene today is less hospitable, for high-density development has come to Mt. Washington. Parking lots, offices for the carriage road and railway, a museum, a weather observatory, a TV and radio installation, and a new summit building—all cluster together on this valuable piece of altitude. A battery of transmitters soars even higher; they pump Muzak and the Red Sox onto the airwaves of New England. Inside the visitor center, a brisk air of commerce prevails: the hikers buy food and drink; the auto and railway riders collect souvenirs —badges, pennants, T-shirts (THIS BODY CLIMBED MT. WASHINGTON). The new building is a big investment for the state of New Hampshire, and only large crowds of non-hikers will make it pay off. Here they can lunch in the clouds, listen to the wind but not feel it. An expert naturalist might locate some of Thoreau's plants at the summit, but most are gone forever. On the trail that leads down into Tuckerman Ravine, hikers have left a hand-lettered sign of protest: "Coming Soon: McDonald's."

Tuckerman Ravine

JOURNAL

About 8.15 A.M., being still in a dense fog, we started direct for Tuckerman's Ravine, I having taken the bearing of it before the fog, but Spaulding also went some ten rods with us and pointed toward the head of the ravine, which was about S. 15° W. Hoar tried to hire Page to go with us, carrying part of our baggage,—as he had already brought it up from the shanty,—and he professed to be acquainted with the mountain; but his brother, who lived at the summit, warned him not to go, lest he should not be able to find his way back again, and he declined. The landlords were rather anxious about us. I looked at my compass every four or five rods and then walked toward some rock in our course, but frequently after taking three or four steps, though the fog was no more dense, I would lose the rock I steered for. The fog was very bewildering. You would think that the rock you steered for was some large boulder twenty rods off, or perchance it looked like the brow of a distant spur, but a dozen steps would take you to it, and it would suddenly have sunk into the ground. I discovered this illusion. I said to my companions, "You see that boulder of a peculiar form, slanting over another. Well, that is in our course. How large do you think it is, and how far?" To my surprise, one answered three rods, but the other said nine. I guessed four, and we all thought it about eight feet high. We could not see beyond it, and it looked like the highest part of a ridge before us. At the end of twenty-one paces or three and a half rods, I stepped upon it,—less than two feet high,—and I could not have distinguished it from the hundred similar ones around it, if I had not kept my eye on it all the while.

It is unwise for one to ramble over these mountains at any time, unless he is prepared to move with as much certainty as if he were solving a geometrical problem. A cloud may at any moment settle around him, and unless he has a compass and knows which way to go, he will be lost at once. One lost on the summit of these mountains should remember that if he will travel due east or west eight or nine miles, or commonly much less, he will strike a public road. Or whatever direction he might take, the average distance would not be more than eight miles and the extreme distance twenty. Follow some watercourse running easterly or westerly. If the weather were severe on the summit, so as to prevent searching for the summit houses or the path, I should at once take a westward course from the southern part of the range or an eastward one from the northern part. To travel there with security, a person must know his bearings at every step, be it fair weather or foul. An ordinary rock in a fog, being in the apparent horizon, is exaggerated to, perhaps, at least ten times its size and distance. You will think you have gone further than you have to get to it.

Descending straight by compass through the cloud, toward the head of Tuckerman's Ravine, we found it an easy descent over, for the most part, bare rocks, not very large, with at length moist springy places, green with sedge, etc., between little sloping shelves of green meadow, where the hellebore grew, within half a mile of top, and the *Oldenlandia cœrulea* was abundantly out (!) and very large and fresh, surpassing ours in the spring. And here, I think, *Juncus trifidus* (?),* and *Lycopodium Selago*, and *Lonicera cœrulea*, or mountain fly-honeysuckle, in bloom, only two specimens; it is found in the western part of Massachusetts.† Saw a few little ferns of a narrow triangular form, somewhat like the *Woodsia Ilvensis*, but less hairy and taller; small clintonias in bloom, and *Viola palustris*, in prime, from three quarters of a mile below summit down to snow; and a fine juncus or scirpus, *cæspitosus*-like, *i.e.* a single-headed or spiked rush;

*Yes.

†Oakes makes the plain above the ravine twelve hundred feet or more below summit.

and trientalis, still in bloom, rather depauperate; and, I think, a few small narrow-leaved blueberry bushes; at least one minute mountain-ash. Also the *Geum radiatum* var. *Peckii* was conspicuous in prime hence down to the snow in the ravine. These chiefly in those peculiar moist and mossy sloping shelves on the mountain-side, on way to the ravine, or within a mile of the summit.

Some twenty or thirty rods above the edge of the ravine, where it was more level and wet and grassy under low cliffs, grew the *Phyllodoce taxifolia*, not in tufts, under the jutting rocks and in moss, somewhat past prime. The *Uvularia grandiflora* apparently in prime, and, part way down into ravine, *Loiseleuria (Azalea) procumbens*, on rocks, still in bloom, and *Cassiope hypnoides*, about done. These four on a moist southeast slope. Also *Rubus triflorus*, reaching to camp, in prime.

Just on the edge of the ravine I began to see the *Heracleum lanatum* in prime, and the common archangelica, not out; and as I descended into the ravine on the steep side moist with melted snows, *Veronica alpina*, apparently in prime, and *Nabalus Boottii* (?) budded, down to snow, and *Epilobium alpinum* in prime, and *Platanthera dilatata* in prime, and the common rue and the first *Castilleja septentrionalis (Bartsia pallida)*, apparently not long, which was more common about our camp. I recollect seeing all the last eight (except the rue and veronica and nabalus, which I do not remember) about our camp and yet more flourishing there and *Solidago Virgaurea* var. *alpina*, not quite out, edge of ravine. Should have included *Arnica mollis* among those on side of ravine reaching to camp, and, according to Hoar, raspberry and linnæa.

ROUTE FROM MT. WASHINGTON: *Summit to Tuckerman Junction, to Headwall and Little Headwall, to Hermit Lake Shelter* — The path to Tuckerman Ravine is now well marked, but dense fogs are common at the summit and hikers can easily lose their way. Thoreau's skill as a surveyor kept him on track as he headed downhill in a heavy mist; today bright yellow blazes on the cairns provide welcome points of reference. The best view of Tuckerman Ravine is along Lion Head Trail, which skirts the north ridge and descends to Hermit Lake. From the summit, Thoreau apparently headed west into Bigelow Lawn, where Edward Tuckerman had collected so many lichen specimens.

We crossed a narrow portion of the snow, but found it unexpectedly hard and dangerous to traverse. I tore up my nails in my efforts to save myself from sliding down its steep surface. The snow-field now formed an irregular crescent on the steep slope at the head of the ravine, some sixty rods wide horizontally, or from north to south, and twenty-five rods wide from upper to lower side [drawing]. It may have been half a dozen feet thick in some places, but it diminished sensibly in the rain while we were there. Is said to be all gone commonly by end of August. The surface was hard, difficult to work your heels into, and a perfectly regular steep slope, steeper than an ordinary roof from top to bottom. A considerable stream, a source of the Saco, was flowing out from beneath it, where it had worn a low arch a rod or more wide. Here were the phenomena of winter and earliest spring, contrasted with summer. On the edge of and beneath the overarching snow, many plants were just pushing up as in our spring. The great plaited elliptical buds of the hellebore had just pushed up there, even under the edge of the snow, and also bluets. Also, close to edge of snow, the bare upright twigs of a willow, with small silvery buds not yet expanded, of a satiny lustre, one to two feet high (apparently *Salix repens*),* but not, as I noticed, procumbent, while a rod off on each side, where it had been melted some time, it was going to seed and fully leaved out. The surface of the snow was dirty, being covered with cinder-like rubbish of vegetation, which had blown on to it. Yet from the camp it looked quite white and pure. For thirty or forty rods, at least, down the stream, you could see the point where the snow had recently melted. It was a dirty-brown flattened stubble, not yet at all greened, covered with a blackish slimy dirt, the dust of the snow-crust. Looking closely, I saw that it was composed in great part of the stems and flowers apparently of last year's goldenrods (if not asters), —perhaps large *thyrsoidea*, for they grew there on the slides,—now quite flattened, with other plants. A pretty large dense-catkined willow grew in the upper part of the ravine, *q.v.* Also, near edge of snow,

*Also apparently *S. phylicifolia*.

vanilla grass, a vaccinium,* budded, with broad obovate leaves *(q.v.)*, *Spiræa salicifolia* (and *on slides*), and nabalus *(Boottii?)* leaves.

From the edge of the ravine, I should have said that, having reached the lower edge of the cloud, we came into the sun again, much to our satisfaction, and discerned a little lake called Hermit Lake, about a mile off, at the bottom of the ravine, just within the limit of the trees. For this we steered, in order to camp by it for the sake of the protec-

Tuckerman Ravine and Mt. Washington, from Hermit Lake

tion of the wood. But following down the edge of the stream, the source of Ellis River, which was quite a brook within a stone's throw of its head, we soon found it very bad walking in the scrubby fir and spruce, and therefore, when we had gone about two thirds the way to the lake, decided to camp in the midst of the dwarf firs, clearing away a space with our hatchets. Having cleared a space with some

°This is apparently *V. cæ*spitosum, for the anthers are two-awned, though I count but ten stamens in the flower I open, and I did not notice that the plant was tufted. Apparently the same, with thinner leaves, by Peabody River at base, but noticed no flowers there. Yet Gray refers it only to the alpine region!

difficulty where the trees were seven or eight feet high, Wentworth kindled a fire on the lee side, without—against my advice—removing the moss, which was especially dry on the rocks and directly ignited and set fire to the fir leaves, spreading off with great violence and crackling over the mountain, and making us jump for our baggage; but fortunately it did not burn a foot toward us, for we could not have run in that thicket. It spread particularly fast in the procumbent creeping spruce, scarcely a foot deep, and made a few acres of deer's horns, thus leaving our mark on the mountainside. We thought at first it would run for miles, and W. said that it would do no harm, the more there was burned the better; but such was the direction of the wind that it soon reached the brow of a ridge east of us and then burned very slowly down its east side. Yet Willey says (page 23), speaking of the dead trees or "buck's horns," "Fire could not have caused the death of these trees; for fire will not spread here, in consequence of the humidity of the whole region at this elevation;" and he attributes their death to the cold of 1816. Yet it did spread above the limit of trees in the ravine.

Finally we kept on, leaving the fire raging, down to the first little lake, walking in the stream, jumping from rock to rock with it. It may have fallen a thousand feet within a mile below the snow, and we camped on a slight rising ground between that first little lake and the stream, in a dense fir and spruce wood thirty feet high, though it was but the limit of trees there. On our way we found the *Arnica mollis* (recently begun to bloom), a very fragrant yellow-rayed flower, by the side of the brook (also half-way up the ravine). The *Alnus viridis* was a prevailing shrub all along this stream, seven or eight feet high near our camp near the snow. It was dwarfish and still in flower, but in fruit only below; had a glossy, roundish, wrinkled, green, sticky leaf. Also a little *Ranunculus abortivus* by the brook, in bloom.

Close by our camp, the *Heracleum lanatum,* or cow-parsnip, masterwort, grew quite rankly, its great leaves eighteen inches wide and umbels eight or nine inches wide; the petioles had inflated sheaths. I afterward saw it, I think in Campton, as much as seven feet high. It was quite common and conspicuous in the neighborhood of the mountains, especially in Franconia Notch. Our camp was opposite a great slide on the south, apparently a quarter of a mile wide, with the stream between us and it, and I resolved if a great storm should occur that we would flee to higher ground northeast. The little pond by our side was perfectly clear and cool, without weeds, and the meadow by it was dry enough to sit down in. When I looked up casually toward the crescent of snow I would mistake it for the sky, a white glowing sky or cloud, it was so high, while the dark earth on [the] mountainside above it passed for a dark cloud.

In the course of the afternoon we heard, as we thought, a faint shout, and it occurred to me that Blake, for whom I had left a note at the Glen House, might possibly be looking for me; but soon Wentworth decided that it must be a bear, for they make a noise like a woman in distress. He has caught many of them. Nevertheless, we shouted in return and waved a light coat on the meadow. After an hour or two had elapsed, we heard the voice again, nearer, and saw two men, and I went up the stream to meet Blake and Brown, wet, ragged, and bloody with black flies. I had told Blake to look out for a smoke and a white tent, and we had made a smoke sure enough. They were on the edge of the ravine when they shouted and heard us answer, or about a mile distant,—heard over all the roar of the stream!! You could hear one shout from Hermit Lake to the top of the ravine above snow, back and forth, which I should think was a mile. They also saw our coat waved and ourselves. We slept five in the tent that night, and it rained, putting out the fire we had set. It was quite warm at night in our tent.

The wood thrush, which Wentworth called the nightingale, sang at evening and in the morning, and the same bird which I heard on Monadnock, I think, and then thought might be the Blackburnian warbler; also the veery.*

> At the upper edge of Tuckerman Ravine stands one of the classic forms of glacial action, an immense bowl-shaped cirque. For thousands of years, snow and ice packed against the Headwall; then cycles of freeze and thaw plucked away its rock, slowly cutting a rim into the

*In that entry, Thoreau wrote: "Going up a mountain is like travelling half a day through a tan-yard, till you get into a fog, and then, when the fog blows away, you discover yourself and a buzzing fly on the sunny mountain-top."—WH

mountainside. The cirque is a cloud-maker: cold prevailing winds sweep across from the west, condensing warm
air from below and spilling streams of fog back over the
edge. Nervous hikers welcome the fog, which helps to
obscure a sheer drop of nearly six hundred feet. Beyond
its Headwall, Tuckerman has the characteristic V-shape
of a glacial ravine. The main stream fans out into cascades, gathers to plunge over short falls, then disappears
far below—still cutting a ragged incision into the valley
floor. Along the stream, ground moisture sustains a great
variety of life, including hellebore (Indian poke), a thick,
broadleaf plant that grows here in lush beds, so luxuri-
ant they seem more suited to the tropics. *(see page 253)*

The steep, narrow trail is generally wet; crews have
reduced the hazards Thoreau faced by building rock
stairways and dry walls at difficult passes. The present
trail heads to the right of Thoreau's line of descent; the
"snowfield," a great bank of impacted snow, is not a true
glacier, for it generally melts away by late summer. The
stream that runs beneath the bank carves a deep, fluted
channel, about seven feet high. Above, the snow is gritty
with dirt and rock dust; but within the arch lies a gleaming cave of translucent blue. For Thoreau, this sight was *(see page 253)*
a living paradox, the place where purity and cinders,
summer and winter, stood together.

His party probably attempted to camp first at Little
Headwall, where the floor of the ravine makes a second *(see page 254)*
drop and descends to Hermit Lake. Today open fires are
prohibited, and the ranger on duty has Thoreau on a list
of incendiaries: "We revoked his permit. He never came
back." Wentworth's casual attitude about the fire does *(see page 255)*
not conceal the fact that it was severe; apparently, it
reached the ridge above Little Headwall (at 4,380′).
Heading farther downstream, a descent of 800 feet in less
than a mile, they camped at the small pool just south of
Hermit Lake. Today this area is a campground and ski- *(see page 256)*
ing center, with an information hut and several lean-to

shelters for packers. The shelters face down the ravine, out of the wind and looking east.

(see page 256) Thoreau treated the arrival of Blake and Brown with sober good humor: his fellow philosophers were sweaty and fly-bitten; his trusted guide thought their shouts might have been a bear. Apparently Blake and Brown had been trailing Thoreau for several days; they followed him to the summit and then down into the ravine. The acoustics here are surprisingly good; trail crews working at the top of Lion Head can be heard below. *(see page 256)* Sleeping five in a tent was crowded; today's shelters comfortably house dozens. A few days later, one of the party returned to Summit House for supplies and met some visiting journalists. One of them dramatically reported to the New York *Tribune* on July 17:

". . . they woke up in the morning perfectly dry, although they had only a cotton tent for shelter. The water ran down hill under them, through the crevices of their bed of fir and spruce boughs, without damping the highest stratum. Mr. Thoreau doubtless understands as well as any mountaineer how to make himself comfortable under such circumstances, but we could not help shivering, as we looked down the ravine the next morning and saw the banks of snow that are all but eternal, and the little black pools a mile below, beside which the party camped for four nights."

July 9. Friday. Walked to the Hermit Lake, some forty rods northeast. *Listera cordata* abundant and in prime in the woods, with a little *Platanthera obtusata,* also apparently in prime. (The last also as far up as the head of the ravine sparingly.) This was a cold, clear lake with scarcely a plant in it, of perhaps half an acre, and from a low ridge east of it was a fine view up the ravine. Hoar tried in vain for trout here. The *Vaccinium Canadense* was the prevailing one here and by our camp. Heard a bullfrog in the lake, and afterward saw a large toad part way up the ravine. Our camp was about on the limit of trees here, and may have been from twenty-five hundred to three thousand feet below the summit.

I was here surprised to discover, looking down through the fir-tops, a large, bright, downy fair-weather cloud covering the lower world far beneath us, and there it was the greater part of the time we were there, like a lake, while the snow and alpine summit were to be seen above us on the other side, at about the same angle. The pure white crescent of snow was our sky, and the dark mountainside above, our permanent cloud.

We had the *Fringilla hyemalis* with its usual note about our camp, and Wentworth said it was common and bred about his house. I afterward saw it in the valleys about the mountains. I had seen the white-throated sparrow near his house. This also, he said, commonly bred there, on the ground.

The wood we were in was fir and spruce. Along the brook grew the *Alnus viridis*, *Salix Torreyana* (?), canoe birch, red cherry, mountain-ash, etc., and prominent among lesser plants, *Heracleum lanatum*, *Castilleja septentrionalis*, the swamp gooseberry in flower and in green fruit, and a sort of *Ribes floridum* without resinous-dotted leaves! The *Hedyotis cœrulea* was surprisingly large and fresh, in bloom, looking as much whiter than usual as late snows do. I thought they must be a variety. And on a sand-bar by the brook, *Oxyria digyna*, the very pretty mountain sorrel, apparently in prime.* Apparently *Viola blanda*, as well as wool-grass, in the meadow, and apparently *Aster prenanthes* and *Juncus filiformis;* also rhodora, fetid currant, amelanchier (variety *oligocarpa*), trientalis, mountain maple, tree-cranberry with green fruit, *Aster acuminatus*, and *Aralia nudicaulis* a salix *humilis*-like, and *Polystichum aculeatum* (? ?), and *Lycopodium annotinum* (variety).

I ascended the stream in the afternoon and got out of the ravine at its head, after dining on chiogenes tea, which plant I could gather without moving from my log seat. We liked it so well that Blake gathered a parcel to carry home. In most places it was scarcely practicable to get out of the ravine on either side on account of precipices. I judged it to be one thousand or fifteen hundred feet deep, but with

*Seen in Kane's expedition by Hans, etc., at the furthest north point, or 80°+.

care you could ascend by some slides. I found that we might have
camped in the scrub firs above the edge of the ravine, though it would
have been cold and windy and comparatively unpleasant there, for we
should have been most of the time in a cloud.

The dense patches of dwarf fir and spruce scarcely rose above the
rocks which they concealed, and you would often think the trees not
more than a foot or two deep,—as, indeed, they might not be generally,
—but, searching within, you would find hollow places six or eight feet
deep between the rocks, where they filled up all level, and by clearing a
space here with your hatchet you could find a shelter for your tent, and
also fuel, and water was close by above the head of the ravine. Nevertheless, at a glance, looking over, or even walking over, this dense
shrubbery, you would have thought it nowhere more than a foot or two
deep, and the trees at most only an inch or two in diameter; but by
searching you would find deep hollow places in it, as I have said, where
the firs were from six to ten inches in diameter. The strong wind and
the snow are said to flatten these trees down thus. Such a shrubbery
would begin with a thin and shallow but dense edge of spruce, not more
than a foot thick, like moss upon a rock, on which you could walk, but in
many places in the middle of it, though its surface was of a uniform
slope, it would be found to be six or eight feet deep. So that these very
thickets of which the traveller complains afford at the same time an
indispensable shelter. I noticed that this shrubbery just above the
ravine, as well as in it, was principally fir, while the yet more dwarfish
and prostrate portion on the edge was spruce.

Returning, I sprained my ankle in jumping down the brook, so that
I could not sleep that night, nor walk the next day. We had commonly
clouds above and below us, though it was clear where we were. These
clouds commonly reached about down to the edge of the ravine.

The black flies, which pestered us till into evening, were of various
sizes, the largest more than an eighth of an inch long. There were
scarcely any mosquitoes here, it was so cool.

A small owl came in the evening and sat within twelve feet of us,
turning its head this way and that and peering at us inquisitively. It
was apparently a screech owl.*

*Or *Acadica ? ?* Saw-whet?

Views of the ravine from Hermit Lake can be clear or clouded, but always the high, rounded cirque dominates, rising far above this clearing. Thoreau could see two cloud layers, one above the Headwall and the other down *(see page 259)* in Pinkham Notch. Again he was struck by a paradoxical contrast, seeing a land that lies between clouds and earth. His solitary hike back up the ravine took him to *(see page 260)* Bigelow Lawn, which he now realized would make a miserable campsite, too wet and windy. Today the ravine is heavily forested and more difficult to explore on foot, but the stream bed does offer an alternative to the main trail. Thoreau's fall probably occurred below Little *(see page 260)* Headwall, where the talus, a jumble of loose rock, forms a treacherous slope for walking.

This incident later provoked different recollections by Thoreau's friends. Emerson said that Thoreau fell near a bed of *Arnica mollis,* a yellow daisy-like flower with broad leaves, which he boiled and used as a poultice. Thoreau actually saw the flower much earlier. Chan- *(see page 255)* ning reported that Thoreau "preferred the ice-cold water of the mountain stream, into which he boldly plunged his tortured limb to reduce the swelling."

July 10. *Saturday.* Wentworth says he once collected one hundred pounds of spruce gum and sold it at Biddeford for forty cents per pound. Says there are "sable lines" about here. They trap them, but rarely see them. His neighbor, who lives on the hill behind where we camped on the 6th, has four hours more sun than he. He can, accordingly, make hay better, but W. beats him in corn. The days are about forty minutes longer on top of Mt. Washington than at seashore, according to guide-book. The sun set to us here at least an hour earlier than usual.

This ravine at the bottom of which we were, looking westward up it, had a rim somewhat like that of the crater of a volcano. The head of it bore from camp about N. 65° W., looking nearer than it was; the highest rock, with the outline of a face on it on the south rim, S. 32° W.; a very steep cliff on the opposite side, N. 20° W.; and over the last we judged was the summit of Mt. Washington. As I understood Wentworth, this was in Pingree's Grant; the Glen House in Pinkham's Grant. To-day and yesterday clouds were continually drifting over the summit, commonly extending about down to the edge of the ravine. When we looked up that way, the black patch made by our fire looked like a shadow on the mountainside.

When I tasted the water under the snow arch the day before, I was disappointed at its warmth, though it was in fact melted snow; but half a mile lower it tasted colder. Probably, the ice being cooled by the neighborhood of the snow, it seemed thus warmer by contrast.

The only animals we saw about our camp were a few red squirrels. W. said there were striped ones about the mountains. The *Fringilla hyemalis* was most common in the upper part of the ravine, and I saw a large bird of prey, perhaps an eagle, sailing over the head of the ravine. The wood thrush and veery sang regularly, especially morning and evening. But, above all, the peculiar and memorable songster was that Monadnock-like one, keeping up an exceedingly brisk and lively strain. It was remarkable for its incessant twittering flow. Yet we never got sight of the bird, at least while singing, so that I could not identify it, and my lameness prevented my pursuing it. I heard it afterward, even in the Franconia Notch. It was surprising for its steady and uninterrupted flow, for when one stopped, another appeared to take up the strain. It reminded me of a fine corkscrew stream issuing with incessant lisping tinkle from a cork, flowing rapidly, and I said that he had pulled out the spile and left it running.* That was the rhythm, but with a sharper tinkle of course. It had no more variety than that, but it was more remarkable for its continuance and monotonousness than any bird's note I ever heard. It evidently belongs only to cool mountainsides, high up amid the fir and spruce. I saw once flitting through the fir-tops restlessly a small white and dark bird, sylvia-like, which may have been it. Sometimes they appeared to be attracted by our smoke. The note was so incessant that at length you only noticed when it ceased.

The black flies were of various sizes here, much larger than I

---

*Torrey and Allen, original editors of the Journal, identify this bird as the winter wren.—WH

noticed in Maine. They compelled me most of the time to sit in the smoke, which I preferred to wearing a veil. They lie along your forehead in a line, where your hat touches it, or behind your ears, or about your throat (if not protected by a beard), or into the rims of the eyes, or between the knuckles, and there suck till they are crushed. But fortunately they do not last far into the evening, and a wind or a fog disperses them. I did not mind them much, but I noticed that men working on the highway made a fire to keep them off. I find many of them accidentally pressed in my botany and plant book. A botanist's books, if he has ever visited the primitive northern woods, will be pretty sure to contain these specimens of the black fly. Anything but mosquitoes by night. Plenty of fly-blowing flies, but I saw no ants in the dead wood; some spiders.

In the afternoon, Hoar, Blake, and Brown ascended the slide on the south to the highest rock. They were more than an hour getting up, but we heard them shout distinctly from the top. Hoar found near the edge of the ravine there, between the snow there and edge, *Rhododendron Lapponicum,* some time out of bloom,* growing in the midst of empetrum and moss; *Arctostaphylos alpina,* going to seed; *Polygonum viviparum,* in prime;† and *Salix herbacea,*‡ a pretty, trailing, roundish-leaved willow, going to seed, but apparently not so early as the *S. Uva-ursi.*

July 11. *Sunday.* Mizzling weather. Were visited by three men from Glen House, who thought it was well named *"Tucker's* Ravine," because it tuckered a man out to get to it!

It rained hard all Sunday night, wetting us but little, however. One of the slender spruce trees by our camp, which we cut down, though it looked young and thrifty, being twenty-eight feet high and only six and a half inches in diameter, had about eighty rings, and the firs were at least as old.

Wentworth said that he had five hundred acres, and would sell the whole with buildings for $2000. He knew a dead log on the fire to be spruce, and not fir, because the stubs of the lower part slanted downward, and also by its "straight rift." He called a rotten cane "dozy."

*According to Durand, at 68° in Greenland.
†According to Durand, at all Kane's stations.
‡According to Durand, at 73° in Greenland.

After some observation I concluded that it was true that the *base* of the lower limbs of the spruce slanted downward more generally than those of the fir.

(see page 261)

(see page 262)

(see page 262)

(see page 263)

Thoreau's injury accounts for the chatty, meandering nature of his entries for the next few days. Conversations with Wentworth yielded bits of local color: the "neighbor" was Charles C. Fernald, who lived on a ridge north of Spruce Mountain (west of NH 16B, Carter Notch Road). Although immobile, Thoreau could put his senses to work; his description of that "memorable songster" is a fine attempt to convey sight and sound. This devotion to actuality *is* the "philosophy" of his later years. Blackfly, a perennial pest in northern forests, is most plentiful in seasons of high water. The female (she alone is the aggressor) injects an enzyme that prevents blood from clotting.

Thoreau's three friends climbed up Boott Spur; today the Link and Boott Spur trails lead there from Hermit Lake. Boott Spur commemorates the work of three botanist brothers: Francis, Wright, and William Boott, who explored this area thoroughly in the early nineteenth century. In 1862, William Boott found near Lakes of the Clouds a rare species he called Cloudy Reedgrass *(Calamagrostis nubila)*. He may have collected all the extant specimens, for it has not been sighted since then. The Boott Spur trail is difficult climbing, especially in hot weather; it rises swiftly out of the tree line to an exposed ridge, then crosses a series of spurs and gullies, each growing less steep. From here, the view north takes in both Tuckerman and Huntington, the two principal ravines on the eastern slope of Mt. Washington.

July 12. *Monday.* It having cleared up, we shouldered our packs and commenced our descent, by a path about two and a half or three miles to carriage-road, not descending a great deal.

The prevailing under-plants at first, as we descended, were *Oxalis*

Acetosella (abundantly in bloom), *Cornus Canadensis, Clintonia borealis,* chiogenes, *Vaccinium Canadense,* gold-thread, *Listera cordata, Smilacina bifolia. Solidago thyrsoidea,* large and prevalent, on more open and grassy parts, from top of ravine to base of mountain, where it was in prime, three feet high and spikes eighteen inches long. Trees, at first, fir and spruce; then canoe birches* increased, and after two miles yellow birch began. Half-way down the mountain, on the road, saw a whiteweed and one *Alsine Grœnlandica.* It [is] surprising how much of that white froth, the nidus of an insect, there was on the grass and weeds on and about the mountains. They were white with it. *Carex trisperma* (?), three-quarters down. Hear the oven-bird near base. Dined by Peabody River, three quarters of a mile south of Glen House. Found *Lonicera ciliata* in fruit there† and saw a little white pine, and *Alnus incana* was common, and that large, fragrant *Aster macrophyllus* (?) was budded.

I had noticed that the trees at the ravine camp—fir and spruce—did not stand firmly. Two or three of us could have pulled over one thirty feet high and six or seven inches thick. They were easily rocked, lifting the horizontal roots each time, which reminded me of what is said about the Indians sometimes bending over a young tree, burying a chief under its roots, and letting it spring back for his monument and protection. W. said they had found the fir the best material for bridge planking in his town, outlasting other woods!

In the afternoon we rode along, three of us, northward and northwestward on our way round the mountains, going through Gorham. We camped about a mile and a half west of Gorham, by the roadside, on the bank of Moose River.

Raymond Path joins the Carriage Road at milepost 2 and descends thereafter to Glen House. On this walk, Thoreau continued to record plant zones, verifying data gathered on the ascent. In his day, some of this forest was still first growth, but now mostly second- and third-generation trees are here. The shift from conifers to hard-

ROUTE FROM TUCKERMAN RAVINE: *Raymond Path to Carriage Road, NH 16 to Gorham*

---

*Oakes says the white birch (here, meaning the canoe) come in after a burning.
†Found in Essex woods.

(see page 265) woods is also a change in color, from dark blues to a more lively green. The Peabody River is a rocky stream along NH 16 that attracts many insect-feeding birds in early or late hours. Shallow roots of trees in the ravine are not inherent but an adaptation to soil and water conditions. Thoreau was surprised to see bridges built of fir, since the wood is weak and coarse-grained. The camp spot that *(see page 265)* evening was near the present site of Moose Brook State Park, on US 2.

Lafayette

JOURNAL

July 13. *Tuesday.* This morning it rained, keeping us in camp till near noon, for we did not wish to lose the view of the mountains as we rode along.

We dined at Wood's tavern in Randolph, just over Randolph Hill, and here had a pretty good view of Madison and Jefferson, which rose from just south the stream there, but a cloud rested on the summits most of the time.

As we rode along in the afternoon, I noticed that when finally it began to rain hard, the clouds settling down, we had our first distinct view of the mountain outline for a short time.

Wood said they had no spruce but white spruce there, though I called it black, and that they had no white pine nor oak.

It rained steadily and soakingly the rest of the afternoon, as we kept on through Randolph and Kilkenny and Jefferson Hill, so that we had no clear view of the mountains.

We put up at a store just opposite the town hall on Jefferson Hill.

It here cleared up at sunset, after two days' rain, and we had a fine view of the mountains, repaying us for our journey and wetting, Mt. Washington being some thirteen miles distant southeasterly. South-westward we looked down over a very extensive, uninterrupted, and level-looking forest, which our host said was very valuable on account of its white pine, their most valuable land, indeed. Over this the fog clouds were rolling beneath us, and a splendid but cloudy sunset was preparing for us in the west. By going still higher up the hill, in the wet grass north of the town house, we could see the whole White Mountain range from Madison to Lafayette.

The alpine, or rocky, portion of Mt. Washington and its neighbors was a dark chocolate-brown, the extreme summits being dark topped or edged,—almost invariably this dark saddle on the top,—and, as the sun got lower, a very distinct brilliant and beautiful green, as of a thick mantle, was reflected from the vegetation in the ravines, as from the fold of a mantle, and on the lower parts of the mountains. They were chiefly Washington and the high northern peaks that we at-tended to. The waifs of fog-like cloud skirting the sides of Cherry Mountain and Mt. Deception in the south had the appearance of rocks, and gave to the mountainsides a precipitous look. I saw a bright streak looking like snow, a narrow bright ribbon where the source of the Ammonoosuc, swollen by the rain, leaped down the side of Mt. Washington from the Lake of the Clouds. The shadows on Lafayette betrayed ridges running toward us. That brilliant green on the north-ern mountains was reflected but a moment or two, for the atmosphere at once became too misty. It several times disappeared and was then brought out again with wonderful brilliancy, as it were an invisible writing, or a fluid which required to be held to the sun to be brought out.

After the sun set to us, the bare summits were of a delicate rosa-ceous color, passing through violet into the deep dark-blue or purple of the night which already invested their lower parts, for this night-shadow was wonderfully blue, reminding me of the blue shadows on snow. There was an afterglow in which these tints and variations were repeated. It was the grandest mountain view I ever got. In the meanwhile, white clouds were gathering again about the summits, first about the highest, appearing to form there, but sometimes to send off an emissary to initiate a cloud upon a neighboring peak. You could tell little about the comparative distance of a cloud and a peak till you saw that the former actually impinged on the latter. First Washington, then Adams, then Jefferson put on their caps, and you saw the latter, as it were, send off one small nucleus to gather round the head of Madison.

Mt. Adams and Mt. Jefferson

This was the best point from which to observe these effects that we *saw* in our journey, but it appeared to me that from a hill a few miles further westward, perhaps in Whitefield, the view might be even finer. I made the accompanying two sketches of the mountain outline here, as far south only as what the landlord called Mt. Pleasant, the route from the Notch house being visible no further. [drawing]

This was said to be a fine farming town. I heard the ring of toads and saw a remarkable abundance of buttercup (the tall) yellowing the fields in this town and the next, somewhat springlike.

ROUTE FROM GORHAM: *US 2 to NH 116, to Whitefield* (see page 266) Thoreau's dining spot in Randolph is just beyond the present site of Ravine House, on US 2. His disagreement with the tavern owner over white and black spruce had a long background. For years Thoreau believed that "few inhabitants of Concord" (other than he) could properly identify the two species; then in May 1857 he admitted: "After all, I seem to have distinguished only one spruce, and that the black, judging by the cones." The needles of white and black spruce are quite similar, but white-spruce cones are much longer and rarely persist on the tree after autumn. (For his troubles with red spruce, see p. 275.)

The town hall of Jefferson Highlands is still standing: *(see page 266)* from its side yard the Presidentials are visible eleven miles directly south. Of this rainy day Thoreau set down mostly afterthoughts, prompted also by his greater distance from the mountains. Having gathered facts about plant zones, he now delivered impressions of their shape and color. Cherry Mountain (3,050') and Mt. Deception (3,658') were seven and eight miles south of his position. His sight of Ammonoosuc Ravine (seventeen miles southeast) recalled the trip of 1839 with John; the fading *(see page 267)* light of late afternoon seemed to bring forth larger inferences, less scientific and more reflective.

July 14. *Wednesday.* This forenoon we rode on through Whitefield to Bethlehem, clouds for the most part concealing the higher mountains. Found the *Geum strictum* in bloom in Whitefield; also common flax by a house. Got another fine view of the mountains—the higher ones much more distant than before—from a hill just south of the public house in Bethlehem, but might have got a better view from a higher hill a little more east, which one said was the highest land between the Green and the White Mountains, of course on that line. Saw the Stratford Peaks, thirty or forty miles north, and many mountains east of them. Climbed the long hill from Franconia to the Notch, passed the Profile House, and camped half a mile up the side of Lafayette. . . .*

The journey to Franconia Notch passed swiftly in Thoreau's account; a traveler today will find startling contrasts along the roadside. In Jefferson the traditional ROUTE FROM WHITEFIELD: *NH 116 to NH 142, US 3 to Mt. Lafayette*

---

*At this point Thoreau quotes extensively from Loudon on alpine plants and their circumpolar distribution, from Europe to North America.—WH

The Stratford Peaks

crafts of New England grace Waumbek Village, yet
nearby is Six Gun City, where blazing gun battles are
(see page 269) staged every half hour. The "higher hill" from which
Thoreau anticipated a better vantage is now the site of
Kimball Hill Inn, where tall, thick trees obscure most
views. Stratford (2,405′), the Percy peaks (3,220′), and
Long (3,615′) are all thirty to thirty-five miles northeast.
Along Butter Hill Road, Thoreau was returning to scenes
of his earlier visit, now greatly changed. Franconia had
become a bustling summer resort. In place of the modest
Lafayette Inn stood an imposing hotel, Profile House,
boasting one hundred and ten rooms for prosperous visitors. (Schoolteachers and artists congregated at Flume
House, farther south.)
(see page 269)   Thoreau ascended Lafayette via the Old Bridle Path,
opened in the early 1850s, which connected Profile House
with Eagle Lakes. Over the years, ironshod hoofs have
worn a deep trench into the soil and rock. The path is
now a self-guided nature trail, where hikers (some 15,000

a year) can study the area's history and ecology. Thoreau's campsite was near point 2 on this trail, well
within the hardwood forest at 1,500 feet. He probably
climbed Lafayette because it was the highest peak in
Franconia Notch (sixth highest in the White Mountains)
and thus gave him an eastern view of the Presidentials.

July 15. *Thursday.* Continued the ascent of Lafayette, also called the
Great Haystack. It is perhaps three and a half miles from the road to
the top by path along winding ridge.

At about a mile and a half up by path, the spruce began to be small.
Saw there a silent bird, dark slate and blackish above, especially head,
with a white line over the brows, then dark slate next beneath, white
throat and reddish belly, black bill. A little like a nuthatch. Also saw
an *F. hyemalis* on top of a dead tree. The wood was about all spruce
here, twenty feet high, together with *Vaccinium Canadense*, lambkill in bloom, mountain-ash, *Viburnum nudum*, rhodora, *Amelanchier oligocarpa*, nemopanthes. As I looked down into some very broad
and deep ravines from this point, their sides appeared to be covered
chiefly with spruce, with a few bodkin points of fir here and there (had
seen two days before some very handsome firs on low ground which
were actually concave on sides of cone) [drawing], while the narrow
bottom or middle of the ravine, as far up and down as trees reached,
where, of course, there was most water, was almost exclusively hard-
wood, apparently birch chiefly.

As we proceeded, the number of firs began to increase, and the
spruce to diminish, till, at about two miles perhaps, the wood was
almost pure fir about fourteen feet high; but this suddenly ceased at
about half a mile further and gave place to a very dwarfish fir, and
to spruce again, the latter of a very dwarfish, procumbent form, dense
and flat, one to two feet high, which crept yet higher up the mountain
than the fir,—over the rocks beyond the edge of the fir,—and with this
spruce was mixed *Empetrum nigrum*, dense and matted on the
rocks, partly dead, with berries already blackening, also *Vaccinium
uliginosum*. Though the edges all around and the greater part of
such a thicket high up the otherwise bare rocks might be spruce, yet
the deeper hollows between the rocks, in the midst, would invariably

be filled with fir, rising only to the same level, but much larger round. These firs especially made the stag-horns when dead.

The spruce was mostly procumbent at that height, but the fir upright, though flat-topped. In short, spruce gave place to fir from a mile and a half to a mile below the top,—so you may say firs were the highest trees,—and then succeeded to it in a very dwarfish and procumbent form yet higher up.

At about one mile or three quarters below the summit, just above the limit of trees, we came to a little pond, maybe of a quarter of an acre (with a yet smaller one near by), the source of one head of the Pemigewasset, in which grew a great many yellow lilies *(Nuphar advena)* and I think a potamogeton. In the flat, dryish bog by its shore, I noticed the *Empetrum nigrum* (1), ledum (2), *Vaccinium Oxycoccus, Smilacina trifolia, Kalmia glauca* (3) (in bloom still), *Andromeda calyculata* (4) (and I think *Polifolia??*), *Eriophorum vaginatum, Vaccinium uliginosum* (5), *Juncus filiformis,* four kinds of sedge *(e.g. Carex pauciflora?), C. irrigua* with dangling spikes, and a *C. lupulina*-like, and the *Scirpus cæspitosus* (?) of Mt. Washington, brown lichens *(q.v.),* and cladonias, all low and in a moss-like bed in the moss of the bog; also rhodora of good size. 1, 2, 3, 4, and 5 were quite dwarfish. The outlet of the pond was considerable, but soon lost beneath the rocks. A willow, *rostrata*-like but not downy, grew there. In the dwarf fir thickets above and below this pond, I saw the most beautiful linnæas that I ever saw. They grew quite densely, full of rose-purple flowers,—deeper reddish-purple than ours, which are pale,—perhaps nodding over the brink of a spring, altogether the fairest mountain flowers I saw, lining the side of the narrow horse-track through the fir scrub. As you walk, you overlook the top of this thicket on each side. There also grew near that pond red cherry, *Aster prenanthes* (??) and common rue.

We saw a line of fog over the Connecticut Valley. Found near summit apparently the *Vaccinium angustifolium* of Aitman (variety of *Vaccinium Pennsylvanicum,* Gray), bluets, and a broadleaved vaccinium lower down *(q.v.).* Just below top, reclined on a dense bed of *Salix Uva-ursi,* five feet in diameter by four or five inches deep, a good spot to sit on, mixed with a rush, amid rocks. This willow was generally showing its down.

We had fine weather on this mountain, and from the summit a good view of Mt. Washington and the rest, though it was a little hazy in the horizon. It was a wild mountain and forest scene from south-southeast round easterwardly to north-northeast. On the northwest the country was half cleared, as from Monadnock,—the leopard-spotted land. I saw, about west-northwest, a large *Green* Mountain, perhaps Mansfield Mountain, though the compass was affected here.

The *Carex scirpoidea* (?) grew at top, and it was surprising how many large bees, wasps, butterflies, and other insects were hovering and fluttering about the very apex, though not particularly below. What attracts them to such a locality?*

Heard one white-throated sparrow above the trees, and also saw a little bird by the pond. Think I heard a song sparrow about latter place. Saw a toad near limit of trees, and many pollywogs in the pond above trees.

Boiled tea for our dinner by the little pond, the head of the Pemigewasset. Saw tracks in the muddy bog by the pond-side, shaped somewhat like a small human foot *sometimes*, perhaps made by a bear.

We made our fire on the moss and lichens, by a rock, amid the shallow fir and spruce, burning the dead fir twigs, or "deer's-horns." I cut off a flourishing fir three feet high and not flattened at top yet. This was one and a quarter inches in diameter and had thirty-four rings. One, also flourishing, fifteen inches high, had twelve rings at ground. One, a dead one, was twenty-nine inches in circumference, and at four feet from ground branched horizontally as much as five feet each way, making a flat top, curving upward again into stag-horns, with branches very large and stout at base, thus: [drawing] Another fir, close by and dead, was thirty inches in circumference at ground and only half an inch in diameter at four and a half feet. Another fir, three feet high, fresh and vigorous, without a flat top as

---

*In an account of C. Piazzi Smyth's scientific mission under the English Government to the Peak of Teneriffe, in 1856, it is said, "In the hollow of this crater [the topmost] 12,200 feet above the sea level, though at a lesser altitude they had left all signs of animal life, they found a population of bees, flies, spiders, as well as swallows and linnets—the birds and insects flying about in numbers."

And of a lower altitude, speaking of the flowers, it is said that during the early summer "the townspeople [of Orotava] find it worth their while to pack their hives of bees on mules and bring them to these upper regions to gather honey from the myriads of mountain flowers."

yet, had its woody part an inch and an eighth thick (or diameter) at base (the bark being one eighth inch thick) and sixty-one rings. There was no sign of decay, though it was, as usual, mossy, or covered with lichens.

I cut off at ground one of the little procumbent spruce trees, which spread much like a juniper, but not curving upward. This rose about nine inches above the ground, but I could not count the rings, they were so fine. (*Vide* piece [of spruce].) The smallest diameter of the *wood* is forty-one eightieths of an inch. The number of rings, as near as I can count with a microscope, taking much pains, is about seventy, and on one side these are included within a radius of nine fortieths of an inch, of which a little more than half is heart-wood, or each layer on this side is less than one three-hundredth of an inch thick. The bark was three fortieths of an inch thick. It was quite round and easy to cut, it was so fresh.

If the fir thirty inches in circumference grew no faster than that an inch and an eighth in diameter, then it was about five hundred and forty-nine years old. If as fast as the *little* spruce, it would be nearly fourteen hundred years old.

When half-way down the mountain, amid the spruce, we saw two pine grosbeaks, male and female, close by the path, and looked for a nest, but in vain. They were remarkably tame, and the male a brilliant red orange,—neck, head, breast beneath, and rump,—blackish wings and tail, with two white bars on wings. (Female, yellowish.) The male flew nearer inquisitively, uttering a low twitter, and perched fearlessly within four feet of us, eying us and pluming himself and plucking and eating the leaves of the *Amelanchier oligocarpa* on which he sat, for several minutes. The female, meanwhile, was a rod off. They were evidently breeding there. Yet neither Wilson nor Nuttall speak of their breeding in the United States.

At the base of the mountain, over the road, heard (and saw), at the same place where I heard him the evening before, a splendid rose-breasted grosbeak singing. I had before mistaken him at first for a tanager, then for a red-eye, but was not satisfied; but now, with my glass, I distinguished him sitting quite still, high above the road at the entrance of the mountain-path in the deep woods, and singing steadily for twenty minutes. It was remarkable for sitting so still and where

yesterday. It was much richer and sweeter and, I think, more powerful than the note of the tanager or red-eye. It had not the hoarseness
of the tanager, and more sweetness and fullness than the red-eye.
Wilson does not give their breeding-place. Nuttall quotes Pennant as
saying that some breed in New York but most further north. They,
too, appear to breed about the White Mountains.

Heard the evergreen-forest note on the sides of the mountains
often. Heard no robins in the White Mountains.

Rode on and stopped at Morrison's (once Tilton's) Inn in West
Thornton. *Heracleum lanatum* in Notch and near, very large, some
seven feet high. Observed, as we rode south through Lincoln, that the
face of cliffs on the hills and mountains east of the river, and even the
stems of the spruce, reflected a pink light at sunset.

The trail up Lafayette is a series of long, gradual ascents
with three broad switchbacks, each one having a turnout
that affords views of the Notch (U-shaped, plowed by a
moving glacier) and the smaller ravines (V-shaped, cut
by streams). Thoreau's description of plant zones is accurate, but not the species: at 3,000 feet, balsam fir and *red*
spruce appear; at 4,500 feet, spruce drops out, leaving fir
and some birch or ash. The tree sizes change as the soil
grows thinner and drier; up here, nutrients are scarce
and the wind is constant. The trail climbs over humps
called "the three Agonies"; at each one, trees stand taller
on the protected south side. Above 4,500 feet, alpine
flowers appear, especially near the two ponds that form
Eagle Lakes.

ROUTE FROM
LAFAYETTE BASE: *Trail to
Greenleaf Hut
(AMC), to
summit and
return, US 3 to
Thornton.*

At this site, where Thoreau boiled tea for his dinner, *(see page 273)*
the AMC Greenleaf hut offers meals and bunks for
thirty-six persons. Day hikers can picnic on an embank-
ment overlooking the glacial pools. Thoreau botanized in
the nearby bogs, but hikers should stay on the trails, *(see page 272)*
since the matted organic materials—roots, grasses,
shrubs—are extremely fragile. *Linnea borealis,* the
twinflower with its pairs of pink, nodding blooms, still *(see page 272)*
puts on an abundant show in mid-July. Thoreau had

fairly clear views: the Connecticut River valley is sixteen miles northwest, Mt. Washington is eighteen miles northeast. The "wild mountain and forest scene" he saw (see page 273) is Pemigewasset Wilderness, still a grand expanse of unchanged country, crossed only by foot trails and fast-running streams.

(see page 273)   To him, the "deer's horns" seemed an inversion of normal values; the trees were mature and yet oddly stunted, ripped by prevailing winds but thick enough to protect an understory of mosses and flowers. He understood how slowly the dwarfs grow, but his method of dating exaggerated their age: most specimens are seventy to one hundred years old.

Thoreau forgot to say here that he went on to the summit. (see page 282) Beyond Greenleaf Hut, the trail is clearly marked for another mile along a moderate grade, leading above the tree line to steps lined with stone walls, built by AMC crews in 1974. At the top are the foundations of the old Summit House, erected in the 1840s but virtually destroyed by the time of Thoreau's visit. The rocks here are encrusted with lichens, far more ancient than the dwarf spruce he admired below—some lichens are known to live more than two thousand years.

Thoreau returned on the bridle path, but a more interesting descent is along the Franconia Ridge, part of the Appalachian Trail. This walk crosses over Mt. Lincoln (5,108′) and gives a fine view of the Pemigewasset Wilderness, lying east. A return via the Falling Waters trail passes Shining Rock, a massive exposure created by a major landslide in 1927, and several fine waterfalls, some with vein-like cascades, eighty feet high. Thoreau saw none of this; instead, he watched for birds on his descent, noting the relation of their feeding and breeding to plant (see page 274) zones. On his trip south through Franconia Notch, he apparently did not visit the sights—Profile, Basin, Flume —that had become popular with tourists since his trip in 1839.

July 16. *Friday.* Continue on through Thornton and Campton. The butternut is first noticed in these towns, a common tree. *Urtica Canadensis* in Campton.

About the mountains were wilder and rarer birds, more or less arctic, like the vegetation. I did not even *hear* the robin on them, and when I had left them a few miles behind, it was a great change and surprise to hear the lark, the wood pewee, the robin, and the bobolink (for the last had not done singing). On the mountains, especially at Tuckerman's Ravine, the notes even of familiar birds sounded strange to me. I hardly knew the wood thrush and veery and oven-bird at first. They sing differently there.* In two instances,—going down the Mt. Jefferson road and along the road in the Franconia Notch,—I started an *F. hyemalis* within two feet, close to the roadside, but looked in vain for a nest. They alight and sit thus close. I doubt if the chipping sparrow is found about the mountains.

We were not troubled at all by black flies after leaving the Franconia Notch. It is apparently only in primitive woods that they work. We had grand views of the Franconia Mountains from Campton, and were surprised by the regular pyramidal form of most of the peaks, including Lafayette, which we had ascended. I think that there must be some ocular illusion about this, for no such regularity was observable in ascending Lafayette. I remember that when I got more than half a mile down it I met two men walking up, and perspiring very much, one of whom asked me if a cliff within a stone's throw before them was the summit. Indeed the summit of a mountain, though it may appear thus regular at a distance, is not, after all, the easiest thing to find, even in clear weather. The surface was so irregular that you would have thought you saw the summit a dozen times before you did, and in one sense the nearer you got to it, the further off it was. I told the man it was seven or eight times as far as that. I suspect that such are the laws of light that our eye, as it were, leaps from one prominence to another, connecting them by a straight line when at a distance and making one side balance the other. So that when the summit viewed is fifty or a hundred miles distant, there is but very

---

Torrey and Allen identify Thoreau's wood thrush and veery as the olive-backed thrush and the Bicknell thrush. They are now called Swainson's thrush and the gray-cheeked thrush.—WH

general and very little truth in the impression of its outline conveyed to the mind. Seen from Campton and lower, the Franconia Mountains show three or four sharp and regular blue pyramids, reminding you of pictures of the Pyramids of Egypt, though when near you suspected no such resemblance. You know from having climbed them, most of the time out of sight of the summit, that they must be at least of a scalloped outline, and it is hardly to be supposed that a nearer or more distant prominence always is seen at a distance filling up the irregularities. It would seem as if by some law of light and vision the eye inclined to connect the base and apex of a peak in the horizon by a straight line. Twenty-five miles off, in this case, you might think that the summit was a smooth inclined plane, though you can reach it only over a succession of promontories and shelves.

Cannon Mountain on the west side of the Franconia Notch (on whose side is the profile) is the most singularly lumpish mass of any mountain I ever saw, especially so high. It looks like a behemoth or a load of hay, and suggests no such pyramid as I have described. So my theory does not quite hold together, and I would say that the eye needs only a hint of the general form and completes the outline from the slightest suggestion. The huge lumpish mass and curving outline of Cannon Mountain is yet more remarkable than the pyramidal summits of the others. It would be less remarkable in a mere hill, but it is, in fact, an elevated and bald rocky mountain.

My last view of these Franconia Mountains was from a hill in the road just this side of Plymouth village. Campton apparently affords the best views of them, and some artists board there.

Gathered the *Carex straminea (?),* some three feet high, *scoparia-*like, in Bridgewater. Nooned on west bank of the Pemigewasset, half a mile above the New Hampton covered bridge. Saw first pitch pines in New Hampton. Saw chestnuts first and frequently in Franklin and Boscawen, or about 43 1/2° N., or half a degree higher than Emerson put it. It was quite common in Hollis. Of oaks, I saw and heard only of the red in the north of New Hampshire. The witch-hazel was very abundant and large in the north part of New Hampshire and about the mountains.

Lodged at tavern in Franklin, west side of river.

As he left behind the mountains, Thoreau's comments grew more reflective, moving from particulars to larger vistas. He considered the presence of birds, wondered why the blackfly was scarce. (In the larval stage, it needs fast-running rapids for adequate food and oxygen.) Having developed a strong set of working details, he looked now for patterns; a method unlike most travelers' genial views of the landscape. By noting how "very little truth" exists in a distant impression, he criticized the tendency to simplify, to make irregularities smooth and straight— this from the man who urged his readers to simplify, simplify in *Walden*. Cannon Mountain (4,040′), seen twenty miles to the north, even qualified *that* generality, for it has a massive, simple shape; a large rounded loaf scoured by glacial action. South of the mountains, Thoreau went along back roads. His lodging that night was in present-day West Franklin.

ROUTE FROM WEST THORNTON: *US 3 to Ashland, NH 3B to Gaza, NH 127 to West Franklin*

(see page 278)

(see page 278)

July 17. *Saturday.* Passed by Webster's place, three miles this side of the village. Some half-dozen houses there; no store nor public buildings. A very quiet place. Road lined with elms and maples. Railroad between house and barn. The farm apparently a level and rather sandy interval, nothing particularly attractive about it. A plain public graveyard within its limits. Saw the grave of Ebenezer Webster, Esq., who died 1806, aged sixty-seven, and of Abigail, his wife, who died 1816, aged seventy-six, probably Webster's father and mother; also of other Websters, and Haddocks. Now belongs to one Fay [?] of Boston. W. was born two or more miles northwest, but house now gone.

Spent the noon on the bank of the Contoocook in the northwest corner of Concord, there a stagnant river owing to dams. Began to find raspberries ripe. Saw much elecampane by roadsides near farmhouses, all the way through New Hampshire.

Reached Weare and put up at a quiet and agreeable house, without any sign or barroom. Many Friends in this town. Know Pillsbury and Rogers here. The former lived in Henniker, next town.

July 18. *Sunday.* Keep on through New Boston, the east side of

Mount Vernon, Amherst to Hollis, and noon by a mill-pond in the woods, on Pennichook Brook, in Hollis, or three miles north of village. At evening go on to Pepperell. A marked difference when we enter Massachusetts, in roads, farms, houses, trees, fences, etc.,—a great improvement, showing an older-settled country. In New Hampshire there is a greater want of shade trees, but long bleak or sunny roads from which there is no escape. What barbarians we are! The convenience of the traveller is very little consulted. He merely has the privilege of crossing somebody's farm by a particular narrow and maybe unpleasant path. The individual retains all other rights,—as to trees and fruit, and wash of the road, etc. On the other hand, these should belong to mankind inalienably. The road should be of ample width and adorned with trees expressly for the use of the traveller. There should be broad recesses in it, especially at springs and watering-places, where he can turn out and rest, or camp if he will. I feel commonly as if I were condemned to drive through somebody's cowyard or huckleberry pasture by a narrow lane, and if I make a fire by the roadside to boil my hasty pudding, the farmer comes running over to see if I am not burning up his stuff. You are barked along through the country, from door to door.

July 19. Get home at noon.

For such an excursion as the above, carry and wear:—

Three strong check shirts.
Two pairs socks.
Neck ribbon and handkerchief.
Three pocket-handkerchiefs.
One thick waistcoat.
One thin (or half-thick) coat.
One thick coat (for mountain).
A large, broad india-rubber knapsack, with a *broad* flap.
A flannel shirt.
India-rubber coat.
Three bosoms (to go and come in).
A napkin.
Pins, needles, thread.
A blanket.

A cap to lie in at night.

Tent (or a large simple piece of india-rubber cloth for the mountain tops?).

Veil and *gloves* (or enough millinet to cover all at night).

Map and compass.

Plant book and paper.

Paper and stamps.

Botany, spy-glass, microscope.

Tape, insect-boxes.

Jack-knife and clasp-knife.

Fish-line and hooks.

Matches.

Soap and dish-cloths.

Waste-paper and twine.

Iron spoon.

Pint dipper with a pail-handle added (not to put out the fire), and perhaps a bag to carry water in.

Frying-pan, only if you ride.

Hatchet (sharp), if you ride, and perhaps in any case on mountain, with a sheath to it.

Hard-bread (sweet crackers good); a moist, sweet plum cake very good and lasting; pork, corned beef or tongue, sugar, tea or coffee, and a little salt.

As I remember, those dwarf firs on the mountains grew up straight three or four feet without diminishing much if any, and then sent forth every way very stout branches, like bulls' horns or shorter, horizontally four or five feet each way. They were stout because they grew so slowly. Apparently they were kept flat-topped by the snow and wind. But when the surrounding trees rose above them, they, being sheltered a little, apparently sent up shoots from the horizontal limbs, which also were again more or less bent, and this added to the horn-like appearance.

We might easily have built us a shed of spruce bark at the foot of Tuckerman's Ravine. I thought that I might in a few moments strip off the bark of a spruce a little bigger than myself and seven feet long, letting it curve as it naturally would, then crawl into it and be protected against any rain. Wentworth said that he had sometimes stripped off birch bark two feet wide, and put his head through a slit in the middle, letting the ends fall down before and behind, as he walked.

The slides in Tuckerman's Ravine appeared to be a series of deep gullies side by side, where sometimes it appeared as if a very large rock had slid down without turning over, plowing this deep furrow all the way, only a few rods wide. Some of the slides were streams of rocks, a rod or more in diameter each. In some cases which I noticed, the ravine-side had evidently been undermined by water on the lower side.

It is surprising how much more bewildering is a mountain-top than a level area of the same extent. Its ridges and shelves and ravines add greatly to its apparent extent and diversity. You may be separated from your party by only stepping a rod or two out of the path. We turned off three or four rods to the pond on our way up Lafayette, knowing that Hoar was behind, but so we lost him for three quarters of an hour and did not see him again till we reached the summit. One walking a few rods more to the right or left is not seen over the ridge of the summit, and, other things being equal, this is truer the nearer you are to the apex.

If you take one side of a rock, and your companion another, it is enough to separate you sometimes for the rest of the ascent.

On these mountain-summits, or near them, you find small and almost uninhabited ponds, apparently without fish, sources of rivers, still and cold, strange as condensed clouds, weird-like,—of which nevertheless you make tea!—surrounded by dryish bogs, in which, perchance, you may detect traces of the bear or *loup-cervier*.

We got the best views of the mountains from Conway, Jefferson, Bethlehem, and Campton. Conway combines the Italian (?) level and softness with Alpine peaks around. Jefferson offers the completest view of the range a dozen or more miles distant; the place from which to behold the manifold varying lights of departing day on the summits. Bethlehem also afforded a complete but generally more distant view of the range, and, with respect to the highest summits, more diagonal. Campton afforded a fine distant view of the pyramidal Franconia Mountains with the lumpish Profile Mountain. The last view, with its smaller intervals and partial view of the great range far in the north, was somewhat like the view from Conway.

Belknap in his "History of New Hampshire," third volume, page 33, says: "On some mountains we find a shrubbery of hemlock (?) and spruce, whose branches are knit together so as to be impenetrable. The snow lodges on their tops, and a cavity is formed underneath. These are called by the Indians, Hakmantaks."

Willey quotes some one* as saying of the White Mountains, "Above this hedge of dwarf trees, which is about 4000 feet above the level of the sea, the scattered fir and spruce bushes, shrinking from the cold mountain wind, and clinging to the ground in sheltered hollows by the sides of the rocks, with a few similar bushes of white and yellow (?) birch, reach almost a thousand feet high."

Willey says that "the tops of the mountains are covered with snow from the last of October to the end of May;" that the alpine flowers spring up under the shelter of high rocks. Probably, then, they are most abundant on the southeast sides?

To sum up (omitting sedges, etc.), plants prevailed thus on Mt. Washington:—

1st. *For three quarters of a mile:* Black (?) spruce, yellow birch, hemlock, beech, canoe birch, rock maple, fir, mountain maple, red cherry, striped maple, etc.

2d. *At one and three quarters miles:* Spruce prevails, with fir, canoe and yellow birch. Rock maple, beech, and hemlock disappear. (On Lafayette, lambkill, *Viburnum nudum,* nemopanthes, mountain-ash.) Hardwoods in bottom of ravines, above and below.

3d. *At three miles, or limit of trees* (colliers' shanty and Ravine Camp): Fir prevails, with *some spruce* and canoe birch; mountain-ash, *Alnus viridis* (in moist ravines), red cherry, mountain maple, *Salix* (*humilis*-like and *Torreyana*-like, etc.), *Vaccinium Canadense, Ribes lacustre, prostratum,* and *floridum* (?), rhodora, *Amelanchier oligocarpa,* tree-cranberry, chiogenes, *Cornus Canadensis, Oxalis Acetosella,* clintonia, gold-thread, *Listera cordata, Smilacina bifolia, Solidago thyrsoidea, Ranunculus abortivus, Platanthera obtusata* and *dilatata, Oxyria digyna, Viola blanda, Aster prenan-*

---

*This is Oakes in his "Scenery," etc.

thes (?). *A. acuminatus, Aralia nudicaulis, Polystichum aculea-tum* (?), wool-grass, etc.

4th. *Limit of trees to within one mile of top,* or as far as dwarf firs: Dwarf fir, spruce, and some canoe birch, *Vaccinium uliginosum* and *Vitis-Idæa, Salix Uva-ursi,* ledum, *Empetrum nigrum, Oxalis Acetosella, Linnæa borealis, Cornus Canadensis, Alsine Grœn-landica, Diapensia Lapponica,* gold-thread, epigæa, sorrel, *Geum radiatum* var. *Peckii, Solidago Virgaurea* var. *alpina, S. thyr-soidea* (not so high as last), hellebore, oldenlandia, clintonia, *Viola palustris,* trientalis, a little *Vaccinium angustifolium* (?), ditto of *Vaccinium cæspitosum, Phyllodoce taxifolia, Uvularia gran-diflora, Loiseleuria procumbens, Cassiope hypnoides, Rubus triflorus, Heracleum lanatum,* archangelica, *Rhododendron Lap-ponicum, Arctostaphylos alpina, Salix herbacea, Polygonum viviparum, Veronica alpina, Nabalus Boottii, Epilobium al-pinum, Platanthera dilatata,* common rue, *Castilleja septentrion-alis, Arnica mollis, Spiræa salicifolia, Salix repens,* * *Solidago thyrsoidea,* raspberry (Hoar), *Lycopodium annotinum* and *Selago,* small fern, grass, sedges, moss and lichens. (On Lafayette, *Vac-cinium Oxyococcus, Smilacina trifolia, Kalmia glauca, An-dromeda calyculata,* red cherry, yellow (water) lily, *Eriophorum vaginatum.*)

5th. *Within one mile of top: Potentilla tridentata,* a very little fir, spruce, and canoe birch, one mountain-ash, *Alsine Grœnlandica,* diapensia, *Vaccinium Vitis-Idæa,* gold-thread, *Lycopodium an-notinum* and *Selago,* sorrel, *Silene acaulis, Solidago Virgaurea* var. *alpina,* hellebore, oldenlandia, *Lonicera cœrulea,* clintonia, *Viola palustris,* trientalis, *Vaccinium angustifolium* (?), a little fern, *Geum radiatum* var. *Peckii,* sedges, rush, moss, and lichens, and probably more of the last list.

6th. At apex: Sedge, moss, and lichens, and a little alsine, diapensia, *Solidago Virgaurea* var. *alpina* (?), etc.

The 2d may be called the Spruce Zone; 3d, the Fir Zone; 4th, the Shrub, or Berry, Zone; 5th, the Cinquefoil, or Sedge, Zone; 6th, the Lichen, or Cloud, Zone.

Durand in Kane (page 444, 2d vol.) thinks that plants suffer more

---

*And apparently *S. phylicifolia* (?).

in alpine regions than in the polar zone. Among authorities on northern plants, names E. Meyer's "Plantæ Labradoricæ" (1830) and Giesecke's list of Greenland plants in Brewster's Edinburgh Encyclopedia (1832).

It is remarkable that what you may call trees on the White Mountains, *i.e.* the forests, cease abruptly with those about a dozen feet high, and then succeeds a distinct kind of growth, quite dwarfish and flattened and confined almost entirely to fir and spruce, as if it marked the limit of *almost* perpetual snow, as if it indicated a zone where the trees were peculiarly oppressed by the snow, cold, wind, etc. The transition from these flattened firs and spruces to shrubless rock is not nearly so abrupt as from upright or slender trees to these dwarfed thickets.

Daniel Webster birthplace

West Franklin is the site of Daniel Webster's birthplace, a state monument open for tours in the summer. Like many New England liberals, Thoreau grew disenchanted with Webster's conciliatory response to slavery during the 1850s. The lunch spot was either at Daviesville or Contoocook; this river has its source on Monadnock, as Thoreau had discovered a month earlier. Parker Pillsbury and Nathaniel Rogers were leading Abolitionists, personally known to Thoreau.

ROUTE FROM WEST FRANKLIN: *NH 127 to Henniker, NH 114 to Weare, NH 77 to New Boston, NH 13 to Amherst, NH 122 to Pepperell, MA 111 to MA 119, MA 2 to Concord*

(see page 279)

For his final entry, Thoreau wrote a conclusion that

(see page 227) contrasted Massachusetts to New Hampshire and brought him back to his opening theme on July 2. After his adventures in the mountains, he welcomed returning to settled and cultivated regions. The call for public (see page 280) campgrounds was prompted by his knowledge of Indian customs, but also by the fact that Franconia Notch was then largely owned by one family, which managed all the public houses and stage lines. Today's public supervision, a cooperative effort of state and federal agencies, is far closer to his ideal.

Reaching home after eighteen days of travel, Thoreau began to write these entries. The chore probably took several days; at the end he drew up a final summary, (see page 280) similar to his "Appendix" in *The Maine Woods.* This listing suggested potential themes for a future narrative: the exact facts—what he wore, ate, carried, saw. The summaries are faulty as narrative; they belatedly reveal that he *did* go to the summit of Lafayette, also that he (see page 282) briefly lost track of Edward Hoar. But the final listing of (see page 283) plant zones is a natural climax, Thoreau's major contribution to alpine ecology.

Monadnock

They who simply climb to the peak of Monadnock
have seen but little of the mountain. I came not
to look off from it, but to look at it.

O f all the mountains Thoreau visited, Monadnock was his favorite. Between 1844 and 1860, he climbed there four different times, camping a total of eleven days at the summit. The sight of Monadnock in the west was an early memory; on his deathbed he wrote about his last camp there. Monadnock therefore best reflects the changes of mind and art that gave shape to his life.

Monadnock has long attracted writers, artists, and geologists, largely because this mountain is so accessible. Lying sixty-five miles northwest of Boston, Monadnock State Park contains fifty miles of hiking trails. On a clear day, the summit view takes in six New England states. Generations of visitors have looked at these rocks and imagined personality (the Imp, the Tooth) or antiquity (Sarcophagus, Doric Temple, Matterhorn). The mountain also has a singular form, which inspired a generic term in geology.

Once the bed of a great ocean, the sedimentary rock of this area was forced upward by collision of the Atlantic and North American plates. Escaping magma cooled into granite and also rose, exerting heat and pressure on the sediments. They metamorphosed into hard mica schist and bent into a downward crescent, a syncline folding, which later fractured and jointed. Before and after this uplifting, long ages of erosion reduced the weaker rock layers to a rolling plain, or peneplain, leaving the more resistant rock to stand as an isolated mountain. Finally, great ice sheets, 2,000 feet higher than the mountain, pushed across and cut ledges, "sheep backs," and deep angular grooves. When the Indians found this place, they called it Monadnock, "mountain that stands alone."

Thoreau knew little of this history; he came to Monadnock because it was nearby and distinctive as a physical locale. Because the mountain stood alone, he could study it as an environment, a prominent and independent world where plants, animals, and the climate worked together. In Concord he was studying natural history on a broad scale; Monadnock gave it to him in a single dramatic landscape.

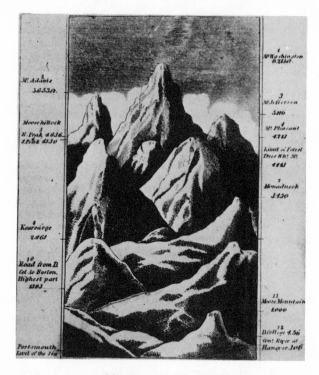

Schematic view of N.H. peaks

He first visited Monadnock in July 1844, during his trip to the Berkshires (see p. 54). No contemporary record of this journey survives, only some offhand remarks made several years later. His route from Concord to the mountain is unknown; the time spent hiking there was at least two days. In the Journal entry for June 28, 1852, he recalled camping all night on four mountaintops, including Monadnock, "and I usually took a ramble over the summit at midnight by moonlight."

With only a blanket for warmth, he made his bed in a rocky cavity, out of the wind. In 1858 he built a fire and boiled tea in the same spot (see p. 319). This location may have been "a stone's throw . . . on the north side, under some spruce trees," which he described as "a good place if you would be near the top."

In 1860 he returned to Monadnock a fourth time, for on each previous visit his fascination had grown. At first he had only general thoughts about the scenic views, but later he came to study the entire mountain closely. He set up an observation post, secure from the elements—and other visitors. He surveyed the summit, walking repeatedly around its five spurs, then drew a careful map of his own. He studied rock forms, the bogs and pools, and every type of plant or animal life.

These interests supplemented his works-in-progress on the natural history of Concord, projects that were cut short by his death in 1862. He also left instructions—bring a small pillow, take only salt beef, make further observations—"next time." Did he plan to write a book about mountains? Perhaps. Yet he tended to work on subjects without any clear purpose in mind. The Journal entries on Monadnock require no justification; like the mountain they honor, these pages can stand alone.

. . .

The trip in September 1852 came at the end of a desultory summer. Thoreau had turned thirty-five; his career seemed to be losing its course. He was not ready to publish *Walden,* not certain how to make literary use of his Journal entries about walking and boating in Concord. Friends offered him no clear models for life; after years of bachelorhood, Blake had married in late August; Channing was neglecting his family and slipping virtually into divorce. Thoreau asked Channing to go with him to Monadnock, and he accepted. He was an unpredictable companion, but always interesting.

J O U R N A L

Sept. 6. *Monday.* To Peterboro. Railroad to Mason Village.

Observed from cars at 7.30 A.M. the dew, or fog rather, on the fine grass in meadows,—a dirty white, which, one of these mornings, will be frozen to a white frost. A woman who wished to go to Nashua was left behind at Groton Junction,—to which she said, "Why, I was *he-ar.*" Girls picking hops in Townsend. Some fields are completely yellow—one mass of yellow—from the solidago. It is the prevailing flower the traveller sees. Walked from Mason Village over the mountain-*tops* to Peterboro. Saw, sailing over Mason Village about 10 A.M., a white-headed and *white-tailed* eagle with black wings,—a grand sight. The "doubly compound racemed panicles" of the spikenard berries, varnish-colored berries, or color of varnished mahogany. Met a crazy man, probably being carried to a hospital, who must take us both by the hand and tell us how the spirit of God had descended on him and given him all the world, and he was going to make every man a present of half a million, etc., etc. High blackberries by the roadside abundant still, the long, sweet, mulberry-shaped ones, mostly confined to the road, and very grateful to the walker. A stone by the roadside in Temple, whitewashed, with an inscription in black, evincing the vulgarity of the Yankees, "Here Jesse Spofford was killed," etc., etc., not telling how. Thus we record only the trivial, not the important event, as the advent of a thought. Who cares whether Jesse Spofford was killed or not, if he does not know whether he was worthy to live?

The tavern-keeper at Temple said the summit just south of the Peterboro road, covered with wood, was the highest (probably a mistake),—980 feet above Temple Common, which is itself very high. Went across lots from here toward this. When part way up, or on a lower part of the ridge, discovered it was not the highest, and turned northward across the road to what is apparently the highest, first having looked south to Kidder's mountain, between New Ipswich and Temple and further west and quite near to Boundary Mountain between Sharon and Temple. Already we had had experience of a mountain-side covered with bare rocks, as if successive thunder [*sic*] spouts had burst over it, and bleached timber lying across the rocks, the woodbine red as blood about a tall stump, and the strong, sweet, bracing scent of ferns between the rocks, the raspberry bushes still retaining a few berries. They usually tell you how many mountain-houses you can see from a mountain, but they are interesting to me in proportion to the number you cannot see. We went down the west side of this first mountain, from whose summit we could not see west on account of another ridge; descended far, and across the road, and up the southernmost of what I have called the Peterboro Hills. The raw edge of a forest of canoe birches on the side of this hill was remarkable on account of the wonderful contrast of the white stems with the green leaves; the former glaringly white, as if whitewashed and varnished or polished. You now hear that grating, creaking flight of the grasshopper. There is something in the aspect of the evergreens, the dwarfed forests and the bare rocks of mountain-tops, and the scent of the ferns, stern yet sweet to man. Hazy. Monadnock would probably look better toward evening. It was now two or three P.M. In the woods near the top, the *Viburnum lantanoides*, hobble-bush, American wayfaring-tree, in fruit, mostly large and red, but the ripe dark blue or black like the *V. nudum*,—what I have formerly falsely called moose-berry. Probably it does not grow in Concord.

Went, still across lots, to Peterboro village, which we could not see from the mountain. But first we had seen the Lyndeboro Mountain, north of these two,—partly in Greenfield,—and further Crotched Mountain, and in the northeast Uncannunuc. Descended where, as usual, the forest had been burned formerly,—tall bleached masts still standing, making a very wild and agreeably [*sic*] scenery,—keeping on a westward spur or side, that we might see north and south. Saw the pond on the "embenchement" between the two mountains. Some sheep ran from us in great fear. Others put their heads down and together, and stood *perfectly still*, resembling rocks, so that I did not notice them at first. Did they not do it for concealment? After we got down, the prevailing trees were hemlock, spruce, black and yellow birch, and beech, the ground very cleanly and smoothly carpeted with the old leaves of the last two especially, without weeds. Saw some ground-hemlock with some fruit still. Had seen on the hill *Polygonum cilinode,* running polygonum, but no flower,—*alias* fringe-jointed false-buckwheat.

A man in Peterboro told me that his father told him that Monadnock used to be covered with forest, that fires ran through it and killed the turf; then the trees were blown down, and their roots turned up and formed a dense and impenetrable thicket in which the wolves abounded. They came down at night, killed sheep, etc., and returned to their dens, whither they could not be pursued, before morning; till finally they set fire to this thicket, and it made the greatest fire they had ever had in the county, and drove out all the wolves, which have not troubled them since. He himself had seen one wolf killed there when he was a boy. They kill now raccoons, hedgehogs, and wildcats there. I thought that I did not see so great a proportion of forest from their hilltops as about Concord, to which they agreed. I should say their hills were uncommonly rocky,—more stone than soil.

ROUTE FROM CONCORD: *MA 2A to MA 119 and Townsend, MA 123 to Greenville, NH 45 to NH 101 and Peterborough*

Today's highway route follows the old Boston and Maine railroad tracks. After car service reached Concord in 1845, Thoreau became an enthusiastic rider. At the end of this trip, he praises the convenience of traveling fifty miles in only two hours. But speed tended to reduce his notes to mere impressions; *Solidago* (goldenrod) comes in more than sixty varieties, which can be identified only *(see page 290)* by close comparative study.

Thoreau did not purchase a spyglass until April 1854, but he already needed one in 1852: the white-headed, white-tailed bird he saw was unmistakably a bald eagle. Throughout this entry, a similar myopia seems to govern his comparisons of nature and people. The old woman who missed her train, the crazy man who offered him a fortune, the "trivial" roadside inscription—all are meant to pale beside nature's bounty, the abundant berries that grow by the road.

(see page 290)　The summit he discussed with the tavern-keeper is

Temple Mountain (2,084'); Pack Monadnock (2,198', three miles north) is definitely higher, as he found on his hike. Kidder (1,814') and Boundary (now Burton Peak, 2,005') mountains are south and west of Temple, respectively. All these hills are heavily forested today, making bare rocks far less visible. Thoreau's reference to "thunder spouts" may indicate that he thought these mountains *(see page 291)* were of volcanic origin, as many geologists believed until the 1860s. In place of sound facts, this entry offers sensory impressions—smells, colors, tastes—and some mildly antisocial remarks. These qualities also dominated his current work-in-progress, *Walden.*

By mid-afternoon, Thoreau and Channing had walked eight miles and ascended Pack Monadnock, the present site of Miller State Park. They continued across lots to Peterborough, seeing on the way Lyndeborough Mountain (1,686', six miles northeast), Crotched Mountain (2,055', nine miles north), and Uncannunuc (1,329', sixteen miles northeast).

The story he heard about Monadnock's history was ac- *(see page 292)* curate. Before 1800, the mountain was covered with red spruce; thereafter came the cycles of fire and erosion that left the summit bare. The wolves were driven out between 1810 and 1820. (In 1860, Thoreau cut a tree and counted its rings; it had sprouted after 1816.) Thus, one of Monadnock's singular features is a bare summit, well below the normal tree line for this latitude, which gives the mountain its form, its views, and its zones of vegetation. All these benefits resulted from a man-made disaster: given a natural history of plant succession, Monadnock would be densely forested today.

Sept. 7. Tuesday. Went, across lots still, to Monadnock, the base some half-dozen miles in a straight line from Peterboro,—six or seven miles. (It had been eleven miles *(by road)* from Mason Village to Peterboro.) My clothes sprinkled with ambrosia pollen. Saw near the mountain a field of turnips whose leaves, all but the midribs, were

eaten up by grasshoppers and looked white over the field, and sometimes the turnips were eaten also. Joe Eavely's, the house nearest the
top, that we saw under the east side, a small red house a little way
up. The summit hardly more than a mile distant in a straight line, but
about two miles as they go. Bunch-berries everywhere now. *Acer
Pennsylvanicum,* striped maple or moosewood or striped dogwood,
but no keys to be seen,—a very large-leaved, three-lobed maple with

a handsome striped bark. This, I believe, the Indians smoke. Also *Acer spicatum,* mountain maple, with upright racemes in fruit. Between the rocks on the summit, an abundance of large and fresh blueberries still, apparently *Vaccinium Pennsylvanicum,* very large, fresh and cooling to eat, supplying the place of water. They said they did not get ripe so early as below, but at any rate they last much longer; both, perhaps, because of the greater coolness of the atmosphere. Though this vegetation was very humble, yet it was very productive of fruit. In one little hollow between the rocks grew blueberries, choke-berries, bunch-berries, *red* cherries, wild currants (*Ribes prostratum,* with the berry the odor of skunk-cabbage, but a not quite disagreeable wild flavor), a few raspberries still, holly berries, mountain cranberries (*Vaccinium Vitis-Idæa*), all close together. The little soil on the summit between the rocks was covered with the *Potentilla tridentata,* now out of bloom, the prevailing plant at the extreme summit. Mountain-ash berries also.

Descending toward Troy, a little after 1 P.M., plucked the *Trillium erythrocarpum* with the large red berry, painted trillium. The *Aster acuminatus,* with its leaves in a whorl, white; methinks we may have it. When we had got down, we could see that the mountain had spurs or buttresses on every side, by whose ridge you might ascend. It is an interesting feature in a mountain. I have noticed that they will send out these buttresses every way from their centre.

Were on the top of the mountain at 1 P.M. The cars left Troy, four or five miles off, at three. We reached the depot, by running at last, at the same instant the cars did, and reached Concord at a quarter after five, *i.e.* four hours from the time we were picking blueberries on the mountain, with the plants of the mountain fresh in my hat.

Thoreau's route continued across lots, saving about four to five miles of road hiking. Although several trails went to the summit in 1852, he chose to create his own. At the junction of Mountain and Dublin roads (by the edge of Thorndike Pond) stood the house of Joseph Eveleth—"Joe Eavely's" to Thoreau. The most direct path to the top would go along Eveleth Brook, a rise of 2,100 feet, and moderate walking. Today's hikers should register at the

ROUTE FROM PETERBOROUGH: NH 101 to Dublin, Mountain Road to Monadnock State Park

State Park and visit the Monadnock Eco Center. From there, they can hike to the summit via the White Cross or White Dot trails (so called because of their paint blazes).

ROUTE FROM
EVELETH BROOK:
Birchtoft trail to
Cascade Link
and Old Ski
trails, White
Cross and White
Dot trails to
summit

(see page 295)

The best approximation of Thoreau's ascent starts near Gilson Pond and follows a ravine to 2,000 feet, jogs right and left to 2,800 feet, then climbs by various pitches across broad ledges to the top. Thoreau's route saved him about a mile of hiking as compared to White Arrow trail on the southwest, the oldest footpath on Monadnock.

At the top, he made the briefest of botanical notes, merely practicing his novice skills, and eating all the berries in sight because he had not brought water. (On later trips he found several good springs on the spurs but did not realize that some also lie close to the summit.)

ROUTE FROM TROY:
NH 12 to
Fitchburg, MA
2A to Concord

(see page 295)

His descent was probably on a direct course for Troy, straight down Fassett Brook (a route he climbed in 1858, without hesitation). Only after leaving did he look back and see the mountain's spurs, a feature examined more closely on later visits. He took the Fitchburg railroad home, carrying plants in his customary fashion—inside the lining of his straw hat.

·   ·   ·

The third journey to Monadnock differed considerably from the 1852 trip. Thoreau was now quite proficient as a naturalist, and he had begun to use this knowledge in his work. Since 1855 he had published writings on Cape Cod and the Maine woods; now he was about to launch a series of works—on leaves, fruits, and seeds—in which science and poetry would mingle. The mountains also attracted him as a potential theme. On the July 1857 trip to Maine, Mt. Kineo revived his interest in climbing, and in October 1857 he described Monadnock in admiring but playful terms.

(see page 162)

Look from the high hill, just before sundown, over the pond. The mountains are a mere cold slate-color. But what a perfect crescent of mountains we have in our northwest horizon! Do we ever give thanks for it? Even as pines and larches and hemlocks grow in communities in the wilderness, so, it seems, do mountains love society and form a community in the horizon. Though there may be two or more ranges, one behind the other, and ten or twelve miles between them, yet if the farthest are the highest, they are all seen as one group at this distance. I look up northwest toward my mountains, as a farmer to his hill lot or rocky pasture from his door. I drive no cattle to Ipswich hills. I own no pasture for them there. My eyes it is alone that wander to those blue pastures, which no drought affects. They are my flocks and herds. See how they look. They are shaped like tents, inclining to sharp peaks. What is it lifts them upward so? Why not rest level along the horizon? They seem not perfect, they seem not satisfied, until their central parts have curved upward to a sharp summit. They are a succession of pickets with scallops between. That side my pasture is well fenced. This being their upper side, I fancy they must have a corresponding under side and roots also. Might they not be dug up like a turnip? Perhaps they spring from seeds which some wind sowed. Can't the Patent Office import some of the seed of Himmaleh with its next rutabagas? Spore of mountains has fallen there; it came from the gills of an agaric. Ah, I am content to dwell there and see the sun go down behind my mountain fence.

By the spring of 1858 he was ready to plan summer excursions. Again Monadnock drew his attention, as he wrote on May 17.

I thought yesterday that the view of the mountains from the bare hill on the Lincoln side of Flint's Pond was very grand. Surely they do not look so grand anywhere within twenty miles of them. And I reflected what kind of life it must be that is lived always in sight of them. I looked round at some windows in the middle of Lincoln and considered that such was the privilege of the inhabitants of these chambers; but their blinds were closed, and I have but little doubt that they are *blind* to the beauty and sublimity of this prospect. I doubt if in the landscape there can be anything finer than a distant mountain-range. They are a constant elevating influence.

He quickly arranged with Harrison Blake to make a journey. They went by railroad to Troy, then hiked to the
summit and camped there for three days in June. The
trip was a great success; Blake's good company and Thoreau's discovery of several plant zones prompted plans
for their trip to the White Mountains in July.

June 2. 8.30 A.M.—Start for Monadnock.

Between Shirley Village and Lunenburg, I notice, in a meadow on
the right hand, close to the railroad, the *Kalmia glauca* in bloom, as
we are whirled past. The conductor says that he has it growing in his
garden. Blake joins me at Fitchburg. Between Fitchburg and Troy
saw an abundance of wild red cherry, now apparently in prime, in full
bloom, especially in burnt lands and on hillsides, a small but cheerful
lively white bloom.

Arrived at Troy Station at 11.5 and shouldered our knapsacks,
steering northeast to the mountain, some four miles off,—its top. It
is a pleasant hilly road, leading past a few farmhouses, where you
already begin to snuff the mountain, or at least up-country air. By the
roadside I plucked, now apparently in prime, the *Ribes Cynosbati*,
rather downy leaved, and, near by, the same with smooth berries. I
noticed, too, the *Salix lucida*, by the roadside there on high land; the
S. rostrata, etc., were common.

Almost without interruption we had the mountain in sight before
us,—its sublime gray mass—that antique, brownish-gray, Ararat
color. Probably these crests of the earth are for the most part of one
color in all lands, that gray color of antiquity, which nature loves;
color of unpainted wood, weather-stain, time-stain; not glaring nor
gaudy; the color of all roofs, the color of things that endure, and the
color that wears well; color of Egyptian ruins, of mummies and all
antiquity; baked in the sun, done brown. Methought I saw the same
color with which Ararat and Caucasus and all earth's brows are
stained, which was mixed in antiquity and receives a new coat every
century; not scarlet, like the crest of the bragging cock, but that hard,
enduring gray; a terrene sky-color; solidified air with a tinge of earth.*

The red elder was in full bloom by the road, apparently in prime.

*Best view of mountain about two and a half miles this side of summit.

We left the road at a schoolhouse, and, crossing a meadow, began to ascend gently through very rocky pastures. Previously an old man, a mile back, who lived on a hilltop on the road, pointed out the upper corner of his pasture as a short way up. Said he had not been up for seven years and, looking at our packs, asked, "Are you going to carry them up?" "Well," said he, with a tone half of pity and half regret, adding, "I shall never go up again."

Here, at the base, by the course of a rocky rill, where we paused in the shade, in moist ground, I saw the *Tiarella cordifolia,* abundant and apparently in prime, with its white spike sometimes a foot and more high; also the leaves of the *Geranium Robertianum,* emitting their peculiar scent, with the radical reddish tinge, not yet budded. The cress in the water there was quite agreeable to our taste, and methinks would be good to eat fresh with bread.

The neighboring hills began to sink, and entering the wood we soon passed Fassett's shanty,—he so busily at work inside that he did not see us,—and we took our dinner by the rocky brook-side in the woods just above. A dozen people passed us early in the afternoon, while we sat there, men and women on their way down from the summit, this suddenly very pleasant day after a louring one having attracted them. We met a man (apparently an Indian or Canadian half-breed) and a boy, with guns, who had been up after pigeons but only killed five crows.

Thereabouts first I noticed the *Ribes prostratum,* abundantly in bloom, apparently in prime, with its pretty erect racemes of small flowers, sometimes purplish with large leaves. There, too, the *Trillium erythrocarpum,* now in prime, was conspicuous,—three white lanceolate waved-edged petals with a purple base. This the handsomest flower of the mountain, coextensive with the wooded sides. Also the *Viburnum lantanoides,* apparently in prime, with its large and showy white outer florets, reminding me by its marginal flowering of the tree-cranberry, coextensive with last; and *Uvularia grandiflora,* not long begun to bloom. Red elder-berry not open, apparently, there; and *Amelanchier Canadensis* var. *Botryapium* not long in bloom.

Having risen above the dwarfish woods (in which mountain-ash was very common), which reached higher up along this ravine than elsewhere, and nearly all the visitors having descended, we proceeded to find a place for and to prepare our camp at mid-afternoon. We wished it to be near water, out of the way of the wind, which was northwest, and of the path, and also near to spruce trees for a bed. (There is a good place if you would be near the top within a stone's throw of the summit, on the north side, under some spruce trees.) We chose a sunken yard in a rocky plateau on the southeast side of the mountain, perhaps half a mile from the summit, by the path, a rod and a half wide by many more in length, with a mossy and bushy floor about five or six feet beneath the general level, where a dozen black spruce trees grew, though the surrounding rock was generally bare. There was a pretty good spring within a dozen rods, and the western wall shelved over a foot or two. We slanted two scraggy spruce trees, long since bleached, from the western wall, and, cutting many spruce boughs with our knives, made a thick bed and walls on the two sides to keep out the wind. Then, putting several poles transversely across our two rafters, we covered [them] with a thick roof of spruce twigs, like shingles. The spruce, though harsh for a bed, was close at hand, we cutting away one tree to make room. We crawled under the low eaves of this roof, about eighteen inches high, and our extremities projected about a foot.

ROUTE FROM CONCORD: *MA 2A to Fitchburg, MA 12 to Troy, NH 119 to NH 124 and Perkins Pond, White Arrow and Dot trails to summit* Thoreau opened his 1858 journey as though he were continuing the account of 1852, by describing the mountain's general shape and color. (At the end, p. 324, he alluded to that previous story, which may indicate that he reread it). His two references to Ararat may have been suggested by a large farmhouse, called "The Ark" (now Monadnock Bible Conference Center), which stood on the lower southeast slope, on Dublin Road. The color Thoreau ascribed to antiquity was more varied than he realized, for the principal rock of Monadnock is banded mica schist, in three colors: two gray and one rusty. A close look at specimens reveals the banded structure, light layers sandwiched between dark.

Thoreau and Blake approached via the Troy Road, where the best view is from Bigelow Hill. The schoolhouse was at the T-junction of Marlboro, Troy, and Jaffrey roads; here the men cut across a field and (reversing the descent of 1852) climbed up Fassett Brook. These former pastures are now heavily wooded, and the ground cover is, accordingly, different. Where Thoreau entered the woods, Cart Path and Twisted Birch trails now cross; Fassett's shanty (built in 1855–56) was a frame cabin lying on the present White Arrow trail, just northwest of *(see page 299)* Halfway House.

Fassett built the original Mountain House, where he offered "refreshments of all kinds and horse-keeping at reasonable prices," and he also cut a trail to the summit (parallel to White Arrow). He ran a busy enterprise here on summer days, serving the visitors who stopped to rent horses, to buy food and drink, or to use his picnic grove and bowling alley. Fasset died suddenly in the fall of 1858; his sons did not maintain the business much longer. Blake and Thoreau stayed apart from this scene; they lunched near Fassett Brook and then hiked up its ravine to the summit, avoiding the crowded White Arrow trail.

With great care they selected a campsite, one so private that some controversy exists about its exact location. Thoreau gave precise references, which have only *(see page 300)* confused later searchers. In 1936, Allen Chamberlain located the site as "a small, brush-filled depression" between Red Cross and White Arrow trails. A map of that period (called "Walks and Rambles") placed this site at 3,000 feet, on a faint line between the trails. A map dated 1911 called the area "Purgatory," probably because it was linked to Paradise Valley trail. (Ellery Channing, who saw both campsites in 1860, said one of them had a clear view of Purgatory.) A group of hikers from Concord, Mass., disputed this claim and made a fresh search in 1973, but they did not agree on a new site. In his *Monadnock Guide* (1980), Henry Baldwin tentatively located the camp north of White Dot trail. Possibly the site was farther south, near the spring and present fire warden's cabin, at 3,000 feet. The mystery is not likely to be re-

solved, for many areas correspond to Thoreau's description: a sunken yard, a rocky plateau full of berries, a
(see page 300) southeastern view. Hikers may wish to search for the
camp, or just to spend some hours as Thoreau did, alone
on the summit at the end of day.

Having left our packs here and made all ready for the night, we went
up to the summit to see the sun set. Our path lay through a couple
of small swamps and then up the rocks. Some forty or fifty rods below
the very apex southeast, or quite on the top of the mountain, I saw
a little bird flit out from beneath a rock close by the path on the left
of it, where there were only very few scattered dwarf black spruce
about, and, looking, I found a nest with three eggs. It was the *Fringilla hyemalis,* which soon disappeared around a projecting rock. It
was near by a conspicuous spruce, six or eight feet high, on the west
edge of a sort of hollow, where a vista opened south over the precipice,
and the path ascended at once more steeply. The nest was sunk in the
ground by the side of a tuft of grass, and was pretty deep, made of
much fine dry grass or sedge (?) and lined with a little of a delicate
bluish hair-like fibre (?) *(q.v.)* two or three inches long. The eggs were
three, of a regular oval form, faint bluish-white, sprinkled with fine
pale-brown dots, in two of the three condensed into a ring about the
larger end. They had apparently just begun to develop. The nest and
tuft were covered by a projecting rock. Brewer says that only one nest
is known to naturalists.* We saw many of these birds flitting about
the summit, perched on the rocks and the dwarf spruce, and disap-
pearing behind the rocks. It is the prevailing bird now up there, *i.e.*
on the summit. They are commonly said to go to the fur countries to
breed, though Wilson says that some breed in the Alleghanies. The
New York Reports make them breed on the mountains of Oswego
County and the Catskills.† This was a quite interesting discovery.
They probably are never seen in the surrounding low grounds at this
season. The ancestors of this bird had evidently perceived on their
flight northward that here was a small piece of arctic region, contain-

Torrey and Allen note that Brewer described a Snow Bunting, not the F. hyemalis—WH
†Prevail in Nova Scotia according to Bryant and Cabot.

ing all the conditions they require,—coolness and suitable food, etc., etc.,—and so for how long have builded here. For ages they have made their home here with the *Arenaria Grœnlandica* and *Potentilla tridentata*. They discerned arctic isles sprinkled in our southern sky. I did not see any of them below the rocky and generally bare portion of the mountain. It finds here the same conditions as in the north of Maine and in the fur countries,—Labrador mosses, etc. Now that the season is advanced, migrating birds have gone to the extreme north or gone to the mountain-tops. By its color it harmonized with the gray and brownish-gray rocks. We felt that we were so much nearer to perennial spring and winter.

I observed rabbit's dung commonly, quite to the top and all over the rocky portion, and where they had browsed the bushes. For the last fifteen or twenty rods the ground between the rocks is pretty thickly clothed or carpeted with mountain cranberry and *Potentilla tridentata*, only the former as yet slightly budded, but much lower than this the mountain cranberry is not common. The former grows also in mere seams on the nearly upright sides of rocks, and occasionally I found some of last year's cranberries on the latter, which were an agreeable acid. These were the prevailing plants of a high order on the very summit. There was also on the same ground considerable fine grass,* and radical leaves of a sericocarpus-like aster (?),†—I saw some withered heads,—springing up commonly, and a little (hardly yet conspicuously budded except in the warmest places) *Arenaria Grœnlandica* in dense tufts, succulent. There were a few very dwarfish black spruce there, and a very little dry moss, and, on the rocks, many of that small leather-colored lichen, and *Umbilicaria pustulata*, and the two common (?) kinds of cladonia, white and green, between them.‡

Scarcely, if at all, lower than the above-named plants, grew the *Vaccinium Pennsylvanicum*, also *Pyrus arbutifolia*, very minute and but just budded, and minute mountain-ashes, a few inches high only. From these one may judge what plants, among others, grow far north.

---

*Was it not *Juncus trifidus?*
†Was it not the *Solidago thyrsoidea* of Aug., 1860?
‡*Vide* specimens of Aug., 1860.

We heard the hylodes peeping from a rain-water pool a little below the summit toward night.

As it was quite hazy, we could not see the shadow of the mountain well, and so returned just before the sun set to our camp. We lost the path coming down, for nothing is easier than to lose your way here, where so little trail is left upon the rocks, and the different rocks and ravines are so much alike. Perhaps no other equal area is so bewildering in this respect as a rocky mountain-summit, though it has so conspicuous a central point.

(see page 302) Thoreau's long account about finding a slate-colored junco is no great tribute to his bird lore. Over the years he used several names for this species, and apparently he thought it ranged farther north in the summer. Finding the bird here in June suggested to him that Monadnock was an arctic isle in the southern sky, a wondrous place that merged spring and winter. The snowfield at Tuckerman Ravine would evoke a similar paradox, but *(see page 253)* with more justification.

In his botanizing, Thoreau was on firmer ground. Here he was studying two different systems of natural order: the food chain that links animals and plants, and the zones of plants that change with altitude. These lessons *(see page 303)* were preparing him for the White Mountains trip in July: "From these one may judge what plants, among others, grow far north." (He made the cross-references, dated 1860, after his fourth trip to Monadnock.)

Notwithstanding the newspaper and egg-shell left by visitors, these parts of nature are still peculiarly unhandselled and untracked. The natural terraces of rock are the steps of this temple, and it is the same whether it rises above the desert or a New England village. Even the inscribed rocks are as solemn as most ancient gravestones, and nature reclaims them with bog and lichens. They reminded me of the grave and pass of Ben Waddi (?). These sculptors seemed to me to court such alliance with the grave as they who put their names over tombstones along the highway. One, who was probably a blacksmith, had sculptured the emblems of his craft, an anvil and hammer, beneath his name. Apparently a part of the regular outfit of mountain-climbers is a hammer and cold-chisel, and perhaps they allow themselves a supply of garlic also. Certainly you could not hire a stone-cutter to do so much engraving for less than several thousand dollars. But no Old Mortality will ever be caught renewing these epitaphs. It reminds what kinds of steeps do climb the false pretenders to fame, whose chief exploit is the carriage of the tools with which to inscribe their names. For speaking epitaphs they are, and the mere name is a sufficient revelation of the character. They are all of one trade,—stone-cutters, defacers of mountain-tops. "Charles & Lizzie!" Charles carried the sledge-hammer, and Lizzie the cold-chisel. Some have carried up a paint-pot, and painted their names on the rocks.

We returned to our camp and got our tea in our sunken yard. While one went for water to the spring, the other kindled a fire. The whole rocky part of the mountain, except the extreme summit, is strewn with the relics of spruce trees, a dozen or fifteen feet long, and long since dead and bleached, so that there is plenty of dry fuel at hand. We sat out on the brink of the rocky plateau near our camp, taking our tea in the twilight, and found it quite dry and warm there, though you would not have thought of sitting out at evening in the surrounding valleys. It was evidently warmer and drier there than below. I have often perceived the warm air high on the sides of hills late into the night, while the valleys were filled with a cold damp night air, as with water, and here the air was warmer and drier the greater part of the night. We perceived no dew there this or the next night. This was our parlor and supper-room; in another direction was our washroom. The chewink sang before night, and this, as I have before observed, is a very common bird on mountain-tops. It seems to love a cool atmosphere, and sometimes lingers quite late with us. And the wood thrush, indefinitely far or near, a little more distant and unseen, as great poets are. Early in the evening the nighthawks were heard to spark and boom over these bare gray rocks, and such was our serenade at first as we lay on our spruce bed. We were left alone with the nighthawks. These withdrawn bare rocks must be a very suitable place for them to lay their eggs, and their dry and unmusical, yet supramundane and spirit-like, voices and sounds gave fit expression to this rocky mountain solitude. It struck the very key-note of the stern, gray, barren solitude. It was a thrumming of the mountain's rocky chords; strains from the music of Chaos, such as were heard when the earth was rent and these rocks heaved up. Thus they went sparking and booming, while we were courting the first access of sleep, and I could imagine their dainty limping flight, circling over the kindred rock, with a spot of white quartz in their wings. No sound could be more in harmony with that scenery. Though common below, it seemed peculiarly proper here. But ere long the nighthawks were stilled, and we heard only the sound of our companion's breathing or of a bug in our spruce roof. I thought I heard once faintly the barking of a dog far down under the mountain, and my companion thought he heard a bullfrog.

A little after 1 A.M, I woke and found that the moon had risen, and heard some little bird near by sing a short strain of welcome to it, somewhat song-sparrow-like. But every sound is a little strange there, as if you were in Labrador. Before dawn the nighthawks commenced their sounds again, and these sounds were as good as a clock to us, telling how the night got on.

The paths on Monadnock are now so clearly marked, and so heavily traveled, that one can hardly get lost. More than 125,000 visitors climb these trails each year, following their semaphoric code of crosses, dots, and arrows; and this heavy traffic dramatically increases the rate of (see page 305) erosion. Thoreau's harangue against the public, which scattered debris and carved initials in the rock, is still pertinent today; but garbage and graffiti are less evident, and daily guide service at the summit does help to control vandalism. Most of the chiseled inscriptions date from 1800 to 1860; the earliest is "S. Eakin 1801," a man who lived in Concord, Mass., that year. Painted letters wear away quickly, but those cut into the stone are enduring memorials. One Boy Scout came prepared; his tribute is to "Troop 113 BSA."

Thoreau's camp seemed warm because it faced southeast and the rocks retained heat after sundown. As he

described the fall of evening, his prose became clear and *(see page 305)*
evocative, joining together images of coolness and dis-
tance to characterize the late hour. He equated the nighthawk call with mountain solitude, like "strains from the
music of Chaos," but he was not alluding to the turmoil *(see page 306)*
felt on Katahdin twelve years before. On Monadnock he
sensed a harmony between the elements; no longer did
the face of brute Matter seem quite so alien to his sensi-
bility. The passage on nighthawks is one of his better
descriptions; it showed how elevation could transform a
common lowland experience.

June 3. At length, by 3 o'clock, the signs of dawn appear, and soon
we hear the robin and the *Fringilla hyemalis,*—its prolonged jingle,
—sitting on the top of a spruce, the chewink, and the wood thrush.
Whether you have slept soundly or not, it is not easy to lie abed under
these circumstances, and we rose at 3.30, in order to see the sun rise
from the top and get our breakfast there. Concealing our blankets
under a shelving rock near the camp, we set out.

It was still hazy, and we did not see the shadow of the mountain
until it was comparatively short. We did not get the most distant
views, as of the Green and White Mountains, while we were there. We
carried up fuel for the last quarter of a mile. A *Fringilla hyemalis*
seemed to be attracted by the smoke of our fire, and flew quite near
to us. They are the prevailing bird of the summit, and perhaps are
baited by the crumbs left by visitors. It was flitting about there, and
it would sit and sing, on the *top* of a dwarf spruce, the strain I have
often heard.

I saw just beneath the summit, and commencing some fifteen or
twenty rods from it, dwarfish *Rhodora Canadensis,* not yet anywhere quite out, much later than in the valley, very common; lambkill;
and checkerberry; and, in slightly boggy places, quite dwarfish specimens of *Eriophorum vaginatum,* quite common in similar localities
all over the rocky part, six inches high or more. A little water andromeda with it, scarcely out, and Labrador tea, scarcely suggesting
flowers. (This I observed only in two or three places on the northerly
side.) A viburnum (probably *nudum* or a form of it) was quite com-

mon, just begun to leaf, and with nemopanthes, showing its *transparent* leaflets not yet expanded, a little behind the other, was quite sizable, especially the latter. These two, with the spruce, the largest shrubs at this height. In the little thickets made by these bushes, grew the two-leaved Solomon's-seal, not nearly out, and *Clintonia borealis,* not budded, though out in the valley. Within the folded leaves of the last, was considerable water, as within the leaves of the seaside goldenrod on the sands of the Cape. *Cornus Canadensis, along* the base of the rocks, not out. Diervilla. And, on the moist ground or in the small bogs, *Lycopodium annotinum,* resembling at first sight the *L. lucidulum,* but running, was very common in boggy places, sometimes forming quite conspicuous green patches.

The above plants of the mountain-top, except perhaps the mountain cranberry, extended downward over the whole top or rocky part of the mountain and were there mingled with a little *Polypodium vulgare;* a peculiar *Amelanchier Canadensis,* apparently variety *oligocarpa,* just begun to bloom, with few flowers, short roundish petals, and *finely* serrate leaves; red cherry, not out; *Populus tremuliformis,* not common and quite small; small willows, apparently *discolor,* etc., also *rostrata,* and maybe *humilis;* canoe birch and yellow birch, for the most part scrubby, largest in swampy places; meadow-sweet; *Lycopodium clavatum; Amelanchier Canadensis* var. *oblongifolia,* not quite out, a little of it; and also a little very dwarfish hemlock and white pine (two or three feet high); a *little* mayflower and *Chiogenes hispidula.*

We concluded to explore the whole rocky part of the mountain in this wise, to saunter slowly about it, about the height and distance from the summit of our camp, or say half a mile, more or less, first going north from the summit and returning by the western semicircle, and then exploring the east side, completing the circle, and return over the summit at night.

To sum up, these were the *Plants of the Summit, i.e.* within a dozen rods of it: *Potentilla tridentata* (and lower); *Vaccinium Vitis-Idæa;* fine grass;* sericocarpus-like radical leaves;† *Arenaria Grœnlandica;* dwarf black spruce; a little dry moss; the two kinds of cla-

---

*Was it not *Juncus trifidus* of August, 1860?

†Was it not *Solidago thyrsoidea* of August, 1860?

donia, white and green, and the small leather-colored lichen of rocks,* mingled with the larger *Umbilicaria pustulata.* All these but the *V. Vitis-Idæa* generally dispersed over the rocky part.†

Within fifteen or twenty rods of it, or scarcely, if at all, lower than the last: Vaccinium Pennsylvanicum and perhaps the variety *angustifolium* (?); *Pyrus arbutifolia;* mountain-ash. Generally distributed.

Commencing fifteen or twenty rods below it: Rhodora; lambkill; checkerberry; *Eriophorum vaginatum;* water andromeda; Labrador tea; *Viburnum (nudum?);* nemopanthes; two-leaved Solomon's-seal; clintonia; *Cornus Canadensis; Lycopodium annotinum;* diervilla.

Generally lower than the above, on the rest of the bare rocky part, with all of the above: *Ribes prostratum; Polypodium vulgaris; Amelanchier Canadensis* var. *oligocarpa (?);* red cherry; *Populus tremuliformis; Salix* apparently *discolor,* perhaps also *humilis,* certainly *rostrata;* meadow-sweet; canoe birch; yellow birch; *Lycopodium clavatum; Amelanchier oblongifolia;* a little red elder; hemlock; white pine; mayflower; chiogenes.‡

Did not examine particularly the larger growth of the swamps, but think it was chiefly spruce, white and yellow birch, mountain-ash, etc.

The *Vaccinium Pennsylvanicum* and the *Abies nigra* are among the most prevailing conspicuous plants.

Thoreau's sunrise view disappointed him, but the mountains of Franconia and Pinkham Notch are quite distant —88 to 105 miles from Monadnock. Near at hand, he gathered data about the summit, a compact area that yielded an inventory of its vegetation. His exploratory walk, two intersecting semicircles, can be duplicated over the bare rocks, if one moves in a spiral pattern down to about 2,500 feet and back. *(see page 307)* *(see page 308)*

He described the plant zones in a topical summary, rather than chronological narrative. Ironically, these layers were a consequence of fires and erosion, but they

---

U. erosa (?) or *hyperborea* (?). *Vide* Sept. 21, 1858, and a specimen from Lafayette. *Vide* specimen of August, 1860,

†The *Vaccinium Vitis-Idæa* also in patches lower down. *Vide* August, 1860.

‡Saw the raspberry in '52 and '60.

gave him a model of zone transition, which he confirmed
and refined on the White Mountains trip in July. His
summary also reflects how rapidly Monadnock had
changed from its forested condition fifty years earlier:
(see page 308)   the *Juncus trifidus* is a true arctic-alpine species, able to
survive because the bare summit had a more severe cli-
mate. Either the plant was already established in patches, or its seeds traveled a great distance to lodge there.

We first descended somewhat toward the north this forenoon, then
turned west over a ridge by which some ascend from the north. There
are several large ponds not far from the mountain on the north, and
I thought there was less forest to be seen on this side than on the
south. We crossed one or two now dry watercourses, where, however,
judging from the collections of rubbish or drift, much water must
have flown at some other season.

Jackson in his map in the Report on the Geology of Massachusetts
calls this mountain "mica slate and porphyritic granite," and [says]
that the rocks on the summit are "a hard variety of gneiss filled with
small crystals of garnets."

We observed that the rocks were remarkably smoothed, almost
polished and rounded; and also scratched. The scratches run from
about north-northwest to south-southeast. The sides of the rocks
often straight, upright walls, several rods long from north to south
and five to ten feet high, with a very smooth, rounded edge. There
were many of these long, straight, rounded walls of rock, especially
on the northwest and west. Some smaller or lower ones were so
rounded and smooth as to resemble at a little distance long-fallen
trunks of trees. The rocks were, indeed, singularly worn on a great
scale. Often a vertical cross-section would show some such profile as
this: [drawing] as if they had been grooved with a tool of a corresponding edge. There were occasionally conspicuous masses and also veins
of white quartz, and very common were bright-purple or wine-colored
garnets imbedded in the rock, looking like berries in a pudding. In
many parts, as on the southeast plateau especially, the rocks were
regularly stratified, and split into regular horizontal slabs about a
foot in thickness, projecting one beyond another like steps.

The little bogs or mosses, sometimes only a rod in diameter, are a singular feature. Ordinarily the cladonia and other lichens are crackling under your feet, when suddenly you step into a miniature bog filling the space between two rocks and you are at a loss to tell where the moisture comes from. The amount of it seems to be that some spongy moss is enabled to grow there and retain some of the clouds which rest on it. Moisture and aridity are singularly near neighbors to each other up there. The surface is made up of masses of rock more or less smoothed and rounded, or else jagged, and the little soil between is a coarse, gravelly kind, the ruins of the rocks and the decayed vegetation that has grown there. You step unexpectedly from Arabia Petræa, where the dry lichens crackle under your feet, into a miniature bog, say Dismal Swamp, where you suddenly sink a foot in wet moss, and the next step carries you into Arabia Petræa again. In more extensive swamps I slumped through moss to water sometimes, though the bottom was of rock, while a fire would rapidly spread in the arid lichens around. Perhaps the mosses grow in the wettest season chiefly, and so are enabled to retain some moisture through the driest. Plants of the bogs and of the rocks grow close to each other. You are surprised to see a great many plants of bogs growing close to the most barren and driest spots, where only cladonias cover the rocks. Often your first notice of a bog in the midst of the arid waste, where the lichens crackle under your feet, is your slumping a foot into wet moss. Methinks there cannot be so much evaporation going on up there,—witness the water in the clintonia leaves, as in the solidago by the sandy seashore,—and this (which is owing to the coolness), rather than the prevalence of mist, may account for the presence of this moisture forming bogs.

In a shallow rain-water pool, or rock cistern, about three rods long by one or one and a half wide, several hundred feet below the summit, on the west side, but still on the bare rocky top and on the steepest side of the summit, I saw toad-spawn (black with white bellies), also some very large spawn new to me. There were four or five masses of it, each three or four inches in diameter and of a peculiar light misty bluish white as it lay in the water near the surface, attached to some weed or stick, as usual. Each mass consisted of but few large ova, more than a quarter of an inch in diameter, in which were pale-brown tadpoles flattened out. The outside of the mass when taken up was found to consist of large spherical or rounded gelatinous projections three quarters of an inch wide, and blue in the light and air, while the ova within were greenish. This rain-water pool was generally less than a foot deep, with scarcely a weed in it, but considerable mud concealing its rocky bottom. The spawn was unusually clean and clear. I suspect it to be that of bullfrogs,* though not a frog was to be seen; they were probably lurking beneath the rocks in the water at that hour. This pool was bounded on one or two sides by those rounded walls of rock five or six feet high. My companion had said

that he heard a bullfrog the evening before. Is it likely that these toads and frogs ever hopped up there? The hylodes peeped regularly toward night each day in a similar pool much nearer the summit. Agassiz might say that they originated on the top. Perhaps they fell from the clouds in the form of spawn or tadpoles or young frogs. I think it more likely that they fell down than that they hopped up. Yet how can they escape the frosts of winter?

The descent north and west cut across Dublin Path, which dates from 1843; the ponds they saw were Dublin Lake and Dark Pond, about three miles north; and the "dry watercourses" were the upper reaches of Gleason *(see page 310)* and Shaker brooks, which flow east toward Marlboro.

Thoreau's informant on the rocks of Monadnock was Charles T. Jackson, who also prepared a geological map of New Hampshire in 1844. Despite his lack of geological

*Probably *Rana fontinalis. Vide* August, 1860.

theory, Thoreau accurately described jointing, the
northwest to southeast scratches left by glacial movement, and the "stratified" zones of folding. He correctly
identified quartz and garnets, yet he failed to remark on
the prominent network of sillimanite crystals, which resemble bird tracks. *(see page 310)*

As a skilled botanist, not a geologist, he was more
drawn to observing the alternation between moist,
spongy bogs and dry, sandy deserts; a contrast that
echoed his earlier equation of spring and winter. His *(see page 304)*
mind explored these contrasts, avoiding conclusions and
lingering over the facts instead. Bullfrogs still dwell at
the pool where he found spawn; by August they form a *(see page 312)*
lively chorus in the late afternoons. To Thoreau, this
creature raised the whole problem of biological distribution: how do species reach new habitats and adapt to
their conditions?

Having reached the neighborhood of our camp again and explored the
wooded portion lower down along the path up the mountain, we set
out northeast along the east side of the mountain. The southeast part
of the mountain-top is an extended broad rocky *almost* plateau, consisting of large flat rocks with small bogs and rain-water pools and
easy ascents to different levels. The black spruce tree which is scattered here and there over it, the prevailing tree or shrub of the mountain-top, evidently has many difficulties to contend with. It is generally
of a yellowish green, its foliage. The most exposed trees are very
stout and spreading close to the rock, often much wider close to the
rock than they are high, and these lower, almost their only, limbs
completely filling and covering openings between the rocks. I saw one
which grew out of a narrow crack in the rock, which was three feet
high, five inches in diameter at the ground, and six feet wide on the
rock. It was shaped like a bodkin,—the main stem. The spruce commonly grows in clefts of the rocks; has many large limbs, and longer
than the tree is high, perhaps, spreading close and flat over the rock
in every direction, sometimes eight or ten within a foot of the rock;
then, higher up the stem, or midway for three or six feet, though

perfectly perpendicular, is quite bare on the north side and commonly smooth, showing no trace of a limb, no stubs, but the limbs at this height all ray out southward, and the top is crowned with a tuft of tender twigs. This proves the violence of the storms which they have to contend with. Its branches love to run along flat on the rocks, filling the openings between the rocks. It forms dense coverts and forms, apparently, for the rabbits, etc. A single spruce tree of this habit would sometimes make a pretty good shelter, while the rocks on each side were your walls.

As I walked over this plateau, I first observed, looking toward the summit, that the steep angular projections of the summit and elsewhere and the brows of the rocks were the parts chiefly covered with dark-brown lichens,—umbilicaria, etc.,—as if they were to grow on the ridge and slopes of a man's nose only [drawing]. It was the steepest and most exposed parts of the high rocks alone on which they grew, where you would think it most difficult for them to cling. They also covered the more rounded brows on the sides of the mountain, especially the east side, where they were very dense, fine, crisp, and firm, like a sort of shagreen, giving a firm footing or hold to the feet where it was needed. It was these that gave that Ararat-brown color of antiquity to these portions of the mountain, which a few miles distant could not be accounted for compared with the more prevalent gray. From the sky-blue you pass through the misty gray of the rocks, to this darker and more terrene color. The temples of the mountain are covered with lichens, which color the mountain for miles.

The west side descends steeply from the summit, but there is a broad almost plateau on the southeast and east, not much beneath the summit, with a precipitous termination on the east, and the rounded brows of the last are covered with the above-named lichens. A spur of moderate length runs off northerly; another, but lower, southwesterly; another, much longer, a little higher than the last, southerly; and one longer and higher than these, one or two miles long, northeasterly. As you creep down over those eastern brows to look off the precipice, these rough and rigid lichens, forming a rigid crust, as it were baked, done brown, in the sun of centuries, afford a desireable hand and foot hold.

They seemed to me wild robins that placed their nests in the spruce up there. I noticed one nest. William Emerson, senior, says they do not breed on Staten Island. They do breed at least at Hudson's Bay. They are certainly a hardy bird, and are at home on this cool mountain-top.

We boiled some rice for our dinner, close by the edge of a rain-water pool and bog, on the plateau southeast from the summit. Though there was so little vegetation, our fire spread rapidly through the dry cladonia lichens on the rocks, and, the wind being pretty high, threatened to give us trouble, but we put it out with a spruce bough dipped in the pool.* I thought that if it had spread further, it must soon have come to a bog. Though you could hardly tell what was moist and what dry till the fire came to it. Nothing could be drier than the cladonia, which was often adjacent to a mass of moss saturated with moisture.

These rain-water pools or cisterns are a remarkable feature. There is a scarcity of bubbling springs,but this water was commonly cool enough in that atmosphere and warm as the day was. I do not know why they were not warmer, for they were shallow and the nights were not cold. Can there be some concealed snow or ice about? Hardly. They are quite shallow, but sometimes four or five rods over and with considerable mud at the bottom at first, decayed lichens, and disintegrated rock. Apparently these were the origin of the bogs, *Eriophorum vaginatum,* moss, and a few other boggy plants springing up in them and gradually filling them; yet, though sometimes filled with sedge (?) or fine grass, and generally the dwarfish *Eriophorum vaginatum* in the moss, they were singularly barren, and, unless they were fairly converted into swamps, contained very little variety. You never have to go far to find water of some kind. On the top, perhaps, of a square half-acre of almost bare rock, as in what we called our wash-room by our camp, you find a disintegrated bog, wet moss alternating with dry cladonia (sign and emblem of dryness in our neighborhood), and water stands in little holes, or if you look under the edges of a boulder there, you find standing water, yet cool to drink.

On their journey down the east side, Thoreau and Blake apparently went partway down the White Arrow trail, then (near 2,500 feet) turned east. On this spur Thoreau

*And wet the ground with it. You cook beside such a moss for the sake of water.

(see page 271)
(see page 313)
(see page 314)

closely examined the dwarf spruce and its variations, an interest he also pursued in July on Mt. Lafayette. Although he could see how well the trees sheltered other plants and animals, he persisted in misidentifying "black spruce." The trees on Monadnock are *red* spruce, as on Lafayette, a variety taller and with longer cones than black spruce.

His main authority on lichens was Edward Tuckerman, whose handbooks Thoreau had used to identify twenty-eight species in the Concord area. Although he says little about this plant's structure, a symbiotic merging of algae and fungus, he does note how it helps to decompose rocks, slowly turning them back into clay. In March 1854 he boiled *umbilicaria* (rock tripe) for several hours to see how it tasted. In February 1859, six months after the present trip, he wrote a remarkable description of how lichens, "the color of antiquity" itself, nourished his inner life.

Going along the Nut Meadow or Jimmy Miles road, when I see the sulphur lichens on the rails brightening with the moisture I feel like studying them again as a relisher or tonic, to make life go down and digest well, as we use pepper and vinegar and salads. They are a sort of winter greens which we gather and assimilate with our eyes. That's the true use of the study of lichens. I expect that the lichenist will have the keenest relish for Nature in her every-day mood and dress. He will have the appetite of the worm that never dies, of the grub. To study lichens is to get a taste of earth and health, to go gnawing the rails and rocks. This product of the bark is the essence of all times. The lichenist extracts nutriment from the very crust of the earth. A taste for this study is an evidence of titanic health, a sane earthiness. It makes not so much blood as soil of life. It fits a man to deal with the barrenest and rockiest experience. A little moisture, a fog, or rain, or melted snow makes his wilderness to blossom like the rose. As some strong animal appetites, not satisfied with starch and muscle and fat, are fain to eat that which eats and digests,—the contents of the crop and the stomach and entrails themselves,—so the lichenist loves the tripe of the rock,—that which eats and digests the rocks. He eats the eater. "Eat-all" may be his name. A lichenist fats where others starve. His provender never fails. What is the barrenest waste to him, the barest rocks? A rail is the sleekest and fattest of coursers for him. He picks anew the bones which have been picked a generation since, for when their marrow is gone they are clothed with new flesh for him. What diet drink can be compared with a tea or soup made of the very crust of the earth? There is no such collyrium or salve for sore eyes as these brightening lichens in a moist day. Go and bathe and screen your eyes with them in the softened light of the woods.

After exploring the mountain from all sides, and again noting the shape of its various spurs, Thoreau prepared dinner near the campsite. His trouble containing a fire *(see page 292)* verifies the history he had learned in 1852, that Monadnock burned easily. Yet the summit bogs and pools pro- *(see page 315)* vided a natural extinguisher. Monadnock was not a formless Chaos, but a balanced structure, wet and dry.

After dinner we kept on northeast over a high ridge east of the summit, whence was a good view of that part of Dublin and Jaffrey immediately under the mountain. There is a fine, large lake extending north and south, apparently in Dublin, which it would be worth the while to sail on. When on the summit of this, I heard the ring of toads from a rain-pool a little lower and northeasterly. It carried me back nearly a month into spring (though they are still ringing and copulating in Concord), it sounded so springlike in that clear, fresh air. Descending to that pool we found toads copulating at the bottom of the water.

In one or two places on this side of the mountain, which, as I have said, terminated in an abrupt precipice, I saw bogs or meadows four or six rods wide or more, but with only grass and moss and eriophorum, without bushes, in them, close to the edge of the mountain or precipice, where, if you stood between the meadow and the summit, looking east, there would appear to be a notch in the rim of the cup or saucer on the east and the meadow ready to spill over and run down the mountain on that side [drawing]; but when you stood on this notched edge, the descent was seen to be much less precipitous than you had expected. Such spongy mountain bogs, however, are evidently the sources of rivers. Lakes of the clouds when they are clear water. Between this and the northeast spur or ridge was the largest swamp or bog that I saw, consisting, perhaps, of between one and two acres, as I remember. It was a grassy and mossy bog without large bushes, in which you sank a foot, with a great many fallen trees in it, showing their bleached upper side here and there but almost completely buried in the moss. This must once have been a dense swamp, full of pretty large trees. The trees buried in the moss were much larger than any now standing at this height. The outlet of this, if it had any, must have been northwesterly. This was a wild place enough.

Having ascended the highest part of the northeastern ridge north of this bog, we returned to the summit, first to the ridge of the plateau, and west on it to the summit, crossing a ravine between. I noticed, in many places upon the mountain, sandy or gravelly spaces from a few feet to a rod in diameter, where the thin sward and loam appeared to have been recently removed or swept away. I was inclined to call them scars, and thought of very violent winds and tempests of rain as the cause, perhaps, but do not know how to account for them.

We had thus made a pretty complete survey of the top of the mountain. It is a very unique walk, and would be almost equally interesting to take though it were not elevated above the surrounding valleys. It often reminded me of my walks on the beach, and suggested how much both depend for their sublimity on solitude and dreariness. In both cases we feel the presence of some vast, titanic power. The rocks and valleys and bogs and rain-pools of the mountain are so wild and unfamiliar still that you do not recognize the one you left fifteen minutes before. This rocky region, forming what you may call the top of the mountain, must be more than two miles long by one wide in the middle, and you would need to ramble about it many times before it would begin to be familiar. There may be twenty little swamps so much alike in the main that [you] would not know whether you had seen a particular one before, and the rocks are trackless and do not present the same point. So that it has the effect of the most intricate labyrinth and artificially extended walk.

This mountain is said in the Gazetteer to extend northeast [and] southwest five miles, by three wide, and the streams on the east to empty into the Contoocook and Merrimack, on the west into the Ashuelot and Connecticut; is 3718 feet high; and, judging from its account, the top was wooded fifty years ago.

Thoreau's northeast walk was along the 2,500-foot level, *(see page 317)* a course lying close to the present Spellman trail, which links the White Dot and Pumpelly trails. The town lines of Dublin and Jaffrey cross just north of Pumpelly; from there he admired Dublin Lake, two and a half miles north.

Again, a mountain phenomenon—the sound of toads—stirred his imagination, just as bogs explained to him the origin of rivers, deep in prehistoric times. The largest pool, now called "Thoreau Bog," lies between Pumpelly and Dublin trails, on the northeast side: it forms the head of Mountain Brook.

His return to the summit, following the course of Pumpelly trail, passed (without comment) a large erratic known as "The Sarcophagus." Thoreau instead noted the "scars" of sandy gravel, spots that probably measure deeper levels of snow cover, where plant growth has been retarded. These sandy places are another example *(see page 318)* of balanced opposites, mountain and shore, in one locale.

We proceeded to get our tea on the summit, in the very place where I had made my bed for a night some fifteen years before. There were a great many insects of various kinds on the topmost rocks at this hour, and among them I noticed a yellow butterfly and several large brownish ones fluttering over the apex.

It was interesting to watch from that height the shadows of fair-weather clouds passing over the landscape. You could hardly distinguish them from forests. It reminded me of the similar shadows seen on the sea from the high bank of Cape Cod beach. There the perfect equality of the sea atoned for the comparatively slight elevation of the bank. We do not commonly realize how constant and amusing a phenomenon this is in a summer day to one standing on a sufficiently

elevated point. In the valley or on the plain you do not commonly
notice the shadow of a cloud unless you are in it, but on a mountain-
top, or on a lower elevation in a plain country or by the seaside, the
shadows of clouds flitting over the landscape are a never-failing
source of amusement. It is commonly easy to refer a shadow to its
cloud, since in one direction its form is preserved with sufficient accuracy. Yet I was surprised to observe that a long, straggling downy
cumulus extending north and south a few miles east of us, when the
sun was perhaps an hour high, cast its shadow along the base of the
Peterboro Hills, and did not fall on the other side, as I should have
expected. It proved the clouds not so high as I supposed. It suggested
how with tolerable accuracy you might easily calculate the height of
a cloud with a quadrant and a good map of the country; *e.g.*, observe
at what distance the shadow of a cloud directly overhead strikes the
earth, and then take the altitude of the sun, and you may presume that
you have the base and two angles of a right-angled triangle, from
which the rest may be calculated; or you may allow for the angle of
elevation of the mountain as seen from the place where the shadow
falls. Also you might determine the breadth of a cloud by observing
the breadth of the shadow at a given distance, etc., etc. Many such
calculations would be easy in such a locality. It was pleasant enough
to see one man's farm in the shadow of a cloud,—which perhaps he
thought covered all the Northern States,—while his neighbor's farm
was in sunshine. It was still too hazy to allow of our seeing the shadow
of the mountain, so we descended a little before the sun set, but
already the hylodes had been peeping for some time.

Again the wood thrush, chewink, etc., sang at eve. I had also heard
the song sparrow.

As the sky was more cloudy this evening, we looked out a shelving
rock near our camp, where we might take shelter from the rain in the
night if necessary, *i.e.*, if our roof did not prove tight enough. There
were plenty of clefts and small caverns where you might be warm and
dry. The mosquitoes troubled us a little this night.

Lying up there at this season, when the nighthawk is most musical,
reminded me of what I had noticed before, that this bird is crepuscular
in its habits. It was heard by night only up to nine or ten o'clock and
again just before dawn, and marked those periods or seasons like a

clock. Its note very conveniently indicated the time of night. It was sufficient to hear the nighthawk booming when you awoke to know how the night got on, though you had no other evidence of the hour. I did not hear the sound of any beast. There are no longer any wolves to howl or panthers to scream. One man told me that many foxes took refuge from dogs and sportsmen on this mountain.

The plants of cold northern bogs grow on this mountain-top, and even they have a boreal habit here, more dwarfish than such of them as grow in our swamps. The more memorable and peculiar plants of the mountaintop were the mountain cranberry and the *Potentilla tridentata*, the *dwarfish* spruce, *Arenaria Grœnlandica* (not now conspicuous). The *Ribes prostratum*, or fetid currant, was very abundant from quite near the summit to near the base, and its currant-acid fragrance was quite agreeable to me, partly, perhaps, from its relation to the currant of the gardens. You also notice many small weed-like mountain-ashes, six or eight inches high, which, on trying to pull up, you find to be very firmly rooted, having an old and large root out of proportion to their top. I might also name in this connection not only the blueberry but the very common but dwarfish *Eriophorum vaginatum* and the *Lycopodium annotinum*, also the amelanchier, variety *oligocarpa*. I was not prepared to find vegetation so much later there than below or with us, since I once found blueberries ripe on Wachusett unexpectedly early. However, it was a pleasing lateness, and gives one a chance to review some of his lessons in natural history. On the rocky part, the only plants, as I noticed, which were or had been in bloom were the salix, now generally done; *Ribes prostratum*, in prime; *Eriophorum vaginatum; Vaccinium Pennsylvanicum,* just begun; *Amelanchier oligocarpa*, little, not long; water andromeda, ditto, ditto; and *probably* (?) the populus, birches (?), mayflower, and spruce.

Insects and butterflies are still plentiful on Monadnock, where forty-five different species have been sighted. The large brown specimens were probably wood satyr, quite *(see page 319)* common in June.

Many of Thoreau's experiences on this last day prepared him for his trip to the White Mountains in July: the problem of elevation, the relation of clouds and sunlight, the bogs and their dwarfed plants—all differed greatly from Concord and required further study. As he noted, the late berries here reminded him of Wachusett in 1842, providing "a chance to review some of his lessons in natural history."

(see page 321)

June 4. Friday. At 6 A.M. we began to descend. Near the upper edge of the wood, I heard, as I had done in ascending, a very peculiar lively and interesting strain from some bird, which note was new to me. At the same time I caught sight of a bird with a very conspicuous deep-orange throat and otherwise dark, with some streaks along the head. This may have been the Blackburnian warbler, if it was not too large for that, and may have been the singer. We descended or continued along the base of the mountain southward, taking the road to the State Line Station and Winchendon, through the west part of Rindge.

It is remarkable how, as you are leaving a mountain and looking back at it from time to time, it gradually gathers up its slopes and spurs to itself into a regular whole, and makes a new and total impression. The lofty beaked promontory which, when you were on the summit, appeared so far off and almost equal to it, seen now against the latter, scarcely deepens the tinge of bluish, misty gray on its side. The mountain has several spurs or ridges, bare and rocky, running from it, with a considerable depression between the central peak and them; *i.e.*, they attain their greatest height half a mile or more from the central apex. There is such a spur, for instance, running off southward about a mile. When we looked back from four or five miles distant on the south, this, which had appeared like an independent summit, was almost totally lost to our view against the general misty gray of the side of the principal summit. We should not have suspected its existence if we had not just come from it, and though the mountain ranges northeasterly and southwesterly, or not far from north and south, and is much the longest in that direction, it now presented a pretty regular pyramidal outline with a broad base, as if it were broadest east and west. That is, when you are on the mountain, the different peaks and ridges appear more independent; indeed, there is a bewildering variety of ridge and valley and peak, but when you have withdrawn a few miles, you are surprised at the more or less pyramidal outline of the mountain and that the lower spurs and peaks are all subordinated to the central and principal one. The summit appears to rise and the surrounding peaks to subside, though some new prominences appear. Even at this short distance the mountain has lost most of its rough and jagged outline, considerable ravines are smoothed over, and large boulders which you must go a long way round make no impression on the eye, being swallowed up in the air.

We had at first thought of returning to the railroad at Fitzwilliam, passing over Gap Mountain, which is in Troy and Fitzwilliam quite near Monadnock, but concluded to go to Winchendon, passing through the western part of Rindge to the State Line Station, the latter part of the road being roundabout. We crossed the line between Jaffrey and Rindge three or four miles from the mountain. Got a very good view of the mountain from a high hill over which the road ran in the western part of Rindge.

But the most interesting part of this walk was the three miles along the railroad between State Line and Winchendon Station. It was the best timbered region we saw, though its trees are rapidly falling. The railroad runs very straight for long distances here through a primitive forest. To my surprise I heard the *tea-lea* of the myrtle-bird* here, as in Maine, and suppose that it breeds in this primitive wood. There was no house near the railroad but at one point, and then a quarter of a mile off. The red elder was in full bloom and filled the air with its fragrance. I saw some of the handsomest white pines here that I ever saw,—even in Maine,—close by the railroad. One by which I stood was at least three and a half feet in diameter at two feet from the ground, and, like several others about it, rose perfectly straight without any kind of limb to the height of sixty feet at least. What struck me most in these trees, as I was passing by, was not merely their great size, for they appeared less than they were, but their perfect perpendicularity, roundness, and apparent smoothness, taper-ing very little, like artificial columns of a new style. Their trunks were so very round that for that reason they appeared smoother than they were, marked with interrupted bands of light-colored lichens. Their

*White-throat, probably.

regular beauty made such an impression that I was forced to turn aside and contemplate them. They were so round and perpendicular that my eyes slid off, and they made such an impression of finish and even polish as if they had had an enamelled surface. Indeed they were less rough than I might have expected. Beneath them grew the *Trillium pictum* and clintonia, both in bloom.

For last expedition to Monadnock, *vide* September, 1852.

ROUTE FROM SUMMIT: *White Cross trail to Jaffrey, NH 123 to West Rindge, US 202 to Winchendon, MA 12 to Fitchburg, MA 2A to Concord.*

After two nights Thoreau and Blake descended, probably via White Cross trail, and headed southwest for Jaffrey. Looking east at the mountain, Thoreau gave his story a summary ending, as he did in July when leaving the White Mountains (see p. 280). Monadnock gave him a model for nature; confusing at close hand, whole and integrated from a distance—if studied in that order.

The projected route over Little Monadnock (1,883′, seven miles southwest) would certainly have added extra miles to the trip; Thoreau held on a briefer course and was rewarded by the sight of a primitive white pine

(see page 323) forest, more perfect than human architecture. His final note, to review the story of his 1852 expedition, suggests that he hoped to bring these entries together—perhaps building them into a future publication.

.   .   .

The final trip to Monadnock in 1860 came during a period of intense activity in Thoreau's writing career. Early in the year, he had read *The Origin of Species* (1859), and this "development theory" influenced several works he was then creating on Concord's natural history: "Wild Apples," "Wild Fruits," "The Succession of Forest Trees," "The Dispersion of Seeds," and "Huckleberries." In various stages of progress when he visited Monadnock, these projects strongly affected his experiences there.

As in 1852, his companion was Ellery Channing, who proved this time to be poor company. In all his travels

Channing had never camped, so he did not respond to
Thoreau's invitation for several weeks. Blake then asked
Thoreau to return to the White Mountains, whereupon
Channing quickly agreed to see Monadnock in early August. Answering Blake, Thoreau joked that Channing
feared a "beast . . . might nibble his legs there." On the
trip Channing was never comfortable. In the 1870s he
wrote: "I cannot remember ever spending a free or
happy moment there as I look back. When I first went
there with H., he entirely spoilt it."

Aug. 4. 8.30 A.M.—Start for Monadnock.

Begins to rain at 9 A.M., and rains from time to time thereafter all
day, the mountain-top being constantly enveloped in clouds.

Notice in Troy much of the *cyperinus* variety of wool-grass, now
done, of various heights. Also, by roadside, the *Ribes Cynosbati*, with
its prickly berries now partly reddened but hardly ripe. Am ex-
hilarated by the peculiar raspberry scent by the roadside this wet day
—and of the dicksonia fern. Raspberries still quite common, though
late. The high blackberries, the mulberry kind, all still green and red;
and also on the 9th, except one berry on a rock.

There was a little sunshine on our way to the mountain, but the
cloud extended far down its sides all day, so that one while we mistook
Gap Monadnock for the true mountain, which was more to the north.

According to the guide-board it is two and one fourth miles from
Troy to the first fork in the road near the little pond and schoolhouse,
and I should say it was near two miles from there to the summit,—
all the way uphill from the meadow [map].

We crossed the immense rocky and springy pastures, containing at
first raspberries, but much more hardhack in flower, reddening them
afar, where cattle and horses collected about us, sometimes came
running to us, as we thought for society, but probably not. I told
Bent* of it,—how they gathered about us, they were so glad to see
a human being,—but he said I might put it in my book so, it would
do no harm, but then the fact was they came about me for salt.

*Apparently a local resident. The pastures Thoreau was crossing were owned by Aaron Bolster.—WH

"Well," said I, "it was probably because I had so much salt in my constitution." Said he, "If you had had a little salt with you [you] could hardly have got away from them." "Well," said I, "[I] had some salt in my pocket." "That's what they smelt," said he. Cattle, young and old, with horns in all stages of growth,—young heifers with budding horns,—and horses with a weak [?] Sleepy-David look, though sleek and handsome. They gathered around us while we took shelter under a black spruce from the rain.

We were wet up to our knees before reaching the woods or steep ascent where we entered the cloud. It was quite dark and wet in the woods, from which we emerged into the lighter cloud about 3 P.M., and proceeded to construct our camp, in the cloud occasionally amounting to rain, where I camped some two years ago.

Choosing a place where the spruce was thick in this sunken rock yard, I cut out with a little hatchet a space for a camp in their midst, leaving two stout ones six feet apart to rest my ridge-pole on, and such limbs of these as would best form the gable ends. I then cut four spruces as rafters for the gable ends, leaving the stub ends of the branches to rest the cross-beams or girders on, of which there were two or three to each slope; and I made the roof very steep. Then cut an abundance of large flat spruce limbs, four or five feet long, and laid them on, shingle-fashion, beginning at the ground and covering the stub ends. This made a foundation for two or three similar layers of smaller twigs. Then made a bed of the same, closed up the ends somewhat, and all was done. All these twigs and boughs, of course, were dripping wet, and we were wet through up to our middles. But we made a good fire at the door, and in an hour or two were completely dried.

The most thickly leaved and flattest limbs of the spruce are such as spread flat over the rocks far and wide (while the upper ones were more bushy and less flat); not the very lowest, which were often partly under the surface and but meagrely leafed, but those close above them.

Standing and sitting before the fire which we kindled under a shelving rock, we could dry us much quicker than at any fireside below, for, what with stoves and reduced fireplaces, they could not have furnished such blaze or heat in any inn's [?] kitchen or parlor. This fire was exactly on the site of my old camp, and we burned a hole deep into the withered remains of its roof and bed.

It began to clear up and a star appeared at 8 P.M. Lightning was seen far in the south. Cloud, drifting cloud, alternated with moonlight all the rest of the night. At 11.30 P.M. I heard a nighthawk. Maybe it hunted then because prevented by the cloud at evening.

I heard from time to time through the night a distant sound like thunder or a falling of a pile of lumber, and I suspect that this may have been the booming of nighthawks at a distance.

Virtually retracing his journey of 1858, Thoreau hiked past Pack ("Gap") Monadnock (2,288', sixteen miles east) via his previous trail, then up Fassett Brook and along the White Arrow trail to his 1858 site, near 3,000 feet. He was obviously in a good mood at the outset, joking with "Bent" about his cows, cheerfully clearing and rethatching the spruce hut. Channing declared the result handsome, Thoreau later wrote, but then "He never camped out before, and was, no doubt, prejudiced in its favor."

ROUTE FROM CONCORD: *MA 2A to Fitchburg, MA 12 to Troy, NH 119 to NH 124, to Perkins Pond*

(see page 325)

Aug. 5. The wind changed to northerly toward morning, falling down from over the summit and sweeping through our camp, open on that side, and we found it rather cold!

About an hour before sunrise we heard again the nighthawk; also the robin, chewink, song sparrow, *Fringilla hyemalis;* and the wood thrush from the woods below.

Had a grand view of the summit on the north now, it being clear. I set my watch each morning by sunrise, and this morning the lichens on the rocks of the southernmost summit (south of us), just lit by the rising sun, presented a peculiar yellowish or reddish brown light (being wet) which they did not any morning afterward. The rocks of the main summit were olive-brown, and C. called it the Mount of Olives.

I had gone out before sunrise to gather blueberries,—fresh, dewy (because wet with yesterday's rain), almost crispy blueberries, just in prime, much cooler and more grateful at this hour,—and was surprised to hear the voice of people rushing up the mountain for berries in the wet, even at this hour. These alternated with bright light-scarlet bunchberries not quite in prime.

The sides and angles of the cliffs, and their rounded brows (but especially their southeast angles, for I saw very little afterward on the north side; indeed, the cliffs or precipices are not on that side), were clothed with these now lively olive-brown lichens (umbilicaria), alike in sun and shade, becoming afterward and generally dark olive-brown when dry. *Vide* my specimens. Many of the names inscribed on the summit were produced by merely rubbing off the lichens, and they are thus distinct for years.

At 7.30 A.M. for the most part in cloud here, but the country below in sunshine. We soon after set out to walk to the lower southern spur of the mountain. It is chiefly a bare gray and extremely diversified rocky surface, with here and there a spruce or other small tree or bush, or patches of them, or a little shallow marsh on the rock; and the whole mountain-top for two miles was covered, on countless little shelves and in hollows between the rocks, with low blueberries of two or more species or varieties, just in their prime. They are said to be later here than below. Beside the kinds (black and blue *Pennsylvanicum*) common with us, there was the downy *Vaccinium Canadense* and a form or forms intermediate between this and the former, *i.e.* of like form but less hairy. The *Vaccinium Canadense* has a larger leaf and more recurved and undulating on its surface, and generally a lighter green than the common. There were the blue with a copious bloom, others simply black (not shiny, as ours commonly) and on largish bushes, and others of a peculiar blue, as if with a skim-coat of blue, hard and thin, as if glazed, such as we also have. The black are scarce as with us.

These blueberries grew and bore abundantly almost wherever anything else grew on the rocky part of the mountain,—except perhaps the very wettest of the little swamps and the thickest of the little thickets,—quite up to the summit, and at least thirty or forty people came up from the surrounding country this Sunday to gather them. When we behold this summit at this season of the year, far away and blue in the horizon, we may think of the blueberries as blending their color with the general blueness of the mountain. They grow alike in the midst of the cladonia lichens and of the lambkill and moss of the

little swamps. No shelf amid the piled rocks is too high or dry for
them, for everywhere they enjoy the cool and moist air of the mountain. They are evidently a little later than in Concord,—say a week or
ten days later. Blueberries of every degree of blueness and of bloom.
There seemed to be fewer of them on the more abrupt and cold
westerly and northwesterly sides of the summit, and most in the
hollows and shelves of the plateau just southeast of the summit.

Perhaps the prettiest berry, certainly the most novel and interesting to me, was the mountain cranberry, now grown but yet hard and
with only its upper cheek red. They are quite local, even on the mountain. The vine is most common close to the summit, but we saw very
little fruit there; but some twenty rods north of the brow of this low
southern spur we found a pretty little dense patch of them between
the rocks, where we gathered a pint in order to make a sauce of them.
They here formed a dense low flat bed, covering the rocks for a rod
or two, some lichens, green mosses, and the mountain potentilla mingled with them; and they rose scarcely more than one inch above the
ground. These vines were only an inch and a half long, clothed with
small, thick, glossy leaves, with two or three berries together, about
as big as huckleberries, on the recurved end, with a red cheek upper-
most and the other light-colored. It was thus a dense, firm sward [?]
of glossy little leaves dotted with bright-red berries. They were very
easy to collect, for you only made incessant dabs at them with all your
fingers together and the twigs and leaves were so rigid that you
brought away only berries and no leaves.

I noticed two other patches where the berries were thick, *viz.* one
a few rods north of the little rain-water lake of the rocks, at the first,
or small, meadow (source of Contoocook) at northeast end of the
mountain, and another not more than fifty rods northwest of the
summit, where the vines were much ranker and the berries larger.
Here the plants were four or five inches high, and there were three
or four berries of pretty large huckleberry size at the end of each, and
they branched like little bushes. In each case they occupied almost
exclusively a little sloping shelf between the rocks, and the vines and
berries were especially large and thick where they lay up against the
sloping sunny side of the rock.

We stewed these berries for our breakfast the next morning, and thought them the best berry on the mountain, though, not being quite ripe, the berry was a little bitterish—but not the juice of it. It is such an acid as the camper-out craves. They are, then, somewhat earlier than the common cranberry. I do not know that they are ever gathered hereabouts. At present they are very firm berries, of a deep, dark, glossy red. Doubtless there are many more such patches on the mountain.*

We heard the voices of many berry-pickers and visitors to the summit, but neither this nor the camp we built afterward was seen by any one.

P.M.—Walked to the wild swamp at the northeast spur. That part is perhaps the most interesting for the wild confusion of its variously formed rocks, and is the least, if at all, frequented. We found the skull and jaws of a large rodent, probably a hedgehog,—larger than a woodchuck's,—a considerable quantity of dry and hard dark-brown droppings, of an elliptical form, like very large rat-droppings, somewhat of a similar character but darker than the rabbit's, and I suspect that these were the porcupine's.

Returned over the top at 5 P.M., after the visitors, men and women, had descended, and so to camp.

On his walk to the southern spur, Thoreau passed over the promontory called Bald Rock (2,640'), once the only open spot on Monadnock. Just below is an old lead mine, last worked in 1849; Thoreau did not notice this site, despite his years of work in the graphite business. His mind was on botany, especially the thick clusters of lichens. (In 1852, Thoreau wrote in the Journal that Channing had tried to study lichens but gave it up, saying, "Why, the whole of it wasn't more than an inch thick.") Those clusters actually represent long years of slow, steady growth, responding to alternate shade and sun. Monadnock has more than a hundred types of lichens, from New Hampshire varieties at low altitude to Cana-

---

*Brought some home, and stewed them the 12th, and all thought them quite like, and as good as, the common cranberry. Yet George Emerson speaks of it as "austere" and inferior to the common cranberry.

dian species on the upper slopes. Thoreau was in the best
area for observing them, near Monte Rosa on the southwest side. *(see page 328)*

Moving along the White Cross trail, he found thick
patches of low-bush blueberry, thriving there in the
open sunlight. He was writing about berries in "Wild
Fruits" and could therefore describe them expertly. To
him, these berries were a supernal fruit; they thrived on
cool, moist air and spread into patches of dry ground. He
had a similar affection for mountain cranberries, which
he boiled for breakfast the next morning and declared
"such an acid as the camper-out craves." Channing's *(see page 330)*
opinion is unrecorded, but not Allen Chamberlain's:
"What a breakfast with which to appease a mountain
appetite!" This notion, that wild flavors are superior to
insipid table fruits, is a central theme in "Wild Fruits."

Aug. 6. The last was a clear, cool night. At 4 A.M. see local lake-like
fogs in some valleys below, but there is none here.

This forenoon, after a breakfast on cranberries, leaving, as usual,
our luggage concealed under a large rock, with other rocks placed
over the hole, we moved about a quarter of a mile along the edge of
the plateau eastward and built a new camp there. It was [a] place
which I had noticed the day before, where, sheltered by a perpendicular ledge some seven feet high and close to the brow of the mountain,
grew five spruce trees. Two of these stood four feet from the rock and
six or more apart; so, clearing away the superfluous branches, I rested
stout rafters from the rock-edge to limbs of the two spruces and
placed a plate beam across, and, with two or three cross-beams or
girders, soon had a roof which I could climb and shingle. After filling
the inequalities with rocks and rubbish, I soon had a sloping floor on
which to make our bed. Lying there on that shelf just on the edge of
the steep declivity of the mountain, we could look all over the south
and southeast world without raising our heads. The rock running east
and west was our shelter on the north.

Our huts, being built of spruce entirely, were not noticeable two or
three rods off, for we did [not] cut the spruce amid which they were

built more than necessary, bending aside their boughs in order to enter. My companion, returning from a short walk, was lost when within two or three rods, the different rocks and clumps of spruce looked so much alike, and in the moonlight we were liable to mistake some dark recess between two neighboring spruce ten feet off for the entrance to our house. We heard this afternoon the tread of a blueberry-picker on the rocks two or three rods north of us, and saw another as near, south, and, stealing out, we came round from another side and had some conversation with them,—two men and a boy,—but they never discovered our house nor suspected it. The surface is so uneven that ten steps will often suffice to conceal the ground you lately stood on, and yet the different shelves and hollows are so much alike that you cannot tell if one is new or not. It is somewhat like travelling over a huge fan. When in a valley the nearest ridge conceals all the others and you cannot tell one from another.

This afternoon, again walked to the larger northeast swamp, going directly, *i.e.* east of the promontories or part way down the slopes. Bathed in the small rocky basin above the smaller meadow. These two swamps are about the wildest part of the mountain and most interesting to me. The smaller occurs on the northeast side of the main mountain, *i.e.* at the northeast end of the plateau. It is a little roundish meadow a few rods over, with cotton-grass in it, the shallow bottom of a basin of rock, and out the east side there trickles a very slight stream, just moistening the rock at present and collecting enough in one cavity to afford you a drink. This is evidently a source of the Contoocook, the one I noticed two years ago as such.

The larger swamp is considerably lower and more northerly, separating the northeast spur from the main mountain, probably not far from the line of Dublin. It extends northwest and southeast some thirty or forty rods, and probably leaked out now under the rocks at the northwest end,—though I found water only half a dozen rods below,—and so was a source probably of the Ashuelot. The prevailing grass or sedge in it, growing in tufts in the green moss and sphagnum between the fallen dead spruce timber, was the *Eriophorum vaginatum* (long done) and the *E. gracile.* Also the *Epilobium palustre,* apparently in prime in it, and common wool-grass *(Scirpus Eriophorum).* Around its edge grew the *Chelone glabra* (not yet out), meadow-sweet in bloom, black choke-berry just ripening, red elder (its fruit in prime), mountain-ash, *Carex trisperma* and *Deweyana* (small and slender), and the fetid currant in fruit (in a torrent of rocks at the east end), etc., etc.

I noticed a third, yet smaller, quite small, swamp, yet more southerly, on the edge of the plateau, evidently another source of a river, where the snows melt.

At 5 P.M. we went to our first camp for our remaining baggage. From this point at this hour the rocks of the precipitous summit (under whose south side that camp is placed), lit by the declining sun, were a very light gray, with reddish-tawny touches from the now drying *Aira flexuosa* on the inaccessible shelves and along the seams. Returned to enjoy the evening at the second camp.

Evening and morning were the most interesting seasons, especially the evening. Each day, about an hour before sunset, I got sight, as it were accidentally, of an elysium beneath me. The smoky haze of the day, suggesting a furnace-like heat, a trivial dustiness, gave place to a clear transparent enamel, through which houses, woods, farms, and lakes were seen as in [a] picture indescribably fair and expressly made to be looked at. At any hour of the day, to be sure, the surrounding country looks flatter than it is. Even the great steep, furrowed, and rocky pastures, red with hardhack and raspberries, which creep so high up the mountain amid the woods, in which you think already that you are half-way up, perchance, seen from the top or brow of the mountain are not for a long time distinguished for elevation above the surrounding country, but they look smooth and tolerably level, and the cattle in them are not noticed or distinguished from rocks unless you search very particularly. At length you notice how the houses and barns keep a respectful, and at first unaccountable, distance from these near pastures and woods, though they *are* seemingly flat, that there is a broad neutral ground between the roads and the mountain; and yet when the truth flashes upon you, you have to imagine the long, ascending path through them.

To speak of the landscape generally, the open or cleared land looks like a thousand little swells or tops of low rounded hills,—tent-like or like a low hay-cap spread,—tawny or green amid the woods. As you look down on this landscape you little think of the hills where the traveller walks his horse. The woods have not this swelling look. The most common color of open land (from apex at 5 P.M.) is tawny brown, the woods dark green. At midday the darker green of evergreens amid the hardwoods is quite discernible half a dozen miles off. But, as the most interesting view is at sunset, so it is the part of [the] landscape nearest to you and most immediately beneath the mountain, where, as usual, there is that invisible gelid haze to glass it.

The nearest house to the mountain which we saw from our camp —one on the Jaffrey road—was in the shadow even of the low southern spur of the mountain which we called the Old South, just an hour before the sun set, while a neighbor on a hill within a quarter of a mile eastward enjoyed the sunlight at least half an hour longer. So much shorter are their days, and so much more artificial light and heat must they obtain, at the former house. It would be a serious loss, methinks, one hour of sunlight every day. *We* saw the sun so much longer. Of course the labors of the day were brought to an end, the sheep began to bleat, the doors were closed, the lamps were lit, and preparations for the night were made there, so much the earlier.

The landscape is shown to be not flat, but hilly, when the sun is half an hour high, by the shadows of the hills. But, above all, from half an hour to two hours before sunset many western mountain-ranges are revealed, as the sun declines, one behind another, by their dark outlines and the intervening haze; *i.e.*, the ridges are dark lines, while the intervening valleys are a cloud-like haze. It was so, at least, from 6 to 6.30 P.M. on the 6th; and, at 5 P.M. on the 8th, it being very hazy still, I could count in the direction of Saddleback Mountain eight distinct ranges, revealed by the darker lines of the ridges rising above this cloud-like haze. And I might have added the ridge of Monadnock itself within a quarter of a mile of me.

Of course, the last half of these mountain-ridges appeared successively higher and seemed higher, all of them (*i.e.* the last half), than the mountain we were on, as if you had climbed to the heights of the sky by a succession of stupendous terraces reaching as far as you could see from north to south. The Connecticut Valley was one broad gulf of haze which you were soon over. They were the Green Mountains that we saw, but there was no greenness, only a bluish mistiness, in what we saw; and all of Vermont that lay between us and their summit was but a succession of parallel ranges of mountains. Of course, almost all that we mean commercially and agriculturally by Vermont was concealed in those long and narrow haze-filled valleys. I never saw a mountain that looked so high and so melted away at last cloud-like into the sky, as Saddleback this eve, when your eye had clomb to it by these eight successive terraces. You had to begin at this end and ascend step by step to recognize it for a mountain at all. If you had first rested your eye on *it*, you would have seen it for a cloud, it was so incredibly high in the sky.

After sunset the ponds are white and distinct. Earlier we could distinguish the reflections of the woods perfectly in ponds three miles off.

I heard a cock crow very shrilly and distinctly early in the evening of the 8th. This was the most distinct sound from the lower world that I heard up there at any time, not excepting even the railroad whistle, which was louder. It reached my ear perfectly, to each note and curl, —from some submontane cock. We also heard at this hour an occasional bleat from a sheep in some mountain pasture, and a lowing of a cow. And at last we saw a light here and there in a farmhouse window. We heard no sound of man except the railroad whistle and, on Sunday, a church-bell. Heard no dog that I remember. Therefore I should say that, of all the sounds of the farmhouse, the crowing of the cock could be heard furthest or most distinctly under these circumstances. It seemed to wind its way through the layers of air as a sharp gimlet through soft wood, and reached our ears with amusing distinctness.

Possibly Thoreau moved to a new campsite because his *(see page 331)* old one was on the blueberry ledges, and thus crowded with pickers. Channing may also have disliked the first site: he later said it had no fireplace or closet, only a perpetual shower bath—when it rained. He recalled that Thoreau walked a straight line from the Road ledges (those just beyond Halfway House, on the southeast) and then laid a path of stones between the two sites. The second camp was located by Herbert Gleason in 1918 at a level of 2,600 feet, in a loop of the White Cross trail. In

(see page 332) this place the two men enjoyed their privacy, even to the
extent of playing boyish tricks on the berry pickers.

(see page 332) Returning to "Thoreau Bog" (via the Red Spot trail), he
again reflected upon the fact that these mountain pools
were sources of large rivers such as the Contoocook and
Ashuelot. The smaller swamp he saw is at the head of
Eveleth Brook, which flows into Thorndike Pond and
also reaches the Contoocook River.

(see page 333) From this point on, his entries grew less chronological
and more topical, as he gathered subjects into thematic
groups: the reflective, meditative qualities of morning
and evening; the advantage of a high perspective, which
allowed a broader view of objects and their relations.

(see page 334) The second camp was selected both for privacy and for
its fine views, looking down a broad ledge toward sunset,
which produced deep shadows and changing colors. The
house they saw on Jaffrey Road, opposite Cummings
Pond, was owned by Oliver Bailey, Jr. (1796–1862), who
operated a mill on Meads Brook. From his camp, Thoreau could scan the horizon and see mountains he had
climbed: south to Wachusett, west for "Saddleback" and
Wantastiquet, north to Washington and Lafayette.
Monadnock was the finale of his mountain life. Here was
the view he had long imagined from Concord's hills, and
he wrote about this moment superbly—as in the closing
description of a cockcrow, piercing the air like "a sharp
(see page 335) gimlet through soft wood."

Aug. 7. Morning—dawn and sunrise—was another interesting season. I rose always by four or half past four to observe the signs of
it and to correct my watch. From our first camp I could not see the
sun rise, but only when its first light (yellowish or, rather, pinkish)
was reflected from the lichen-clad rocks of the southern spur. But
here, by going eastward some forty rods, I could see the sun rise,
though there was invariably a low stratum or bar of cloud in the
horizon. The sun rose about five. The tawny or yellowish pastures
about the mountain (below the woods; what was the grass?) reflected

the auroral light at 4.20 A.M. remarkably, and they were at least as distinct as at any hour.

There was every morning more or less solid white fog to be seen on the earth, though none on the mountain. I was struck by the localness of these fogs. For five mornings they occupied the same place and were about the same in extent. It was obvious that certain portions of New Hampshire and Massachusetts were at this season commonly invested with fog in the morning, while others, or the larger part, were free from it. The fog lay on the lower parts only. From our point of view the largest lake of fog lay in Rindge and southward; and southeast of Fitzwilliam, *i.e.* about Winchendon, very large there. In short, the fog lay in great spidery lakes and streams answering to the lakes, streams, and meadows beneath, especially over the sources of Miller's River and the region of primitive wood thereabouts; but it did [not] rest on lakes always, *i.e.*, where they were elevated, as now some in Jaffrey were quite clear. It suggested that there was an important difference, so far as the health and spirits of the inhabitants were concerned, between the town where there was this regular morning fog and that where there was none. I shall always remember the inhabitants of State Line as dwellers in the fog. The geography and statistics of fog have not been ascertained. If we awake into a fog, it does not occur to us that the inhabitants of a neighboring town which lies higher may have none, neither do they, being ignorant of this happiness, inform us of it. Yet, when you come to look down thus on the country every morning, you see that here this thick white veil of fog is spread and not there. It was often several hundred feet thick, soon rising, breaking up, and drifting off, or rather seeming to drift away, as it evaporated. There was commonly such a risen fog drifting through the interval between this mountain and Gap Monadnock.

One morning I noticed clouds as high as the Peterboro Hills,—a lifted fog,—ever drifting easterly but making no progress, being dissipated. Also long rolls and ant-eaters of cloud, at last reduced by the sun to mere vertebræ. That morning (the 8th) the great and general cloud and apparently fog combined over the lowest land running southwest from Rindge was apparently five hundred or more feet deep, but our mountain was above all.

This forenoon I cut and measured a spruce on the north side the mountain, and afterward visited the summit, where one of the coast surveyors had been signalling, as I was told, to a mountain in Laconia, some fifty-five miles off, with a glass reflector.

After dinner, descended into the gulf and swamp beneath our camp. At noon every roof in the southern country sloping toward the north was distinctly revealed,—a lit gray.

In the afternoon, walked to the Great Gulf and meadow, in the midst of the plateau just east of and under the summit.

Aug. 8. *Wednesday.* 8.30 A.M. Walk round the west side of the summit. Bathe in the rocky pool there, collect mountain cranberries on the northwest side, return over the summit, and take the bearings of the different spurs, etc. Return to camp at noon.

Toward night, walk to east edge of the plateau.

Aug. 9. At 6 A.M., leave camp for Troy, where we arrive, after long pauses, by 9 A.M., and take the cars at 10.5.

Thoreau's punctilious habits—rising at sunrise and correcting his watch—must have galled Channing; and by now the discomfort of camping had taken its toll. On their trips to Canada or Cape Cod they had stayed at inns, eaten regular meals, studied botany in a casual manner. Thoreau took his eastward walk alone, along the Red Spot trail that crosses between White Dot and White Cross trails. The points he could see through morning *(see page 337)* fog are eight miles southeast and fifteen miles southwest.

(see above)   The surveyors he met later that day were from the U.S. Coast Survey, which worked on Monadnock in the summers of 1858, 1860, and 1861. (Their 1861 camp was on the White Arrow trail, near Halfway spring.) In 1860 their stay was from July 24 to August 6, so Thoreau's date of August 7 is incorrect. They were signaling Gunstock Mountain (2,394', fifty-eight miles northeast) with a heliotrope, or mirror reflector.

The perfunctory nature of his final entries may reflect difficulties with Channing, who had declared, as Thoreau later told Blake, "that 6 working days made a week, & . . . he was ready to *de-camp.*" (In the 1870s, Channing often camped alone on Monadnock and wrote some of his best poetry there.) Their route down the mountain, to Troy and Concord, exactly reversed the approach hike. *(see page 338)*

I observed these plants on the rocky summit of the mountain, above the forest:—

Raspberry, not common.

Low blueberries of two or three varieties.

Bunchberry.

Solidago thyrsoidea.

Fetid currant, common; leaves beginning to be scarlet; grows amid loose fallen rocks.

Red cherry, some ripe, and handsome.

Black choke-berry.

Potentilla tridentata, still lingering in bloom.

Aralia hispida, still lingering in bloom.

Cow-wheat, common, still in bloom.

Mountain cranberry, not generally abundant; full grown earlier than lowland ditto.

Black spruce.

Lambkill, lingering in flower in cool and moist places.

Aster acuminatus, abundant; not generally open, but fairly begun to bloom.

Red elder, ripe, apparently in prime, not uncommon.

Arenaria Grœnlandica, still pretty common in flower.

Solidago lanceolata, not uncommon; just fairly begun.

Epilobium angustifolium, in bloom; not common, however.

Epilobium palustre, some time, common in mosses, small and slender.

Wild holly, common; berries not quite ripe.

Viburnum nudum, common; berries green.

White pine; saw three or four only, mostly very small.

Mountain-ash, abundant; berries not ripe; generally very small, largest in swamps.

Diervilla, not uncommon, still.

Rhodora, abundant; low, *i.e.* short.

Meadow-sweet, abundant, apparently in prime.

Hemlocks; two little ones with rounded tops.

Chelone glabra, not yet; at northeast swamp-side.

Yarrow.

Canoe birch, very small.

Clintonia borealis, with fruit.

Checkerberry.

Gold-thread.

One three-ribbed goldenrod, northwest side (not *Canadense*).

Tall rough goldenrod, not yet; not uncommon.

Populus tremuliformis, not very common.

Polygonum cilinode, in bloom.

Yellow birch, small.

Fir, a little; four or five trees noticed.

Willows, not uncommon, four or five feet high.

Red maple, a very little, small.

Water andromeda, common about the bogs.

Trientalis.

Pearly everlasting, out.

Diplopappus umbellatus, in bloom, not common (?); northeast swamp-side, also northwest side of mountain.

Juncus trifidus.

Some *Juncus paradoxus?*

Some *Juncus acuminatus?*   about edge of marshes.

CYPERACEÆ

Eriophorum gracile, abundant, whitening the little swamps.

Eriophorum vaginatum, abundant, little swamps, long done, (this the coarse grass in tufts, in marshes).

Wool-grass, not uncommon, (common kind).

Carex trisperma (?) or *Deweyana*, with large seeds, slender and drooping, by side of northeast swamp. *Vide* press.

Carex scoparia? or *straminea?* a little.

C. debilis.

Carex, small, rather close-spiked, *C. canescens*-like (?), common.

A fine grass-like plant very common, perhaps *Eleocharis tenuis;* now without heads, but marks of them.

GRASSES

Aira flexuosa.

Glyceria elongata, with appressed branches (some purplish), in swamp.

Blue-joint, apparently in prime, one place.

Festuca ovina, one place.

Cinna arundinacea, one place.

Agrostis scabra (?), at our spring, *q.v.*

FERNS AND LICHENS, ETC.

A large greenish lichen flat on rocks, of a peculiarly concentric growth, *q.v.*

Some common sulphur lichen.

The very bright handsome crustaceous yellow lichen, as on White Mts., *q.v.*

Two or three umbilicaria lichens, *q.v.*, giving the dark brown to the rocks.

A little, in one place, of the old hat umbilicaria, as at Flint's Pond Rock.

Green moss and sphagnum in the marshes.

Two common cladonias, white and greenish.

Stereocaulon.

Lycopodium complanatum, one place.

Lycopodium annotinum, not very common.

Common polypody.

Dicksonia fern, *q.v.*

Sensitive fern, and various other common ones.

I see that in my last visit, in June, '58, I also saw here Labrador tea (on the north side), two-leaved Solomon's-seal, *Amelanchier Canadensis* var. *oligocarpa* and var. *oblongifolia,* one or two or three kinds of willows, a little mayflower, and chiogenes, and *Lycopodium clavatum.*

The prevailing trees and shrubs of the mountain-top are, in order

of commonness, etc., low blueberry, black spruce, lambkill, black
choke-berry, wild holly, *Viburnum nudum*, mountain-ash, meadow-
sweet, rhodora, red cherry, canoe birch, water andromeda, fetid currant.

The prevailing and characteristic smaller plants, excepting grasses,
cryptogamic, etc.: *Potentilla tridentata, Solidago thyrsoidea*,
bunchberry, cow-wheat, *Aster acuminatus, Arenaria Grœnlandica*, mountain cranberry, *Juncus trifidus, Clintonia borealis,
Epilobium palustre, Aralia hispida.*

Of *Cyperaceæ* the most common and noticeable now were *Eriophorum gracile* and *vaginatum*, a few sedges, and perhaps the
grass-like *Eleocharis tenuis.*

The grass of the mountain now was the *Aira flexuosa*, large and
abundant, now somewhat dry and withered, on all shelves and along
the seams, quite to the top; a pinkish tawny now. Most would not have
noticed or detected any other. The other kinds named were not common. You would say it was a true mountain grass. The only grass that
a careless observer would notice. There was nothing like a sod on the
mountain-top. The tufts of *J. trifidus*, perhaps, came the nearest to
it.

The black spruce is the prevailing tree, commonly six or eight feet
high; but very few, and those only in the most sheltered places, as
hollows and swamps, are of regular outline, on account of the strong
and cold winds with which they have to contend. Fifteen feet high
would be unusually large. They cannot grow here without some kind
of lee to start with. They commonly consist of numerous flat branches
close above one another for the first foot or two, spreading close over
the surface and filling and concealing the hollows between the rocks;
but exactly at a level with the top of the rock which shelters them they
cease to have any limbs on the north side, but all their limbs now are
included within a quadrant between southeast and southwest, while
the stem, which is always perfectly perpendicular, is bare and smooth
on the north side; yet it is led onward at the top by a tuft of tender
branches a foot in length and spreading every way as usual, but the
northern part of these successively die and disappear. They thus
remind you often of masts of vessels with sails set on one side, and
sometimes one of these almost bare masts is seen to have been broken

short off at ten feet from the ground, such is the violence of the wind there. I saw a spruce, healthy and straight, full sixteen feet without a limb or the trace of a limb on the north side. When building my camp, in order to get rafters six feet long and an inch and a half in diameter at the small end, I was obliged to cut down spruce at least five inches in diameter at one foot from the ground. So stout and tapering do they grow. They spread so close to the rocks that the lower branches are often half worn away for a foot in length by their rubbing on the rocks in the wind, and I sometimes mistook the creaking of such a limb for the note of a bird, for it is just such a note as you would expect to hear there. The two spruce which formed the sides of my second camp had their lower branches behind the rock so thick and close, and, on the outsides of the quadrant, so directly above one another perpendicularly, that they made two upright side walls, as it were, very convenient to interlace and make weather-tight.

I selected a spruce growing on the highest part of the plateau east of the summit, on its north slope, about as high as any tree of its size, to cut and count its rings. It was five feet five inches high. As usual, all its limbs except some of the leading twigs extended toward the south. One of the lowermost limbs, so close to the ground that I thought its green extremity was a distinct tree, was ten feet long. There were ten similar limbs (though not so long) almost directly above one another, within two feet of the ground, the largest two inches thick at the butt. I cut off this tree at one foot from the ground. It was there five inches in diameter and had forty-four rings, but four inches of its growth was on the south side the centre and only one inch on the north side. I cut it off again nineteen inches higher and there there were thirty-five rings.

Our fuel was the dead spruce—apparently that which escaped the fire some forty years ago!!—which lies spread over the rocks in considerable quantity still, especially at the northeast spur. It makes very good dry fuel, and some of it is quite fat and sound. The spruce twigs were our bed. I observed that, being laid bottom upward in a hot sun, as at the foot of our bed, the leaves turned pale-brown, as if boiled, and fell off very soon.

The black spruce is certainly a very wild tree, and loves a primitive soil just made out of disintegrated granite.

After the low blueberry I should say that the lambkill was the commonest shrub. The black choke-berry also was very common, but this and the rhodora were both dwarfish. Though the meadow-sweet was very common, I did not notice any hardhack; yet it was exceedingly prevalent in the pastures below.

The *Solidago thyrsoidea* was the goldenrod of the mountain-top, from the woods quite to the summit. Any other goldenrod was comparatively scarce. It was from two inches to two feet high. It grew both in small swamps and in the seams of the rocks everywhere, and was now in its prime.

The bunchberry strikes one from these parts as much as any,— about a dozen berries in a dense cluster, a lively scarlet on a green ground.

Spruce was the prevailing tree; blueberry, the berry; *S. thyrsoidea*, the goldenrod; *A. acuminatus*, the aster (the only one I saw, and very common); *Juncus trifidus*, the juncus; and *Aira flexuosa*, the grass, of the mountain-top.

The two cotton-grasses named were very common and conspicuous in and about the little meadows.

The *Juncus trifidus* was the common grass (or grass-like plant) of the very highest part of the mountain,—the peak and for thirty rods downward,—growing on the shelves and especially on the edges of the *scars* rankly, and on this part of the mountain almost alone had it fruited,—for I think that I saw it occasionally lower and elsewhere on the rocky portion without fruit.

The apparently common green and white cladonias, together with yet whiter stereocaulon, grew all over the flat rocks in profusion, and the apparently common greenish rock lichen (*q.v.* in box)* grew concentricwise in large circles on the slopes of rocks also, not to mention the common small umbilicaria *(q.v.)* of one or two kinds which covered the brows and angles of the rocks.

The berries now ripe were: blueberries, bunchberries, fetid currant, red cherry, black choke-berry (some of them), mountain cranberry (red-cheeked and good cooked), red elder (quite showy), *Clintonia borealis*, raspberry (not common). And berries yet green were:

Thoreau is probably referring to specimens he collected.—WH

Aralia hispida (ripe in Concord, *much* of it), wild holly (turning), *Viburnum nudum* (green), mountain-ash.

At the close of his dated entries Thoreau wrote up a long topical summary, gathered from his field notes and previous Journal entries. This material, which suggests that he had a future project in mind (it resembles the "Appendix" he included in *The Maine Woods*), concentrates on the mountain's summit zone and treats in order its plants, animals, visitors, rocks, water, weather, and camping (with some variations).

Botany chiefly held his interest, and this list reflects the skill he had developed in field identification— grasses, for example, are extremely difficult to distinguish. Yet he continued to misidentify "black spruce," *(see page 342)* and he erred in saying that it grew from the primitive soil of "granite." Here the red spruce grows mostly from *(see page 343)* mica schist; lichens would serve as a better emblem for the life that emerges from decomposition.

The birds which I noticed were: robins, chewinks, *F. hyemalis*, song sparrow, nighthawk, swallow (a few, probably barn swallow, one flying over the extreme summit), crows (sometimes flew over, though mostly heard in the woods below), wood thrush (heard from woods below); and saw a warbler with a dark-marked breast and yellowish angle to wing and white throat, and heard a note once like a very large and powerful nuthatch. Some small hawks.

The bird peculiar to the mountain was the *F. hyemalis*, and perhaps the most common, flitting over the rocks, unless the robin and chewink were as common. These, with the song sparrow and wood thrush, were heard regularly each morning. I saw a robin's nest in one of the little swamps. The wood thrush was regularly heard late in the afternoon, its strain coming up from the woods below as the shadows were lengthening.

But, above all, this was an excellent place to observe the habits of the nighthawks. They were heard and seen regularly at sunset,—one night it was at 7.10, or exactly at sunset,—coming upward from the lower and more shaded portion of the rocky surface below our camp, with their *spark spark*, soon answered by a companion, for they seemed always to hunt in pairs,—yet both would dive and boom and, according to Wilson, only the male utters this sound. They pursued their game thus a short distance apart and some sixty or one hundred feet above the gray rocky surface, in the twilight, and the constant *spark spark* seemed to be a sort of call-note to advertise each other of their neighborhood. Suddenly one would hover and flutter more stationarily for a moment, somewhat like a kingfisher, and then dive almost perpendicularly downward with a rush, for fifty feet, frequently within three or four rods of us, and the loud booming sound or rip was made just at the curve, as it ceased to fall, but whether voluntarily or involuntarily I know not. They appeared to be diving for their insect prey. What eyes they must have to be able to discern it *beneath* them against the rocks in the twilight! As I was walking about the camp, one flew low, within two feet of the surface, about me, and lit on the rock within three rods of me, and uttered a harsh note like *c-o-w, c-o-w,*—hard and gritty and allied to their common notes,—which I thought expressive of anxiety, or to alarm me, or for its mate.

I suspect that their booming on a distant part of the mountain was the sound which I heard the first night which was like very distant thunder, or the fall of a pile of lumber.

They did not fly or boom when there was a cloud or fog, and ceased pretty early in the night. They came up from the same quarter—the shaded rocks below—each night, two of them, and left off booming about 8 o'clock. Whether they then ceased hunting or withdrew to another part of the mountain, I know not. Yet I heard one the first night at 11.30 P.M., but, as it had been a rainy day and did not clear up here till some time late in the night, it may have been compelled to do its hunting then. They began to boom again at 4 A.M. (other birds about 4.30) and ceased about 4.20. By their color they are related to the gray rocks over which they flit and circle.

As for quadrupeds, we saw none on the summit and only one small gray rabbit at the base of the mountain, but we saw the droppings of rabbits all over the mountain, and they must be the prevailing large animal, and we heard the motions probably of a mouse about our camp at night. We also found the skull of a rodent larger than a woodchuck or gray rabbit, and the tail-bones (maybe of the same) some half-dozen inches long, and saw a large quantity of dark-brown oval droppings (*q.v.*, preserved). I think that this was a porcupine, and I hear that they are found on the mountain. Mr. Wild saw one recently dead near the spring some sixteen years ago. I saw the ordure of some large quadruped, probably this, on the rocks in the pastures beneath the wood, composed chiefly of raspberry seeds.

As for insects: There were countless ants, large and middle-sized, which ran over our bed and inside our clothes. They swarmed all over the mountain. Had young in the dead spruce which we burned. Saw but half a dozen mosquitoes. Saw two or three common yellow butter-flies and some larger red-brown ones, and moths. There were great flies, as big as horse-flies, with shining black abdomens and buff-colored bases to their wings. Disturbed a swarm of bees in a dead spruce on the ground, but they disappeared before I ascertained what kind they were. On the summit one noon, *i.e.* on the very apex, I was pestered by great swarms of small black wasps or winged ants about a quarter of an inch long, which fluttered about and settled on my head and face. Heard a *fine* (in the sod) cricket, a dog-day locust once or twice, and a *creaking* grasshopper.

Saw two or three frogs,—one large *Rana fontinalis* in that rocky pool on the southwest side, where I saw the large spawn which I supposed to be bullfrog spawn two years ago, but now think must have been *R. fontinalis* spawn; and there was a dark pollywog one inch long. This frog had a raised line on each side of back and was as large as a common bullfrog. I also heard the note once of some familiar large frog. The one or two smaller frogs which I saw else-where were perhaps the same.

There were a great many visitors to the summit, both by the south and north, *i.e.* the Jaffrey and Dublin paths, but they did not turn off from the beaten track. One noon, when I was on the top, I counted forty men, women, and children around me, and more were constantly arriving while others were going. Certainly more than one hundred ascended in a day. When you got within thirty rods you saw them seated in a row along the gray parapets, like the inhabitants of a castle on a gala-day; and when you behold Monadnock's blue summit fifty miles off in the horizon, you may imagine it covered with men, women, and children in dresses of all colors, like an observatory on a muster-field. They appeared to be chiefly mechanics and farmers' boys and girls from the neighboring towns. The young men sat in rows with their legs dangling over the precipice, squinting through spy-glasses and shouting and hallooing to each new party that issued from the woods below. Some were playing cards; others were trying to see their house or their neighbor's. Children were running about and playing as usual. Indeed, this peak in pleasant weather is the most trivial place in New England. There are probably more arrivals daily than at any of the White Mountain houses. Several were busily engraving their names on the rocks with cold-chisels, whose incessant clink you heard, and they had but little leisure to look off. The mountain was not free of them from sunrise to sunset, though most of them left about 5 P.M. At almost any hour of the day they were seen wending their way single file in various garb up or down the shelving rocks of the peak. These figures on the summit, seen in relief against the sky (from our camp), looked taller than life. I saw some that camped there, by moonlight, one night. On Sunday, twenty or thirty, at least, in addition to the visitors to the peak, came up to pick blueberries, and we heard on all sides the rattling of dishes and their frequent calls to each other.

The rocky area—or summit of the mountain above the forest—which I am describing is of an irregular form from a mile and a half to two miles long, north and south, by three quarters to a mile wide at the widest part, in proportion as you descend lower on the rocks.

There are three main spurs, *viz.* the northeast, or chief, one, toward Monadnock Pond and the village of Dublin; the southerly, to Swan's [?]; and the northerly, over which the Dublin path runs. These afford the three longest walks. The first is the longest, wildest, and least-frequented, and rises to the greatest height at a distance from the central peak. The second affords the broadest and smoothest walk. The third is the highest of all at first, but falls off directly. There are also two lesser and lower spurs, on the westerly side,—one quite short, toward Troy, by which you might come up from that side, the other yet lower, but longer, from north 75° west. But above all, for walking, there is an elevated rocky plateau, so to call it, extending to half a mile east of the summit, or about a hundred rods east of the ravine. This slopes gently toward the south and east by successive terraces of rock, and affords the most amusing walking of any part of the mountain.

The most interesting precipices are on the south side of the peak. The greatest abruptness of descent (from top to bottom) is on the west side between the two lesser ravines.

The northeast spur (of two principal summits beyond the swamp) has the most dead spruce on it.

The handsome ponds near the mountain are a long pond chiefly in Jaffrey, close under the mountain on the east, with a greatly swelling knoll extending into it on the east side; Monadnock Pond in Dublin, said to be very deep, about north-northeast (between the northeast spur and Dublin village); a large pond with a very white beach much further off in Nelson, about north (one called it Breed's?); Stone Pond, northwesterly, about as near as Monadnock Pond. Also large ponds in Jaffrey, Rindge, Troy; and many more further off.

The basis of my map was the distance from the summit to the second camp, measured very rudely by casting a stone before. Pacing the distance of any easy cast, I found it about ten rods, and thirteen such stone's throws, or one hundred and thirty rods, carried me to the camp. As I had the course, from the summit and from the camp, of the principal points, I could tell the rest nearly enough. It was about fifty rods from the summit to the ravine and eighty more to the camp.

It was undoubtedly Saddleback Mountain which I saw about S. 85° W. What was that elevated part of the Green Mountains about N. 50° W., which one called falsely Camel's Hump?—the next elevated summit north of Saddleback.

It would evidently be a noble walk from Watatic to Goffstown perchance, over the Peterboro mountains, along the very backbone of this part of New Hampshire,—the most novel and interesting walk that I can think of in these parts.

They who simply climb to the peak of Monadnock have seen but little of the mountain. I came not to look *off from* it, but to look *at* it. The view of the pinnacle itself from the plateau below surpasses any view which you get from the summit. It is indispensable to see the top itself and the sierra of its outline from one side. The great charm is not to look off from a height but to walk over this novel and wonderful rocky surface. Moreover, if you would enjoy the prospect, it is, methinks, most interesting when you look from the edge of the plateau immediately down intc the valleys, or where the edge of the lichen-clad rocks, only two or three rods from you, is seen as the lower frame of a picture of green fields, lakes, and woods, suggesting a more stupendous precipice than exists. There are much more surprising effects of this nature along the edge of the plateau than on the summit. It is remarkable what haste the visitors make to get to the top of the mountain and then look away from it.

Northward you see Ascutney and Kearsarge Mountains, and faintly the White Mountains, and others more northeast; but above all, toward night, the Green Mountains.

In his summary of animals, Thoreau's best prose turned the nighthawks into timeless memories, shaped by the *(see page 346)* daily rhythms of hunting and calling. Had he visited during the fall migratory season, the entry would have listed more varieties of birds. Human beings bring up the rear of his account—an appropriate position, consid- *(see page 348)* ering the behavior he observed. Visitors today can be just as "trivial," climbing up in sneakers (or barefoot) and sprawling on the summit for a celebratory smoke.

Thoreau's survey of the mountain revealed a balanced form, its contrasting spurs—wild, smooth, high—held to- *(see page 348)* gether as a single entity. The ponds he saw were Thorn-dike Pond and Dublin Lake; "Breed's" was Nubanusit Lake (twelve miles northeast) and "Stone Pond" was probably Cranberry Meadow Pond. The compass bearing for Greylock should be 75 degrees; the mountain he queried was possibly Stratton (3,850'); his later view- *(see page 349)* points were Ascutney (3,186') and "Kearsarge," or Mt. Warner (2,943').

Having criticized trivial visitors, he summarized the kind of traveler he represented: one who looked *at* nature, not away from it, who saw objects closely and for their intrinsic worth. In *Walden* he said that we must

know where we are, and why we live there, to get the full
measure of life; here he challenged the American preoccupation with getting swiftly to the top. The sides of an
experience, the process of exploring them, were the elements of life that he most valued.   *(see page 350)*

But what a study for rocks does this mountain-top afford! The rocks
of the pinnacle have many regular nearly right-angled slants to the
southeast, covered with the dark-brown (or olivaceous) umbilicaria.
The rocks which you walk over are often not only worn smooth and
slippery, but grooved out, as if with some huge rounded tool, or they
are much oftener convex: [drawing] You see huge buttresses or walls
put up by Titans, with true joints, only recently loosened by an earth-
quake as if ready to topple down. Some of the lichen-clad rocks are
of a rude brick-loaf form or small cottage form: [drawing] You see
large boulders, left just on the edge of the steep descent of the
plateau, commonly resting on a few small stones, as if the Titans were
in the very act of transporting them when they were interrupted;
some left standing on their ends, and almost the only convenient rocks
in whose shade you can sit sometimes. Often you come to a long, thin
rock, two or three rods long, which has the appearance of having just
been split into underpinning-stone,—perfectly straight-edged and
parallel pieces, and lying as it fell, ready for use, just as the mason
leaves it. Post-stones, door-stones, etc. There were evidences of recent
motion as well as ancient.

I saw on the flat sloping surface of rock a fresher white space
exactly the size and form of a rock which was lying by it and which
had lately covered it. What had upset it? There were many of these
whitish marks where the dead spruce had lain but was now decayed
or gone.

The rocks were not only coarsely grooved but finely scratched from
northwest to southeast, commonly about S. 10° E. (but between 5° and
20° east, or, by the true meridian, more yet).* I could have steered
myself in a fog by them.

*Hitchcock, p. 387, calls the rock of Monadnock granite, and says the scratches are north and south, nearly, and very striking.

Piles of stones left as they were split ready for the builder. I saw one perfect triangular hog-trough [drawing]—except that it wanted one end—and which would have been quite portable and convenient in a farmer's yard. The core, four or five feet long, lay one side.

The rocks are very commonly in terraces with a smooth rounded edge to each. The most remarkable of these terraces that I noticed was between the second camp and the summit, say some forty rods from the camp. These terraces were some six rods long and six to ten feet wide, but the top slanting considerably back into the mountain, and they were about four or five feet high each [drawing]. There were four such in succession here, running S. 30° E. The edges of these terraces, here and commonly, were rounded and grooved like the rocks at a waterfall, as if water and gravel had long washed over them.

Some rocks were shaped like huge doughnuts: [drawing] The edges of cliffs were frequently lumpishly rounded, covered with lichens, so that you could not stand near the edge. The extreme east and north-east parts of the plateau, especially near the little meadow, are the most interesting for the forms of rocks. Sometimes you see where a huge oblong square stone has been taken out from the edge of a terrace, leaving a space which looks like a giant's grave unoccupied.

On the west side the summit the strata ran north and south and dipped to east about 60° with the horizon. There were broad veins of white quartz (sometimes one foot wide) running directly many rods [drawing].

Near the camp there was a succession of great rocks, their corners rounded semicircularly and grooved at the same time like the capital of a column reversed [drawing]. The most rugged walking is on the steep westerly slope.

We had a grand view, especially after sunset, as it grew dark, of the *sierra* of the summit's outline west of us,—the teeth of the sierra often turned back toward the summit,—when the rocks were uniformly black in the shade and seen against the twilight.

In Morse's Gazetteer (1797) it is said, "Its base is five miles in diameter north to south, and three from east to west. . . . Its summit is a bald rock." By the summit he meant the very topmost part, which, it seems, was always a "bald rock."

There were all over the rocky summit peculiar yellowish gravelly spots which I called scars, commonly of an oval form, not in low but elevated places, and looking as if a little mound had been cut off there [drawing]. The edges of these, on the very pinnacle of the mountain, were formed of the *Juncus trifidus,* now gone to seed. If they had been in hollows, you would have said that they were the bottom of little pools, now dried up, where the gravel and stones had been washed bare. I am not certain about their origin. They suggested some force which had suddenly cut off and washed or blown away the surface there, like a thunder-spout [*sic*], or lightning, or a hurricane. Such spots were very numerous, and had the appearance of a fresh scar.

Much, if not most, of the rock appears to be what Hitchcock describes and represents as graphic granite (*vide* his book, page 681).

Hitchcock says (page 389) that he learns from his assistant, Abraham Jenkins, Jr., that "on the sides of and around this mountain (Monadnock) diluvial grooves and scratches are common; having a direction about N. 10° W. and S. 10° E. The summit of the mountain, which rises in an insulated manner to the height of 3250 feet, is a naked rock of gneiss of several acres in extent, and this is thoroughly grooved and scored. One groove measured fourteen feet in width, and two feet deep; and others are scarcely of less size. Their direction at the summit, by a mean of nearly thirty measurements with a compass, is nearly north and south."

According to Heywood's Gazetteer, the mountain is "talc, mica, slate, distinctly stratified," and is 3718 feet high.

Though there is little or no soil upon the rocks, owing apparently to the coolness, if not moisture, you have rather the vegetation of a swamp than that of sterile rocky ground below. For example, of the six prevailing trees and shrubs—low blueberry, black spruce, lamb-kill, black choke-berry, wild holly, and *Viburnum nudum*—all but the first are characteristic of swampy and low ground, to say nothing of the commonness of wet mosses, the two species of cotton-grass, and some other plants of the swamp and meadow. Little meadows and swamps are scattered all over the mountain upon and amid the rocks. You are continually struck with the proximity of gray and lichen-clad rock and mossy bog. You tread alternately on wet moss, into which you sink, and dry, lichen-covered rocks. You will be surprised to see the vegetation of a swamp on a little shelf only a foot or two over,—a bog a foot wide with cotton-grass waving over it in the midst of cladonia lichens so dry as to burn like tinder. The edges of the little swamps—if not their middle—are commonly white with cotton-grass. The *Arenaria Grœnlandica* often belies its name here, growing in wet places as often as in dry ones, together with eriophorum.

One of the grandest views of the summit is from the east side of the central meadow of the plateau, which I called the Gulf, just beneath the pinnacle on the east, with the meadow in the foreground.

Water stands in shallow pools on almost every rocky shelf. The largest pool of open water which I found was on the southwest side of the summit, and was four rods long by fifteen to twenty feet in width and a foot deep. Wool- and cotton-grass grew around it, and there was a dark green moss and some mud at the bottom. There was a smoother similar pool on the next shelf above it. These were about the same size in June and in August, and apparently never dry up. There was also the one in which I bathed, near the northeast little meadow. I had a delicious bath there, though the water was warm, but there was a pleasant strong and drying wind blowing over the ridge, and when I had bathed, the rock felt like plush to my feet.

The cladonia lichens were so dry at midday, even the day after rain, that they served as tinder to kindle our fire,—indeed, we were somewhat troubled to prevent the fire from spreading amid them,—yet at night, even before sundown, and morning, when we got our supper and breakfast, they would not burn thus, having absorbed moisture. They had then a cool and slightly damp feeling.

(see page 351) Thoreau's "study for rocks" was a close examination of geological details. He recognized all the evidence of glacial motion, but apparently not its cause. Hitchcock called the grooves and scratches "diluvial," created by an ancient flood. Channing—equally ignorant in 1860—lived to see glaciation theory become common knowledge: his poem "Monadnoc" (1875) described the movement of a "polar host." Most of the rock features are still *(see page 352)* recognizable, except for that "hog trough." The "ter-

races" are round-shouldered ledges, their blunt ends fac-
ing south. This configuration is uniform—gradual rises
on the north, sharp cliffs on the south—because the ice
moved in that direction, first pushing and smoothing,
then pulling and plucking. On the west side, Thoreau
saw an example of drag folding, which he described as
angular "strata." Hitchcock called the summit rock *(see page 352)*
granite; actually, that lies far below—most of the summit
is mica schist. The summit views are similar today, al- *(see page 354)*
though heavier forest growth lies just below.

Every evening, excepting, perhaps, the Sunday evening after the rain
of the day before, we saw not long after sundown a slight scud or mist
begin to strike the summit above us, though it was perfectly fair
weather generally and there were no clouds over the lower country.

First, perhaps, looking up, we would see a small scud not more than
a rod in diameter drifting just over the apex of the mountain. In a few
minutes more a somewhat larger one would suddenly make its appearance, and perhaps strike the topmost rocks and invest them for
a moment, but as rapidly drift off northeast and disappear. Looking
into the southwest sky, which was clear, we would see all at once a
small cloud or scud a rod in diameter beginning to form half a mile
from the summit, and as it came on it rapidly grew in a mysterious
manner, till it was fifty rods or more in diameter, and draped and
concealed for a few moments all the summit above us, and then
passed off and disappeared northeastward just as it had come on. So
that it appeared as if the clouds had been attracted by the summit.
They also seemed to rise a little as they approached it, and endeavor
to go over without striking. I gave this account of it to myself. They
were not attracted to the summit, but simply generated there and not
elsewhere. There would be a warm southwest wind blowing which
was full of moisture, alike over the mountain and all the rest of the
country. The summit of the mountain being cool, this warm air began
to feel its influence at half a mile distance, and its moisture was
rapidly condensed into a small cloud, which expanded as it advanced,
and evaporated again as it left the summit. This would go on, apparently, as the coolness of the mountain increased, and generally the

cloud or mist reached down as low as our camp from time to time, in the night.

One evening, as I was watching these small clouds forming and dissolving about the summit of our mountain, the sun having just set, I cast my eyes toward the dim bluish outline of the Green Mountains in the clear red evening sky, and, to my delight, I detected exactly over the summit of Saddleback Mountain, some sixty miles distant, its own little cloud, shaped like a parasol and answering to that which capped our mountain, though in this case it did not rest on the mountain, but was considerably above it, and all the rest of the west horizon for forty miles was cloudless [drawing]. I was convinced that it was the local cloud of that mountain because it was directly over the summit, was of small size and of umbrella form answering to the summit, and there was no other cloud to be seen in that horizon. It was a beautiful and serene object, a sort of fortunate isle,—like any other cloud in the sunset sky.

That the summit of this mountain is cool appears from the fact that the days which we spent there were remarkably warm ones in the country below, and were the common subject of conversation when we came down, yet we had known nothing about it, and went warmly clad with comfort all the while, as we had not done immediately before and did not after we descended. We immediately perceived the difference as we descended. It was warm enough for us on the summit, and often, in the sheltered southeast hollows, too warm, as we happened to be clad, but on the summits and ridges it chanced that there was always wind, and in this wind it was commonly cooler than we liked. Also our water, which was evidently rain-water caught in the rocks and retained by the moss, was cool enough if it were only in a little crevice under the shelter of a rock, *i.e.* out of the sun.

Yet, though it was thus cool, and there was this scud or mist on the top more or less every night, there was, as we should say, no dew on the summit any morning. The lichens, blueberry bushes, etc., did not feel wet, nor did they wet you in the least, however early you walked in them. I rose [?] to observe the sunrise and picked blueberries every morning before sunrise, and saw no dew, only once some minute dewdrops on some low grass-tips, and that was amid the wet moss of a little bog, but the lambkill and blueberry bushes above it were not wet. Yet the Thursday when we left, we found that though there was no dew on the summit there was a very heavy dew in the pastures below, and our feet and clothes were completely wet with it, as much as if we had stood in water.

I should say that there were no true springs (?) on the summit, but simply rain-water caught in the hollows of the rocks or retained by the moss. I observed that the well which we made for washing—by digging up the moss with our hands—half dried up in the sun by day, but filled up again at night.

The principal stream on the summit,—if not the only one,—in the rocky portion described, was on the southeast side, between our two camps, though it did not distinctly show itself at present except a little below our elevation. For the most part you could only see that water had flowed there between and under the rocks.

I fancied once or twice that it was warmer at 10 P.M. than it was immediately after sunset.

The voices of those climbing the summit were heard remarkably far. We heard much of the ordinary conversation of those climbing the peak above us a hundred rods off, and we could hear those on the summit, or a hundred and thirty rods off, when they shouted. I heard a party of ladies and gentlemen laughing and talking there in the night (they were camping there), though I did not hear what they said. We heard, or imagined that we heard, from time to time, as we lay in our camp by day, an occasional chinking or clinking sound as if made by one stone on another.

In clear weather, in going from one part of the summit to another it would be most convenient to steer by distant objects, as towns or mountains or lakes, rather than by features of the summit itself, since the former are most easily recognized and almost always in sight.

I saw what I took to be a thistle-down going low over the summit, and might have caught it, though I saw no thistle on the mountain-top nor any other plant from which this could have come. (I have no doubt it was a thistle by its appearance and its season.) It had evidently come up from the country below. This shows that it may carry its seeds to higher regions than it inhabits, and it suggests how the seeds of some mountain plants, as the *Solidago thyrsoidea,* may be conveyed from mountain to mountain, also other solidagos, asters, epilobiums, willows, etc.

The descent through the woods from our first camp to the site of the shanty is from a third to half a mile. You then come to the raspberry and fern scented region. There were some raspberries still left, but they were fast dropping off.

There was a good view of the mountain from just above the pond, some two miles from Troy. The varying outline of a mountain is due to the crest of different spurs, as seen from different sides. Even a small spur, if you are near, may conceal a much larger one and give its own outline to the mountain, and at the same time one which extends directly toward you is not noticed at all, however important, though, as you travel round the mountain, this may gradually come into view and finally its crest may be one half or more of the outline presented. It may partly account for the peaked or pyramidal form of mountains that one crest may be seen through the gaps of another and so fill up the line.

Think I saw leersia or cut-grass in bloom in Troy.

I carried on this excursion the following articles (beside what I wore), *viz.:*—

One shirt.
One pair socks.
Two pocket-handkerchiefs.
One *thick* waistcoat.
One flannel shirt (had no occasion to use it).
India-rubber coat.
Three bosoms.
Towel and soap.
Pins, needles, thread.
A blanket (would have been more convenient if stitched up in the form of a bag).
Cap for the night.
Map and compass.
Spy-glass and microscope and tape.
Saw and hatchet.
Plant-book and blotting-paper.

Paper and stamps.

Botany.

Insect and lichen boxes.

Jack-knife.

Matches.

Waste paper and twine.

Iron spoon and pint dipper with handle.

  All in a knapsack.

Umbrella.

N.B.—Add to the above next time a small bag, which may be stuffed with moss or the like for a pillow.

For provision for one, six days, carried:—

2½ lbs. of salt beef and tongue.	Take only salt beef next time, 2 to 3 lbs.
18 hard-boiled eggs.	Omit eggs.
2½ lbs. sugar and a little salt	2 lbs. of sugar would have done.
About ¼ lb. of tea.	⅔ as much would have done.
2 lbs. hard-bread.	The right amount of bread,
½ loaf home-made bread and a piece of cake.	but might have taken more but home-made and more *solid* sweet cake.

N.B.—Carry salt (or some of it) in a wafer-box. Also some sugar in a small box.

N.B.—Observe next time: the source of the stream which crosses the path; what species of swallow flies over mountain; what the grass which gives the pastures a yellowish color seen from the summit.

The morning would probably never be ushered in there by the chipping of the chip-bird, but that of the *F. hyemalis* instead,—a dry, hard occasional chirp, more in harmony with the rocks. There you do not hear the *link* of the bobolink, the chatter of red-wings and crow blackbirds, the wood pewee, the twitter of the kingbird, the half [*sic*] strains of the vireo, the passing goldfinch, or the occasional plaintive note of the bluebird, all which are now commonly heard in the lowlands.

That area is literally a chaos, an example of what the earth was before it was finished.

(see page 356) Thoreau correctly explained how clouds move across the mountains, for air cools as it rises up the slopes, forming either caps or streamers. Seeing the same type of cloud over "Saddleback" was a striking coincidence. In 1844 he (see page 76) saw the clouds there as a symbol of transcendence; now his view was precise and explanatory: "I gave this ac- (see page 355) count of it to myself." He did not study the mountain's springs as carefully, for several exist on its surface. In the 1860s this "mineral water" was touted as a health cure—until a Harvard geologist verified that the water contained no substances of medicinal value.

(see page 357)   At the close, Thoreau wrote about seed dispersal, the subject of his largest current project in Concord. He took a final admiring glance from Perkins Pond at the mountain's pyramidal shape, then looked forward to "next time." This area was "literally a chaos," and so were his thoughts—not disorderly but incomplete, needing to (see page 360) grow in time.

In late August, he added notes about minor details: the view of a pond, the sound of birds, and, on September 1, the changes of mind he had felt:

We could not judge correctly of distances on the mountain, but greatly exaggerated them. That surface was so novel—suggested so many thoughts,—and so uneven, a few steps sufficing to conceal the least ground, as if it were half a mile away, that we would have an impression as if we had travelled a mile when we had come only forty rods. We no longer thought and reasoned as in the plain.

After Blake returned from the White Mountains, Thoreau sent him an account of the days spent at Monadnock with Channing. The elements of human interest—

Crawford Notch

joking about his companion, the visitors, the tourists in
Crawford Notch—suggest the themes that might have
emerged in a future version.

Concord Nov. 4 1860

Mr Blake,
    I am glad to hear any particulars of your excursion. As for myself,
I looked out for you somewhat on that Monday, when, it appears, you
passed Monadnock—turned my glass upon several parties that were
ascending the mountain half a mile on one side of us. In short, I came
as near to seeing you as you to seeing me. I have no doubt that we
should have had a good time if you had come, for I had, all ready, two
good spruce houses, in which you could stand up, complete in all
respects, half a mile apart, and you & B[rown] could have lodged by
yourselves in one, if not with us.
    We made an excellent beginning of our *mt* life. You may remember
that the Saturday previous was a stormy day. Well, we went up in the

rain—wet through, and found ourselves in a cloud there at mid *pm.* in no situation to look about for the best place for a camp. So I proceeded at once, through the cloud, to that memorable stone "chunk yard," in which we made our humble camp once, and there, after putting our packs under a rock, having a good hatchet, I proceeded to build a substantial house, which C[hanning] declared the handsomest he ever saw. (He never camped out before, and was, no doubt, prejudiced in its favor.) This was done about dark, and by that time we were nearly as wet as if we had stood in a hogshead of water. We then built a fire before the door, directly on the site of our little camp of two years ago, and it took a long time to burn thro' its remains to the earth beneath. Standing before this, and turning round slowly, like meat that is roasting, we were as dry if not drier than ever after a few hours, & so, at last we "turned in."

This was a great deal better than going up there in fair weather, & having no adventure (not knowing how to appreciate either fair weather or foul) but dull common-place sleep in a useless house, & before a comparatively useless fire—such as we get every night. Of course, we thanked our stars, when we saw them, which was about midnight, that they had seemingly withdrawn for a season. We had the *mt* all to ourselves that *pm* & night. There was nobody going up that day to engrave his name on the summit, nor to gather blueberries. The Genius of the *mts.* saw us starting from Concord & it said,—There come two of our folks. Let us get ready for them—Get up a serious storm, that will send a packing these holiday guests (They may have their say another time) Let us receive them with true *mt.* hospitality—kill the fatted cloud—Let them know the value of a spruce roof, & of a fire of dead spruce stumps. Every bush dripped tears of joy at our advent. Fire did its best & received our thanks.—What could fire have done in fair weather?—Spruce roof got its share of our blessings. And then such a view of the wet rocks with the wet lichens on them, as we had the next morning, but did not get again!

We & the *mt* had a sound season, as the saying is. How glad we were to be wet in order that we might be dried!—how glad we were of the storm which made our house seem like a new home to us! This day's experience was indeed lucky for we did not have a thunder shower during all our stay. Perhaps our host reserved this attention in order to tempt us to come again.

Our next house was more substantial still. One side was rock, good for durability, the floor the same, & the roof which I made would have upheld a horse. I stood on it to do the shingling.

I noticed, when I was at the White *Mts* last, several nuisances which render travelling there-abouts unpleasant. The chief of these was the *mt* houses. I might have supposed that the main attraction of that region even to citizens, lay in its wildness and unlikeness to the city, & yet they make it as much like the city as they can afford to. I heard that the Crawford House was lighted with gas, & had a large saloon, with its band of music, for dancing. But give me a spruce house made in the rain.

An old Concord farmer tells me that he ascended Monadnock once, & danced on the top. How did that happen? Why, he being up there, a party of young men & women came up bringing boards & a fiddler, and having laid down the boards they made a level floor, on which they danced to the music of the fiddle. I suppose the tune was "Excelsior." This reminds me of the fellow who climbed to the top of a very high spire, stood upright on the ball, & then hurrahed for—what? Why for Harrison & Tyler. That's the kind of sound which most ambitious people emit when they culminate. They are wont to be singularly frivolous in the thin atmosphere they can't contain themselves, though our comfort & their safety require it; it takes the pressure of many atmospheres to do this; & hence they helplessly evaporate there. It would seem, that, as they ascend, they breathe shorter and shorter, and at each *expiration,* some of their wits leave them, till, when they reach the pinnacle, they are so light headed as to be fit only to show how the wind sits. I suspect that Emersons criticism called Monadnock* was inspired not by remembering the inhabitants of N.H. as they are in the valleys, so much as by meeting some of them on the *mt* top.

After several nights' experience C came to the conclusion that he was "lying out doors," and inquired what was the largest beast that might nibble his legs there. I fear that he did not improve all the night,

*A poem in R. W. Emerson's Poems (1847).—WH

as he might have done, to sleep. I had asked him to go and spend a week there. We spent 5 nights, being gone 6 days, for C suggested that 6 working days made a week, & I saw that he was ready to *de-camp.* However, he found his account in it, as well as I.

We were seen to go up in the rain, grim & silent like 2 Genii of the storm, by Fassett's men or boys, but we were never identified afterward, though we were the subject of some conversation which we overheard. Five hundred persons at least came onto the *mt.* while we were there, but not one found our camp. We saw one party of three ladies & two gentlemen spread their blankets and spend the night on the top, & heard them converse, but they did not know that they had neighbors, who were comparatively old settlers. We spared them the chagrin which that knowledge would have caused them, & let them print their story in a newspaper accordingly.

From what I heard of Fassett's infirmities I concluded that his partner was Tap. He has moved about thirty rods further down the *mt.,* & is still hammering at a new castle there when you go by, while Tap is probably down cellar. Such is the Cerberus that guards *this* passage. There always is one you know. This is not so bad to go by as the Glen House. However, we left those Elysian fields by a short cut of our own which departed just beyond where he is stationed.

Yes, to meet men on an honest and simple footing, meet with rebuffs, suffer from sore feet, as you did, aye & from a sore heart, as perhaps you also did,—all that is excellent. What a pity that that young prince could not enjoy a little of the legitimate experience of travelling, be dealt with simply & truly though rudely. He might have been invited to some hospitable house in the country, had his bowl of bread & milk set before him, with a clean pin-a-fore, been told that there were the punt & the fishing rod, and he could amuse himself as he chose—might have swung a few birches, dug out a woodchuck, & had a regular good time, & finally been sent to bed with the boys,— and so never have been introduced to Mr. [Edward] Everett at all. I have no doubt that this would have been a far more memorable & valuable experience than he got.

The snow-clad summit of *Mt.* Washington must have been a very interesting sight from Wachusett. How wholesome winter is seen far or near, how good above all mere sentimental warm-blooded—short-lived, soft-hearted *moral* goodness, commonly so called. Give me the goodness which has forgotten its own deeds,—which God has seen to be good and let be. None of your *just made perfect*—pickled eels! All that will save them will be their picturesqueness, as with blasted trees Whatever is and is not ashamed to be is good. I value no moral goodness or greatness unless it is good or great even as that snowy peak is. Pray how could thirty feet of bowels improve it? Nature is goodness crystalized. You looked into the land of promise. Whatever beauty we behold, the more it is distant, serene, and cold, the purer & more durable it is. It is better to warm ourselves with ice than with fire.

Tell Brown that he sent me more than the price of the book—viz a word from himself, for which I am greatly his debtor.

H.D.T.

Thoreau did not live to visit the land of mountains again. One month later, he contracted a cold that turned into bronchitis, then to tuberculosis. In May of 1861 he made a long trip to Minnesota, vainly seeking a climate that would improve his health. Out West he saw no mountains, only high bluffs along the Mississippi River where Indians had once camped. Back in Concord by July, he could travel nowhere; yet, when a group of ministers from Worcester sought his advice about a trip to the White Mountains, he sent a long, detailed letter listing the supplies they would need.

His condition steadily worsened; by late November of 1861 he was confined to a sickbed and no longer able to write his daily Journal. In one of its last entries, he recorded news of better days: "Young Macey, who has been camping on Monadnock this summer, tells me that he found one of my spruce huts made last year in August, and that as many as eighteen, reshingling it, had camped in it while he was there." Thoreau drew satisfaction from knowing that others would follow him to the mountains of New England. When he died in May 1862, his highest climb—to fame and lasting recognition—had only just begun.

SELECTED BIBLIOGRAPHY

NOTES ON ILLUSTRATIONS

INDEX

Selected Bibliography

GENERAL WORKS

Casewit, Curtis W. *The Mountain World.* New York: Random House, 1976.

Costello, David F. *The Mountain World.* New York: Thomas Y. Crowell, 1975.

Farb, Peter. *Face of North America.* New York: Harper & Row, 1963.

Jerome, John. *On Mountains.* New York: Harcourt Brace Jovanovich, 1978.

Lane, Ferdinand C. *The Story of Mountains.* Garden City, N.Y.: Doubleday, 1950.

Milne, Lorus J. and Margery. *The Mountains.* New York: Time, Inc., 1962.

Smythe, Francis S. *The Mountain Vision.* London: Hodder and Stoughton, 1946.

MOUNTAINS IN HISTORY AND ART

Alden, Edmund Kimball. "Mountains and History," *Annual Report of the American Historical Association,* 519–29. Washington, D.C.: Government Printing Office, 1895.

Feininger, Andreas. *The Mountains of the Mind.* New York: Viking, 1977.

Meade, Charles. *High Mountains.* London: Harvill, 1954.

Nicolson, Marjorie H. *Mountain Gloom and Mountain Glory: The Development of the Aesthetics of the Infinite.* Ithaca, N.Y.: Cornell University Press, 1959.

Noyce, Wilfrid. *Scholar Mountaineers.* London: Dennis Dobson, 1949.

Spectorsky, A. C. *The Book of the Mountains.* New York: Appelton-Century-Crofts, 1955.

ALPINE LIFE

Habeck, James R. and Ernest Hartley. *A Glossary of Alpine Terminology.* Missoula, Mont.: Department of Botany, University of Montana, 1968.

Huxley, Anthony J. *Mountain Flowers in Color.* New York: Macmillan, 1968.

Long, Tony. *Mountain Animals.* New York: Harper & Row, 1971.

Ricciuti, Edward R. *Wildlife of the Mountains.* New York: Harry Abrams, 1979.

Zwinger, Ann. *Land Above the Trees: A Guide to American Alpine Tundra.* New York: Harper & Row, 1972.

MOUNTAINEERING

Bernstein, Jeremy. *Ascent: Of the Invention of Mountain Climbing & Its Practice.* New York: Random House, 1965.

Blackshaw, Alan. *Mountaineering: From Hill Walking to Alpine Climbing.* Harmondsworth: Penguin, 1965.

Clark, Ronald. *The Victorian Mountaineers.* London: Batsford, 1953.

Collomb, R. G. *A Dictionary of Mountaineering.* Glasgow: Blackie & Son, 1957.

Engel, Claire Elaine. *Mountaineering in the Alps: An Historical Survey.* London: George Allen & Unwin, 1971.

Jones, Chris. *Climbing in North America.* Berkeley: University of California Press, 1976.

Lyman, Tom and Bill Riviere. *The Field Book of Mountaineering and Rock Climbing.* New York: Winchester Press, 1975.

Newby, Eric. *Great Ascents: A Narrative History of Mountaineering.* New York: Viking, 1977.

Shipton, Eric E. *Mountain Conquest.* New York: American Heritage, 1966.

Ullman, James Ramsey. *High Conquest: The Story of Mountaineering.* Philadelphia: J. B. Lippincott, 1941.

HIKING AND TOURING

Appalachian Trail Conference. *Guide to the Appalachian Trail in Maine,* 7th ed. Washington, D.C.: The Maine Appalachian Trail Club, 1969.

———. *Guide to the Appalachian Trail in Massachusetts and Connecticut.* Washington, D.C.: Appalachian Trail Conference, 1968.

———. *Guide to the Appalachian Trail in New Hampshire and Vermont,* 2nd ed. Harpers Ferry, W.Va.: Appalachian Trail Conference, 1968.

Deedy, John. *Literary Places: A Guided Pilgrimage: New York and New England.* Kansas City: Sheed Andrews and McMeel, 1978.

Fletcher, Colin. *The Complete Walker: The Joys and Techniques of Hiking and Backpacking.* New York: Alfred A. Knopf, 1969.

George, Jean Craighead. *The American Walk Book.* New York: E. P. Dutton, 1978.

Harting, Emilie C. *A Literary Tour Guide to the United States: Northeast.* New York: William Morrow, 1978.

Henley, Thomas A. and Neesa Sweet. *Hiking Trails in the Northeast.* Matteson, Ill.: Greatlakes Living Press, 1976.

Meves, Eric. *Guide to Backpacking in the United States.* New York: Macmillan, 1977.

National Park Service. *Back-Country Travel in the National Park System.* Washington, D.C.: U.S. Government Printing Office, 1974.

Rudner, Ruth. *Off and Walking: A Hiker's Guide to American Places.* New York: Holt, Rinehart and Winston, 1977.

NEW ENGLAND MOUNTAINS

Appalachia: The Journal of the Appalachia Mountain Club. Boston: Houghton Mifflin, 1876–

Clark, Thomas H. *Appalachian Tectonics.* Toronto: University of Toronto Press, 1967.

Connelly, Thomas L. *Discovering the Appalachians.* Harrisburg, Pa.: Stackpole Books, 1968.

Peattie, Roderick. *The Friendly Mountains: Green, White, Adirondacks.* New York: Vanguard, 1942.

Rodgers, John. "The Northeast—A Billion Years of History," *Geological Highway Map: Northeastern Region.* Tulsa, Okla.: American Association of Petroleum Geologists, n.d.

Tanner, Ogden. *New England Wilds.* New York: Time–Life Books, 1974.

Thomson, Betty Flanders. *The Changing Face of New England.* New York: Macmillan, 1958.

Wilson, Harold Fisher. *The Hill Country of Northern New England: Its Social and Economic History, 1790–1930.* New York: Columbia University Press, 1936.

HENRY DAVID THOREAU

Basset, Charles. "Katahdin, Wachusett, and Kilimanjaro: the Symbolic Mountains of Thoreau and Hemingway," *Thoreau Journal Quarterly* 3 (April 1971), 1–10.

Collins, Christopher. "Thoreau, the Mountain-Climber," *The Uses of Observation,* 58–81. The Hague: Mouton, 1971.

Lane, Lauriat, Jr. "Mountain Gloom and Yankee Poetry: Thoreau, Emerson, Frost," *Dalhousie Review* 55 (Winter 1975–76), 612–30.

Vicker, Jim Dale. "Profile of a Pioneer: Henry David Thoreau," *Backpacking Journal* 3 (Fall–Winter 1977), 21ff, 28ff (two parts).

MASSACHUSETTS

WACHUSETT (1842)

Fuller, Richard. "Visit to the Wachusett. July 1842," *Thoreau Society Bulletin* 121 (Fall 1972), 1–4.

Moran, John B. "Every Man's Landmark," *New England Outdoors* 4 (August 1978), 30–31.

Thurston, Anthony. "Restless Earth: Geological Forces That Produced Wachusett," *Massachusetts Audubon* 49 (Autumn 1964), 236–38.

GREYLOCK (1844)

Anon. "A Short History of Greylock Mountain." Pittsfield, Mass.: Greylock State Reservation, 1980.

Carman, Bernard R. "Thoreau on Greylock," *Berkshire Eagle* (Pittsfield, Mass.) (July 11, 1956), 18.

Cleland, Herdman Fitzgerald. *Geological Excursions in the Vicinity of Williams College.* Williamstown, Mass.: n.p., 1916.

Evers, Alf. *The Catskills: From Wilderness to Woodstock,* 488–91. Garden City, N.Y.: Doubleday, 1972.

Federal Writers' Project. *The Berkshire Hills.* New York: Funk & Wagnalls, 1939.

H., W. W. "Mt. Greylock Wilder Now Than in Thoreau's Time," *The Boston Sunday Herald* (August 11, 1963).

Murray, D. M. "The Dark Lady in *A Week*—Who Was She?" *Thoreau Society Bulletin* 158 (Winter 1982), 1–2.

Oleson, Hedvig (Town Clerk of Florida, Mass.). Letter to William Howarth, August 1980.

Peattie, Roderick. *The Berkshires: The Purple Hills.* New York: Vanguard, 1948.

Woodson, Thomas. "Thoreau's Excursion to the Berkshires and Catskills," *Emerson Society Quarterly* 21 (1975), 82–92.

MAINE

KATAHDIN (1846)

Blair, John G. and Augustus Trowbridge. "Thoreau on Katahdin," *American Quarterly* 12 (Winter 1960), 508–17.

Clark, Stephen. *A Guide to Baxter State Park and Katahdin.* Bangor, Me.: Fort Halifax, 1978.

Hamlin, C. E. "Observations upon the Physical Geography and Geology of Mount Ktaadn and the Adjacent District," *Bulletin of the Museum of Comparative Zoology* 7 (1881), 189–223.

Laverty, Dorothy Bowler. *Millinocket: Magic City of Maine's Wilderness.* Freeport, Me.: Bond Wheelwright, 1973.

Leavitt, H. Walter. *Kahtahdin Skylines.* University of Maine Studies No. 90. Orono, Me.: University of Maine Press, 1970.

MacKaye, Benton. "Thoreau on 'Ktaadn'," *The Living Wilderness* 9 (September 1944), 3–10.

Nitkin, Nathaniel. "Wild, the Mountain of Thoreau," *New England Quarterly* 9 (Fall 1967), 35–43.

Stibbs, John H. "Mountain Fantasy," *The Living Wilderness* (December 1946), 10–13.

Worthington, John W. "Thoreau's Route to Katahdin," *Appalachia* 26 (June 1946), 3–14.

K I N E O (1857)

Bearse, Ray. *Maine: A Guide to the Vacation State,* 2nd ed. Boston: Houghton Mifflin, 1969.

Clepper, Henry. "The Allegash of Thoreau and 100 Years Later," *American Forests* 68 (November 1962), 12ff.

Smith, Edmund Ware. "Along Thoreau's Canoe Trail," *Ford Times* 51 (March 1959), 2–9.

Starr, John T. "Moosehead: Thoreau's North Woods Lake," *American Forests* 70 (June 1964), 19–23.

VERMONT & NEW HAMPSHIRE

WANTASTIQUET AND FALL MOUNTAIN (1856)

Allison, Elliott S. "Thoreau in Vermont," *Vermont Life* 9 (Autumn 1954), 11–13.

Basset, T. D. Seymour. *A History of the Vermont Geological Surveys and State Geologists.* Burlington, Vt.: Vermont Geological Survey, 1976.

THE WHITE MOUNTAINS

Atkinson, Brooks and W. Kent Olson. *New England's White Mountains: At Home in the Wild.* San Francisco: Friends of the Earth, 1978.

Eastman, Samuel Coffin. *The White Mountain Guidebook,* 10th ed. Boston: Lee & Shepard, 1872.

King, Thomas Starr. *The White Hills: Their Legends, Landscape, and Poetry.* Boston: Crosby, Nichols, Lee, 1860.

Oakes, William. *Scenery of the White Mountains.* Boston: Crosby, Nichols, 1848.

Spaulding, John H. *Historical Relics of the White Mountains.* Mount Washington, N.H.: J. R. Hitchcock, 1855.

Sweetser, Moses Foster. *The White Mountains: A Handbook for Travellers.* Boston: Houghton Mifflin, 1891.

WASHINGTON (1839)

Anon. *Mount Washington.* Gorham, N.H.: Mount Washington Observatory, Inc., 1962.

Evans, Robert. "Blazing a Trail with Thoreau," *The Boston Sunday Globe* (September 11, 1960), 30A.

Flynn, John H. Jr. "Two Days on the Concord and Merrimack," *Concord Journal* (July 29, 1965), 18A.

Holden, Raymond P. "New Men for a New World," *The Merrimack,* 243–59. New York: Rinehart, 1958.

Kilbourne, Frederick W. "Thoreau and the White Mountains," *Appalachia* 14 (June 1919), 356–67.

McKee, Christopher. "Thoreau's First Visit to the White Mountains," *Appalachia* 31 (December 1956), 199–209.

Randall, Peter. *Mount Washington: A Guide and Short History.* Hanover, N.H.: University Press of New England, 1974.

WASHINGTON AND TUCKERMAN RAVINE (1858)

Allison, Elliott S. "A Thoreauvian on Red Hill," *Yankee* 14 (June 1950), 36–43ff.

Anon. "A White Mountain Excursion," *New York Tribune* (July 17, 1858).

Antevs, Ernst. *Alpine Zone of Mt. Washington Range.* Auburn, Me.: Merrill & Webber, 1932.

Bark, John and Marjorie Sackett. "Alpine Gardens," *Appalachia Bulletin* 45 (April 1979), 16–19.

Erickson, Richard. "Transcendentalists Among the Hills," *New England Galaxy* 17 (Summer 1975), 43–50.

Graustein, Jeanette E. "Thoreau's Packer on Mt. Washington, with Some Bits of Jackson History," *Appalachia* 33 (June 1956), 414–17.

Harding, Walter. "Thoreau and the Worcester Ministers," *Nature Outlook* 9 (Spring 1951), 12ff.

McKee, Christopher. "Thoreau: A Week on Mt. Washington and in Tuckerman Ravine," *Appalachia* 30 (December 1954), 169–83.

———. "Thoreau's Sister in the White Mountains," *Appalachia* 31 (December 1957), 551–56.

FRANCONIA NOTCH (1839, 1858)

McNair, Andrew Hamilton. *The Geologic Story of Franconia Notch and the Flume.* Concord, N.H.: State Planning and Development Commission, 1949.

Welch, Sarah N. Brooks. *Franconia Notch: History and Guide.* Littleton, N.H.: Courier Printing, 1952.

MONADNOCK (1844, 1852, 1858, 1860)

Allison, Elliott. "Alone on the Mountain," *Yankee* 37 (June 1973), 158–65.

———. "Thoreau of Monadnock," *Thoreau Journal Quarterly* 5 (October 1973), 15–21.

Allison, Hildreth M. "Man on a Mountain," *Appalachaia* 26 (June 1947), 361–63.

Baldwin, Henry I. *Monadnock Guide,* 3rd ed. Concord, N.H.: Society for the Protection of New Hampshire Forests, 1980.

———. "The Vegetation of Mt. Monadnock," *Forest Notes* 99 (Fall 1968), 12–13.

Byron, Gilbert. "Thoreau's Mountain: Monadnock," *The Living Wilderness* 30 (Autumn 1967), 45–47.

Chamberlain, Allen. *The Annals of the Grand Monadnock,* 2nd ed. Concord, N.H.: Society for the Protection of New Hampshire Forests, 1968.

Edgett, Edwin Francis. "Thoreau and Emerson on Monadnock," *Boston Evening Transcript* (September 5, 1931).

Hausman, Leon A. "Thoreau on Monadnock," *Thoreau Society Bulletin* 25 (October 1948), 1–2.

Herrick, Gerri. "To Mount Monadnock with Henry Thoreau," *The Grand Monadnock,* 13–18. Keene, N.H.: Keene State College, 1974.

Morrel, Richard. "Monadnock is a Mountain Strong," *Yankee* 32 (October 1968), 96ff.

Roe, Mary. "Site of Thoreau Camp Sought on Monadnock," *Keene* (N.H.) *Sentinel* (August 28, 1973), 6.

Rothovius, Andrew. "'Great Dissenter' Was a Friend of Monadnock," *Peterborough* (N.H.) *Transcript* (July 27, 1967), 12.

Notes on Illustrations

MAPS

21. Massachusetts
83. Maine
189. Vermont & New Hampshire

WOODCUTS

iii. From *Snowbound* . . . by John Greenleaf Whittier (Boston: Ticknor & Fields, 1868), p. 65.

3. From *A Collection of One Hundred and Seventy Engravings by Alexander Anderson, M.D. Executed on Wood after his Ninetieth Year* (New York: Charles L. Moreau, 1872), n.p.

19. From *A Collection . . . by Alexander Anderson*, n.p.

29. "Residence of R. W. Emerson, Concord, Mass." from *Homes of American Authors . . . Comprising Anecdotal, Personal, and Descriptive Sketches by Various Authors* (New York: G. P. Putnam, 1853), p. 245.

34. "Distant view of Wachusett Mountain" from *Historical Collections . . . of Every Town in Massachusetts . . .* by John Warner Barber (Worcester: Dorr, Howland, 1839), p. 599.

38. "Trees on Boulders" from "The Hudson from the Wilderness to the Sea" by Benson J. Lossing, *The Art Journal* (London, 1860–61), I, p. 81.

43. "South-western view of the central part of Lancaster" from *Historical Collections . . .* by John Warner Barber, p. 578.

46. From *A Collection . . . by Alexander Anderson*, n.p.

55. From *The Rhyme and Reason of Country Life: Or, Selections from Fields Old and New* by Susan Fenimore Cooper (New York: G. P. Putnam, 1854), p. 251.

58. "View at the Confluence of Deerfield and Connecticut Rivers" from *The American Magazine of Useful and Entertaining Knowledge* (Boston: John L. Sibley, James B. Dow, 1834) I, p. 265.

59. "Eastern view in the central part of Charlemont" from *Historical Collections* . . . by John Warner Barber, p. 241.

61. "The Hudson from the Queensbury Line" from Benson J. Lossing, *The Art Journal*, I, p. 53.

66. "Western view of the Center of North Adams" from *Historical Collections* . . . by John Warner Barber, p. 63.

67. "North-eastern view of Saddle Mountain, (Adams)" from *Historical Collections* . . . by John Warner Barber, p. 64.

74. "Western view of Williams College and other buildings" from *Historical Collections* . . . by John Warner Barber, p. 105.

75. From *A Collection . . . by Alexander Anderson*, n.p.

79. "The Catskills: Sunrise over South Mountain" from *Picturesque America*, ed. William Cullen Bryant (New York: D. Appleton, 1972–74), Part 26, frontispiece.

86. "Eagle Lake" from *Picturesque America*, Part 1, p. 14.

100. From *Forest Life and Forest Trees: Comprising Winter Camp-Life Among the Loggers, and Wild Woods Adventures* by John S. Springer (New York: Harper & Brothers, 1851), p. 146.

111. "Indian Carry, Upper Saranac" from *Picturesque America*, Part 42, p. 423.

119. "The Hudson, Twenty Miles from its Source" from *Picturesque America*, Part 42, p. 435.

123. From *Forest Life and Forest Trees*, p. 165.

125. "Lower Falls, Rumford" form *The Water Power of Maine* by Walter Wells (Augusta, Me.: Sprague, Owen, & Nash, 1869), p. 408.

131. "A Carry near Little Tupper Lake" from *Picturesque America*, Part 42, p. 428.

134. "The Trout" from *Thrilling Adventures among the Indians* . . . by John Frost (Philadelphia: J. W. Bradley, 1850), p. 128.

153. From *Adventures in the Wilderness: Or, Camp-Life in the Adirondacks* by William H. H. Murray (Boston: Fields, Osgood, 1869), n.p.

155. "Fire on the Beach" from *Marco Paul's Voyages & Travels: Maine* by Jacob Abbott (New York: Harper & Brothers, 1852), p. 114.

159. "The Loon" from Benson J. Lossing, *The Art Journal*, I, p. 81.

164. "View of Lily Bay, on Moose-head Lake" from *Forest Life and Forest Trees*, p. 228.

166. From *The Hudson Legends: Rip Van Winkle, Sleepy Hollow, From the Sketch Book* by Washington Irving (New York: G. P. Putnam, 1864), p. 33.

173. "St. Regis Lake" from *Picturesque America*, Part 42, p. 424.

193. "Brattleboro" from *Picturesque America*, Part 28, p. 86.

197. "Mount Chesterfield" from *Picturesque America*, Part 28, p. 85.

201. "The West Branch of Bellows Falls" from *Picturesque America*, Part 28, p. 93.

203. "Bellows Falls from Distance" from *Picturesque America*, Part 28, p. 90.

208. "Confluence of the Hudson and Batten-kill" from Benson J. Lossing, *The Art Journal*, I, p. 145.

211. "Mount Washington, from the Conway Road" from *Picturesque America*, Part 7, p. 152.

213. "The Pemigewaset" from *The Merrimac and Its Incidents: An Epic Poem* by Robert B. Caverly (Boston: Innes & Niles, 1866), p. 69.

214. From *The White Hills: Their Legends, Landscape, and Poetry* by Thomas Starr King (Boston: Crosby, Nichols, Lee, 1860), p. 15.

217. "Profile Mountain" from *Picturesque America*, Part 7, p. 168.

218. From *The White Hills*, p. 116.

221. The Notch House, White Mountains" from *A Pictorial Description of the United States* . . . by Robert Sears (New York: Robert Sears, 1855), p. 36.

223. "Mount Washington" from *The American Magazine* . . . , I, p. 297.

224. From Benson J. Lossing, *The Art Journal*, I, p. 5.

226. "The Raft" from *Marco Paul's Voyages & Travels: Maine*, p. 97.

231. "Centre Harbor, and Lake Winnipiseogee" from *A Pictorial Description of the United States* . . . , p. 34.

233. From *The White Hills*, p. 67.

235. "Squam Lake" from *A Pictorial Description of the United States* . . . , p. 27.

237. "The White Mountains, from the Conway Meadows" from *Picturesque America*, Part 7, p. 150.

239. "The White Mountain Notch" from *The Christmas Stocking*, p. 121.

240. From *The White Hills*, p. 315.

242. "Glen House" from *The Christmas Stocking* by Virginia Wales Johnson (New York: Thomas O'Kane, 1874), p. 83.

246. "Mount Washington from top of Thompson's Falls, Pinkham Pass" from *Picturesque America*, Part 7, p. 164.

248. "The Mount Washington Road" from *Picturesque America*, Part 7, p. 1.

254. "Tuckerman's Ravine, from Hermit's Lake" from *Picturesque America*, Part 7, p. 160.

268. "Mounts Moriah, Adams, and Jefferson, from Gilead" from *The Christmas Stocking*, p. 54.

270. "Stratford Peaks" from *The Christmas Stocking*, p. 135.

285. "Webster" from *Homes of American Authors*, p. 317.

288. "Comparative View of the Heights of Mountains etc. in N. Hampshire" from *A Gazetteer of the State of New Hampshire* by John Farmer and Jacob B. Moore (Concord, N. H.: Jacob B. Moore, 1823), p. 112.

294. From *The Song of the Sower* by William Cullen Bryant (New York: D. Appleton, 1871), p. 34.

312. From *A Collection . . . by Alexander Anderson*, n.p.

361. "Elephant's Head, Gate of Crawford Notch" from *Picturesque America*, Part 7, p. 153.

Index

Abol Falls, 141, 142
Aboljacarmegus Falls, 126, 132, 153, 183
Aboljacarmegus Lake, 126
Aboljacknagesic Stream, 126, 132, 133, 136
Abol Pond, 141
Abol Slide, 86, 141, 142, 146
Abol Stream, 135, 141, 142, 151
Abol Stream Road, 135
Abol Trail, 141, 142, 151
Achilles, 28
Acton, MA, 28, 31, 46
Adam, 96
Adirondacks, 161, 199
Aeschylus, 144
Agassiz, Louis, 15, 312
Agiocochook (Mt. Washington), 219
Albany, NY, 234
Alcott, Amos Bronson, 46, 192, 203
Allagash River, 117, 151, 162, 184; lakes of, 151, 152
Alleghanies, 41, 302
Allen, Francis H., 277
Allenstown, NH, 228
Alps, 3, 7
Amazon River, 76
Ambajejus Falls, 126, 127, 155
Ambajejus Lake, 122, 123, 124, 126, 128, 155
Ambajejus Stream, 126

America, 23, 46, 158, 160, 178; Civil War of, 68; Manifest Destiny of, 24
Amherst, NH, 280
Amherst College, 14, 245
Ammonoosuc Ravine, 220, 222, 269
Ammonoosuc River, 219, 220, 267
Amoskeag Falls, NH, 59
Andes, 8, 14, 25
Androscoggin River, 89
Annursnuck, 3, 23
Appalachian Mountain Club; huts of, 219–20, 241, 275
Appalachians, 7, 42
Appalachian Trail, 6, 74, 78, 146, 151, 215, 220, 276
Arabia Petraea, 35, 311
Ararat, 3, 4, 298, 300, 314
Arctic, 14
Argonauts, 112, 114
Ark, The (Monadnock), 300
Aroostook River, 88; valley of, 102
Aroostook Road, 87, 95
Aroostook War, 92
Ascutney, 197, 199, 203, 350
Ashburnham, MA, 49
Ashby, MA, 196
Ashland, NH, 279
Ashuelot River, 319, 332, 336

Index

Asnebumskit, 23

Assabet River, 28, 45

Atlantic Monthly, 192

Atlantic Ocean, 67, 212

Atlas, 143

Aurora, 76

Avalanche Falls, 215

Babboosuck Brook, 228

Bailey, Oliver Jr., 336

Bailey, Prof. J. W., 88, 146

Baker, George, 50

Baker River, 209

Balboa, Vasco Nuñez de, 151

Bald Rock, 330

Baldwin, Henry: *Monadnock Guide,* 301

Ball, Dr., 225

Bancroft, George, 202

Bangor, ME, 85, 87, 88, 89, 92, 94, 96, 102, 113, 115, 128, 139, 146, 157, 161, 162, 163, 167, 168

Bartlett Corner (Glen), NH, 237, 239, 241

Base Road, 219

Basin, The, 214, 215, 216, 276

Baxter Peak, 141, 146

Baxter State Park, 113, 135

Bearcamp River, 234

Bear Mountain, 235

Beck, T. R., 194

Bedford, NH, 228

"Beggar's Daughter of Bednall-Green, The," 65

Belknap, Jeremy, 228, 283

Belknap Mountain, 230, 231; *see also* Suncook Mountain

Belknap Street, 28

Bellows, Benjamin, 203

Bellows Falls, VT, 192, 200, 201, 216; bridge, 203

Bellows Fort, 202

Bellows Pipe, 65, 68, 71

Belphoebe, 58, 59

Bent, Mr., 325, 327

Ben Waddi, 304

Berkshires, 4, 16, 17, 65, 288

Bethlehem, NH, 219, 269, 282

Bible, 3, 4, 65, 115

Biddeford, NH, 261

Bigelow, Jacob, 14, 229

Bigelow Hill, 300

Bigelow Lawn, 221, 252, 261

Big Spencer Mountain, 167

Big Squaw Mountain, 167

Birchtoft Trail, 296

Blake, Harrison Gray Otis, 51, 224, 225, 256, 258, 259, 263, 289, 298, 300, 301, 312, 315, 324, 325, 360, 361

Blue Ridge Mountain, 235

Boardman, map by, 247

Boise, Mr., 216

Bolster, Aaron, 325

Bolton, MA, 30, 31

Bolton Pond Trail, 37

Boott, Francis, 264

Boott, William, 264

Boott, Wright, 264

Boott Spur, 242, 264

Boott Spur Trail, 264

Boscawen, NH, 278

Boston, MA, 24, 33, 37, 42, 72, 88, 96, 99, 100, 103, 162, 205, 287

Boston *Daily Advertiser,* 85

Boston Harbor, 52

Boston Miscellany, The, 24

Boston Road, 47

Boundary Bald Mountain, 174, 177

Boundary Mountain (Burton Peak), 291, 293

Boylston, MA, 31, 32

Bradford, George, 245

Brattleboro, VT, 191, 192, 193, 194, 196, 198, 199, 200, 202, 204, 234

Breed's Pond, 349, 350

Brewer, Thomas M., 302

Brewster: Edinburgh Encyclopedia, 285

Bridgewater, NH, 278

Brown, Addison, 193, 197, 198; family of, 195, 198

Brown, Frances, 196, 198

Brown, John, 6
Brown, Mary, 196, 198
Brown, Theophilus, 225, 256, 258, 263, 361
Bryant, Dr. Henry, 302
Burnt Land, 108, 149, 152
Burt Ravine, 219
Burying-Hill, 11
Butter Hill Road, 270

Cabot, John, 160
Cabot, Dr. Samuel, 302
California, 161
Cambridge, MA, 24
Cambridge Turnpike, 28
Camel's Hump, 349
Campton, NH, 212, 255, 277, 278, 282
Canada, 98, 102, 114, 116, 151, 177, 338
Cannon Mountain, 218, 278, 279
Canterbury, NH, 229
Cape Ann, 245
Cape Cod, 4, 296, 308, 319, 338
Carter Notch Road, 264
Carthage, 31
Cart Path Trail, 301
Cascade Brook, 216
Cascade Link Trail, 296
Catskill, NY, 80
Catskills, 4, 41, 55, 56, 77, 78–80, 302
Caucasus, 3, 144, 298
Center Harbor, NH, 230, 231, 232, 234
Cerebrus, 364
Chamberlain, Allen, 301, 331
Champdore, Sieur, 134
Channing, William Ellery, 55, 78, 80, 261,
    289, 293, 301, 324–25, 327, 331, 332, 338, 339,
    360, 362, 363, 364
Channing, William Francis, 85, 88
Chaos, 140, 142, 149, 306, 307
Charlemont, MA, 58, 59, 63, 64
Charlevoix, Pierre François Xavier de, 90
Chaucer, Geoffrey, 9
Chaudiere River, 116
Cherry Mountain, 267, 269

Chester, MA, 80
Chesterfield Mountain (Wantastiquet), 196,
    234
Chesuncook Lake, 89, 92, 113, 145, 151, 152,
    157, 183
Cheviot Hills, 36
Chocorua, 230, 231, 232, 234, 235, 236, 237
Cholmondeley, Thomas, 51
Church, Benjamin, 43
Cliffs, The, 50
Coast Survey, U.S., 338
Cold River, 202
Cold Stream Pond, 92
Coldwater Path, 194, 195, 196, 198
Collins, William: *Persian Ecloques*, 34
Columbus, Christopher, 160
Concord, MA, 3, 4, 9, 11, 12, 13, 14, 23, 24, 25,
    28, 29, 31, 43, 45, 46, 52, 54, 55, 56, 70, 80, 85,
    87, 103, 105, 150, 192, 193, 194, 203, 204, 207,
    218, 223, 226, 229, 231, 239, 244, 268, 288,
    289, 295, 300, 301, 306, 316, 317, 329, 336,
    339, 345, 362, 363, 365
Concord, NH, 209, 211, 222, 228, 229, 279
Concord Antiquarian Society, 28
Concord Free Public Library, 28
Concord River, 32, 169, 194, 206, 207, 229
Concord Turnpike, 28, 31, 47, 229
Connecticut River, 37, 39, 40, 54, 56, 58, 194,
    196, 202, 319; valley of, 192, 203, 204, 271,
    276, 334
Contoocook, NH, 285
Contoocook River, 209, 279, 319, 329, 332, 336
Conway, NH, 205, 220, 222, 236, 238, 282, 283
Conway Meadows, 237
Copple-Crown Mountain, 232, 235
Corner Spring, 48
Cranberry Meadow Pond, 350
Crane, Stephen, 8
Crawford, Thomas J., 218, 219
Crawford Notch, 205, 361
Crawford Notch House, 218, 219, 220, 221,
    222, 268, 363
Crawford Path, 219, 220, 221, 222
"Criminal Calendar," 106

Crocker, Mr., 99, 104
Cromwell, Oliver, 99
Crotched Mountain, 291, 293
Cummings Pond, 336
Cyclops, 143

Dante, 3
Dark Pond, 312
Darwin, Charles, 14; *Origin of Species, The*, 324
Davis Path, 220
Davisville, NH, 285
Deep Cove, 122, 155, 170
Deerfield River, 54, 58, 59
Deer Hill, 238
Deer Island, 165, 166, 170
Defoe, Daniel: *Robinson Crusoe*, 147
Delantee, John, 153
Dial, The, 23, 24, 54
Dionysius, 63
Disco Island, 244
Dismal Swamp, 311
Dolby Pond, 105
Doric Temple, The, 287
Doublehead Mountain, 236
Double Top Mountain, 124
Dryads, 208
Dublin, NH, 295, 300, 317, 319, 332, 348, 349
Dublin Lake, 312, 319, 350
Dublin Path, 312
Dublin Trail, 319
Dummerston, VT, 200
Dunstable, MA, 227
Durand, Elias, 243, 244, 245, 263, 284
Dwight, Timothy, 202

Eagle Cliff, 218
Eagle Lakes, 270, 275
Eakin, S., 306
East Charlemont (Lower Village), MA, 59
Eastern Point, 245

East Millinocket, ME, 105
Echo Lake, 218
Egypt, 278
Ellis River, 237, 254
Emerson, George B., 194–95, 196, 330
Emerson, Ralph Waldo, 5, 8, 13, 28, 29, 51, 261; "Emancipation in the British West Indies," 115; "Monadnock" (poem), 363
Emerson, William Sr., 315
Enfield, ME, 91, 92, 97
Enfield Road, 92
England, 124, 161
English, 169
Etruria, 25
Europe, 56, 67, 160, 161
Eveleth, Joseph, 294, 295
Eveleth Brook, 295, 296, 336
Everett, Edward, 364

Fabyan, Horace, 219
Fabyan, NH, 220
Fairhaven Bay, 54
Fairhaven Hill, 47, 48
Falling Waters Trail, 276
Fall Mountain, 4, 192, 200–4; *see also* Mt. Kilbourne
Farm Hill (Wentworth Road), 203
Farm Island, 177
Fassett, Joseph, 299, 364
Fassett Brook, 296, 301, 327
Fay, Mr., 279
Fernald, Charles C., 264
Ferrin's Pond (Profile Lake), 216
Field, Darby, 205, 241
Fisk, Mr., 100, 104
Fiske Cemetery, 104
Fitchburg, MA, 42, 192, 298, 300
Fitchburg Railroad, 296
Fitzwilliam, NH, 323, 337
Five Islands, 92, 97, 109, 157
Fletcher, Giles, 78
Flint's Pond, 297

Florida, MA, 59, 63, 64, 65

Flume, The, 214, 216, 276

Flume Brook, 214

Flume House, 215, 270

Fort Dummer, 227

Foster, Mr., 52, 53

Fowler, Betsy Martin, 110, 113

Fowler, George W., 110, 112, 113

Fowler, Thomas Jr., 108, 112, 113, 148, 156, 157

Fowler, Thomas Sr., 109, 113

France, 29

Franconia, NH, 212, 218, 219, 269

Franconia Notch, 205, 212, 214, 226, 232, 235, 255, 262, 269, 271, 275, 276, 277, 278, 282, 286, 309

Franconia Notch State Reservation, 212

Franconia Ridge, 276

Franklin, NH, 278

Frederickton, NB, 97

Frost, Charles, 193, 194, 195, 196

Fruitlands Museums, 45–46

Fuller, Margaret, 23, 24, 51

Fuller, Richard, 23, 24, 34, 46

Fulton, Robert, 160

Gap Mountain, 323

Gaza, NH, 279

Georgia, 6

Gesner, Conrad, 7

Gibbon, Edward, 3

Gibson, Mr., 109, 150

Giesecke, 285

Gilmanton, NH, 229, 230, 236, 237

Gilson Pond, 296

Gleason Brook, 312

Glen, NH, 238, 239, 241; *see also* Bartlett Corner, NH

Glen Bridle Path, 243

Glen Ellis Falls, 240, 241

Glen House, 240, 242, 256, 262, 263, 265, 364

Glen Mary (inn), 80

Gloucester Harbor, 245

Goethe, Johann Wolfgang von, 3

Goffstown, NH, 349

Golgotha, 3

Gorham, NH, 265, 268

Gosnold, Bartholomew, 160

Goths, 43

Grand Falls, 107, 109, 113, 156

Grand Portage, 151

Gray, Asa, 194, 196, 254

Great Brook, 30, 31

Great Gulf, The, 338

Great Haystack (Lafayette), 208, 271

Great Northern Paper and Pulp, 105

Great Pasture, The, 245, 249

Greece, 23

Greek, 178

Greenfield, MA, 54, 58

Greenland, 243, 244, 245, 247, 263, 285

Greenleaf AMC Hut, 275, 276

Green Mountains, 37, 39, 40, 41, 53, 191, 269, 307, 334, 349, 350, 356

Greenville, ME, 163, 167, 170, 175

Greenville, NH, 291, 292

Greylock, 4, 9, 16, 54–80, 86, 142, 151, 334, 335, 336, 349, 350, 356; *see also* Saddleback Mountain

Greylock State Reservation, 68, 74

Groton, MA, 24, 32, 45

Groton Junction, MA, 290

Guernsey, "Aunt Jesse," 214

Gulf, The (Monadnock), 354

Gulf of Mexico (in White Mountains), 247

Gunstock Mountain, 338

Hale, Edward Everett, 85, 88

Halfway House: Monadnock, 301; Washington, 241, 243, 247

Halfway Spring, 338

Hall, Mr., 247

Hamlin, Charles, 146

Harford Point, 167

Harrington Trail, 52
Harrison, William Henry, 363
Harvard, MA, 24, 44, 45, 46
Harvard College, 3, 15
Harvard University, 38
Hassan, 32
Hawk's Brook, 59
Hawthorne, Nathaniel, 24; "Great Stone Face, The," 216
Headwall, 252, 256, 257, 261
Hecker, Isaac, 56
Heetopades of Veeshnoo-Sarma, 59, 65
Helicon, 208
Helvellyn, 36
Hemingway, Ernest, 13
Henniker, NH, 279
Hermit Lake, 244, 252, 254, 256, 257, 258, 261, 264
Hermit Lake Shelter, 252
Heywood's Gazetteer, 353
Himalayas, 3, 7, 297
Hinsdale, NH, 196, 198
Hippocrene, 208
Hitchcock, Edward, 351, 353
Hoar, Edward, 162, 177, 224, 225, 227, 250, 252, 258, 263, 282, 286
Hoar, John, 45
Hodge, James T., 108, 151, 176
Holley, Myron, 115
Hollis, NH, 278, 280
Hollow Road, 229
Homer, 24, 25, 28, 36
Hooksett, NH, 207, 209, 210, 219, 223, 228
Hooksett Falls, 210
Hooksett Pinnacle, 210, 228
Hoosac Mountain, 40, 42, 53, 65
Hoosac Tunnel, 64
Hopper Trail, 74, 75
Horseshoe Pond, 228
Houlton, ME, 94, 96
Houlton Road, 87, 91, 92, 94
Howard, Mrs., 99, 104
Hubbbardston, MA, 53

Hudson Bay, 315
Hudson River, 55, 78, 160
Huguenots, 66, 67, 69
Humboldt, Alexander von, 14, 25, 28
Huntington Ravine, 242, 264
Hunt Trail, 151

Imp, The, 287
Indians, 43, 45, 46, 161; Abenaki, 90; Abnaquiois, 114; Chippewa, 169; Eskimo, 244; Incas, 178; King Philip, 43; Mohawk, 94; Paugus, 43; Penobscot, 161, 162, 170, 210; St. Francis, 169; Utawas, 118
Intervale, NH, 239
Ipswich, MA, 297
Iron Mountain, 239
Isthmus of Darien, 151
Italy, 29

Jackson, Charles T., 88, 92, 97, 144, 146, 175, 232, 233, 235, 310, 312
Jackson, NH, 238
Jackson Center, NH, 237
Jaffrey, NH, 49, 300, 317, 319, 323, 324, 334, 337, 349
Jaffrey Road, 336
Jefferson, NH, 266, 282
Jefferson, Thomas, 216
Jefferson Highlands, NH, 269
Jenkins, Abraham Jr., 353
Jesuits, 114
Johnson, Samuel, 3; *Rasselas,* 24, 27, 28
Jo-Mary Lakes, 122
Jo-Mary Mountain, 114, 120, 124
Jordan Mills, ME, 104
Jupiter, 31, 39

Kaaterskill Clove, 80
Kaaterskill Creek, 80
Kaaterskill Falls, NY, 80

Kane, Elisha, 243, 244, 259, 263, 284; *Arctic Explorations,* 194
Kant, Immanuel, 8
Katahdin, 4, 6, 9, 12, 15, 16, 71, 85–161, 162, 182, 193, 307
Katahdin Stream, 135, 136, 142, 151; *see also* Murch Brook
Katepskonegan Carry, 154
Katepskonegan Falls, 126
Katepskonegan Lake, 126
Katepskonegan Stream, 126
Kauterskill Falls, 78
Kearsarge Mountain (Mt. Warner), 208, 232, 236, 239, 350
Kennebec River, 89, 103, 105, 116, 124, 125, 165; East Outlet of, 170, 173
Kennedy Channel, 244
Kidder Mountain, 291, 293
Kilbourn fort, 202
Kilkenny, NH, 266
Kimball Hall Inn, 270
Kineo, 4, 162–81, 296
Kineo Cove, 167, 174
Kineo House, 172, 174
Knight's Tavern, 214

Labrador, 4, 15, 247, 306
Laconia, NH, 222, 231, 338
Lafayette, 4, 10, 225, 226, 244, 266–86, 309, 316, 336; *see also* Great Haystack
Lafayette Inn, 270
Lake Onota, 78
Lake Pontoosuc, 78
Lakes of the Clouds, 220, 221, 264, 267; AMC Hut, 219–20
Lake Superior, 156
Lake Winnipesaukee, 207, 209, 230, 231, 232, 233
Lancaster, MA, 30, 31, 32, 43, 45
Latin, 178
Leominster State Forest, 45
Lescarbot, Marc, 133

Lexington Road, 28
Libbey, Mr., 95
Lily Bay, 164
Lincoln, MA, 297
Lincoln, ME, 92, 156
Lincoln, NH, 212, 214, 215, 275
Link Trail, 264
Linnaeus, Carolus, 13, 14
Lion Head, 258
Lion Head Trail, 252
Little Headwall, 252, 257, 261
Little Monadnock, 324
Little Porus Island, 121
Little Schoodic River, 102
Littleton, MA, 52
Long Mountains, 270
Long-wharf (Boston, MA), 75
Lost Pond, 152
Loudon, John Claudius, 244, 269
Loudon, NH, 228–29
Loudon Ridge, 229
Lovewell, Capt. John, 43
Lowell, MA, 42, 207
Lower Gilmanton, NH, 231
Lower Village (East Charlemont), MA, 59
Lumberman's Museum, 104
Lunenburg, MA, 298
Lyceum (Brattleboro, VT), 193
Lyell, Charles: *Principles of Geology,* 15
Lynch Cemetery, 104
Lyndeborough Mountain, 291, 293

McCauslin, George, 102, 103, 105, 109, 112, 117, 118, 119, 121, 124, 125, 129, 130, 133, 136, 139, 148, 150, 151, 152, 154, 158
McCauslin, Mrs. George, 156
Macey, Mr., 365
McKee, Christopher, 206
Madawaska River, 151
Madison, NH, 236, 238
Madison Boulder, 238
Mad River, 209, 234

Maine, 4, 5, 6, 10, 85, 87, 92, 103, 104, 105, 115,
    121, 130, 139, 140, 144, 145, 148, 152, 158, 161,
    175, 181, 192, 224, 225, 263, 296, 302, 323;
    Gazetteer of, 146; Greenleaf's Map of, 97,
    98; Map of the Public Lands of, 97
Maine Forest Service, 127
Main Street: Concord, MA, 28; Walpole, NH,
    203
Mammon, 24
Manchester, NH, 207, 228
Mann, Thomas, 13
Mansfield Mountain, 273
Marlborough, NH, 300, 312
Marsh, Sylvester, 243
Mars' Hill, ME, 91
Mason Village, NH, 290, 293
Massachusetts, 9, 23, 40, 41, 76, 80, 102, 121,
    130, 145, 158, 176, 207, 230, 251, 280, 286, 310,
    337; Map of the Public Lands of, 97
Mattaseunk Stream, 99, 104
Mattawamkeag, ME, 97, 104
Mattawamkeag Lake, 97
Mattawamkeag Point, 88, 92, 94, 97, 100, 102,
    109, 115, 158, 182
Mattawamkeag River, 92, 94, 95, 96, 97
Matterhorn: Alps, 8; Monadnock, 287
Meadow Pond, 152
Meadow Road, 31
Meads Brook, 336
Medway, ME, 104
Melville, Herman, 8
Meredith, NH, 222, 231
Meredith Bay, 232
Meredith Bridge, 230
Merrill, John, 215
Merrimack, NH, 223, 229
Merrimack River, 40, 56, 206, 207, 212, 219,
    225, 228, 229, 319; valley of, 210; *see also*
    Sturgeon River
Meyers, E.: "Plantae Labradoricae," 285
Michaux, François André, 124
Miles, Jimmy, 316
Milford, ME, 90

Mill Brook, 59
Miller's River, 337
Miller State Park, 293
Millinocket, ME, 113, 183
Millinocket Lake, 104, 108, 113, 117, 145
Millinocket River, 108, 109, 156, 157, 158
Millinocket Road, 113, 135
Millinocket Stream, 113
Milton, John, 3, 9, 99; *Paradise Lost*
    (quoted), 144
Minerva, 24
Minnesota, 365
Mississippi River, 365
Mitchel, Mr., 209, 210
Moat Mountain, 235, 236
Mohawk Trail, 58
Molly Stark Trail, 198
Molunkus, ME, 95, 96, 97, 182
Molunkus House (inn), 95
Monadnock, 3, 4, 5, 12, 15, 16, 23, 25, 35, 37, 39,
    40, 41, 42, 54, 56, 197, 199, 203, 225, 232, 245,
    256, 262, 273, 285, 287–365
Monadnock Bible Conference Center, 300
Monadnock Pond, 348, 349
Monadnock State Park, 295
Monroe Road, 65
Monte Rosa (Monadnock), 331
Montreal, QB, 4
Montresor, John, 183
Monts, Sieur de, 134
Mont Vernon, NH, 280
Moody Island, 177
Moose Brook State Park, 266
Moosehead, ME, 173
Moosehead Lake, 5, 122, 145, 162, 163, 164, 165,
    166, 167, 170, 174, 175, 182
Moosehillock Mountain, 208
Moose Island, 167
Moose River, 170, 173, 265
Moosilauke Mountain, 235
Morrison, John, 115
Morrison's Inn, 275
Morse's Gazetteer, 352

Moultonborough, NH, 232, 234, 236

Mountain Brook, 319

Mountain House, 301

Mountain Road, 198, 295

Mount of Olives (Monadnock), 327

Mt. Adams, 236, 239, 247, 268

Mt. Carrigan, 235

Mt. Carter, 237

Mt. Clinton (Mt. Pierce), 220

Mt. Deception, 267, 269

Mt. Eisenhower, 220

Mt. Hancock, 235

Mt. Jefferson, 247, 266, 268, 277

Mt. Kilbourne (Fall Mountain), 203

Mt. Kinsman, 235

Mt. Liberty, 215

Mt. Lincoln, 276

Mt. Madison, 266, 267, 268

Mt. Monroe, 220, 221

Mt. Pierce (Mt. Clinton), 220

Mt. Pleasant, 268

Mt. Shaw, 231, 235; *see also* Ossipee Mountain

Mt. Warner, 350; *see also* Kearsarge Mountain

Mt. Washington Carriage Road, 241, 247, 248, 265

Mt. Washington Summit Road Company, 242

Mt. Williams, 71

Mt. Winnipesaukee, 235

Murch Brook (Katahdin Stream), 132, 136, 139, 142, 147, 151

Muses, 36

Musketaquid (Thoreau's boat), 206

Naiads, 208

Nashua, NH, 207, 290

Nashua River, 32, 44, 45, 48, 53, 209

Nashville, NH, 65

Nawshawtuct, 3, 204

Nelson, NH, 349

Neosowadnehunk Deadwater, 135

Neptune, Louis, 92, 97, 157

New Bedford, MA, 229

New Boston, NH, 279

New Brunswick (Canada), 92, 98

Newfound Lake, 209

Newfoundland, 220

New Hampshire, 3, 4, 6, 9, 10, 15, 23, 40, 49, 67, 124, 198, 202, 205, 207, 216, 225, 229, 230, 231, 236, 249, 278, 279, 280, 286, 312, 330, 337, 363; Gazetteer of, 202, 318

New Hampton, NH, 278

New Holland, 160

New Ipswich, NH, 291

New Jersey, 66; Highlands of, 41, 67

New York, 4, 76, 160, 275, 302

New York, NY, 33, 54, 67, 72, 85, 96, 99

New York *Tribune,* 258

Niagara Falls, 154

Nicholai, Peal, 183

Nickatou Island (the Forks), 90, 100, 104, 185

Nietzsche, Friedrich, 13

Nimrod, 137

Noliseemack (Shad Pond), 108, 182

Norcross, Mr., 234

Norcross, ME, 121

North Adams, MA, 54, 65, 66, 67

North Bay, 174

North Chelmsford, MA, 227

North Conway, NH, 205, 236, 238

North Moat Mountain, 239

North Nashua River, 45

North Road, 203

North Tamworth, NH, 235

North Twin Lake, 85

Northwest Passage, 8

Notch Brook, 68

Notch Road, 67

Nova Scotia, 220

Noyce, Wilfrid, 13

Nubanusit Lake, 350

Nut Meadow, 316

Nuttall, Thomas, 274, 275

Index

Oakes, William, 14, 195, 196, 245, 251, 265, 283

Oak Hall, 130, 154

Old Bridle Path, 270

Old Indian Trail, 37

Old Man of the Mountains, The, 214, 216, 217; *see also* Profile, The

Old Ski Trail, 296

Old Testament, 115

Oldtown, ME, 85, 88, 89, 90, 92, 158, 161, 162, 168, 173, 182

Olemmon Stream, 91, 185

Olympus, 3, 25, 78, 120

Oreads, 208

Oregon, 161

Orinoco River, 76

Orono, ME, 122, 153, 161

Orotava, 273

Ossa, 208

Ossipee Lakes, 235

Ossipee Mountain (Mt. Shaw), 212, 230, 231, 232, 233, 234, 235, 236

Oswego County, NY, 302

Overlook Trail, 74

Pacific Ocean, 35, 151, 161

Pack Monadnock Mountain, 293, 325, 327, 337

Page, Mr., 241, 250

Pan, 24

Paradise Valley Trail, 301

Parish's Geography, 106

Parnassus, 3, 36

Passadumkeag, ME, 92

Passadumkeag Stream, 91, 185

Passamagamet Falls, 128, 155

Passamagamet Lake, 126

Passamagamet Stream, 126

Passamaquoddy River, 89, 161

Patent Office, U.S., 297

Patten, ME, 104

Pattison Road, 67

Peabody River, 254, 265, 266

Peeling (Woodstock) NH, 212

Pelion, 208

Pemadumcook Lakes, 108, 121, 123, 128, 155, 183

Pembroke, NH, 228

Pemigewasset River, 207, 208, 212, 213, 216, 219, 273, 278

Pemigewasset Wilderness, 276

Pennant, Thomas, 275

Pennichook Brook, 280

Penobscot Bay, 171

Penobscot County, ME, 146

Penobscot River, 90, 116, 151, 157, 161, 183; East Branch, 90, 100, 102, 104, 145, 162; Falls of, 88; South Branch, 174, 177; Valley of, 85; West Branch, 87, 92, 97, 98, 99, 100, 103, 104, 105, 108, 109, 113, 128, 129, 149, 162

Pepperell, MA, 280

Percy Peaks, 270

Perkins Pond, 300

Peterborough, NH, 25, 290, 291, 292, 293, 295, 349

Peterborough Hills, 291, 320, 337

Peters, Samuel A.: *History of Connecticut*, 201

Petrarch, 3

Pierce Bridge, 219

Pillsbury, Parker, 279, 285

Pindar, 78

Pingree's Grant, 262

Pinkham Notch, 205, 225, 226, 239, 240, 241, 246, 261, 309; AMC Camp, 241

Pinkham's Grant, 240, 262

Piscataquoag River, 209

Pittsfield, MA, 55, 78

Plum Island, 207

Plymouth, NH, 212, 278

Pockwockamus Falls, 131, 135, 154

Pockwockamus Lake, 126

Polis, Joseph, 162, 163, 167, 168, 170, 173, 174, 177, 178

Polynesia, 35

Pomola, 92, 97, 144, 146

Pond Falls, 107

Ponkawtasset, 3

Pool, The, 215

Potter, Judge C. E., 182

Potter's History of Manchester, 194

Presidential Range, 219, 220, 235, 269, 271

Princeton, MA, 35, 38

Profile, The, 216, 276; *see also* Old Man of the Mountains, The

Profile House, 269, 270

Profile Lake, 216

Profile Mountain, 282

Prometheus, 143, 144, 146

Prospect Hill Road, 45

Proteus, 133

Pumpelly Trail, 319

Purgatory, 3, 301

Puritans, 160

Putney, VT, 200

Quakers, 157

Quakish Dam, 113

Quakish Lake, 110, 113, 114, 120, 156

Ragged Mountain, 68, 71, 232

Ragmuff Stream, 184

Raleigh, Sir Walter, 160

Randolph, NH, 266, 268

Randolph Hill, 266

Rasles, Fr. Sebastien, 182, 183

Ravine House, 268

Raymond Path, 265

Red Cross Trail, 301

Redemption Rock, 45

Red Hill, 4, 230, 231, 232, 234, 235, 236, 238

Red Hill Road, 234

Red Spot Trail, 336, 338

Rice, Capt. Luke, 54, 57, 59–63, 64, 65, 70

Rice's Brook, 59

Rindge, NH, 49, 322, 323, 337, 349

Rines Pitch, 113

Rio Bravo, 161

Rippogenus Falls, 153

Rippogenus Portage, 151

Rip Van Winkle Trail, 80

River Road, 65

Roaring Brook Road, 113

Robin Hood, 44, 45

Rockabema Stream, 100, 104

Rockies, 8

Rockwell Road, 78

Rockwood, ME, 167, 173

Rogers, Nathaniel, 279, 285

Rome, 31, 90

Rousseau, Jean Jacques, 3

Rowlandson, Mary, 43, 45

Rum Mountain, 142

Ruskin, John, 12; *Modern Painters*, 7

Russell, John, 245

Sabine River, 161

Saco River, 89, 222, 236, 253

Saddleback Mountain (Greylock), 55, 67, 78, 334, 335, 336, 349, 356

St. John River, 89, 116, 117, 134, 151

St. Lawrence River, 114, 151

Salmon River, 99

Salmon Stream, 104

Sanbornton, NH, 211, 222

Sandbar Island, 169, 170, 173

Sandwich, NH, 234

Sandwich Mountains, 207, 230, 232

Sandy Hook, 67

San Salvador, 178

Sarcophagus, The, 287, 319

Satan, 140, 142, 146

Saturn, 39

"Satyrus," 64

Sault de Ste. Marie: rapids of, 156

Saussure, Horace Benedict de, 7

Savoy, MA, 63

Schoodic Stream, 105

Scribner, Ira, 80

Sebago Lake, 222

Shad Pond, 107, 108, 113, 156, 182; *see also* Noliseemack

Shaker Brook, 312

Shakers, 46

Shakespeare, William, 78; *King Lear,* 65

Sharon, NH, 291

Shelburne, MA, 59

Shelburne Falls, MA, 54, 58, 59

Shelter Rock, 216

Shining Rock, 276

Shirley, MA, 32, 298

Silenus, 63

Silver Cascade, 222

Silver Lake, 238

Sinai, 3

Six Gun City, 270

Smith, Capt. John, 160

Smith River, 209

Smith's Sound, 244

Smythe, C. Piazzi, 273

Soucook River, 209

Souhegan River, 209

South Adams, MA, 69

South Peak, 141, 142, 146

Sowadnehunk Deadwater, 126, 132

Sowadnehunk River, 109, 183

Sowadnehunk Stream, 150

Spain, 161

Spaulding, Mr., 247, 250

Spellman Trail, 319

Spencer Bay, 173

Spencer Bay Mountain, 165

Spenser, Edmund: *Faerie Queene, The,* 59

Spofford, Jesse, 290

Springer, John S., 101, 124, 148

Spruce Mountain, 264

Squam Lake, 209, 232, 235

Squam Mountains, 207, 212, 235

Squaw Mountain, 165

Squaw Point, 170

Stage Coach Trail, 52

Standish, Miles, 43

Staten Island, NY, 66, 68, 69, 75, 315

Sterling, MA, 31, 33, 43, 45

Still River, MA, 43, 44

Stillwater, ME, 88

Stillwater River, 24, 33, 34

Stone Pond, 349, 350

Stow, MA, 24, 28, 31

Stratford Peaks, 269, 270

Stratton, 350

Sturgeon (Merrimack) River, 207

Sudbury River, 45

Sugar Island, 165, 169, 175, 177

Sumehenna Trail, 39

Summit House: Lafayette, 276; Washington, 243, 247, 249, 258

Suncook (Belknap) Mountain, 231, 232

Suncook River, 209

Sunkhaze Stream, 91, 185

Swasen, Tahmunt, 183

Swift River, 234

Symplegades, 112

Table Rock: Flume, The, 214; Niagara Falls, 154

Tamworth, NH, 234, 237, 238

Temple, NH, 290, 291, 293

Temple Common, 290

Temple Mountain, 293

Teneriffe, 25, 273

Thatcher, George, 85, 114, 162

Thessaly, 25

Thoreau, Henry David: "Allegash and the East Branch, The," 162; "Chesuncook," 167; "Dispersion of Seeds, The," 324; *Excursions,* 25; "Huckleberries," 324; Journal, 51, 52, 192, 206, 218, 226, 288, 289, 345, 365; "Ktaadn," 9, 86, 162; *Maine Woods, The,* 86, 162, 167, 181, 286, 345; "Succession of Forest Trees, The," 324; *Walden,* 5, 51, 56, 80, 92, 104, 192, 279, 289, 293, 350; "Walk to Wachusett, A," 24; *Week on the Concord and Merrimack Rivers, A,* 9, 46, 56,

59, 65, 71, 80, 206, 207, 209, 215, 218, 220; "Wild Apples," 324; "Wild Fruits," 324, 331

Thoreau, John Jr., 23, 28, 46, 205, 206, 220, 222, 269

Thoreau, Sophia, 25, 215, 218

Thoreau Bog, 319, 336

Thoreau Lyceum, 28

Thoreau Spring, 146

Thorndike Pond, 295, 336, 350

Thornton, NH, 212, 213, 275, 277

Tilton, James, 212, 275

Timias, 58, 59

Tiptop House, 247, 249

Titans, 144, 150, 207

Toque Pond Gate, 113

Toque Pond Road, 135

Tooth, The, 287

Torrey, Bradford, 277

Townsend, MA, 290, 292

Transcendentalism, 8, 46, 51, 78

Trent, William of, 44

Trolhate, 33

Troy, NH, 295, 296, 298, 300, 323, 325, 338, 339, 348, 349, 358

Tuckerman, Edward, 14, 224, 253, 316

Tuckerman Junction, 252

Tuckerman Ravine, 6, 14, 16, 222, 225, 236, 242, 249, 250–66, 277, 281, 282, 304

Twin Lakes: North, 116, 150, 155; South, 116, 121

Twisted Birch Trail, 301

Tyler, John, 363

Umbazookskus River, 164, 183

Uncannunuc Mountain, 4, 210, 291, 293

Union Magazine, The, 86

Ventoux, 3

Vermont, 10, 76, 146, 191, 192, 194, 198, 199, 334, 335

Vespucci, Amerigo, 160

Victoria, Queen, 7

Vikings, 160

Virgil, 24, 25, 28, 35; *Aeneid, The,* 30–31; *Georgics,* 33, 39

Vulcan, 143

Wachusett, 3, 4, 9, 16, 23–53, 142, 151, 225, 322, 336, 364

Wachusett Mountain State Reservation, 37, 52

Wachusett Pond, 53

Wadleigh Brook, 121

Waite, Mr., 102, 105

Walden Pond, 5, 8, 28, 56, 64, 75, 78, 80, 85, 104, 158

Walpole, NH, 192, 203, 204

"Wandering Jew," 106

Wantastiquet, 4, 191–99, 336; *see also* Chesterfield Mountain

Wantastiquet State Forest, 198

Washington, 4, 6, 7, 9, 14, 56, 206–49, 252, 254, 261, 262, 264, 267, 268, 276, 283, 336, 364; *see also* Agiocochook

Washington, MA, 80

Washington House (inn), 219

Wassataquoik River, 87

Watatic, 23, 40, 349

Waterville Valley, NH, 234

Waumbek Village, 270

Weare, NH, 279

Webster, Abigail, 279

Webster, Daniel, 216, 285; birthplace of, 279

Webster, Ebenezer, 279

Weirs Beach, NH, 232

Weld, Mr., 227

Wentworth, William H. H., 238, 239, 240, 241, 255, 256, 257, 259, 261, 262, 264, 265, 282

Wentworth Road (Farm Hill), 203

West Acton Road, 31

West Brattleboro, VT, 194

West Franklin, NH, 279, 285

West Indies, 161

Westminster, MA, 52, 193

Westminster, VT, 200

Westminster Review, 115

West Mountain Road, 67

West River, 194, 197, 198

West Sterling, MA, 24, 33, 34, 37

West Thornton, NH, 211, 212, 275

Whetstone Brook, 194

Whitcomb Hill, 65, 67

Whitcomb Hill Road, 65

White, Mr., 247

White Arrow Trail, 296, 300, 301, 315, 327, 338

White Cross Trail, 296, 324, 331, 338

White Dot Trail, 296, 300, 319, 338

Whitefield, NH, 268, 269

White Mountains, 4, 14, 16, 17, 88, 194, 205–86, 298, 304, 307, 310, 321, 324, 325, 348, 350, 360, 363, 365

White Mountains National Forest, 239

Whittier, NH, 234

Whymper, Edward, 8

Wild, Mr., 347

Willard, Josiah, 227

Willey, Benjamin G., 241, 246, 255, 283; map in, 247

Williams College, 55, 73, 74, 75

Williamson, William D., 182

Williamstown, MA, 69, 74

Willis, William, 182

Willow Street, 31

Wilson, Alexander, 274, 302

Winchendon, MA, 50, 322, 323, 337

Winnipesaukee River, 207

Wood, Mr., 266

Woodstock, NH, 212

Worcester, MA, 51, 225, 365

Wordsworth, William, 3, 9, 35; *Peter Bell*, 24, 36, 39

Yorkshire, 36

Zoar River Road, 58